This r... ...extraordinary life and career:

- An impoverished childhood in the forests of Canada

- The tragic death of her parents when she was only twenty-two

- Her first record contract and her rocky start in Nashville

- Her marriage to the world's most successful and reclusive record producer

- Her astonishing crossover to mainstream pop

SHANIA TWAIN

THE BIOGRAPHY

SHANIA TWAIN

THE BIOGRAPHY

ALSO BY ROBIN EGGAR

Tom Jones: The Biography

SHANIA TWAIN

THE BIOGRAPHY

ROBIN EGGAR

CMT

POCKET BOOKS

New York   London   Toronto   Sydney

CMT

POCKET BOOKS, a division of Simon & Schuster, Inc.
1230 Avenue of the Americas, New York, NY 10020

CMT © 2005 Country Music Television, Inc.,
a division of MTV Networks, a Viacom company.

Copyright © 2002, 2005 by Robin Eggar

Library of Congress Cataloging-in-Publication Data
Eggar, Robin.
Shania Twain : the biography / Robin Eggar.
p.   cm.
Includes bibliographical references (p.   ) and index.
1. Twain, Shania. 2. Country musicians—Canada—Biography. I. Title.
ML420.T953E44 2005
782.421642'092—dc22
[B]
2005051474

ISBN-13: 978-0-7434-9735-0
ISBN-10:   0-7434-9735-X

First CMT/Pocket Books trade paperback edition October 2005

10 9 8 7 6 5 4 3 2 1

POCKET and colophon are registered trademarks of
Simon & Schuster, Inc.

Design by Jan Pisciotta

Manufactured in the United States of America

For information regarding special discounts for bulk purchases,
please contact Simon & Schuster Special Sales at 1-800-456-6798
or business@simonandschuster.com.

For Farah—*a true fan*

As ever, to the loves of my life: Jacqui, Jordan, and Rowan

ACKNOWLEDGMENTS

WHEN I FIRST decided to write a biography of Shania Twain, I was insistent that it must be my take on her career and should not be compromised by being seen as "authorized." However, before I wrote a word I met with Jon Landau, Barbara Carr, and Jan Stabile from Jon Landau Management and told them of my intentions. My thanks to them for being prepared to listen and then to help, and never hinder, my research.

At the very core of the book are some three hours of interviews I conducted with Shania Twain in London in January 1998 and October 1999 for British magazines. They lie at the heart of my take on who she is and where she comes from. When Shania initially learned I was writing this book, she did not take the easy option—it is always easier to withhold cooperation than it is to help—and while she and her immediate family chose not to be interviewed for the book, she has never advised me against talking to anybody, and indeed has made sure that I have access to the correct facts. Her personal assistant, Kim Godreau, has been unfailingly polite and efficient in answering my frequent queries, for which she has my thanks. On August 16, 2002, at the Royal Parc Hotel in Evian, France, Shania and I sat down for an hour's interview for *Marie Claire* magazine. This provided the basis for updating the final chapters and helped clarify her relationship with her father, Clarence Edwards.

During my research, I conducted almost ninety interviews either face-to-face or on the telephone. My thanks to all of them and also to anyone whom I have inadvertently omitted. The mistake is mine. I have seen Northern Ontario in three seasons—autumn, winter, and summer—and driven thousands of miles in snow, hail, rain, and sunshine, which has given me some idea of what the inhabitants of that stunning but tough land live through. The hospitality I received throughout Canada and in Nashville was exemplary and the reaction of those people who know Shania, both now and in her past, speaks volumes to the person she is.

In Canada, essential and invaluable background work and research was carried out with aplomb, grace, and total efficiency by Jeff Silverstein, without whom my job would have been very much harder. Thanks to Declan Hill and Katie and Kees t'Hooft for effecting the introduction.

Extra special thanks to Jeff MacInnis for going far beyond the call of friendship. He provided me with a base in Toronto—plus a taxi service to and from the airport, room, board, skiing, hiking, kayaking, a twenty-four-hour spinning marathon, and countless other ideas, all of which helped provide relaxation and an alternative focus away from Shania. My thanks as well to John Lucato for the loan of a cellular phone.

Searching for Shania's roots would have been impossible without the assistance of her uncle, Don Fraser. Don, his wife, Jan, and their children, Darlene and Shane, made me welcome in their home. Further memories and information on her mother's family in Manitoba came from the family historian, Roger Pearce; May Thompson; and Evelyn Struthers. Despite being rudely awakened one November morning, Jerry Twain's sister, Karen (and her daughter Angela) has helped me understand the depth of Shania's Native heritage. Jerry's cousin Willis McKay told me of her time spent on the Mattagami reserve as a child, while cousin Kenny Derasp told of how he had taught her to play the guitar and gave valuable insight into her early years in Hanmer. In Chapleau, the home of Shania's natural father, Clarence Edwards, thanks are especially due to Lori Edwards, and to Dan Boucher for his comments. Gordon Edwards was generous with his time and honest about his own life.

New perception of Shania's life would not have been possible without the personal insights and memories of conductor and producer John Kim Bell, Helene Bolduc, Mike Taylor, and Laura Surch, none of whom had previously spoken publicly about the times they spent with her. Nor had Mary Bailey, who believed in a young girl's talent when no one else did and who, despite nurturing and losing this once-in-a-lifetime talent, refuses to be bitter and has moved on with her life. Record producer Harry Hinde knows talent when he sees it, but luck and circumstance often conspire against him.

My visits to Timmins were made a great deal easier by Jean-Paul and Charmaine Aubé, who have set remarkable standards in Northern Ontario hospitality. John Emms's knowledge of the local music scene was essential. David Hartt and Mike Chabot, former members of Longshot, shared their memories of those days. Old high school friends Brian Hurst and Rick Thompson gave a different picture. Thanks also to: Lise Dubois; Carole Kiraga; Paul Cousineau; Pam Kardas; Kim Seale; Len Gillis; Jerry Paquette; Claude Gagnon; Roger Richard at the Maple Leaf; Marjan Ilovar; Paul Toffanello, principal of Timmins High and Vocational school; City Clerk Jack Watson; Vic Power (mayor of Timmins 1983–2000); Will Saari; and Georges Quirion, architect of the Shania Twain Centre. In Sudbury, Colette Del Frate kindly drove me around Hanmer to see the old Twain home and the schools Shania attended. Thanks also to Lynn Bond for tales of practical jokes and ponies and to Shania's old teachers Ted Evans, John Browning, Laurie Macdonald, and Keir Kitchen.

In Huntsville, thanks to Laura Kennedy for sorting out my stay at Deerhurst and to Gillian Brunette of *The Forester*. The performers and backstage staff (past and present) of the Deerhurst Resort who helped place the era in perspective included Celia Finley, Dean Malton, Mike Degazio, Gilles Lanthier, Marg Reid, Hilda Montgomery, and Gary Hubbard. And my thanks to the elusive John Kotowski, who finally granted me an interview.

My visit to Nashville, Tennessee, would not have been half as productive without the invaluable advice and help of country PR supreme Richard Wooton, Gillie Crowder, Bob Doyle, and Joni Wilson (and from an earlier but essential background trip, Garth Brooks and Bernie Leadon). At Mercury Nashville, the big boss, Luke Lewis, was generous with his time and praise; Sandy Neese, John Grady, and Retta Harvey were generous with their time answering my nit-picking queries. Thanks to Ron Baird at CAA, Norro Wilson, Harold Shedd, the inimitable Dick Frank, Cecelia Walker at Music Country, Joe Chemay, and especially to that master of American feel and German technology, Paul Leim, who has since shown himself to be a friend and a supporter. Sorry it didn't work out, Paul.

In Toronto, Larry le Blanc, *Billboard*'s Canadian correspondent, and Brian Robertson, president of the Canadian Recording Industry Association, clued me in to the Canadian music scene. Thanks to Samantha Johnson at Universal Music Canada for help, background, and the Tragically Hip CDs.

Discovering Mutt Lange's background would have been much tougher without the assistance of record producer Steve Brown, Geoff Williams, Ralph Simon, Nigel Grainge, Johan du Plooy, and Alison Green. Some of the quotes dealing with Mutt's working habits are taken from the Mutt Lange Zone—the only online resource on Mutt worth looking at. Many thanks to George Frazer for putting me in touch with Geoff Williams and Johan du Plooy. Thank you to James Borthwick, who contacted me to fill in many of the blank areas that still remained in Mutt's early years. Information about Sant Mat came from Lorenz Knauer in Germany and Rachel Storm at Inform in London.

I was first introduced to Shania Twain by Richard Beck at LD Publicity. Special thanks to Richard, Bernard Doherty, Claire Singers, and all the staff at LD for providing press clippings, support, and general background information. Adam White at Universal in London has kept me up-to-date with Shania statistics and in-concert DVDs.

Kate Maiden at Bacall helped arrange my frequent trips to Canada on Air Canada, which flew me there in comfort (and on time!). For helping me track down various numbers and people, I thank: Christa Wenzl, Nic Stern, Frances Schoenberger, Elly Houman, and Jackie Harris.

Thanks to my agents: Julian Alexander at Lucas Alexander Whitley in London for his advice and encouragement, and Sarah Lazin in New York; to Doug Young for greenlighting the project; and to Lindsay Simons and Jo Roberts Miller at Headline for seeing it through. Thanks to Jacob Hoye and Mitchell Ivers in New York for making this US edition possible.

Since the publication of the original British edition, various people have contacted me to further enhance my knowledge of Shania's life. So thanks to Jenny Moutsatos (née Sachsalber) who has corrected my spelling of her maiden name. Members of the Shania Twain North American Online Fan Club were not shy in offering a critique and corrections, so extra special thanks to Roger Baggeley and Desiree Pits. FV—you get a special mention for a great online review and for making sure I had all the information I needed to update the book for America. Marianne at The Shania Twain Traditional UK Fan Club has been very supportive. Farah Whitehead and her grandmother Jean Freer have shown me how Shania's music and personality have reached out to help the less fortunate. My godson Oliver North did some proofreading, but even more tut tutting at my loose use of dependent comma clauses.

As ever, I would never have been able to finish the book without the love and support of my family: my wife, Jacqui, who put up with my frequent visits to Canada and the States, and Jordan and Rowan, who know all the words to Shania's songs and still love them.

Introduction

THE LAND OF DREAMS

THE FIRST OF JULY is Canada Day. It is an important event for all Canadians, a reminder to the world that they are not just a backward, northern outpost of the United States, that they have their own traditions, their own culture, and their own heroes. Canada Day 2001 was the nation's 134th birthday. In Timmins, it was much, much more than that.

Timmins is Shania Twain's hometown, and its people had just spent millions building a museum in her honor. They had also declared Shania Time.

During the buildup to Canada Day, Shania Time was impossible to escape. It circled overhead like the threatening rainclouds, then settled like a carpet of pigeons over Trafalgar Square. Her face, all flawless cheekbones, dishevelled hair, and knowing look, followed you wherever you went. She was omnipresent: on giant billboards, on car stickers, on lapel buttons. The sign outside Casey's restaurant proclaimed "Shania loves our Veggie Burgers." In downtown Timmins, the streets had been barricaded off so that shoppers could visit the Shania Twain Heritage Festival, an opportunistic rebranding of the annual holiday sidewalk sale. The local radio and TV stations seldom stopped chattering about the last opportunities to win tickets to the opening of the Shania Twain Centre.

This small town in northern Ontario was preparing to honor its most famous daughter, the country princess turned international superstar. The center cost C\$11 million to build. The town contributed several million dollars to that sum, while the rest was raised from a series of federal and state grants and corporate investors. In return, they hope, the attraction will bring in fifty thousand tourists a year.

The night before the center opened to the public, there was a gala opening, a black-tie event attended by Timmins's great and good. Of the two hundred who attended, only half a dozen knew Shania when she was simply Eilleen Twain, a tiny, feisty teenager with a startling voice and a lungful of ambition. While local politicians and the Ontario Minister for Tourism glad-handed each other, scarcely anybody spoke to her uncle and aunt, Don and Jan Fraser, for they did not know who they were. A few acknowledged Helene and Larry Bolduc, but then Helene is known to be one of Shania's closest confidants—her sister Flo works for the mayor and Larry drove the bus on Shania's American tour. Shania's adoptive father's sister, Karen Twain, had also been invited to attend, but the Ojibwe woman is shy, does not drive, and nobody had thought to make sure she came. The event was about Shania the superstar, not about Eilleen's working-class roots.

In many ways, Shania Twain remains an enigma in her own hometown. She likes to keep it that way. Many stars would have been in a hurry to forget Timmins. When Shania left town for good, in 1988, she had spent only eleven of her twenty-two years there. Aside from her classmates and those on the local music scene, few knew her and less would have noticed if she never came back. But Shania wanted to belong . . . and Eilleen, the orphan, needed to.

"It's where her family are from. Her mom and dad are still here," says Helene Bolduc. "They are buried in the cemetery, but she feels that they are still here, so she wants to think Timmins is still very special. Eilleen believes it doesn't matter where you come from, which city you're from, which country you're from, how much population there is, it can happen. And Timmins did it for her. Whatever she went through here, it helped her follow that path. Timmins will always have a special place in her heart; her childhood was here, she graduated here. It was a big part of her life. Timmins is very easy to forget if you want to. She doesn't want to forget and by talking about Timmins she has made sure she hasn't."

Right from the moment she signed her record deal in Nashville, Shania brought Timmins into her life. She shot the pictures for the first album sleeve in the snows outside town and gave a concert in the local French high school a year later. Once her career took off she mentioned her hometown at every possible occasion.

In 1996, the city declared Shania Twain Day and renamed a street after her. She attended a massive gala celebration at the Senator Hotel. It was pouring with rain, but Shania delighted the fans waiting outside by joining them in the wet and announcing, "We're not made of sugar, we're northerners." Once inside, recalls local hairdresser Paul Cousineau, "She went up to every single person, even the bathroom attendants, and did not leave until she had said hello to everybody. She got up and signed autographs. I don't know how she smiles so much. She doesn't forget people; she is very down to earth and fame has never gone to her head . . . if it hasn't now, I don't think it can."

On Canada Day 1999, she held the last concert of the first leg of her North American tour in Timmins's Hollinger Park. Despite the extra costs (many of which were covered by the City of Timmins) involved in bringing her spectacular show hundreds of miles north of the regular stadium circuit, Shania refused to consider giving anything other than the full deal. It was the biggest show the town had ever seen, attracting twenty-eight thousand people. They still talk about it today. In the summer of 2000, she quietly drove up from Toronto with her younger sister and arrived unannounced, without a bodyguard, at her high-school reunion, where she posed for photos and signed autographs for anyone who wanted them.

A year later, when Shania was only thirty-five, and the town prepared for the opening of the Shania Twain Centre, a palpable aura of disappointment hung in the air. Months previously, Shania had told the organizers that she would be absent from the July celebrations, by which time she would be heavily pregnant with her first child, due at the end of August. In town, though, hope—tinged with blind faith—refused to accept logic. After all, she had shown up unannounced before. Like Kevin Costner in *Field of Dreams*, Timmins collectively believed that if they built it she would come. She didn't show, of course, just as she had said. Timmins being Timmins and Canadians being Canadians, the townsfolk shrugged their collective shoulders, mumbled the odd tsk-tsk of disapproval, and once the opening party was over went back to living their Shania-free existence. If they were disappointed, they certainly didn't show it to outsiders. They knew Shania would come when she was ready. It took another three years.

The eleven-thousand-square-foot building, designed by local architect Georges Quirion and constructed primarily from local materials, fronted in glass, wood, and granite, would be an attractive feature anywhere. Inside, there is light and space, beckoning visitors to "Come on over, come on in." Interactive exhibits mean people can play musical instruments and watch an excellent video full of unseen footage of Shania, and these are well put-together by the Toronto-based Lord Design Studio, who have worked with the Jimi Hendrix Museum in Seattle and the Muhammad Ali Center. But there are not enough of them, making one feel that too much money was spent on the building and not enough on highlighting its contents.

Shania backed the project from the start, when she told the then mayor, Vic Power, "This looks like it will be an exciting project for the city of Timmins and I am happy to be part of it." Since then she has lived up to her word by donating a million pounds' worth of memorabilia. She has sent so much material, in fact, that only between 10 and 15 percent will be on view at any one time. Her fans making pilgrimages of many thousands of miles would probably prefer it if there was more of her stuff simply housed in an aircraft hangar.

The Shania Twain Centre is certainly a testament to her remarkable achievements. There are racks of awards, a fraction of a cabinet bulging at the seams. (As of October 2004 she has won five Grammys, twelve Junos (Canadian Grammys), two CMAs and twenty-four Canadian CMAs, six American Music Awards, eight Billboard Music Awards, and, perhaps most important to her, twenty-six BMI Pop Awards and twelve SOCAN songwriter awards.) There are costumes, too—notably the leopard-skin-print pantsuit from the legendary "That Don't Impress Me Much" video. Somewhere in the vaults are her wedding dress; a tan suede skirt with fringes handmade by her Native grandmother, Selina, which she wore as a child; handwritten lyric sheets for hit songs like "Don't Be Stupid" and "Black Eyes, Blue Tears"; and the skimpy T-shirt she wore for her breakthrough video, "Whose Bed Have Your Boots Been Under?"

The clothes all seem impossibly tiny for a star so impossibly big. In ten years, she has soared across the music world like a flaming comet that has, as yet, shown no signs of burning out. Shania Twain has shown herself to be a mistress of what video can be; she can deliver a live show to rival those with ten times as much experience. But it is the near exponential curve on the graph of her worldwide record sales that is deeply scary. Her debut album, *Shania Twain*, sold one hundred thousand copies on its original release; that figure rose to seventeen million for *The Woman in Me*, and close to thirty-four million for *Come On Over*, of which a staggering twenty million were sold in the USA. Her fourth album, *UP!*, has also passed the ten million mark, while her *Greatest Hits* compilation released in November 2004 has sold three and a half million in the USA and a further three million around the world. In November 2004 Shania was given a 45-pound Double Diamond plaque for selling more than twenty million copies of *Come On Over* in the USA, making it the highest-selling country album ever. Globally *Come On Over* is the second-highest-selling album of all time. After overtaking *Eagles: Their Greatest Hits 1971–75* (thirty-one million) and the *Saturday Night Fever Original Soundtrack* (thirty million), Shania still remains a long way behind Michael Jackson's *Thriller* (forty-six million).

Like that of her bestselling rivals, Shania's music works on multiple levels. Hers are classic pop songs that hook into the memory so deeply they are all but impossible to extract without surgery; their sound is as close to perfect as money can buy, the result of hundreds of hours spent in the studio weaving instruments and voices together into a seamless whole. They are happiness shrapnel, positive messages appealing across the generations to children, to young teens, and to adults—if seldom to the young and trendy. Much of Shania's fan base is above the age of twenty-eight, the very core of album buyers.

What is on display in the center is a physical manifestation of the Shania Twain legend. It is about what she is perceived to be—not what made her. *That* lies outside the walls. Perhaps it is only confirmation of the legend that people want to see, to be reminded of her Cinderella story, her rags-to-riches rise, her triumph over tragedy. To fans, a star is a blank slate upon which our own preconceptions, our own beliefs and desires, can be placed. They become what we want them to be.

Shania herself knows that Shania Twain is an illusion. When she met Timmins city clerk Jack Watson to discuss the plans for the center, she told him that she is two people whom she tries to keep separate: Eilleen, wife and soon-to-be mother, and Shania, the superstar. "Eilleen has a private life where she likes to do certain things," Watson says, "while Shania Twain is that famous person. And if she can use her to help our community she will."

Timmins and the seemingly infinite bush and forest surrounding it are an essential part of what made her. Much has not changed since she grew up there. Wednesday night was still talent night at the Maple Leaf Tavern—though the club has since closed, a victim to the recession that perches behind the city's shoulders like a vulture. Twenty years ago, Eilleen Twain dropped in every few weeks, sang some of her own songs, maybe a country weepy, accompanying herself on her twelve-string acoustic. The décor has faded a touch (and they have added Shania memorabilia to the wall) but the crowd, lost under a cloud of cigarette smoke and beer, has hardly changed at all. The Mattagami Hotel, where a timid eight-year-old gave her first appearance for twenty-five bucks, was pretty sleazy in 1973. Now it is a strip club. Don's Pizzeria has a Shania vegetarian special, but otherwise its pizzas and the *poutine* (fries covered with cheese and gravy) from Chez Nous taste as good as they ever did after a few beers.

The paraphernalia of the twenty-first century—cable TV, the Internet, cellphones—has brought the thoughts and sounds of the world closer to Timmins. It is no longer a northern backwater forgotten by both high and pop culture. Physically, however, it will always hover on the periphery. It's a hard place to visit, four hundred and fifty miles north of Toronto and above the Arctic Watershed (its rivers flow north into the Arctic Ocean) and just far enough off the Trans-Canada Highway to be an unnecessary detour. The roads are a bit better nowadays, but the railroad no longer runs through town and a round-trip ticket on the ninety-minute flight to Toronto can cost more than a transatlantic hop.

On satellite pictures of the earth at night, one can see Timmins clearly for what it is: a single pinprick of light encompassed on all sides by darkness. It is a pimple of civilization, bordered by mile upon mile of bush, spruce, and pine trees and as many lakes as there are stars in the sky. Timmins's other claim to fame is that it is Canada's largest city. Its limits sprawl over 1,995 square miles, including one hundred lakes and rivers within its boundaries, while trees outnumber the forty-six thousand inhabitants a thousand to one.

Timmins would never have existed at all but for gold. It is a town founded on dreams, a place where fortunes lie unseen, undiscovered, beneath the trees. When the town was incorporated in 1912, few believed it had any more future than the dozens of other abandoned mining camps that litter northern Ontario. It is not a pretty place, for it is a working-class mining town whose architecture reflects its history. Row upon row of wooden mine houses that have not changed externally in decades sit alongside shops and office buildings carved from chunks of prestressed concrete. The climate can be as harsh and unforgiving as the land is beautiful. Winters last six months—and while the locals say they are easier nowadays, the cold still chews at fingers and toes like a ravenous ice demon. In early summer, the mosquitoes and blackflies can drive a man mad.

It is a friendly, hospitable place—in part because nobody has been there long enough to put down roots so deep they need to freeze out visitors. Folks can be a little reserved at the outset, but once they have decided to let go, they love to talk. That's Shania, too: a bit distant at first meeting but a major motormouth once she's comfortable.

Timmins has survived but not thrived, for it walks a thin line between riches and extinction. Its population is the same today as forty years back. In the late sixties, just as the Hollinger gold mine was closing down, Texas Gulf discovered huge zinc deposits at Kidd Creek. And without that base-metal strike it is unlikely that Shania Twain would be claiming Timmins as her hometown; perhaps nobody would be. Now, though the mine remains a major employer, Timmins's economy is suffering. The town has an unemployment rate of 8 percent, half as much again as the province average. One day the mine will close—for mines always do—and when that happens, Timmins may wither away and die unless something is done now. Hence the center.

Timmins needs the attention that a global superstar has brought it. It needs tourists. Until Shania, the celebrities it exported were what one might expect from a chilly frontier town: tough. A series of rugged ice-hockey stars—currently personified by Steve Sullivan of the Nashville Predators—Olympic gold-medal-winning skier Kathy Kreiner, and multimillionaire entrepreneurs Roy Thomson and Jack Kent Cook. Shania Twain is beautiful, but make no mistake: She is as tough, determined, and hardworking as any of them and any of Timmins's original prospectors. The only difference is that she has taken words and melodies and turned her dreams multiplatinum.

Yet long before Shania ever existed, another girl inhabited this unlikely land of dreams. Eilleen Twain: a little girl with goofy teeth, a voice from God, and a mother who believed in her talent almost to the point of madness.

Chapter One

TITANIC BLUES (AND BOOTLEGGING BRAWLERS)

ACCIDENTS MAKE HISTORY. Sometimes a missed connection is a vital one. Shania Twain might not exist if her great-grandfather Francis George Pearce had arrived at Southampton docks one day earlier. The twenty-four-year-old soldier had promised his wife and baby daughter that the voyage taking them to a new life in Canada would be on a brand new ship. Fortunately he arrived too late and all the third-class passages had sold out. The *Titanic* sailed without the Pearces. On April 14, 1912, the unsinkable ship hit an iceberg and sank with the loss of fifteen hundred lives, most of whom were traveling in steerage class.

The Pearces were a solid mixture of English and Irish stock (though they tried to deny their Irish blood for years). Frank, born in 1887, had joined the British army in his late teens and was serving in Norfolk, where he met Lottie Louise Reeves, one of eleven children. A few months younger, she was born in Weybourne, where the winds blow straight down from the Arctic over the North Sea. They were married in St. Michael's Church, Aldershot, on October 2, 1909, after which Frank was posted to keep the peace in Ireland. Their eldest daughter, Eileen, was born in Newbridge, County Kildare, on April 10, 1911. The following year they decided, along with most of her family, to try their luck in the Dominion of Canada.

Frank, Lottie Louise, and baby Eileen made the crossing safely on the next available boat and took the trains as far as Manitoba. Frank had been lured by the promise of a quarter-section farm, one hundred and sixty acres of land to call his own. Until his claim was registered, he worked on the railroads out of Winnipeg, thanks to the man his sister-in-law Mary had met on the boat over and subsequently married. Their second child, a son also named Frank, was born in Winnipeg, but when war broke out, Frank Sr., an army reservist, was immediately called up. He returned to Europe, leaving his wife, pregnant with Jack, sitting in their new homestead in the wild scrubland outside of Badger, six miles north of the US border.

Frank did not worry unduly about his wife. He knew the Reeves women had strength of character, spirit in spades. They knew how to look after themselves and their families. "Lottie and her sister Cyl didn't take a backseat," says Roger Pearce, Frank Jr.'s son. "If someone pissed them off, look out. There were three Irishmen, the Ryans, in town. They were raising hell, fighting all the time, but if they were where Lottie was she would give them a tune up and they would sit in the corner like little boys, wouldn't say 'boo.' They had respect for her because she wouldn't take no BS from anyone. When she and Cyl were older they loved to watch wrestling on TV, they'd get all wild over it."

Gunner F.G. Pearce (No. 37417) did not return home for five years. He served in the Royal Regiment of Field Artillery; his special affinity with horses proved essential for driving the guns and ammunition trailers through the mud behind the front line. Gunners did not have to live in the trenches, or go over the top into the machine guns of no man's land, though Frank regularly volunteered to carry extra ammunition supplies into the trenches. He returned home in 1919 sporting "Pip, Squeak & Wilfred," a full set of medals: the 1914–15 Star, the British War Medal, and the Victory Medal.

He was a quiet, well-mannered, dignified man who never spoke about his wartime experiences and just got on with providing for his family. Two more daughters, Grace and May, arrived and, in 1926, when May was two, the Pearces moved to a new farm just outside Piney. It was a family affair, for Lottie's father, Sidney Reeves, had the farm opposite. The land around Piney was all right but nowhere near as fertile as the Red River Valley where the Great Plains began thirty miles further west. It was mostly flat scrub and bush enlivened by a few hills and East Ridge, with its plunging ravines and towering red pines over one hundred feet tall. Frank ran a mixed farm supporting a few cattle, other livestock, and grain fields, enough to feed the family. The cash crops were oats and alfalfa, excellent cattle forage. Frank produced such high-quality alfalfa seed that he was contacted by the University of Manitoba, which wanted to know how he did it.

During the twenties, while life was tough and money short in rural Manitoba, the Pearces and the Reeveses survived well enough. Thanks to Mary's husband there was always work on the railroads—every day Frank walked the two miles to the railhead in Piney—and the farm provided all the food they needed. They entertained themselves playing cards, Frank Jr. and May loved to sing, Lottie's sister Cyl (Cecilia) had an excellent voice and was a very good piano player, and several times a year there was a let-your-hair-down hoedown. While the farm could feed a growing family, the adults had to find work outside.

Eileen started working in the kitchens and behind the bar of the Piney Hotel when she was eighteen. There she met Walter Fraser, a lad from a local town. They married in 1932 and decided to chance their luck in the mines of northern Ontario. He found work as a shaft sinker in the Hallnor mine in Timmins, where their son Don was born on August 7, 1933. The marriage foundered soon after, and Fraser left town, severing all contact with his family.

Eileen struggled to make ends meet. Money was so tight that when Don was ten, he was sent to live with his grandparents on the farm in Piney for the winter. Eileen scrimped and saved her waitressing tips to buy him a pair of ice skates for Christmas. Things looked up after she fell in love with George Morrison (born 1908), a professional saw filer who sharpened and hammered into shape the huge blades in a sawmill. "George," May recalls, "was very nice-looking. He was a big man, tall and very kind." He, too, was of mixed ancestry. His father, Bert, was Scottish and his mother, Mary, (née Brisbois) was, despite her French name, predominantly Irish with a little dash of Spanish. Their only child, Sharon, was born in Vita, Manitoba, on June 4, 1945, because Eileen wanted to be back with her parents. She returned to Timmins soon after the birth, to the family house on Poplar Street. Later they moved to a small three-bedroomed, wooden bungalow with white walls and a red roof out on Highway 101 between Matheson and Moose Creeks, fifteen miles east of South Porcupine. When Eileen's kids came out to visit on Sundays, the main entertainment was the short walk to the gas station in Hoyle where two brown bears, Yogi and Booboo, were kept in cages.

George made a good wage and the family was well provided for, but like most fathers of his generation he left the child rearing to his wife. Eileen was a gentle woman, happiest milking the cow and tending to her large garden. Her daughter, virtually an only child (Don married and left home when he was nineteen), was headstrong and willful. "As a child, Sharon was a real handful," says May Thompson, Eileen Morrison's youngest sister. "She wanted her way with everything. My brother Jack, who lived in Timmins too, couldn't get over how disciplined our kids were in comparison. Sharon had a nervous complaint of some kind and my sister always worried about her. She would raise heck every morning about going to school on the bus, there was an argument every day about something."

"She was a bright young girl, very enthused with life," remembers Don. "She went to school in Hoyle and then to Roland Michener High School in South Porcupine. She was very headstrong, but she was also high-strung, very high-strung, so she would go into depression fairly easily. She was always on the go, a very busy girl."

In the early 1960s, the Morrisons moved to Field, just outside Sudbury. In a few short years, everything went horribly wrong. George suffered a severe stroke that left him 90 percent paralyzed and unable to speak. Under the added pressure Eileen, who had a congenital heart condition, suffered the first of several minor heart attacks. That did nothing to help Sharon's mood swings, and without any male influence she started to look for a substitute. Sharon had always been interested in boys—even at thirteen when she went to help out her mother's pregnant cousin Evelyn Struthers, who was staying up at Nellie Lake. "She was young, happy-go-lucky, a cute girl," recalls Evelyn. "She was very outgoing and there was a few younger guys in the island and she was certainly interested in them."

At seventeen, she was a pretty girl, tall, five foot seven and very slender—perhaps too thin for some—with blond hair turning to auburn. When she was happy she was wonderful company who loved to talk and talk and talk. When the moods were upon her she could be difficult company as she withdrew into herself. She got engaged to Gilles, a young Frenchman from Sturgeon Falls, whom both her mother and brother liked. Just before the wedding he was killed in a car crash. Sharon was already pregnant. Her daughter, called Jill after her father, was born on April 19, 1963.

Sharon, a once indulged child, found herself flooded by a fistful of adult responsibilities, a baby, an invalid father, a poorly mother, no money. She was not yet eighteen and she should have been out having fun. She found it hard to cope, she could not earn enough to support herself. In 1964, that was a man's job. She needed help. Jill was still a toddler when Sharon met a man who seemed to be the answer to all her problems: Clarence Edwards.

"Those times really hit us all hard, Sharon especially, as she had a little girl," says Don. "When she met Clarence she was still very upset. At that time I thought he was a real nice person."

Clarence Edwards was the eighth of Harold and Regina Edwards's nine children. The Edwardses are a sprawling, brawling clan who emigrated from Ireland in the nineteenth century and fetched up farming in the Ottawa Valley outside Renfrew on the Quebec border. Fed up with life in "Cowshit Valley," Harold's father moved to Chapleau to work on the railroads in the early 1900s.

Timmins, 125 miles to the east, had a reason to exist: the mines. Without the railroad, Chapleau had none. For over a century, it has been the biggest railway terminal between Montreal and Winnipeg and for many years had its own shop and was home to crane drivers, engineers, and drivers. If the railway ever leaves, the town, which is slowly wasting away, will disappear back into the forests. There is logging in abundance, for trucks can go anywhere there is wood and bush road, but little else.

In Chapleau, Harold, who was born in 1906, fell madly in love with fourteen-year-old Regina Benson. Her father was Swedish, while her mother was from an old French family, born and raised in Quebec. Along the way the Quebecois had incorporated some Native genes. "My mother told me one time when I was young that her mother's mother was part Indian," says Gordon Edwards. "Clarence and Ernie, they don't look Indian, but my brother Walter, you put him beside one of these fellas here in the reserve and they are like twins." The Bensons decided to move two hundred miles due north, to Kapuskasing, where the Spruce Falls Power and Paper Plant was promising to build a model town in which the needs of the forestry industry could coexist happily with the community. There is nothing but four hundred miles of river, forest, and lake between Kapuskasing and James Bay, so its location was ideal for an internment camp. During the Great War, thousands of Eastern Europeans, perceived as a threat to national security, were confined there, treated as prisoners of war. After the war, the camp was filled with "dangerous" left-wing radicals, including the leaders of the 1919 Winnipeg general strike.

The smitten Harold followed Regina to Kap and married her in 1927. They set up home on a small farm four miles outside of town. He worked the midnight shift at Spruce Falls Paper, commuting in by dogsled in winter and bicycle in summer, and worked the farm as soon as he got back. As the Great Depression bit, Harold helped support different families, including his in-laws, sending them out into the bush to cut stove wood. "I saw other little kids with nothing to eat, but we lived like millionaires, albeit with no hydro [electricity] and we had to fetch in our own water," recalls Gordon, the second child and the oldest boy, born in 1931.

The secret to Harold's success was simple. He was a bootlegger, distilling moonshine, brewing beer, and selling it to locals, bushwhackers, and Natives. The family was engaged in a perpetual battle to outwit the OPP (Ontario Provincial Police). Despite having no phone, Harold somehow always knew when the cops were coming to search for his still.

"One day, when I was about six, he says, 'Come out for a ride in the sleigh with me,' " says Gordon. "We went out in the bush half a mile or so where he had his still, he picked up all the copper tubing and threw them up into the thick snow in the spruce trees. Then he lights a fire and we sit down. All of a sudden I hear these dogs coming and he says, 'Don't say a word about anything.' The OPPs really scared me, big, big men in fur jackets, fur hats, and fur mitts. The first time I saw them I thought they were bears, I was so scared I couldn't say a word. They asked my father, 'Where's your still? Where's all the paraphernalia for the booze you're making?' They searched all over the place, then they took off again cursing. All they had to do was look above their heads."

One time, when her husband was at work, Regina got word the OPP were on their way. A tiny woman of five foot two, she somehow found the strength to pick up a forty-five-gallon barrel of home brew, stagger out to the porch, and flip it over. Then she washed out the barrel and was sitting comfortably on it when the cops arrived.

Bootlegging was a labor of love for Harold. Drinking to insensible excess was more than blue-collar culture to him, for alcoholism was bred into his bones, a poisoned flagon passed down through the generations. "My father and his two brothers, they could have drunk the lake. Everybody they knew was the same. My father's brother was the only one who went in the army during the war," recalls Gordon, "and when he came home on leave he'd take whatever he could get to drink and go in the bush and lay there for days until the MPs came to find him."

The start of the Second World War was good news for Regina's carpenter brothers. They headed south to work for the car manufacturers in Detroit and Windsor. Harold intended to join up or follow them south, but after the army rejected him for having too many kids to support, he stopped off in Chapleau to see his father, who told him the railroad was desperate for firemen and engineers. He never went back to Kap, just sent word home for them to come and join him. Regina and the kids packed the wagon with furniture, hitched the horse to it, and headed for the station. The train journey was close to 260 miles.

The family settled a mile and a half out of town on Bucciarelli Road. Backwoods kids who had never seen power lines before, they had no idea what the hydro cables that stretched over the peak of the roof did. One day, after Gordon and his mother had walked into town to buy groceries, nine-year-old Ernie went to play on the roof. He was running down the gable, gathering speed as he went, so he thought he'd grab the wires to break his fall, swing on them like Tarzan. The electricity fried his arms so badly he lost them both, and he wore steel hooks from the time he got out of the hospital. The house was cursed, so they moved into town. The hooks never stopped Ernie having fun: When the boys got into fights, he could lay opponents out with one blow.

Music was always there—"Irish people have to have music," says Gordon—part of the furniture. Harold scarcely needed an excuse for a party. He had an old wind-up gramophone and every 78 Hank Snow ever cut, from back when the Nova Scotian could yodel like Jimmie Rodgers, long before "I'm Moving On" made him a Nashville star. Regina's brothers were accomplished musicians, always ready to break out fiddles and guitars. The Edwards boys didn't play anything, but they could all sing. Clarence had a beautiful voice, but he was too shy to use it. Sometimes, when he was a kid and lost in play, he'd start singing. "Christ," says Gordon, "I'm telling you, he had a voice that would drive you up the wall. So good you didn't want him to quit."

The Edwardses were a good-looking clan, especially Clarence—though he had so much body hair that he was too embarrassed to strip off when he was swimming with his brothers. Their sister Irene was a renowned local beauty. "Clarence was so handsome when he was younger," says Shania. "I saw pictures of them and they were a really handsome family. Those young men were so beautiful."

In addition to his looks, Clarence was a good athlete, quick and tough on the basketball court and the ice hockey rink. His cousin Dan Boucher reckons he was the best broomball player (shooting around on ice using a broom and ball instead of a stick and a puck) in Chapleau. He had a temper, though; one night a spectator gave him so much grief that eventually Clarence dropped his broom, vaulted the rail, and repaid the heckler in kind.

There was always a rebellious, screw-authority streak in Clarence. When he was a kid and did not get his own way, he threw himself onto the ground and held his breath until he turned blue. The only person who could talk air back into his lungs was his father. After high school, he joined the army. He looked smart in his uniform, but he constantly clashed with the stripes and the brass. When he didn't fancy his latest posting, he went AWOL until the MPs dragged him back. Eventually the military tired of his antics, banged him up in the glasshouse for six months, and sent him packing with a discharge. For a while he roamed Ontario working odd jobs.

In the fall of 1964, Clarence met Sharon Morrison in a Sudbury bar. They were physical opposites, which might have accounted for some of the attraction. Clarence was dark, with a heavy build, five foot nine (tall for an Edwards), arms like hams. Sharon was skinny, so thin that she seemed taller than she actually was, a twitchy girl forever lighting another cigarette while its predecessor still smoldered, hoping it might calm her jangling nerves, giving her hands something with which to occupy themselves. Even in a culture where everybody smoked all the time, people remember Sharon as a chain-smoker.

Clarence was a handsome guy, black haired and olive skinned, a party boy, full of Irish blarney and bravado. Sharon came from a normal family with traditional values, and here was a gorgeous man with laughing green eyes who didn't seem to care about the mess her life was in. Small wonder that she grabbed on to him, a life raft in her stormy seas. Needy, lonely, and insecure, once she had him she was not going to let go.

Gordon Edwards was working underground at the Levack mine and was living in Chelmsford, just outside Sudbury, when Clarence and Sharon turned up looking for a place to stay, to be alone for a couple of days. Although he has been sober for the past fifteen years, Gordon still retains one family trait. He is quick to judge and slow to forgive. Sharon's arrival in the house was akin to throwing gasoline on a bonfire.

"Three days later I've had it up to here with this girl, but Clarence, he wants to marry her," says Gordon. So he called his younger brothers Walter and Desi together, told them there was an important family meeting that night, and ordered Clarence to send his girl out somewhere, anywhere. The boys got together after work and started downing a few, until Gordon stepped into his elder-brother role and told Clarence, "You can't marry this girl, it's impossible, you marry her and you'll be in the fucking nuthouse in a year."

Clarence took the point, but all he said was: "I have to marry her because we are having a baby." Gordon tried to reason with him, told him he wasn't the first guy to have a baby by accident and anyway she'd already been down that route once and why hadn't the last guy married her? Clarence, who knew about Jill's father, refused to budge; he was going to stand by Sharon and that was it. Gordon told him he was going to be sorry, washed his hands of the affair, and they all got hammered.

Eileen Morrison was too ill to attend the wedding in Garson, so Don Fraser gave Sharon away. Soon after, Clarence and Sharon moved down to Windsor, just across the border from Detroit, where the pay in the Chrysler plant was better than the mines. They rented a house and their daughter was born on August 28, 1965. They christened her Eilleen after her maternal grandmother and Regina after Clarence's mother. Little Eilleen was a true child of the New World, more Irish (coming from all sides) than anything else, with healthy dashes of English, Swedish, and Scottish blood, leavened with exotic touches of French, Native, and Spanish.

The baby girl might have calmed things for a while, but in truth the relationship was doomed before it began. It was a marriage forged in mistake, transferred onto a never-ending battlefield on which there could be no victors, only damaged offspring. Sharon needed someone preternaturally calm who could still the demons in her head. She craved security. Instead, she had a man from a family that considered her to be a nutcase. The Edwards clan still rails about Sharon. To them she has become the monster who destroyed any vestige of a relationship Clarence might have had with his daughters. But they admit "he is no saint." He never was.

"I had a very stressful job, being a railroad engineer," Clarence said in his only interview. "On top of that, Shania's mom was a very jealous, possessive person. She didn't like me to do normal things like go out for a beer with my friends. I had to be home all the time. There was a lot of stress. I had a nervous breakdown and wound up in the hospital for a time. Shortly after I got out, I just decided enough was enough. One day, I just left."

There were times when Sharon's behavior became erratic. She needed stability and there was none, which magnified her mood swings. There are signs of an obsessive compulsive disorder in the way she tackled problems all her life, though her daughter insists that Sharon's problems with Clarence were caused by her circumstances, not a mental condition. Back in the 1960s, the only medication for a working-class mother was tranquilizers. "She was on nerve pills steady, she was always taking pills," says Gordon. "I've seen her with the pills because one time I went into the blues. She was the one who helped me out, gave me these frigging nerve pills and actually talked me out of it. I took a couple of pills, went to sleep, and when I woke up I was okay."

When she was on an up, there was a hyper intensity to Sharon; her energy was phenomenal, her emotions allowed no half measures. The Edwardses say she was jealous and possessive, that she had to know where Clarence was at all times. If his friends phoned, he'd sneak out to join them for a beer. He might neck a couple before Sharon found him. If he stopped by for a drink after a broomball game and came back with a book of matches from an un-known bar, she accused him of having an affair. According to Gordon, Sharon's mental and physical demands on her husband were constant and exhausting.

"They were living in South Porcupine. Me and three other fellas went to go to the winter carnival," says Gordon. "I was hanging around until Clarence came in from work and when he did come in, he said, 'I have to go to the bank to cash my check so we can go to this thing.' Sharon told him, 'You have got fifteen minutes—don't forget it.' He goes and he comes back and it was sixteen minutes and she says to him, 'You were fucking the teller!' It was a fight from then until we went to the carnival and all the time we were there."

Such problems were hardly surprising, for by this point in their disintegrating marriage Sharon knew only too well what Clarence was like. His charm and looks had seduced her, and when the drink was talking it could certainly do the same to others. Shania is adamant that her mother is the wronged party. "How she responded to that situation and dealt with it was not the result of any illness," she says. "If he was a womanizer and he was drinking, of course it would have driven my mother nuts. She had all these insecurities already, having a daughter coming into the marriage, feeling maybe he was doing her a favor.

"She was such a straight woman. She came from a family who are so straight and nice, genuine to the core. She was a good person who got caught up with the wrong people. My mother must have gone through such hell. It was the nightmare of her life. The Edwardses are all pretty wild, so I am glad my mother kept me away from them. If she hadn't I think my future would have been very different."

Clarence moved from one job to another, though he always put food on the table. From Windsor they moved to Toronto, where he worked for CNR (Canadian National Railways) in the car department, and then back to Timmins. They stayed with Sharon's mother in Hoyle while Don, who was a superintendent at Texas Gulf's Kidd Creek mine, fixed Clarence a job.

Eventually it was Clarence who could not cope. In Toronto he'd go to the gym, run for an hour, dripping with sweat, to get everything out of his system for a few minutes. It was a steady fight from the time they got up to the time they went to bed, especially after Clarence had a few drinks. Once, as they were crossing the horseshoe bridge, driving into Chapleau, arguing furiously, Clarence crashed the car straight into the town dairy, demolishing both it and the car. On occasion his temper got him into bar brawls ("If he gets mad enough, get out of his road," warns Gordon).

By the time Carrie Ann was born on December 16, 1967, both Clarence and the marriage were finished. His nerves shot, he committed himself to a mental hospital. Discharging himself after several weeks, he returned home and quickly realized he could not take it anymore. One day he went out for a pack of cigarettes and a loaf of bread. Nobody in the family heard from him for months until he turned up in Toronto, back working for CNR in the boxcar department. Eventually, he returned to Chapleau and went to work on the railway as an engineer.

Clarence never came back. He left his daughters with a powerful genetic inheritance—beauty and a wonderful singing voice—and his wife with a shadow of fear, a worry that one day he might return and demand to take his children away with him. When she was seven, Eilleen asked what her father looked like. Sharon described him. The next day Eilleen was out in the park and saw a man who fit that description. She rushed home and, as children do, announced excitedly, "I saw Clarence. I'm sure I did." She remembers her mother's nervous reaction: "Where did you see him? What do you mean?"

Although they first met formally when she was thirteen, Eilleen still has distinct memories of her father from her early childhood. Not of his face—"I didn't know what he looked like at all"—but of this obscured, shady image.

"I was scared by that image because it was always secretive," she says. "I always got the feeling that he wasn't supposed to be there. My mother didn't want him around, but he came in and out of her life anyway. I didn't need to see him—I was probably in bed—but I knew that was him. He'd surprise my mom and she'd get nervous. My mother was scared of him. I don't know why I was afraid of him but I always sensed fear when he was around."

"It was a very sad marriage," says Don. "Clarence and Sharon were just bad for each other. She was prone to be excitable and high-strung for sure. They were set staying at my mother's place in Hoyle and he [Clarence] just left and never come back. I'd say Clarence was the worst person she could have married and Jerry was the best."

Eileen Morrison adored her three granddaughters. After Clarence left, Sharon and the girls lived with her in Hoyle. She looked after them as well as supporting Sharon financially. Knowing how sick she herself was, Eileen worried about them all the time. "Sharon got depressed and Eileen worried that she wouldn't look after the girls properly. I imagine that Sharon loved her in her way, but she wasn't the easiest person to live with," says May Thompson. "Eileen gave her life up for those three little girls. When she was on her deathbed, she said to me, 'I've been lying here thinking what is going to happen to those kids. I've decided that my sister Grace will take one, my sister-in-law Isla will take one.' I said to her, 'Which one am I going to have?' and she said, 'Carrie Ann.'"

That never happened. Sharon had already met the man who would give her the stability and support she had craved for so long. A man who wanted to be a father to her three little girls.

Chapter Two

THE MAN FROM MATTAGAMI

ABANDONED, LEFT HIGH, dry, and penniless, Sharon wanted nothing more to do with her husband. With the same intense focus with which she had attempted to keep him in her life, she cut him out of it. She refused to let him have anything to do with raising his daughters. She told the girls she didn't need him, that none of them did, and that they never would. It was a brave, if foolhardy, decision. Aged twenty-four with three daughters under five and no professional qualifications, Sharon's prospects were not great. She stayed with her mother and found part-time work in menial jobs, as a cleaner or in hotel kitchens.

On days when the black clouds went away, Sharon was engaging company. Unlike some Timmins locals, who ranted and raved against the Indians, she had no racial prejudices. In town one day, she struck up a friendship with an Ojibwe girl called Audrey Twain. Audrey decided Sharon was just right for her younger brother Jerry and determined to set them up. One night in late 1969, when Jerry had returned home after working on a logging contract out west in British Columbia, Sharon was invited over to the Twain home at 294 Birch Street North.

She liked what she saw. Although he was two years her junior, there was something solid and reassuring about Jerry. A lot of Native people are very quiet and Jerry was, too, a watcher who bided his time; he did not strut into a room and demand attention, but he certainly was not an introvert. He spoke when he had something to say and could carry on a very good conversation. But there was something else there . . . a twinkle, a sparkle behind his eyes. He loved to tease, but gently, without malice. He laughed a lot, used his humor to alleviate Sharon's dark moments. Above all, Jerry was strong, both physically and mentally. "He was everybody's leaning post," says Karen Twain. "When we were going through so much my brother was always the one who told us, 'Be tough.' "

Étienne Brulé would have recognized Jerry Twain. To look at, he was all Native: short—only five foot six—powerfully built with a low center of gravity, jet black hair with matching eyes carved from coal. The name, the clothes, and the language might have changed, but the spirit was the same as the French explorer had seen in the Ojibwe warriors 350 years earlier: the unbending duty toward his extended clan, the love for the forests, the physical presence, and the pride, the absolute certainty in who he was.

Although their name lacks the historical and romantic resonance of such tribes as the Sioux, the Apache, the Commanche, or even small tribes like the Huron and the Mohawk, the Ojibwe have been one of the largest Native groups in North America for most of their known history. The Ojibwe remain unrecognized in cowboy and Indian history primarily because of their geographical remoteness. Secondly, despite being skilled hunters and fierce warriors, they were smart enough to seldom confront white governments in open warfare.

There were always more Woodland Ojibwe than people realized. They lived in the forests on the east banks of Lake Superior and to the north of Lake Huron, stretching all the way up to Hudson Bay. There may have been as many as one hundred thousand living in northern Ontario when they first encountered Brulé in 1623 at Sault Sainte Marie. Prior to that first contact they were a loose confederation of independent clans, bound together by a common language. The Ojibwe are one people with three names—Chippewa, Ojibwe, and Anishinabe—as well as dozens of subgroupings and bands.

Chippewa is the "official" name recognized by the United States government and was used on all their treaties. (Stick an "o" in front of Chippewa and the linguistic link is obvious.) In Canada, they are known as Ojibwe (pronounced "Oh-jib-way"), the name given them by their enemies back in the seventeenth century. It means "to pucker" and comes from the way their moccasins were sewn with a distinctive puckered seam to keep out the snow. They refer to themselves as Anishinabe and more playfully as "nish-nobs."

Their land was never suited to agriculture. The Ojibwe were expert woodcraftsmen, hunter-gatherers who harvested wild rice and used maple syrup and sugar as seasoning and a food preservative. They hunted moose and partridge, trapped beaver or rabbit, and fished for sturgeon. Birch bark was used to make utensils, storage containers, and canoes, and to cover their dome-shaped wigwams. They dressed in buckskin, adding layers of fur when the snow came.

In summer, bands gathered by lakes, living off fish, berries, and wild rice. During winter, the communities (at most a few hundred strong) split into extended families living in isolated camps, which allowed the men to range for miles without encountering any competition. Perhaps owing to those long winters confined inside their tepees, the Ojibwe became renowned as great storytellers. (In one tale explaining the origin of Chicago, the Ojibwe refer to it as "the Place of the Skunk"!) Henry Longfellow's famous narrative poem *The Song of Hiawatha* tells of a young brave growing up on the shores of Lake Superior. After many adventures he marries a Dakota maiden, Minnehaha ("laughing water"), and eventually departs for the Isles of the Blest to rule the kingdom of the Northwest Wind. Longfellow got his tribal alliances and names mixed up. While the geographical locations and stories are all taken from Ojibwe legends, the original Hiawatha was a Mohawk, who, like Minnehaha's Dakota Sioux, were their sworn enemies.

Originally, hereditary chiefs only had limited authority over their own band. However, direct contact with the French fur traders, who admired the high quality of their beaver pelts, changed the social structure of the Ojibwe forever. Seeking to fill a seemingly insatiable demand back home, the French offered steel weapons and firearms in exchange for fur.

To the east, Dutch and French merchants had encouraged an arms race, which, coupled with the virtual eradication of beaver in southern Ontario, had upset the old balance of power. For the seventy years of the Beaver Wars (1630–1700), the Iroquois Alliance and the Huron squabbled and fought for possession of new hunting grounds. Initially, the Ojibwe were too far away to become involved, but when the Iroquois, the best-armed force in North America, started to raid their territory, the Ojibwe did not flee. Instead, they regrouped around Sault Sainte Marie and organized into larger battle groups. In 1662, they surprised a large Mohawk war party just west of Sault Sainte Marie and annihilated it. Still known today as Iroquois Point, the Ojibwe call it "the place of Iroquois bones." Soon afterward, they drove their enemies back east for good.

By 1700, the Ojibwe supplied two-thirds of the French fur trade and Ojibwe had become the unofficial trade language. The larger bands continued to extend their hunting grounds south and east of Lake Superior—an area then of little interest to Europeans—and eventually, after a hundred-year war, wrested the lakes and wild rice–growing areas in northern Michigan, Wisconsin, and Minnesota from the Sioux. In 1820, the Ojibwe were the largest and most powerful Great Lakes tribe and quite probably the strongest in North America.

As French power in Canada waned after 1763, the British established strong trading links with the Ojibwe. During the British-American war of 1812, they helped defend Ontario from invasion. After 1815, the Ojibwe signed a peace treaty and were seldom in direct conflict with the United States—they always preferred to fight the Sioux—though north of the border some did support Louis Riel's Métis (mixed French-Cree-Ojibwe) forces in the Red River Rebellions of 1869 and 1884.

The last official battle of the Indian Wars did involve the Ojibwe. On October 5, 1898, US army troops were sent to the Leech Lake reservation in northern Minnesota to arrest Bugonaygeshig, a dissident elder. As his braves gathered around, an army rifle was accidentally discharged, and the soldiers found themselves surrounded and under fire. Eventually, a truce was agreed and the army withdrew without their quarry. To save face, Private O. Burchard was given the last Medal of Honor awarded in an Indian campaign. As historian Lee Sultzman remarks, "A soldier got the medal, but as was the case with almost every enemy they had ever faced, the Ojibwe had won the battle."

While they were never beaten in war, economics, disease, and the slow, inexorable advance of European settlers proved more effective in destroying Ojibwe power. The total collapse of the fur trade in the mid-nineteenth century destroyed their economic clout, and a series of treaties—fifty-one with the Americans and thirty with the British—slowly whittled away their lands. Western diseases, notably smallpox epidemics, killed thousands, while the insidious effects of alcohol sapped their spirit. However, the Ojibwe remain numerous. There are currently 130,000 in the United States and 60,000 in Canada. Of the 600-plus First Nations recognized by Canada, more than 130 are Ojibwe (at least in part), spread across Ontario, Manitoba, Saskatchewan, and Alberta.

When Jerry Twain was born on September 24, 1947, years of social and economic neglect had eroded much of the Ojibwe's self-respect. Primitive living conditions on the reserves resulted in high infant mortality and low life expectancy. In town, many Indians—they were still called Indians then—found it hard to get jobs and lived off welfare. Inherently shy, coming from a culture where it is impolite to look people straight in the eyes, their problems were compounded by booze. After a few drinks, retiring personalities would flip, leading to fights.

Indians were often dismissed as dysfunctional, unreliable, and lazy, an image founded on ignorance and fanned by prejudice. When the Twain family first moved to Timmins in 1964, there was only one other Native family in the town. "My brother and I had pretty much a hard time," says Karen Twain. "When my mother took us and enrolled us in school, people just surrounded us. They kept asking us where had we lived before and did we live in a tepee. People were ignorant back then. We'd lived all over, but I don't remember being teased anyplace else, maybe because there were other Native families in most of the towns we moved to."

The Twains were a long way from the shiftless Indians of public imagination. Jerry's father—also Gerry (born February 9, 1922)—was brought up on Bear Island on the Lake Temagami reservation, an hour out of North Bay. He first met Selina Luke (born July 10, 1923), whose friends called her "Chi Jo" ("It means squirrel or something like that," says Karen), when she and her mother came down from Mattagami to visit. He was only eight, but told her firmly he was going to marry her. They eventually married on September 25, 1944. Between 1945 and 1958, they had four children (Audrey, Jerry, Karen, and Tim) and moved from small town to small town—Shining Tree, New Liskeard, Latchford—in search of work. Gerry worked as a line cutter and claim staker and instilled in his family such pride in his heritage that his eldest son refused government welfare all his life.

"My dad wanted the family to do well," says Karen. "He liked the bush but he wouldn't sit in the reservation taking welfare; we were taught to try and make it on our own." Gerry moved the family to Timmins after he was hired by the legendary prospector Don McKinnon to stake claims in Kidd Township, eighteen miles north of the town. (The area he staked became part of the valuable Kidd Creek mine, which produces zinc and silver to this day.)

Ojibwe culture had been systematically eradicated. Traditional names were replaced by Tims, Ricks, and Harriets, while, like the slavemasters did to their African-American slaves, surnames were imposed at random. Karen has no idea where the Twain surname came from. "I went back to my reserve," she says, "where they were making a family tree, but it's hard to trace back because there were no birth certificates and records."

While Gerry and Selina spoke Ojibwe and were determined to keep the old tales and traditions alive, their children spoke only a few words. The language, bedeviled with dozens of different dialects, was deliberately targeted by the Canadian educational system. "Our parents couldn't speak it at school. If they were caught, they were punished," says Jerry's cousin Willis McKay, "so they spoke to us in English. After grade six my brother and cousin and I were sent away to a residential school in Sault Sainte Marie—four hundred miles away—and our parents didn't have no say in the matter. There we weren't allowed to speak anything but English. And that is how we lost our language. It is now spoken only by the elderly people and I can't speak or understand it."

The Twain children all attended normal high schools. Jerry was smart, although his schooling was constantly interrupted by the family moving about, and despite attending Timmins High and Vocational School, he never graduated. On his return from British Columbia he buckled down and studied accounting at night school. During the day he worked at the Ministry of Natural Resources marking logs. For all they lived in towns, the Twains never lost their love of the bush. Close to their ancestral lands they found relief in the old ways. Woodcraft was woven into their being like birch bark. All his life, Jerry hunted and trapped, as much for love of it as for survival. It defined who he was.

Jerry had had a few girlfriends, but nobody serious until he met Sharon. "He took an immediate liking to her, I guess," laughs Karen. "He asked her out on a date straight away. He took her out to dinner—he invited me as well but I wouldn't go—well, they went out and from that night on they were inseparable, it was really quick."

Unlike many other men, it didn't bother him that Sharon was white, nor that she had three little girls. From the beginning they connected, though it wasn't always love's young dream. "I used to laugh at them," says Karen, "because they used to get into a tiff. I knew there was something wrong, because one would show up at my place and then the other would show up a little later, but they were always so close."

Like any other ethnic group, Native Americans have been marrying outside their tribes for centuries. In white society, a Native wife was a cause for social stigma and so the information was often buried and then denied. That is what Shania believes happened in the Edwards family. "She [my mother] told me they were ashamed of it and would never admit it," she told Q magazine. "Apparently, my great-grandmother was Indian and married a white man. In those times it was not unusual for such women to have to renounce their Indian status and leave the reservation, so it's very, very believable that she had to leave her family and never associate again."

It was less common for Native men to marry white women. Sharon's choice of second husband certainly incensed Gordon Edwards, who to this day refers to Jerry as "that Twain fella" and, with little foundation in fact, dismisses him as an alcoholic, claiming "Show me an Indian who isn't an alky; there is something they can't handle in alcohol."

In 1971, such prejudice was the norm in a blue-collar town like Timmins, and an air of tacit disapproval hung over Jerry and Sharon's relationship for years. Gerry senior did enjoy a few drinks, but was so severely beaten up by three youths one night after leaving a bar that he ended up in intensive care.

Sharon's divorce took a while to come through, but they were married on June 4, 1970, after which Jerry formally adopted the three girls. They were members of the Temagami Anishinabe Bear Island First Nation Band, registered as 50 percent Native Canadian and entitled to the same medical, dental, and welfare benefits. Natives did not have to pay 8 percent Provincial Sales Tax. Until the law changed in 1986, a woman marrying a Native man was automatically accepted into the band. Regardless of their genetic bloodlines, Jill, Eilleen, and Carrie Ann were, and still are, legally Native. To Jerry's Ojibwe relatives it was more than that; they were true kin raised in the same nest, if not from the same egg.

Mark (someone had a sense of humor) was born two years later, on August 18, 1972. Darryl was born on February 21, 1974. He was Audrey's son, whom they adopted after she committed suicide in March 1975. Despite this tangled family tree, nobody batted an eyelash; traditionally, Ojibwe childcare has always been spread across extended families and there is no stigma on adoption.

From the start Jerry announced, "There will be no step-anything in this family," a pledge he never broke. All the Twains embraced the responsibility of being family, so that the ties of love became closer than those of blood. The girls had few enough relatives. The Edwards family were at the time little more than names to them. Bert Morrison had died in 1968, his last years spent in a nursing home, trapped inside his body, scarcely moving and unable to communicate. Eileen died in 1971, only sixty, a kind woman worn out by misfortune, worrying to the very end. "My mother on her dying breath said, 'Don, please take care of them little girls,'" says Don Fraser, who had five children of his own to raise. "That was her last breath to me and I've told the girls that. If they were ever in need they knew that Uncle Don was always there. If they ever asked me, my home was there . . . but they were always independent."

Little Eilleen took an immediate shine to Gerry and Selina Twain, who in their turn loved the girls back as if they were their very own, and they were welcomed as family by Jerry's other relatives. The family visited the Mattagami reserve all the time—it was midway between Sudbury and Timmins—staying many weekends and most of the summer. Jerry's cousin Willis McKay remembers Eilleen: "She was four or five when she was first out here. She was always chasing after the other kids. Mostly they played hide and seek at the time, as this place was all bush then.

"Everybody knew Sharon and Jerry. They were devoted to their children. They were raised well even though there wasn't much money. They were fun to be with, they joked around and they enjoyed people's company."

When Eilleen first visited the reserve in 1970, it was a primitive, poor place, cut off from the world, and could only be reached along a back road from Gogama. There were no more than twenty houses and a community hall huddled on a point surrounded by Lake Mattagami on two sides and thirteen thousand acres of trees and bush on the others. The houses were two-roomed wooden shacks built back in 1951, when the Ojibwe were given the land. There was no electricity; in winter, the snow was packed tight around the sides of the shacks, which were heated by wood-burning stoves and lit by oil lamps. Sanitation was "a little pee pot on the porch" or an outhouse. Running water lasted from spring thaw until around Christmas, when the water lines froze and everyone had to haul water up from the lake until the lines opened up again in April. Mattagami finally got hydro in 1971; at the same time it ceased to be called an Indian reserve and became a "First Nation," but it took many years to upgrade the buildings and get in proper plumbing.

Mattagami was a small place and, as most of the inhabitants were related, it enjoyed a communal style of living. "You could sleep pretty much where you wanted and go eat at anyone's house," recalls Eilleen, "like it was one big family." There were singalong parties in the community hall. At Christmas, she'd get up onstage and sing a few country songs. In the summers they never missed the powwows, applauding the competitive dancing displays, joining in the drumming and the barbecues. Instead of chocolate-chip cookies, treats were chunks of moose meat and partridge cooked over a fire or deep-fried bannock dumplings topped with jam.

Living off the land was essential in Mattagami, whose inhabitants were not bound by hunting restrictions. "In those days, there was still a good return on the fur from trapping," says Willis McKay. "My father and some of the older members would go trapping and be gone a week, maybe more. They had to skin them, stretch them, and bring them to the Hudson Bay settlement. Jerry loved the bush, he did a lot of trapping around here; he didn't own a trap line, but he did live on wildlife for a part of his time here. Back then we were more reliant on hunting. Moose meat, beaver, rabbit were the three main ones, and deer, partridge, and fish from the lake."

In wintertime, meat was packed, stripped, labeled on paper, and stored in outdoor sheds (freezers after electricity came). In summertime, the Ojibwe built wells twenty feet down to keep the moose meat cold. If there was a danger of it going rotten it would be distributed to all the families, who would dry and smoke it.

Hunting was a communal occupation. Hunters went out to catch enough for everybody and children were expected to do their bit.

Gerry and Selina taught Eilleen how to track and snare rabbits. "They would take me out into the bush in winter and show me where the rabbit's tracks would intersect. That's where you'd set your snare." The snare was a stick with a loop of wire a bit bigger than a rabbit's head set across the trail, just above the ground. When the animal ran into the loop, it would strangle itself. Like all the children she was taught to use a gun as soon as she was old enough to carry one.

"I was a good little hunter," says Eilleen, who also claims to be a good shot with a bow and arrow, although most of the hunters at Mattagami only used rifles or shotguns. "I was carrying a gun when I was eight years old. Hunting for us was very different, not the whole camouflage GI Joe thing. When we needed food, we'd go hunt. It wasn't a sport, it was about surviving."

Children were automatically taught how to survive in the bush. "We'd have camping trips, the kids would play, some people would fish. We were all taught how to live in the bush the Native way," says Karen Twain. "You can't get me lost in the bush; it's the same with Eilleen. My father taught us that when you are in the bush it all looks the same, so you have to look for certain markers, a mark on a tree, a different sort of rock, and if you keep those in mind you can never get lost."

There are certain experiences in childhood that never leave, which make such an impression that they color the adult forever. Eilleen's time spent in the bush with her adoptive family left her with a yearning that can only ever be assuaged when she is sitting alone among the trees, staring into a fire, watching wisps of woodsmoke dance her memories across the darkness. "I like being secluded. I like solitude. I never want to let go of it. It's a craving for me. I have to be in the bush," she has said. "I like chopping wood. I like making fires. I love smelling like fire. That's my favorite smell. I love it when my hair smells like fire."

Chapter Three

LATE-NIGHT BARS
(FOR A CHILD STAR)

THERE WAS OTHER SMOKE that haunted Eilleen's memories: the fug of stale tobacco smoke that hung over the pools of spilled beer in late-night bars. Times when a terrified little girl was woken in the middle of the night and thrust half-asleep, dressed in a buckskin dress—handsewn by Grandma Selina—and cowboy boots, hiding behind a guitar almost as big as she was, onto a stage to entertain a bunch of half-drunk miners and loggers. She gave them Hank Williams's "Kaw-liga" just the way Charley Pride did, belted out Tanya Tucker's raunchy "Delta Dawn," wrung the beer tears out with Dolly Parton's "Coat of Many Colors," and left them with Kris Kristofferson's "Me and Bobby McGee."

On those late nights at the Mattagami Hotel in Timmins, or whichever bar gig Sharon had found, singing "Freedom's just another word for nothing left to lose," Eilleen truly did not have much left to lose. The family needed the twenty bucks she earned and Sharon kept telling her she needed the experience. She hated it, really hated it, didn't feel like singing at that time of night at all. She was eight years old. She loved to sing . . . but she hated performing.

Eilleen could always sing. She has no memory of a time before music. "When I was three," she says, "I would go out the back of the house into the garden, find a space, and just sing to myself. I needed to be alone. I always wanted to get lost in my own little world where I would hum and sing to myself. Often I could not be found for hours. I remember being put on top of a countertop by my mother when I was three. I would always sing out loud to the jukebox."

She did not sing nursery rhymes like "Twinkle Twinkle Little Star" with a toddler's lisp and a wandering tune; instead she held the melody and experimented with phrasing and tone. At six she was singing the harmony parts because they were more interesting.

For show-and-tell at her primary school, six-year-old Eilleen decided to sing John Denver's "Take Me Home, Country Roads." At home everybody loved it; unfortunately, the horde of first-graders were less impressed and they teased her mercilessly, christening her "Twang" and instilling in her a fear of performing in public that was to last a decade. "All my classmates thought I was being a show-off and it created serious inhibitions for me," she recalled in a letter to her fans written in 1994. "From that point on I was afraid to perform."

Sharon, however, would have none of that. She recognized that her daughter had a special talent because of the way she would harmonize with songs on the radio—Eilleen adored the Mamas and the Papas, the Carpenters, and the Supremes—or extemporize new parts to the country songs on the creaky eight-track player, which included Jerry's favorites: Charley Pride, Waylon Jennings, Dolly, and Tanya.

Don Fraser has never been quite sure where Eilleen's musical talent came from, though Roger Pearce insists it's there in the younger generations. "I don't think there is a musician in our family and as far as I know none on the Morrison side," says Don. "My mother couldn't sing, but she loved music. She was a wonderful lady, everybody loved her, and I think it was her who Eilleen got her talent from. Eilleen does look like her. Her drive she got from Sharon, for sure. Sharon really believed in Eilleen, it was the one thing she really believed in. I know how much she pushed her; she was the driving force. One year, we had our relatives up from Piney. Myrna Lorrie was performing at the Mattagami Hotel and

Sharon said, 'Would you like to hear Eilleen sing?' She was still little. We went down there, she performed, and it was just tremendous. At the end Myrna came up to us and said, 'That young girl
has a lot of talent and she is going to go places.' "

The musical branch of Jerry's family was Selina's side. Her
younger sister had married Romeo Derasp, a French Métis, and the
whole family played music—their son Kenny played guitar and
sang while Romeo and his brother had a pick-up country band on
the weekends. Kenny was thirteen on Christmas 1972, when there
was a family party at his mother's house in Timmins. It was the first
time he had met his cousin Jerry's new wife and family.

"We were having a Christmas get-together at my mother's," says
Kenny. "I was singing, my dad was singing, when Eilleen stepped up
and said, 'I want to sing a song.' She was very young but we were
all shocked by how good she was. Her timing was good, her pitch
was good, it surprised everyone, came out of the blue. She sang her
little heart out. My dad said, 'This kid can sing, you should bring
her down to Sudbury and we'll get her out in public.'

"I have often thought they moved down to Sudbury because of
that. Sharon was a real stage mom, she was so enthusiastic about
the whole music thing."

After Sharon and Jerry married, they rented a small house on
Bannerman Avenue in Timmins. Jerry had a job on the line in the
mines, which he hated; it was physically demanding and kept him
inside. The following year, the Twains moved down south. They
rented a small apartment on King Street, in the Flour Mill area, one
of the poorer sections of Sudbury. Kenny Derasp lived with his dad
on Queen Street, two blocks away across Little Creek, but spent a
lot of time over at his cousins'. Any hand with the babysitting was
greatly appreciated because the family was strapped for cash. Jerry
went to work for a local building supply store while Sharon took
on two part-time jobs. In the day, she was a chambermaid at the
Sorento Hotel. In the evenings, she waited tables at Gus's Restaurant, a Greek-Canadian family eatery at 336 Elm Street W. At
Gus's she earned C$1.30 an hour and could make a further C$5 in

tips. Her shift finished at 1 A.M., after which the owner would always drive her home.

When she was ten, Jill was given an acoustic guitar, but somehow it was her little sister who always ended up hugging it. One day, Jerry was fooling around on it and started showing Eilleen how to hold it so that her left hand could travel up and down the fretboard, while her right hand strummed across the strings—no easy task, as the little girl was dwarfed by the instrument. Jerry was not an accomplished picker but he knew his way around a couple of instrumentals—the old Carter family classic "Wildwood Flower" and "Under the Double Eagle," a standard based on an old German march—and taught her the basic chords. Soon she could play Stompin' Tom Connors songs as well as he could.

Stompin' Tom Connors is a Canadian icon, yet nobody outside the country has a clue who he is. Born into utter poverty in Saint John, New Brunswick, to a single mother, he was taken into care before being adopted. At fifteen, he took off from his hometown of Skinners' Pond, Prince Edward Island, with his guitar and for the next thirteen years hitchhiked across the country subsisting on menial jobs and handouts. His big break came in 1966 at the Maple Leaf Hotel in Timmins (a coincidence that was not lost on Sharon). When he discovered that he was a nickel short of a beer, the bartender, Gaet Lepine, suggested Tom play a few songs instead. He was such a hit that he ended up playing at the hotel for the next thirteen months. CKGB, the local radio station, gave him a weekly spot and issued eight 45-rpm singles of his songs. In 1969, he signed with a national label and soon became a star.

There was nothing complicated about Stompin' Tom. His songs are no-frills, three-chord country, Tom in his roll-brimmed cowboy hat strumming a guitar, stomping out the rhythm with his pointed Western boot. Maybe another guitar and an acoustic bass, but nothing else to detract from the lyrics. His songs, like "Sudbury Saturday Night," "Bud the Spud," "I Am the Wind," "The Bridge Came Tumbling Down," and "The Canadian Lumberjack," are not full of poetic images. They are tales that resonated with the drinking men in the

Maple Leaf because they are all about ordinary working-class Joes like them—truckers, miners, boatmen—who liked to season all their food with ketchup, get hammered on the weekend, and watch other big guys beat the crap out of each other on the hockey rink. (Stompin' Tom is also a dyed-in-the-maple-leaf patriot with a fierce personal integrity. In 1979, railing against the Americanization of the domestic music industry, he handed back all six of his Juno Awards. What relevance, he reasoned, did Dionne Warwick have to Canada? This was not just a symbolic gesture, as he did not tour or release any new records for the next six years. His legend, however, has continued to grow.) Tom Connors stood for all the little guys, because he was one. Small wonder Jerry Twain loved him. Sharon reasoned that if Stompin' Tom could get his break out of Timmins— and they'd seen him many times—so could her daughter.

Kenny, who had been playing guitar since he was six and was pretty proficient, took over teaching Eilleen. "I saw she had a knack for it and so I started showing her chords and stuff." She quickly grasped the rudiments and began practicing with the Derasps. One of her first shows was at the Christmas for the Kids Telethon held in the auditorium at Sudbury High. Her first recordings were just Kenny playing and her singing. "We didn't know what we were doing," he says, "but we were playing the songs at a million miles an hour. We did Tammy Wynette's 'Your Good Girl's Going to Go Bad' so fast we turned it into a rock song. It was hilarious."

Soon Eilleen and her guitar were inseparable. "I started playing guitar at eight, but I was singing long before then," she says. "I was serious about experimenting with my voice harmonies. That was all I wanted to do. I didn't want to play with dolls or anything else but my guitar. I would play until my fingers were bruised. If I'd had it my way, I'd have taken the easy option and remained a songwriter, not a performer. I loved music, but I was never passionate about being a performer."

Sharon was not prepared to let that happen. She was a deter- mined stage mother who "lived for my career. She knew I was tal- ented and she lived with the hope that my abilities were my chance to do something special." When the family moved out to Hanmer, they bought Eilleen her first guitar, an Elvegas copy of a Gibson Hummingbird. She was given music lessons by a local guitar teacher. Then they bought a piano and sent her off for lessons. Sharon pumped every visiting band for information. One night, a singer gave her some advice on microphone technique, how you had to learn to back off and then come up real close, sing in a whisper one moment and a scream the next. A few days later, Sharon came home with a small PA system complete with tiny amp, a mixer, two column speakers, and a Shure SM58 microphone, determined that Eilleen learn how to work with a microphone. Jerry was furious, so Sharon had to get a part-time job pumping gas until she paid for it.

Sharon and Jerry sacrificed a great deal so that Eilleen could have access to everything she needed. They drove her the twelve-hour round-trip to Toronto for voice lessons. Sharon needed her daughter to succeed, for that meant not only escape from the drudgery of her life but a more fundamental affirmation of her worth. Over the next few years she lapsed into long depressions, often triggered when Eilleen's career was not going well.

In the mid-1970s, the Woodland Hotel in Val Caron was one of Sudbury's premier country gigs—a bit faded around the edges, but it could attract out-of-town artists of the caliber of Myrna Lorrie. Sharon convinced the owners to let Eilleen come and perform. To do that she had to wait until after they had finished serving liquor at 1 A.M. By that stage half the audience were too soaked in beer and whiskey to care. "When there was a good band in town, my parents would get permission and ask the club if they minded if I came in to sing," Shania remembers. "Lots of times the band would play past after they started closing the bar and they'd stop serving. But the band would usually play while everybody finished their last-call drinks. There's about an hour there and the band would be tired then anyway and everybody was drunk. So they were happy to have me come up and sing. I would do that quite often.

"I was scared shitless. I had terrible stage fright. My parents forced me to perform, which in the long run was the best thing, because I was quite a recluse," she admits. "If not for them I'd still be singing in my bedroom. From the age of eight, I was doing weekends, the odd gig here and there. I did everything my parents could get me on. Every TV station, every radio station, every community center, every senior citizen center. My great-grandfather Twain was in one, so I'd go and entertain him. I'd have some people going, 'I can't hear anything—is she playing anything?' and others complaining that it was too loud.

"I wasn't just a kid trying to sing, I was actually a musician. I basically taught myself. I used to write out all of my chord charts to my original music. I was very serious. I was actually a professional by the time I was eleven. Sure, I was doing the telethons, little fairs, and country shows locally, but I was getting paid and I was working."

Sudbury was certainly a better place than Timmins to launch the career Sharon knew Eilleen deserved. The local bar culture was thriving, as Stompin' Tom had recognized in "Sudbury Saturday Night." Those after-hours shows were the gigs Eilleen always dreaded the most. Sometimes she was so tired, plucked from the depths of dreamtime, standing up there defenseless and all alone, that when she sang "I'm So Lonesome I Could Cry" there was hardly a dry eye amidst the beer and cigarette fumes (small wonder that she has never smoked and seldom drinks). The bar owners paid cash under the table or passed the hat around to those not too drunk to forget where they had put their wallet. When she turned eleven, she went legit. "The police were either going to have to arrest me, ban me from being in there," she says, "or give me a proper permit." The permit meant she could sing in the bars, but had to be given a separate room . . . and it meant an end to the 1 A.M. shows.

"Our mom had a lot of faith in her," says Carrie Ann. "She was always on the phone trying to book things, taking her to talent contests, traveling out of town to shows, getting her lessons."

At times, Eilleen must have wondered why it was her doing this, not Jill, nor Carrie Ann, nor any of her friends, wondered what her childhood was being mortgaged for. Or perhaps not. "I wasn't really aware of what was going on," she says, "I was just singing and

it was my parents who were more aware of everything. I don't remember what I thought at the time, because a singer is what I've
always been, it's what I've always done.

"My deepest passion was music. It helped. There were moments
when I thought 'I hate this.' I hated going into the bars and being
with drunks. But I loved the music and so I survived. Can you
imagine if I had actually hated the music, too?"

Eilleen was only nine when she learned an important lesson.
Singing like a honky-tonk angel is not enough. To win you do not
have to be the best, you have to know the right people. She learned
it the hard way. "Eilleen was far better than a lot of the singers that
they were pushing that were older than her," says Kenny, who used
to go with Sharon and Eilleen to many of the local talent contests.
Sometimes he'd play guitar behind her. "That was where the politics came in; there were so many jealousies going on. It was awful
what they did to her, she was only a little kid. I saw bands rehearse
with her and do it fine, but when it came to the contest they'd deliberately screw up the song, so it messed her up and she'd be coming off the stage crying. I couldn't believe grown-ups would do that
to kids. Sharon and I used to get really mad."

Angered, Sharon was determined that Eilleen would win talent
competitions, believing that was a way forward. "Mom was so discouraged," said Shania. "She couldn't understand why her little girl
was unable to win a contest." When she was nine, she performed in
a contest at the Native Friendship Center in Sudbury, where she
met the half-Cree, half-Irish singer Lawrence Martin. Smarting at
another failure a few weeks later, Eilleen and her parents, along
with Lawrence and his fiancée, Connie, drove a thousand miles to
Brandon, Manitoba, for an Aboriginal contest. The drive took almost twenty-four hours and they arrived with barely an hour to
spare. Eilleen and Lawrence appeared as a duo and as soloists. They
won everything.

For some years afterward the two would occasionally perform
together. Lawrence, though ten years older, came over to her home
at Proulx Court to watch music shows on TV and then sit around

analyzing the moves, the material, and how to improve their own. However vindicated Sharon felt, winning Native talent contests meant nothing to a record label (though Lawrence did eventually win a Juno award under the Cree name Wapistan and served as mayor of Moose Factory, up in James Bay). While Sudbury was closer to the center of things than Timmins, the local entertainment market remained oblivious to Eilleen's talents. In 1977, she told the *Sudbury Star*, alluding to her experiences in the subtext, "People just don't notice you in Sudbury. They see a lot of performers and you are just an ordinary person. But the first time I played with a band in Toronto, people stood up and took notice. Down there they are always looking for new talent. It is more fun playing with people like Carroll Baker, because you can do what you want. In Sudbury, there was no communication with the band."

While she had struck up a good rapport with Myrna Lorrie at the Woodland Hotel, her best reception was in Toronto, where she gathered some heavyweight admirers. In 1977, she sang with Freddie Fender (which impressed her teachers no end), learning the Spanish verse to his hit "Before the Next Teardrop Falls" phonetically. She had no idea what she was singing, but the crowd in Rockhill Park called her back for three encores, which blew the night's schedule to shreds. She performed with Country Edition in Orchard Park and recorded a demo of ten of her songs with a band called Eastwind.

"They were the cream of the crop of country players down there and they knew she came from a family that didn't have any money," says Kenny Derasp. "So they did a demo for her free of charge. None of the musicians charged anything; a lot of people knew she had something."

It looked like she had cracked it when she was signed to do several appearances with the *Big Country Show*, a traveling concert party sponsored by *Opry North*, the largest syndicated Canadian country radio show. She sang in Ottawa and Sudbury on the same bill as Carroll Baker and Ronnie Prophet (who both had deals in Nashville) and opened shows for Canadian country artists like

Debbie Post, Gary Buck, and Anita Perras. There was even an offer to go and do a TV show in New York, but Sharon and Jerry decided she was too young for the Big Apple. In 1978, in Sudbury, she opened for Mary Bailey, a young singer from Kirkland Lake; their paths were to cross again and again.

Eilleen's set at the time was pure country. The running order for a show in the Soo (Sault Sainte Marie) on May 13, 1977, featured fifteen songs, including such classic country weepies as "Crying Time Again," "Honky Tonk Angels," "Delta Dawn," "Jambalaya," "What's Your Mama's Name Child," "Tennessee Mountain Home," "Me and Bobby McGee," "Harper Valley PTA," "Queen of the Silver Dollar," "Say You'll Stay Until Tomorrow," and finishing up with "I Wish I Was a Teddy Bear" and "Pure Love."

In 1978, her biggest break to date was being invited onto *The Tommy Hunter Show*, the country music TV show in Canada that aired from 1965–92. Everybody who was or indeed wanted to be anybody was desperate to be invited on. For that appearance she was billed as Ellie Twain. Glen Campbell and Ronnie Milsap topped the bill. In contrast to her usual attire, she dressed in a dark velvet jacket and a long skirt; around her neck she wore a simple silver chain with an Austrian crystal given to her by her friend Colette. She also made TV appearances on *Easy Country* and *The Mercey Brothers Show*.

Traveling to one show, she got on the train from Sudbury and after a while realized she was going in the wrong direction. The conductor told her she could transfer at another station in six hours. She recalls, "I said, 'You've got to stop the train right now because I'm going to be on TV.' So they let me off in the middle of the bush with my guitar, like a little hobo. I caught a train going the other way in half an hour, but I did think, 'What if the train never comes?' "

Chapter Four

THE HUNGRY YEARS

SUDBURY LIES SOME two hundred miles south of Timmins, and at four times the size it is in many ways its bigger brother. It was a major terminus for the Canadian Pacific Railway until some of the richest copper and nickel deposits in the world were discovered in 1883–4. Smelting operations were underway by 1888. Sudbury rapidly became the most important mining center in Canada, with the majority of its population employed in that industry. Huge nickel concentrators and smelters were erected at Copper Cliff, Falconbridge, and Levack. Sudbury and its sprawl of surrounding communities still produce around one-fifth of all the nickel mined in the world and almost all of Ontario's copper.

Like many a mining town, it has lain in thrall for almost a century to a single company, Inco (formed in 1902 as the International Nickel Company). Although by the time the Twains moved to Sudbury in 1973, Inco's importance to the local economy had begun to decline, it still employed over twenty thousand people (the population of Greater Sudbury is currently 164,000). If Inco sneezed, the whole town caught a cold. Almost everybody had some link to Inco: If they weren't directly employed, their businesses serviced the mines or the workers.

After Jerry landed a job with Indian Affairs, the Twains moved out to Proulx Court, a horseshoe road right on the northern edge of Hanmer. The house was bought with the aid of an Aboriginal housing grant, but there was still a hefty mortgage with high monthly payments to make. (At the time, if a Native chose to go and live on a reserve, the government was obliged to build him a house, so if he wished to buy one off the reserve, the government kicked in some money to help.) It was a three-bedroom bungalow of fourteen hundred square feet with a dirt floor in the basement, which, after living with four kids in a small apartment, seemed like a mansion. All the houses around were constructed of wood, dotted on lots with scrub and trees filling in the gaps, which did little to dispel the icy winds that swept across the smooth valley floor. There were lakes in abundance for swimming or skating.

In 1975, the population of the Valley, as the four small townships of Val Caron, Blezard Valley, Val Therese, and Hanmer are collectively described, was 90 percent blue collar. People moved there because land was cheap and the rents were low. Hanmer had one Dominion supermarket and a couple of mom-and-pop corner stores. Behind it the roads were gravel, not tarmac. It was an insular working-class community made more so by language—70 percent of the Valley was French, not all of whom spoke English. John Browning, who taught at Pinecrest School in the 1970s, recalls how three twelve-year-olds in his class had never been to Sudbury and how a girl burst into tears when she first saw Ottawa, because "she never ever thought she'd go somewhere like that in her life." Miners disciplined their children the old-fashioned way; if a teacher called, that meant they were in trouble, even if they weren't. A boy turned up one morning with his head shaved bald—his father's solution to a minor disciplinary misdemeanor.

Provided they weren't on strike, regular Inco employees earned a good wage; they could afford fishing boats and new trucks. It was the others like Jerry Twain, the casual lumber or forestry workers and the subsistence farmers—there were still a few working farms in the Valley—who were at the bottom of the economic pile. Less than half a mile from the Twain house on Concession 4 (later renamed

Gravelle Drive) were houses that still had dirt floors and whose nearest water-pipe was four blocks away.

For Eilleen it was not all work and no play. She was still a little girl, with a little girl's enthusiasms. She had to go to school. She attended Redwood Acres for three years, Pinecrest Junior High for grades seven and eight, Capreol High for just one year, and very seldom missed a day. Eilleen and Lynn Bond became firm friends at Redwood Acres when they discovered they both loved horses, and their friendship continued through their move to Pinecrest. Lynn lived three miles away in Val Caron and they would hang out anywhere they could see a horse. On Michelle Drive up the road from Lynn's was a house with a little paint pony in the field behind. The ten-year-old girls thought nothing of knocking on the door and asking, "Can we spend time with your pony?" A warning that the animal had not been ridden much did not deter Eilleen, who leapt on it bareback and rode it back to Lynn's. They tied him up in the backyard and forgot to tell her dad, who woke up and thought he was hallucinating elephants.

No neighborhood house with horses was safe. The Dions, who lived on the curve of Proulx Court, also allowed the girls to look after their pony. Lynn's greatest triumph was being allowed to look after Prince Buddy, who unfortunately lived on a farm way down on Highway 69. The girls decided they were going to enter him in a local horse show. Lynn's mother only agreed to take them on the condition that on Sunday morning they both went to church. The potential cowgirls reluctantly agreed and then went off to the show. Eilleen wore Lynn's checkered shirt while Lynn wore one of Eilleen's.

"We didn't know anything, like what we were getting ourselves into," recalls Lynn, "but we packed that horse up and we were hot girls, we were going to show what we had. Eilleen took Prince Buddy into one class where they would command, 'Okay, walk, trot,' and you had to stop and do this straight away. This pony was a real hothead and went just ballistic. The judges were like, 'You're going to be thrown off, control this horse,' but she was so determined to get him under control and finish her class. That took a lot of guts, because she looked like a real idiot out there. Everybody else was doing their class the way they're supposed to and she's in there, you know . . . but she was staying on her horse whatever. Needless to say we didn't win, but we had a good time."

Lynn was a natural runner, skinny as a whip. Her relationship with Eilleen was always competitive; in grade six they practiced doing backflips for hours. They had the same focus on getting things right. Lynn won most of the sports events, but she got angry when Eilleen won the standing long jump, telling her friends, "Well, I had to let her win one," then going back home and complaining to her mother because she was so frustrated at her friend.

While the teachers seldom saw it, there was another, wilder side to Eilleen. Like Jerry, she enjoyed playing practical jokes on her friends, pretending to throw up green slime at parties. She caught Lynn in one class by offering her a homemade chocolate brownie. After it had been wolfed down she killed herself laughing and admitted to having laced it with Ex-Lax. A few months later, Lynn went for payback with an extra strong laxative. "I doubled over and laughed, and, no, she didn't think it was very funny either, she was a little upset, but hey, what comes around goes around, right?

"There were a few episodes in school when she would do some kinda mean thing, but it never stopped us being friends. I remember going to my locker and there was this letter in there. I wasn't the prettiest thing in those days, but there was this letter and it was about this boy and how he watched me when we had recess and how cute he thought I was. I'm like, 'Eilleen, look at this, check this out, this guy likes me, but I don't know who he is.' We'd be out at recess and I'd be looking like, 'Okay, who's watching me, and . . .' Well it turned out she wrote this letter, so of course the joke was on me again. She did things like that, she had a sense of humor."

Singing took priority in Eilleen's home, for it was the dream rock upon which her mother's fragile psyche rested. At school she preferred to sink into the anonymity of the pack. The only reason that Laurie Macdonald, the music teacher at Pinecrest, knew was that one of her teachers at Redwood Acres told him, "You are getting one hell of a singer." Eilleen had been asked to sing at a parents' evening there and had stunned the teacher by telling her to first check with her mother that she wasn't already booked to perform elsewhere and then asked if there would be a sound system and onstage monitors for her performance.

During Laurie's first singing lesson, in which the whole class would sing popular songs together, he listened out for her. When he could not distinguish her from the crowd he asked her if she wanted to sing something. "Oh no, not really," she replied, perhaps remembering that long-ago first-grade humiliation. Laurie listened some more and realized that most times, if the class was singing a song, he could not pick her out from anybody else. But if she ever wanted to, she could drown them all out—"Her control was that good."

Eilleen was convinced to sing in front of her classmates on the eighth-grade camping trip to Halfway Lake. Teachers Ted Evans and John Browning were in charge of fifty-six young teens, aided only by two eighteen-year-old qualified lifeguards, Wendy Wickstrom and Jenny Sachsalber. Eilleen had brought her guitar along and on the first night—in between hands of euchre—she sat down by the campfire and played a small set, including Randy Vanwarmer's hit "Just When I Needed You Most," Kenny Rogers's "The Gambler," and the traditional scouts' favorite "Barges."

It was not enough for Eilleen to play the song; it had to be just right. Says John, "She would play along for a while and sing, sound just great, and then all of a sudden she'd quit and start over again." It turned out that Wendy and Jenny were good harmony singers and they started to join in, so the following evening the three of them disappeared off from the fire. They sat around experimenting with different harmonies until long after everybody else had gone to bed. Although Eilleen was the best singer, she did not attempt to exert her will, she just let it slide along. "Eilleen was not that kind of personality that she would take charge; she would watch and listen, and then suggest," says Ted.

Well-organized and comfortable in the bush, Eilleen had arranged to share a tent with Leah Mersham, who had turned in early because she was not feeling well. Unfortunately, she had left the zipper undone and the tent was invaded by mosquitoes. John and Ted were enjoying a quiet moment alone by the fire when Eilleen stomped up in a filthy mood. "Leah's in there snoring like a fool," she complained, "the tent is full of mosquitoes, and there's no damn way I'm sleeping in there with a bunch of bugs!" Ted had a truck with a camper in the back, so Eilleen grabbed her blanket and went to sleep in the driver's cabin. Every time she turned over the truck would rock and disturb the teachers in the back.

The next morning, after they had organized the kids to load their gear into the buses, Eilleen made up for giving them a sleepless night. "John and I were starved, I would have eaten his shoes at the time," says Evans. "Eilleen says, 'I've a piece of steak in my cooler,' so she got out this chunk of pounded minute steak. I cut some sticks and we propped it over the coals, and the three of us shared the steak with some salt, and it tasted like heaven. Eilleen was pretty thrilled. She told us, 'This is great, we have real food, we can cook and eat. When my dad takes us camping, all he ever brings is flour and salt!' "

For the two years she was at Pinecrest, Eilleen seldom did anything to show off in front of her peers. "She was pale, mousy," recalls Macdonald, "very small, slight, a cute, nondescript kid who never wore makeup—no eye shadow, no fancy hairdos—she was a very pleasant, nice little thirteen-year-old, with terrible teeth. She never was a fashion plate, just blue jeans and a nice little top, dressed very plainly in clothes that were cheap and easy to look after. She buried herself into the crowd and did her best not to stand out."

"She wasn't a loner," agrees Ted Evans, who taught her English and physical education, "she wasn't a target, nobody picked on her, but she wasn't a joiner. She did want to join the basketball team, and so she orchestrated this meeting between her stepfather and myself."

Eilleen was close to a shoo-in for the team—she had balance, poise, and strength that belied her size. The problem was that team practice was on Sunday mornings, which conflicted with her doing any out-of-town gigs on Saturday nights. One afternoon when Ted Evans was on bus duty, she asked him to talk to Jerry, who had come to pick her up. Ted offered to pick her up and take her home (in those days teachers were allowed to do such things without need of a chaperon). Jerry was too polite to give an outright "no," but Ted knew he was not keen on the idea. A week later, Eilleen told him she would not be able to try out. Her schedule, she explained, was such that she had to go home after school, get her homework done, have something to eat, rest, and then she'd be out singing some-place that evening, and then, when she came home and everything was done, she could go to bed and start again for the next time. Even in grade eight she didn't have very much spare time.

Occasionally, she rebelled against such strictures. On long, cramped car trips she and her sisters might start arguments that brought the car to a halt, followed by a brisk walk allowing every-body a chance to cool down. One day, she and her aunt Karen went into town to watch a fashion show and decided they wanted to go to a movie afterward (Hanmer only had a drive-in theater). Karen phoned home to be told firmly by Jerry, "No, you girls have to come right back. Eilleen, you have a show this evening." They stayed and watched the movie anyway, but there was hell to pay back at Proulx.

That distance between school, where she tried so hard to be just another little girl, and career became increasingly important to Eilleen. Her close friends knew both sides of her and loved to listen to her sing, though she was always uncomfortable playing to those she knew intimately. They joked that if a house had a guitar Eilleen would find it. Lynn Bond begged her to play her own songs but, being a competitive little girl, could never resist teasing her about it. One time at school she crossed the line seriously, called her "twa twa twa Twain" and made fun of her. Eilleen was very upset and it took them a while to be friends again.

Singing was simultaneously her release and her curse. "Shania would always be singing—even just walking down the street. I'd be embarrassed," recalls Carrie Ann. At home the radio was always playing and at every song—Elton John, the Carpenters, Fleetwood Mac, whatever came on—she danced around the room crying, "Oh I love this song." Laura Surch might say tartly, "You love every song," but that never stopped Eilleen. Singing along to the radio or to Jerry's eight-track was how she learned to refine, then to perfect, her harmonies.

"Eilleen was a very serious kid," says Kenny Derasp. "She spent a lot of time in her room. Her and I used to go and sit in her room to get away from everybody and just play." The art of creating, of actually writing songs, was very different from performing them and became progressively important. That was private, where the loner came out. She was ten when she wrote her first songs. Her first two titles—"Is Love a Rose?" and "Just Like the Storybooks"—were wish-fulfillment fantasies, fairy tales in rhyme. In her dreams she waited for Frank Sinatra, the superstar the most removed from northern Ontario imaginable, to kidnap her and take her away from it all. A more down-to-earth fantasy was becoming Stevie Wonder's backing singer. "I wanted to escape this life I had," she has said, "and I knew the only honest way of doing it would be to be kidnapped. Because I'd have felt so guilty if I'd ever left my family willingly."

Writing songs was her escape from reality. They came out of silence, out of solitude. After one performance in the Soo, she sat silent in the back of the car for the whole ride. Then, without a word, she rushed into her bedroom and emerged twenty minutes later with a new song. Sharon admitted to the *Sudbury Star*, "I always wondered what was going through her head then." When she was in one of her hyper modes she found it hard to wait, constantly asking her daughter, "What have you been writing lately? Can I hear something? What have you been doing in there all these hours?" Says Shania, "I would never play her my music. Very rarely would I let her hear something. Unless I felt it was completely finished."

In winter, she wrote in the bedroom she shared with Carrie Ann. She wrote songs on scraps of paper that, like some absent-minded hamster, she left all over the house. Eventually she learned

to store them in boxes under her bed. When it was warm, she retired to her secret place, hidden out in the woods that straggled
around the back of the house. Nobody was invited there, until one
day she beckoned her Aunt Karen out into the bush and then
shushed her to secrecy. She led her by the hand into a little grove
surrounded by scrub and spruce trees, and she proudly pointed out
her little barbecue setup and the rocks that passed for seats
grouped around the fire she loved to watch. "This," she said, "is
where I come when I want to be alone and to write songs."

Pinecrest was a small school with no cafeteria, so at lunchtimes
the kids ate in their homerooms, supervised by their teachers.
They bolted down their food and then rushed off to enjoy whatever activities were on offer. Whenever possible, Eilleen made
some excuse about her lunch and headed for the classroom that
doubled as a music room. There she grabbed a guitar and started
singing. The staff room was right next door, which was how Laurie
Macdonald learned how good she was. Sometimes he played the
piano while she let rip, and next door those who did not know
complained that Laurie had cranked the stereo up too high. What
he did not know was that on many of those days she had eaten no
lunch at all.

Throughout their years in Hanmer, the Twain family was struggling to meet their bills and put food on the kitchen table. In those
pre-PC days, Jerry was an oddity, the only Native on the payroll of
the Sudbury Bureau of Indian Affairs, and when he proudly
showed the pictures of his five children the white staff got more
confused. "He was what they called an Indian agent," recalls Willis
McKay, who is now the Housing Officer at Mattagami First Nation.
"He took care of band affairs, dealing mostly with housing problems and water and membership, too. Jerry was really an outspoken
person, very steadfast in what he believed in, always pushing to get
a better life for himself and his family. He cared for people around
here. If we had problems, he worked for us; he tried to help everybody. He didn't take no for an answer. If he felt [there was] something he didn't agree with, he spoke up, he didn't let it drag by, he

stood up for us. At the time it was a difficult and brave thing to be a go-between between Indian Affairs and the Indian people."

As well as being a frustrating job for a man with drive and intelligence, it was also poorly paid, involving short-term contracts with no civil-service benefits. In winter, Jerry found himself without steady work, struggling to make the rent, a situation not helped, as Karen remembers, by the casual, endemic racism of the day: "In Sudbury, they would always lay off the Natives first." Jerry did not help himself either, for he was a proud, stubborn man who refused to accept government handouts. He would not go on the dole, nor go back to Mattagami or Bear Island. "We would have been better off on the reserve a lot of the time," Shania said, "but my father had much too much pride for that. He had to be independent of the clan and we starved for it a lot of the time. He must have earned a pittance, because we didn't eat half the time, and he got turned off in the winter, which was not good."

Winters in Hanmer were long and hard, made doubly so when the electricity got shut off. When cash was too tight to visit the laundromat, the washing was done in the tub in cold water. "We didn't have a lot of food; often I didn't have a lunch to go to school," Shania has said. "How many days in a row can you not have a lunch? Sometimes I would make up a mustard sandwich because I was so embarrassed, I would make up something, any kind of sandwich I could just to throw the teachers off, or I would get permission to go to the music room for lunch to sit at the piano and write.

"I was very much aware of being poor, because everybody around me had things. My sister Jill and I used to walk home from school and smell everybody's dinner cooking. We were so envious, we'd call them 'roast beef families.' We thought roast beef families were the norm and that everyone with a brick house was rich, because only rich people could afford to have such a sturdy house. Anyone with meat cooking was also rich, because that was not normal to us. If you decided to take an extra potato, someone didn't get a potato at all. The only kind of meat we ever had was ground beef, and in the autumn the reserve sometimes sent a little box with moose or fish—but certainly not enough for seven people. We would snare rabbits and stuff, but beef was a luxury."

Although officially his family were band members at Bear Island, Jerry was so respected at Mattagami for what he did for the community there that they were happy to help out in return. "We considered them more members here than at Bear Island, we recognized them as family," confirms Willis McKay. "If we knew they were hurting, we would pass on whatever we had: moose meat, beaver, rabbit, deer, and partridge." However, living off the land was not a long-term option in the Valley.

"There were definitely hard times, many days when we had to huddle round the stove because we couldn't pay the heating bill," said Shania. "We went to bed wearing our coats, literally freezing. It's not the way you want to live; you can die in those conditions. I don't think our parents would have allowed us to die, they would have taken us to a shelter, but we definitely endured what we could, we pushed it to the limits. We did everything we could to hide it from other people.

"I was very aware, not ashamed, but cautious about concealing the standard of living we had. In Canada, if you are not careful, the Children's Aid will take you away. The schools keep an eye on those sorts of things."

The reality of the social services bogeymen was somewhat different. The teachers at Pinecrest seldom pried into family circumstances unless invited to. The root of the fear might have been that Jerry worried that, like so many Native children in the past, the boys would be sent away to special schools. On the surface, the Twains presented a united front, their clothes were clean and mended, their passive behavior never drew attention to the trouble at home. Those days taught Eilleen how to dissemble, to hide in plain sight behind a polite smile. Pretending everything is fine on the surface when beneath all is raging turmoil is an essential skill for a nascent superstar.

While some doubts have been cast on just how poor the Twains were (most notably in Laurence Leamer's anti-Nashville polemic *Three Chords and the Truth*), there is no doubt that they suffered far tougher times than most of their contemporaries. Kenny Derasp, whose parents were divorced, often lived with Jerry and Sharon, whom he considers to be his second family. When he was eighteen, he had a grant to go back to school, so he paid them for board. "I probably ate up what I paid them; they had a rough go of it. It was tough—one income and five children to clothe and feed—but they seemed to manage. Money was very, very tight. They spent a lot of time worrying about how they were going to pay the electricity bill in winter, they had house payments, then the car would break down. I used to fix Jerry's car a lot. I rode with him to work in the morning and he had this really beat-up old Dodge. The gas gauge didn't work, so we used to carry a jerrycan in the trunk and a lot of times we just barely made it to the gas station. We'd be swerving all around the road to get the gas to swish around in the tank to get a little bit further. One time we ran out and we found a gallon of camp-stove gas in the trunk we had to put in, which got us to the gas station.

"We ate a lot of Kraft dinners—macaroni and cheese in a box, it was maybe twenty cents a box in those days. It's got a few noodles and some cheese you mix with milk. Add in a pound of hamburger and it stretched enough for everybody to have some.

"There was a lot of love in the house, for sure," says Kenny. "There was a lot of yelling too, it was a very loud household, very energetic. Everyone was noisy, kids coming in screaming, 'Darryl did this . . . Mark took my toy.' The house was in a highly excited state all the time, kids running around. Sometimes Sharon would just sit there in the kitchen and go, 'Oh, my God,' and panic."

Family discipline was imposed in a rough and traditional manner by Jerry and his belt. "In our house it was nothing to get a slap for something," recalls Shania matter-of-factly. "Personally, I don't think there was anything wrong with it. We all went back to our room crying, but we weren't devastated; we did not need therapy for having the belt." Sometimes Jerry did overreact. "Parents can go out of control," she says. "There were times when my dad definitely used too many straps, too hard."

Although children are seldom aware of the bigger picture, all of Eilleen's friends recall odd incidents. When she was seven, Colette St. Amande's (now Del Frate) family lived on Gravelle, just a block from Proulx Court. Her mother remembers "a little Eilleen who lived a street over who used to come over and play, and I used to feed her all the time. She was always hungry."

But it is the milk that jumps out of all their memories. To most kids, blue- and white-collar alike, there is always milk; it is omnipresent, a constant in their lives from before they can talk. Nobody rations milk.

"I was aware enough to know that the Twains' house was different from mine," says Colette. "But the only thing that has really stuck in my mind was one time when Eilleen wanted something to drink, she wasn't allowed to have milk. They only had so much milk, and that was saved for the boys." When Laura Surch stayed over for the first time in 1979, she helped herself and drank the family's entire breakfast ration. "I used too much milk and she had to tell me that in her house there wasn't cookies and pop and chips and enough milk to go around. She would actually come to school with no lunches. She didn't complain."

There were days when Eilleen told Lynn, "You can't come over tonight, it's not a good night." Now Lynn knows it was because there wasn't enough food to go around one more plate. Once she was there for tea and the only food on offer was "milk, sugar, and bread. They kind of chunked up the bread, put it in the bowl, added milk and then sugar. I'd never tried it, but so what? Hey, some people have pancakes for supper or macaroni with butter. It was different and Eilleen never complained, so I thought it must be good."

By history and circumstance, the Twains were a dysfunctional family held together, despite the havoc that living below the poverty line brought, by Jerry's will and Sharon's belief in her daughter's talent. "To her parents, Eilleen's career was everything," recalls Laura. "Everything. Any extra money was spent on her, on her singing lessons; her parents were very driven to make sure she succeeded." They were prepared to sacrifice grocery money to pay for her singing lessons, for gas money to get her to gigs, which in turn put extra pressure on the family.

The most acute damage was to Sharon's mental health. The incessant grind of poverty sapped her strength and led to fits of acute depression. "When there wasn't anything to feed us for breakfast," Shania has said, "my mother didn't get out of bed. She didn't want to face that morning. And there were a lot of mornings like that. We'd come home from school, she'd still be in bed. She would get very depressed, but she had very good reason to be depressed. At times it was, 'We can't afford to go grocery shopping, and the cupboards are empty, so I think I'll stay in bed today. Or maybe for three days.'

"When you can't feed your kids, it is really tough," says Shania. "A lot of times my mother gave up. It was as simple as that. She had depressed states, but I always thought she was quite normal. I never saw her as being anything outrageous at all, she was quite a conservative lady. She loved to read. She was well read. She made sure I never drank out of bottles when I was in clubs. Life just dealt her a bad hand. Had her life gone in a different way she would have held on to her innocence a lot more easily.

"My mother's obsession for my music kept her going a lot of the time. She would get up and want to hear my songs. Then she would get on the phone and start working out where I was going to sing. It was her saving grace," she told VH-1's *Behind the Music*. "Her dream was for me to become successful, that was her passion. I think she would have given up if it wasn't for my music. I definitely felt a responsibility as a child to keep my mother happy with my music. My mother didn't say, 'If you quit music, I will wither away.' I just understood that if I said 'I'm quitting,' her world would fall apart."

In 1978, things got even worse: Jill left home. She was only fourteen and why exactly she left no one will discuss, though she certainly chafed under Jerry's rule that there was to be no dating boys or wearing makeup until she was sixteen. (By the time she was sixteen she had Mandy, a daughter of her own.) Ted Evans remembers Jill very well. "She was a very sharp English student. I encouraged writing and Jill wrote a lot for me. I had a journal program, which was of its nature personal. Although she never referred to her personal life, she did have insight into the human condition. Jill was—and Eilleen had some of this—an observer; they both stepped back and watched. Jill was tougher than Eilleen, she didn't have the softness that her sister could have. I often caught her sitting watching. She had almost an adult perspective of the world and was a very strong writer. My impression, my instinct said that there was something hurting in her life, but I never got the details, nor did I pry."

Once Jill had left the house, Eilleen was the oldest and was given a lot more responsibility. Laura remembers her taking control, making sure that everything continued to work. "We were probably in the heart of our difficult times as a family," Shania recalls. "I had to take control and was really an anchor in keeping the family together. I ironed Dad's clothes and made porridge in the morning for the kids."

Sharon's depression may have been exacerbated, because by 1979 Eilleen's career had stalled. While she was earning some money from her shows, it was often not enough to cover the costs of getting there. "My mom was more of the stage parent," said Shania. "My dad was more practical. He made decisions about whether it made sense to drive somewhere to perform for free, or to pay the heating bill that week. Once, my father decided we couldn't afford to travel to a certain town to perform. After I went to bed that night, I snuck out of my window and my mom and I went anyway."

Money drained out on demo tapes and travel, but the record companies never called. A cute little moppet had novelty value but a hesitant teenager did not. When Tanya Tucker sang "Delta Dawn" and "Would You Lay with Me (in a Field of Stone)," her appeal was jailbait raunch. Tanya knew she was sexy and played it to the hilt. Eilleen hated her body and tried to hide it. She developed breasts early. At eleven, her games were all outside—riding horses, running through the bush, climbing trees, ice skating—and suddenly her body had let her down. She kept on doing the same stuff and now boys stared at her in a different way, but she wasn't any different. Not in her head, anyway.

"I spent my whole youth hiding behind a tomboy image, trying to hide my figure," she said later. "I wanted to stay this tomboy, to stay flat-chested forever. I didn't want the curves because of the attention it drew to me. It's like, the better shape you were in, and the more curves you had, the more you stood out. And you didn't want to stand out for that."

"I liked boys," laughs Colette St. Amande. "I wasn't like Eilleen, though, she was very, very developed. People think that she's gotten surgery; not so. She hid it, she wore baggy clothes, big sweatshirts. She was very modest and shy about it. She hated it when in grade nine she had to change for gym class in front of everybody. She didn't flaunt it; a lot of girls wore a lot of tight shirts and low-cut things, and she never dressed like that, never."

By her own admission, Colette was boy crazy, but too scared of the consequences to do much about it. Like Eilleen, she was not allowed to be alone with a boy until she was sixteen, but that did not stop them listening with open mouths to those girls in their class who went all the way—or at least bragged that they had. Eilleen might reciprocate if a boy was interested in her, as Lynn recalls: "There was this boy, Mike Perrault, he was the cutie in the class, I had a really big crush on him, but he ended up liking her. She knew if a person was right for her or wasn't. She knew what she wanted. Then it was carry on, let's move on. But she never did the chasing."

The teenage fashions of the late 1970s were not label-conscious. Girls seldom wore skirts and they were never short unless you wished to be considered tarty. They wore jeans with diamante studs stitched around the pockets and along the back, or bell-bottoms as wide as they could find them. Colette caused a stir with a pair of white super bell-bottoms wide enough to hide skates. They wore baggy work shirts or sweatshirts, and "runners" on their feet.

It was easier for Eilleen when she started to hang with Colette, for Colette liked the comfortable things in life—which meant passing the time at her house where there were milk and cookies aplenty, talking and dreaming about boys and sweaters, listening to records by the Alan Parsons Project and Meatloaf—until Colette's mother heard the lyrics to "Bat Out of Hell" and it went straight into the garbage. Eilleen grounded Colette, showed her that being the richest kid in class wasn't that important, didn't have to be a barrier to making friends, while Eilleen got to escape the pressure of life in Proulx Court. In ninth grade they both bussed out fifteen minutes to Capreol High while Lynn went to the bigger Confed (Colette's folks were worried that there were drugs at Confed, while Jill had also gone to Capreol). Laura Surch was sitting in front of them and they all clicked.

Laura bonded so instantly with Eilleen that they became life-long friends. Raised first by her grandmother and then by an aunt, Laura knew what a dysfunctional family was. She too had her dreams—mainly to get out of Hanmer. Laura saw behind Eilleen's mask, or maybe she let it slip on purpose, showed how much she hated school. Laura stayed over at Proulx a lot and saw her friend struggling to keep everything going. Says Laura, "She'd eat at my place and I'd share my food and stuff, but at home she'd give what food there was to the kids. Darryl and Mark didn't know what was going on. Her brothers were little brats. Always. Always brats. She didn't have much use for school other than having to go. She liked English, I liked math. What did we like together? Nothing."

Jerry's humor could not keep everything together forever. Neither he nor Sharon was particularly physical in public. "The whole family tends to be a little standoffish," Carrie Ann told *People* magazine. "There wasn't a lot of hugging and grabbing between our parents." During their last few years in Hanmer, the Twains' relationship went close to foundering under the combined weight of poverty and failed expectations. When the arguments got worse, Sharon left Jerry. "Most times they just talked it out, but later on when Sharon got moody she'd come and see me," says Karen. "When they'd get angry at each other they'd come visit and calm down."

In late 1978, worn out by Sharon's depression, Eilleen convinced her to take the family to Toronto where she knew they had proper programs to help desperate families find food and shelter. "I told my mother to get in the car the next day when my dad was gone. I said, 'All you've got to do is drive.' I don't know why she listened to me. I think she was numb. We drove to Toronto and went to a shelter. We finally got fed every day.

"My father was furious and couldn't find us for a long time. I told my mother, 'Don't tell him where we are.' I was just so desperate not to go back to what we were in. In Toronto I got a singing job and my mother got a cooking job in the same club, and on weekends I did sales phone work for the club. We left the shelter eventually and got into special housing."

After the family was reunited Jerry realized he had to do something. He had had enough of offices, paperwork, and bureaucracy, of living on the "bread goulash" line, of watching Sharon sink into depression and his family start to fragment. During the summer months, many of his relatives were involved in tree planting. Trees, he realized, were a natural but renewable resource and so, according to Karen, he started asking questions. "How many trees did you plant? How many hours were you out there?" That was when he got the idea to start his own company. His time in Indian Affairs came in useful, because he knew how to play the system at a time when the Canadian government was suffering from a major guilt trip over how it had treated the Natives.

Jerry got a grant to set up a tree-planting operation employing Native workers. Hanmer was too far south and the big concerns had already got it tied up. The business was all in the vicinity or to the north of Timmins. Timmins was their hometown—returning there would certainly please Sharon and maybe help mend their marriage. He insisted that he needed her to get involved, to help run the business. The decision was made and the Twains moved into a small apartment on 137 Balsam Street South, just opposite a funeral home, in the summer of 1980.

The main casualty of the move was Eilleen's career. The extra distance made it impossible to do anything except the most important live shows. Secretly she was relieved. Perhaps she could become just another normal teenager.

Chapter Five

BLACKFLIES AND BRASS BANDS

EILLEEN LOVED THE tree-planting business. "We planted millions of trees every year," she recalls wistfully. "It was a wonderful life: there were no roads unless we made them ourselves, we were completely isolated, everyone we hired was Indian. That is another irony that lives strong in the mind of so many Indians: 'We plant trees and they cut them down.'

"I loved the whole feeling of being stranded. I'm not afraid of being in my own environment, being physical, working hard. I was very strong, I walked miles and miles every day, carried heavy loads of trees, it didn't matter what the weather was like. You can't shampoo, can't use soap, deodorant, or makeup—nothing with any scent—you have to bathe and rinse your clothes in a lake because the bugs are so ferocious they can kill a moose. It was a very rugged existence. I wrote so many things; I was very creative then. I would sit alone in the forest with my dog and a guitar and just write songs."

Financially, Jerry Twain's reforestation business was to prove the family's salvation. The first two years establishing the business were tough. Although he got a government grant, Jerry still had to get a bank loan to buy extra equipment, and then he had to make contacts. One former employer, the Ministry of Natural Resources, issued some early contracts and as the business prospered, more and more private lumber companies came on board. The business commenced operations in April 1981.

Tree-planting is a long-established summer business across northern Ontario. After an area of forest is felled, the ground is cleared and prepared and seedlings planted, not in nature's haphazard manner but in straight lines that will make for easier logging in another decade. Tree-planting is a rite of passage for environmentally conscious students who every summer head north to discover that the forests are full of voracious insects, angry bears, and unfriendly locals who despise their soft southern ways and tree-hugging habits. It is poorly paid, grueling, backbreaking work in the summer heat, often miles from civilization. Seedlings have to be planted the regulation distance of three feet apart and at the right depth. If it is not done correctly, there is no pay. In the early 1980s, the rate was five to six cents a tree. Karen Twain, who "was good for a woman, I guess" averaged one thousand trees a day, earning her C$50 for a working day that started before dawn and lasted between twelve and sixteen hours.

Jerry was well equipped to make a go of it: He was physically strong, totally at home in the bush, and he knew how to motivate Native workers. His employees were primarily Cree and Ojibwe from Manitoulin Island or from Moose Factory and Moosonee up north on James Bay. Coming from communities where unemployment was endemic, the pay was reasonable for six months' work. They were divided into crews of six or seven, each under a crew boss.

Jerry planted trees all over northern Ontario. The gear would be driven up to a base town—Gogama, Matheson, Hearst, Moonbeam—where the tarmac ended and the crews would head out along the graveled bush roads. The camps consisted of a couple of trailers containing supplies, fresh water, and a portable kitchen; most of the workers slept in tents. It was a family affair—Sharon was heavily involved from the outset, Jerry's twenty-three-year-old brother Tim was a crew boss, and so was Karen when she wasn't back in Timmins minding the office, the house, and the children, and getting lumbered with a mountain of dirty laundry every couple of weeks. Gerry and Selina did the cooking, so that when the crews staggered back into camp at seven and eight there was always hot food—"beans, bread, and tea in the morning, roast and steak at night; my brother made sure there was pretty good food for everybody"—waiting for them. Says Karen, "The guys didn't mind being told what to do, because we pretty well hired the same crew every year. We were just one big happy family out there."

Nobody was allowed to bring any alcohol or drugs into the bush. Anybody caught using was immediately fired and left to find their own way home. At the end of every plant there would be a party. Jerry, who did not drink much anymore, brought in a few beers, though never more than two or three bottles, for each worker.

Conditions in the camp were spartan. Washing was done in the lakes and if there was no local water supply they ran a hose out from one of the vans. The weather could turn nasty: torrential rain and sometimes, as late as August, hailstorms chucking down ice the size of pebbles. During summer, the insect life in the northern forests is particularly vicious. Mosquitoes can smell unnatural odors like shampoo or perfume from miles away and home in more effectively than smart cruise missiles. Insect repellents only work sporadically, and if there's a centimeter of bare skin the bugs find it and eat you alive. Worst of all were June and July—blackfly season. Blackflies are little flying sharks that operate in small clouds like some biblical plague. In the midsummer heat, blackflies come in swarms so thick you can swallow them along with your lunch, millions upon millions of unrelenting bugs that take chunks out of the unwary and leave them bleeding. "Imagine the world's worst weather, tremendous cold or oppressive heat, and you can't even come close to being eaten alive by blackflies," says Canadian explorer Jeff MacInnis, who has planted trees in northern Ontario. "At times I felt that if I lay down for just a minute they would slowly take my life away."

By the summer of 1987, Jerry was employing seventy-five people. The crew bosses were John Rodrigues, Dave Rodrigues, Kim Spence, Tim and Karen Twain . . . and Eilleen and Carrie Ann. Eilleen had started out planting whenever she could and after she graduated high school in July 1983, she became a crew boss. The only concession made to the girls was that they slept in a trailer parked some distance away from the main camp so they could enjoy a little privacy. Her twelve-string guitar was always the first thing she brought and the sounds of her and Carrie Ann harmonizing echoed through the trees. On those evenings when she did not crash out early due to sheer exhaustion, Eilleen brought her guitar to the campfire to play and sing after dinner. The family joked— and not without reason—that Eilleen sang extra loud to scare off any curious bears in search of a snack.

In 1982, Kenny Derasp was with a band playing in Geraldton. "About noon there was a knock on the door waking us up. It was Jerry, who was doing a tree-plant in the area," he recalls. "They came into the bar that night. Eilleen, who was sixteen, got up and sang a few songs dressed in her work boots and jeans."

Out in the bush there was nothing feminine about Eilleen. There were no games to play, she could forget about being a sex object. Despite only being knee-high to a moose, she was a tough cookie who took no nonsense from her workers. She expected them to match up to her standards. "Out there dating wasn't ever on my mind," she says. "There were a lot of four in the mornings when I did not feel like getting up to plant a tree. I was one of the guys, I really was. I worked as hard as any of them, if anything even harder. I was determined never to be outwalked or outworked and I gained tremendous respect from my workers. I would tell people how to do things a few times. If they didn't get it right, then they would be let go. If they cheated, they would get fired and have to walk to the nearest road. It could take you a day to do that. Cheating lets other people down."

The Twains always treated their Native workers with respect. When she was not out in the bush, Eilleen kept the books, so she regularly liaised with the CIBC bank and Zudel's Fresh Mart, a small convenience and grocery store at 49 Tisdale, just around the corner from the Twain home.

"Sharon and Jerry had a lot of Natives working for the planting business," recalls Pam Kardas, who started work as Zudel's bookkeeper in 1982, "and they were very good in extending credit for them. They'd come in and be allowed to buy groceries against their pay and Jerry would make sure we were paid for it. The account was always good, but when you are working on contract like that you have to have credit, because the money doesn't come in right away, so we would accommodate them. When somebody came in, I would have to check over the phone with Eilleen. Jerry and Sharon did not have a lot of money themselves—they were well below middle income, if not living in poverty—but there was never any finagling. They were poor but honest." At times the Twains owed in excess of C$25,000—which they always paid.

Paying their workers was a hassle. Most of them did not live in Timmins, some could barely read or write, nor did they have active bank accounts or two forms of photo ID. On Friday afternoons, Eilleen regularly accompanied between five and fifteen employees to the CIBC bank on Pine and Third and stood on line to make sure they had enough money for the weekend. Before the days of ATM cash machines the queues were long and slow.

"Eilleen was very easy to notice," recalls Carole Kiraga, who worked as a teller for CIBC in 1985. "In order to accommodate the workers, we allowed Eilleen to endorse the checks. When anybody came up to the cashier, I would signal to Eilleen and she would come and introduce herself to the teller and say, 'Hi, I'm Eilleen Twain, and my parents have an account here and I can guarantee that this is Mr. John Doe.'

"She was a little cutie, a tiny little girl, she had a ponytail, wore no makeup at all, didn't need any; she was always smiling, she had a very nice personality. She always had jeans on and a little jeans shirt and I used to chitchat with her. It was neat that she came and did this for them. You could tell she had a little bit of control in the company and a lot of trust. I had no idea if it was a successful business, but there was always money to pay those checks they were presenting. They were earning between C$600 and C$2,000, big checks, especially in 1985.

"The Aboriginal workers wouldn't say much, but the guys had all due respect for her. I always find Natives to be very shy. They are very respectful and I could tell she was their leader. They were very pleased that she would do this for them. They'd go, 'Thank you, thank you,' and when she'd done her duty she just kind of went her own way. And they went theirs until the next time."

By the end of October, the onset of winter brought the tree-planting season to an end. During the winter, Jerry switched over to running a mining service company, cutting lines and staking claims. Timmins perpetually dreams of, exists on, the belief in another big strike. Claims are only valid for up to five years, when they have to be renewed. Staking a claim cannot be done in an office, it has to be done physically. Posts are erected at each of the four corners. A line is cut from corner to corner, then a tag is placed on each corner and the claim registered at the mining office. Jerry did not own the mineral rights to the land, because he was subcontracting for Seymour Sears and companies as far afield as Wawa. Most times, Jerry left the actual staking to his Native employees; he would get them to the claim sites, some of which could only be reached by helicopter, snowmobile, or snowshoe, and make sure everything was okay. During the winter, the stakers, who lived under canvas in temperatures up to fifty below zero, relied on Jerry to keep them supplied.

The business proved a welcome respite for Eilleen. Because Sharon was so involved, it took the pressure off, allowed her to have a normal teenage life at high school. If opportunities came up, they would take them, but Sudbury was three hours away and Toronto ten. Her star future was not abandoned, merely put on to simmer.

After Hanmer, Timmins must have seemed a metropolis to a fifteen-year-old girl. Yet, in other ways it was like stepping back twenty years. There was only one pop, one country, and one French radio station and just two channels on the TV (MuchMusic, Canada's answer to MTV, did not exist; MTV only started up in 1981). Some nights when the air was clearer, they could pick up WLS Chicago—real FM radio—full of new sounds, new bands, and lots of Zeppelin. There was not a lot for teenagers to do. There was no Timmins Mall to hang in, no fast food outlets except the McDonald's opposite Hollinger Park. Fun was outdoors.

In summer, there was the skateboard park and the drive-in movie theater. Freedom came with a car. Driving was essential. Once teens turned sixteen and copped a driver's license, they could go camping out by the lakes and rivers or drive up to Hilltop Rendezvous. That was one of the big things once school was out for summer. Drive up the hill to the radio station and make a selection from their musical menu—a choice of fifty rock, twenty country, and ten French popular hits—and dedicate a song to your girl, or friends and relatives if there wasn't a girl, while everyone listened at home.

In winter, which lasted six months, there was hockey. Hockey has always been big in Timmins. The town has a long pedigree of siring tough, no-nonsense hockey stars like Steve Sullivan, brothers Frank and Peter Mahovlich, Allen Stanley, men capable of making the quantum leap from the farm teams to the NHL. There were hockey leagues of all levels for the guys and for the girls there was always . . . cheering hockey. The ski hill was twenty minutes down the road, or there was snowmobiling (you could get a permit at fifteen and pick up a lousy piece of machinery that still ran) and sliding parties, where everyone grabbed a sled or a bin bag and cascaded down the hills. On weekends there was always a house party somewhere, it just depended on how liberal the parents were, or whether they even knew about it.

Everyone drank beer long before they passed the legal age, for Timmins is a drinking town. That was a rite of passage in a conservative town. There were drugs, too, though they came late to Timmins. "Even though we'd watched the Beatles invasion on TV, we didn't get any rock and roll culture until Woodstock came to the cinema screen," says John Emms. "That was a real revelation. It started the drug era in Timmins, mainly pot and a little LSD. Until then, the music scene was old-style country. If there were fifteen bands in town, eleven of them were country."

The drug scene among teenagers was always more widespread than their parents cared to believe. "I knew that that was black hash and that was blond," Shania told *Rolling Stone*, "but I was so high on music, and the music was so good—Supertramp and Rush and Pink Floyd. We're all going to see Pink Floyd, and I'm like, 'You guys want to put a few things on your tongue, do acid, you just go ahead.' Meanwhile, I probably looked high. I used to really rock out. I'd get people coming up to me saying, 'Do you do drugs or what?' I never did, but I looked like I did."

Although Eilleen kept well clear of drugs, she had her flirtations with alcohol, like any normal teenager. "The first time," she said, "was when I was thirteen and my parents got me drunk because I was showing curiosity, you know, what does that taste like? And I think it was like a holiday of some kind and they were having a few drinks, 'cause they never drank normally, they never had liquor in the house. Maybe that's why I was so curious about it.

"So my dad, you know, being smart enough as he was, knowing that at thirteen kids start drinking—experimenting and stuff—so he said, 'Well, do you want to taste it?' And I said, 'Yeah.' So I tasted it and I said, 'Hmm, that's good.' And I didn't really like it, and he goes, 'Oh, you want some more?' 'Sure.' So I don't know how much I had, not that much. But you know he wanted me to be drunk, he wanted me to feel terrible the next day. And it worked, it was good. And I was like singing, I remember so well, singing with my guitar and slurring my words and falling off the chair—I was drunk. I remember the feeling. And then I went to bed and [threw up] all over everything. And they knew, they waited for me, they came, cleaned me all up, treated me like the baby that I was. And then made great fun of me the next day."

In 1982, the Twains bought a small house at 42 Montgomery Avenue. The upstairs apartment was rented out to help the mortgage payments. The front door was up three steps that opened straight into a small room with a battered upright piano to the left of the door. That led into a veritable warren of small, interconnecting rooms: A small sitting room/emergency bedroom led to Jerry and Sharon's bedroom and also to the kitchen. The back corridor led to the bathroom and a tiny bedroom that Jerry converted into an office. The stairs outside the kitchen went down into a semibasement. The "rec room" (about six and a half by ten feet) was mostly taken up by the boys' gear, ice-hockey equipment, and Mark's drum kit. Off it were two bedrooms, the front shared by Mark and Darryl, the back by Eilleen and Carrie Ann. There was little spare space, so Eilleen kept all her songs in a cardboard box under her bed. (According to Laura Surch, a whole trunkload of her stuff—"including a song she wrote about me"—was lost during the move back from Hanmer.) At the back of the basement was the laundry room, which ended in a battered green door that opened to reveal an expanse of wall. The family called it "the door to nowhere."

Back in Timmins, the rocky times that had threatened Jerry and Sharon's marriage in Hanmer vanished back beneath the waves. Those who knew them talk of them as if they were one person, "Jerryandsharon." They appeared to be together all the time. Unlike her first marriage, however, Sharon had no need to force her presence on Jerry; she stood by—and above—him by right. It was no longer a matter of possession.

"They were always close, I never seen one without the other," says Lise Dubois, a half-Ojibwe girl who worked for the Native Friendship Center in Timmins. "They really stuck close together. You know how married couples drift this way and that way? Not with them. Like, if their sons had to go to a hockey tournament, they both went to it. If Eilleen played music at the weekends, then both were there. They seemed a couple to me, very inseparable, they couldn't be split apart."

Mark was still a lanky kid waiting to grow into his body, while Darryl was shorter and tough as nails. Both were talented ice-hockey players, which was the only sport that counted. Although their team was sponsored by a local video store, equipment was not cheap, and over a season the traveling expenses ran into a couple of thousand bucks. Just as they had done with Eilleen's music, Sharon and Jerry found the money to pay for the boys' hockey.

"I would see Jerry supporting his kids; in the Native culture that's what they do, support their children, because we always say our children are the next generation. He taught them well," says Lise, whose younger brother played on the same team as Mark. She and Carrie Ann often sat in the stands cheering the boys on. "They didn't have much money, but I remember if they needed new pairs of skates or anything, they would always manage to get it. As far as I knew, the kids never asked for anything else. Mark used to come over at weekends and say stuff like, 'Cool, you've got a video game,' and 'Does your dad always buy this much chips for us to come over?' "

If money was still tight, the Twains were better off than they had been in Hanmer. In Timmins, outside of grocery stores, there was only one place where a fifteen-year-old could find part-time work—McDonald's. It was a popular teen hangout as well as an employment prospect, for Don's Pizzeria on Rea catered to an older crowd. Eilleen pulled on the blue polyester uniform, with a white hat with a blue stripe around the side covering her hair, and went to work at the cash register. The pay was minimum wage—C$2.30 an hour—but the shifts (11:30 A.M.–3:30 P.M. on weekends, 3:30–7:00 P.M. during the week) could be fitted around school and musical commitments in the evening. When she left the restaurant she filled her pockets with the condiments—sachets of maple syrup and ketchup—that were given to customers. "It was the cheapest way to get them. But I guess I'd still have been fired if I'd been caught." Eilleen appreciated her time at McDonald's, commenting later, "I learned a work ethic, etiquette, and discipline."

"She was very fast and very friendly with the customers," says Marjan Ilovar, who was working French fries at the time. "I remember one time we had a crew incentive and she won Smile of the Week. The only reward was you got your picture over the counter and a free meal.

"I knew that she was a singer, because she mentioned it during the six months she worked at McDonald's and Carrie Ann, who worked there for a lot longer, also mentioned it. Once, when she was playing with the band at the Escapade, I sneaked in to see her. Eilleen never stood out of the crowd. She wore plain ordinary jeans, a shirt, and no makeup. She was beautiful to look at, but when she smiled it threw you off, as she had a huge gap between her teeth."

Sharon knew that stars have to have a perfect smile. Once Eilleen was fully grown, she had her teeth fixed. They embarrassed her. The problem was congenital; her laterals—the teeth between the front teeth and the eyeteeth—never grew, which left four teeth struggling to fill a gap nature designed for six. Her Native status, which helped with basic dental work, did not run to cosmetic surgery. When she was sixteen, the Twains found the money to fill the gap in her smile. "Eilleen had to have a lot of orthodontic work done," says Timmins dentist Gerry Paquette. "My colleague Dr. Davis did some and also my study club, to help with costs, but it cost her a few thousand dollars to get everything done. I used a crown with a bridge to fill the missing gap, but I know she's had it all done again since then."

Timmins High and Vocational School, with twelve hundred students, was daunting after cosy Capreol. In May 1981, at the end of tenth grade, the school moved to new premises off Theriault Boulevard. The facilities were a distinct improvement, with a fully equipped theater and several well-appointed music rooms. As she had in Hanmer, Eilleen went through the motions, never giving the teachers any clue as to how much she despised going to school.

"She sang sometimes two or three nights a week and would come to class the next day," says Maureen Yakabuski, her twelfth-grade English teacher. "She would always make a point of getting the work done and hand it in. She was a conscientious student, although music was the love of her life much more than English literature was."

Years of hiding her family circumstances had made her an accomplished dissembler. She was a rebel but never showed it. She skipped school a lot more than anybody realized, for she was smart enough to write fake sick notes from her mother to cover her absences. "I felt invisible a lot," she said. "I actually wrote a song called 'Feeling Invisible.' I was athletic and into music and not really socializing, and I'm sure a lot of it was because I was introverted." When she cut classes—especially history, which she thought irrelevant—she headed straight for the music rooms.

Her teachers recognized that she had a special ability. "Her talent stood out even then," says Tony Ciccone, who taught music in her final year. "She already had the package: the voice, the delivery, and the ability to project onstage. There are a lot of things you can't teach, like her innate ability to project and a way to touch people with her talent. We had a performance group, a wind band in which Eilleen played trumpet, but because she could sing so well, I did an arrangement of Pat Benatar's 'Hit Me with Your Best Shot' and left out the melody line. For the performance in the theater we grouped the twenty people in the band around her; she stood in the middle of the circle and sang the words. She brought the house down."

For a while, Eilleen was able to lose herself in the anonymity of the bigger school, but that was not enough. The adolescent advances of thirteen-year-olds are far more easily repelled than those of older boys. Eilleen enjoyed sports: she was on the track-and-field team and also played soccer. The problem was that it was her breasts that drew immediate attention, not her athletic abilities. While the boys admired her jiggling, she was embarrassed. "I was very much into sports," she said. "So now I wasn't just running on the soccer team as one of the guys; I was running on the soccer team bouncing! They weren't seeing me as part of the team; they were seeing me as a girl, and I didn't like that.

"Guys at that age, as you know, do tend to cross that line. They might grab your butt—they're not thinking, they're being impulsive," she said. "And that stuff really made me withdraw from wanting to be a girl. There was one girl at my school who didn't care. She had a figure very similar to mine. She was very curvy. We were in track and field together and she just let it fly. She didn't care. She was being natural. And I remember what people thought of her at the time. I would never have been caught being thought of in that way.

"I was so confused about all that stuff, I did everything I could to hide what I had. I started wearing layers of clothing. I would always strap my breasts down so that when I was on the soccer field, the guys were watching me play, not watching me bounce."

She wore baggy track pants and sweatshirts to school and sometimes two bras. "I was a girl physically, but it didn't matter to me, I couldn't have cared less. I didn't think that's what it meant to be a girl. I resented the fact that there was a difference between men and women. I just wanted to be a person. On a hot summer day, I'd wear something over my bathing suit, and then when I'd get into the lake up to my knees, I'd throw it off and dive in." This natural shyness lasted for years, and even in the superstar Shania there is still something of the gauche teenager uncomfortable in a body that has let her down. She never struts the walk of the physically and sexually confident.

Like any girl, Eilleen enjoyed being fancied by boys, though she found their adolescent fumblings irritating and felt demeaned by the way their conversation was directed into her cleavage and not her eyes. Their small-town prejudices—the parents of one boy she was dating forbade him to see her anymore once they discovered she was from a Native family—and ambitions irritated her, too. In return she treated boys badly.

"In my teens I was as hard as a rock, I was so hard and so tough I wasn't very likeable," she says. "I was going to achieve whatever I wanted in life and nothing was going to stop me. I had little relationships with boys where I'd say right up front, 'I want you to know I don't get too attached. My career comes first. If an opportunity comes up I'm gone.' I'd make all these things clear up front. When you come from hardship you know what you don't want to repeat and I knew that if I was going to be independent, financially independent, I was never going to rely on anybody again ever, because there wasn't anybody in my life I could rely on."

She was seventeen when she lost her virginity to Mike Chabot. She was much too sensible to take any risks. "I'm kind of old-fashioned," she told *FHM* magazine, "so I was never really into the do-it-at-a-party-in-the-side-room thing. I wasn't drinking, it was well thought-out and I was like, 'OK, now I'm gonna experiment.' And it was enjoyable."

Such an attitude toward sex, plus her rejection of many of her suitors, gave Eilleen the reputation of being aloof and stuck-up. She found it hard to make close girlfriends, whose primary interests, boys and clothes, did not appeal to her. She palled up with Cynthia Hagen, but her closest friendships were with boys—provided they never tried to put the moves on her.

"She wasn't shy but she was not the center of attention either. She wasn't someone who, when she entered the room, everyone went quiet. I thought she was very pretty, though she wasn't flashy and she dressed fairly plain," says Brian Hurst, who was one grade ahead. He first met Eilleen in the drama class he was attending to pick up an extra credit. "It was a fairly loose class. We did a lot of free-association stuff—pretend you're in an elevator stuff. She was already a performer, but it taught her how to improve her presence in front of people."

Brian was also the lead trumpet in the brass band. Eilleen was fourth trumpet, playing typical high-school material, movie themes, and massacring Beatles hits like "Eight Days a Week." "She could make noise but she wasn't a lead player," says Brian. "She is a much better singer than a trumpet player."

He knew that before they ever met. At Timmins High there were a couple of small practice rooms next to the main rehearsal room. "One day during band practice," says Brian, "there was a lot of noise with people tuning instruments, and our conductor tapped on the stage to get us to pay attention to him . . . but when it was quiet we could hear Eilleen and Carrie Ann singing a country duet. Joe Belinkis, the music teacher, held up his finger and we listened a few minutes. Then he smiled and we started to play. There was everybody making a horrendous noise and there she was in the background making this beautiful music."

Brian's best friend was Rick Thompson ("we met in the crib"), who played tuba in the brass band but had ambitions beyond that. Both Rick and Eilleen also performed with the Timmins Youth Singers. Because of their mutual love for music, Eilleen and the two boys became close friends, and none of them ever endangered this by throwing sex into the equation. Once she relaxed, Eilleen was a chatterbox just like her mother. She was, as Rick recalls, great company. "There are some people that shine pretty bright and some that are pretty dim. She was always a lot more shiny than the rest of us. She loved to know exactly what was going on around her. If she started laughing, that was it, the whole room cracked up. She's got one of those infectious laughs and she loved to use it. She was an absolute howl. When she wanted to start speaking, she'd get all excited, go at a million miles an hour. She had a joie de vivre. She was passionate and enthusiastic about things. She wore her heart on her sleeve for us and we did the same for her. She called me her Big Bear, because we'd always have a big hug.

"She was one of the boys. One time, when she was about seventeen, she insisted she wanted to party with us. 'Come on, let's go over to Brian's place and have a couple of beers.' We were seasoned northern Ontario beer drinkers at that point. She came over. She was always slight and skinny, well-proportioned and gorgeous, a great-looking girl but always a mate to us. Anyway, she had a couple of beers and that was it . . . she passed right out. She could not handle it at all. I tried to carry her, she must have weighed next to nothing, but she was a dead weight, and I could not get her off the ground. So we both threw her in Brian's bed, closed the door, both of us smiling at her, and carried on our merry way, finishing off the rest of the case."

Timmins High might have had the facilities, but it could not provide enough to feed her yearning. Throughout her teen years, music remained the focus of her life. She always knew what she was going to do, as Vic Power (mayor of Timmins 1983–2000 and 2003 to present), recalls: "I was her guidance counselor and it was my job to meet with students to discuss career or academic prospects. I was always impressed that she knew what she wanted and that she was going places even as a teenager. I didn't have to guide her at all, she always knew where she was going."

"I hated high school," she says. "I would never do that again. All I ever wanted to do was music, so the last thing I wanted to do was waste my time in class, and I still look at it that way. When a child has a talent, let them concentrate on that, let them learn what they want, let them excel at that. I didn't want to be in school. I guess one thing it taught me was some kind of discipline.

"When I look back now I think, yes, I could have enjoyed my teen years much, much more. But at the time you could have never told me that because I was so passionate about music that that's all I cared about. I threw myself into music. All I wanted to be was in band practice or writing songs or singing. I loved being in the basement with the band, I loved writing music and that sort of thing, but I didn't care to be the front person; as a matter of fact, I didn't like it at all. I really had to grow into that, it took me a very long time. But music itself could consume me every hour of the day and I would have been content with that, not realizing what I was missing by not socializing with the other kids, because most of the time the people I was playing with were much older. They weren't in school, they were adults. I did miss out a lot, but I don't regret it."

Eilleen's next major break came eighteen months after she moved back to Timmins. She desperately wanted to join a local rock band and had heard about these four young guys called Longshot. One winter night when she was working at McDonald's, they came in after rehearsal . . . and gave her the kiss-off. "We went to eat after rehearsal," says Mike Chabot, "and Eilleen was behind the counter serving us. She said, 'You guys are in a band, aren't you?' Not knowing she had already done *The Tommy Hunter Show*, we just nodded and kind of ignored her."

Her mother convinced her to appear on the annual telethon shown on the local CBC TV station. By coincidence, Longshot were taking a break from rehearsals and switched on the television "to see which local bands were playing and who was making a fool of themselves. There was this girl singing," says Dave Hartt, who did not recognize her from the burger bar, "and she's got an incredible voice. I said, 'Guys, we've got to get her to sing for us.' "

Chapter Six

LONGSHOT

IN THE SUMMER OF 1981, Guy Martin had corralled four of his friends into the basement of Rick Dion's house on 371 Elm Street South, directly opposite Zudel's Fresh Mart. Guy's original plan was to record two songs as a birthday gift for a friend. He had already booked time at a recording studio down in Toronto in October. Rick played lead guitar, the soft-spoken Mike Mitchell bass, Tom Lauzon rhythm guitar, and Mike Chabot drums, while Guy, who, after toying with various stage names, including Jonathan Devonshire, finally settled on David Hartt, played keyboards and sang. The rehearsals went so well that after the recording session was done, the boys—with the exception of Tom—decided to stay together.

As bands do, they bickered over their name almost as long as they rehearsed and spun their fantasies of stardom. One night Dave grumbled, "It's a long shot that anything will ever come out of this." Mike Mitchell retorted, "Well, Longshot's a better name than anything else." It stuck. Longshot did a few gigs as a quartet, but mainly continued to rehearse at Rick's.

Although the band was stunned by Eilleen's voice on the telethon, nobody caught her name. They did hear the station announcer say she attended Timmins High. When Dave mentioned the girl to his friend Brian Hurst, he said he played trumpet with her in the school band. Brian gave Longshot's Toronto tape to

Eilleen and a couple of months later she strolled round the corner from the Twain apartment on Balsam South to meet with Dave, who thought his song "Take My Hand" might work as a duet. He played the piano, she sang the first verse, he sang the second, then they harmonized on the chorus. Upstairs, Mike Mitchell, who had just walked in, heard Eilleen singing and ran down the stairs, almost tripping headfirst on his way. His first breathless words to her were, "You're not going anywhere!"

"The band clicked musically from day one," says Hartt. "It only happens once in a lifetime that you really get that perfect mix. Everybody gets along, you're all friends . . . of course, you always break up."

During the early 1980s, the mines were doing well so the town was booming. "I could make C$35,000 mining in Timmins in 1980 and only C$20,000 in Toronto," recalls John Emms, who has played in local rock bands since the early 1970s, "and I got to play music in hotels at the weekend. Everybody's life revolved around the weekend. The hotels and bars were a way of life and all the twenty-odd bars in Timmins were packed. You would go from one to another. If you met anybody, it was at a bar. Everyone got polluted until the bars shut, then you'd go for a pizza at Don's or to somebody's house and continue the party until four, sleep late, and start again on Saturday night. The bars were full for twenty years, it was a terrific scene . . . then satellite TV arrived and Timmins rejoined the rest of the world!"

On Friday nights, everyone old enough to drink followed the same ritual. Back from work, a quick shower for the guys, a paint, daub, and gossip session for the girls. Forget the movies; there were only two cinemas in town and they showed the same films for a month at a time. Then it was out to the bar playing the music of your choice. Most of the hotels featured country music, but they were all packed out. If you wanted a table, you had to be there by half past eight, as the band went onstage for the first of their four sets at nine. The bars closed at one so there was much serious drinking to be done. Shots of hard liquor with beer chasers were the order of the night and if you couldn't hold your drink until last call, you weren't a man.

The best bars were in a small six-block area south of Algonquin East. A major focus was the corner of Mountjoy and Wilson where the Escapade, the Rocking Tap, and the more traditional Northern Star were but a short stumble apart. The younger crowd also frequented the Empire (the biggest gig in town). The "Riv" (Riverview Hotel), the Algoma Tavern, the GV Hotel, the South End Hotel, and, for a major change of scenery, the Airport Hotel five miles away in South Porcupine. Country fans preferred the Maple Leaf over on Balsam, still virtually unchanged from the days of Stompin' Tom, or the Windsor. They were all small places: JP's Lounge could squeeze in two hundred if everyone breathed in at the same time; the Algoma could not fit a hundred.

Jean-Paul Aubé was an entrepreneur before he was allowed to drink. At seventeen, he was running his own club, putting on bands every weekend. He bought the Escapade Hotel with his brother Ben when he was twenty-five, kept on renting its rooms to construction workers on contract (though the bridal suite featured a round bed and a fur rug), and started a discotheque downstairs. It was not until J.P. canned the disco, rechristened the space "JP's Lounge," and started booking live acts that he struck the paypacket lode. The formula was simple and commercial: He hired in duos from southern Ontario who played easy-listening Top 40 hits. It worked. "I could have had police directing traffic on Friday and Saturday nights," he says.

Late one afternoon in early 1982, there was a timid knock on the door of J.P.'s office in the lobby of the Escapade. A sixteen-year-old girl he had never seen before asked nervously if she could come in. She was good-looking, not stunning, but there was something about her, a presence, something familiar, perhaps a quality he recognized from his own youth. That was why J.P. gave her the time of day.

"We have a group," Eilleen Twain told him—she didn't say "I"—all business, very articulate, very focused and specific. "We have been practicing for a while and we're trying to get into a hotel because we want to play. I'll be upfront with you . . . I'm underage, so nobody will give me a chance." That all but finished the deal as far as J.P. was concerned. Hoteliers in Ontario had to abide by the rules, otherwise the all-powerful LLBOA (Liquor License Board of Ontario Authority) closed them down. Underage drinkers were a definite no-no.

"If you are underage you are not allowed in," he said. "Sorry . . ."

"No, but you can," she said so forcefully he stopped mid-sentence. "The management have to provide me with a place where I can go between sets. I can be on the stage for my set, but after that I have to be in a room."

There were rooms upstairs at the Escapade, so that was not a problem. J.P. was intrigued by the girl's self-confidence in asking him to make an exception for her. She was certainly cute, but could she sing? "We'd like you to hear us first," she said, as if she had been reading his mind. "We practice most nights in the basement at 371 Elm Street South."

J.P. discussed the girl with his brother, who had also been visited by Hartt and Chabot. They checked out the legal situation to find Eilleen was right and went to a rehearsal. "As soon as they started playing and she started singing, I knew," says J.P. "Just hearing the sound, the voice, and the look. I'm not stupid. They were a Top 40 band, better than I was getting from southern Ontario. It was more expensive than what we were paying the duos and I remember thinking 'Do we want to do this?' but I looked at my brother. He agreed. They filled up the place pretty much from the first night on."

J.P. and Ben gave the band a residency at JP's Lounge starting in May. They had only heard them play one song—which was fortunate. "The date was twenty-seven days away," says Hartt. "We had to play four sets a night and we only knew five songs. We practiced every night, marathon practices on weekends, going into the wee hours of Sunday morning. Sunday night, Monday night, every night we'd practice and by the first show we had forty-two songs."

The pay was pretty good at a time when the minimum wage

was C$2.30 an hour: C$1,200 for the first four-night residency at JP's, rising later to C$1,600. Within a few weeks they were booked solid until January. Some of the profit went into buying a small PA, and to start with, Eilleen—who didn't have to buy any gear—was asked to contribute. The other band members knew her family was poor and how much C$300 a week meant to them. Her deductions dropped from fifty bucks to twenty-five and then disappeared for good.

Longshot were such a good draw J.P. had to hire bouncers—after 9:30 nobody could get in. Much of Longshot's appeal was because they attracted the girls. "They loved us, we had attendance records that stood for a long time," says Hartt. "It was simple. With a female lead singer, you attract women, men come into a bar, see lots of women, they stay, they buy the women drinks. Bars make a lot of money. We weren't cheap, we demanded a good price."

"Longshot was not into drinking as much as Smuggler or Elmer Thudd or some of the other rock bands," adds John Emms. "These guys wanted to play it straighter so they had a larger audience of women. My wife would tell me, 'Your band is terrible, but these guys are great because they are playing the songs just like on the radio.'

"As a performer, Eilleen was a mix of halting confidence, but her personal attitude was great. She was kind of shy, but she had to be the lead singer and at times she seemed forced into the role. She was good, she could hit all the high notes. Longshot were there to bang out the hits and they did that better than anybody else in town."

Onstage, Eilleen never flaunted it. She hid her figure behind her Tacoma twelve-string guitar and played percussion when she was not singing. She dressed down, never too sexy, baggy sweatshirts over spandex tights and wool leggings—the *Flashdance* look—and no bare flesh on display. As she grew in confidence her clothes became a little tighter: she favored black satin skintight pants with a matching top and headband—very Olivia Newton John—or black leather trousers. They all wore black satin tour jackets with the Longshot logo on the back. Although her hair was fine and thin she insisted that hairdresser Paul Cousineau give her regular perms. She wanted to wear it big, backcombed to *Dynasty* heights. There was one frizzy perm that was disastrous. Eilleen never wore too much makeup, no foundation or lipstick, just heavy black eyeliner.

To begin with, Eilleen never talked to the audience much. Hartt and Chabot took care of that, but her confidence grew steadily. She learned to use the breaks between sets. Sharon, Jerry, and the extended Twain clan were regulars, but she did not confine herself to family and friends; instead she learned to work the room.

"I never saw her sleazy or flirting with guys, she was just very focused all the time," says Cousineau, a friend of Mike Chabot's, who saw Longshot play all the time with his girlfriend. "She would finish her first set and on her way offstage she would thank whoever was there for coming. She'd take a few minutes' rest, get back up there, she'd play hard, and the next thing you know she'd go through the audience on the second set, same on the third, and anyone she hadn't seen she'd go and say hello. She wasn't allowed to drink because of her age, but she was always the lady, she'd say hello to everybody on her way to the upstairs room."

Longshot did not rely on original songs. They only did three David Hartt compositions: "Thanks for the Good Times," "Sandy," and the duet "Take My Hand," which became an unofficial anthem at several local weddings. Eilleen sang over half the material with Hartt taking lead vocals on about 40 percent, leaving the two Mikes to sing three numbers between them. The material was miles from what Eilleen knew. Hartt loathed country and refused to touch anything with a twang. They concentrated on current hits by melodic hard rockers, leavened with a sprinkling of classic cuts ("We didn't do 'Hotel California' or 'Stairway to Heaven,' those were taboo songs," says Hartt). The Beatles's "Let It Be," Fleetwood Mac's "Don't Stop," Creedence Clearwater Revival's "Travelin' Band," and Grand Funk Railroad's "American Band." Longshot covered hits by Canadian rockers Loverboy, Toronto, and Bryan Adams as well as Bob Seger, Styx, REO Speedwagon, and Journey, whose "Don't Stop Believing" was a particular showstopper, along with Survivor's "Eye of the

Tiger," Foreigner's "Feels Like the First Time" (written and produced by one Robert John "Mutt" Lange) and Orleans's "Still the One" (which has nothing in common with the track on Shania's *Come On Over*). For ballads, Eilleen convinced them to let her sing Linda Ronstadt's quivering version of "Poor Poor Pitiful Me" and Sheena Easton's "When He Shines." Longshot never played any Pat Benatar numbers, although they did rehearse a couple.

All the band members knew that Eilleen wrote songs and they wanted to tackle them, but she always demurred, insisting they weren't ready. Dave Hartt still has a tape of "Stepping Stones," which he begged her to perform with them. "Maybe she wasn't comfortable," says Hartt, "because when you put a song out before other people, you are standing pretty naked there. Also she was writing ballads, which didn't fit with us so well. I remember her sitting on a stool at JP's Lounge singing this line: 'the flickering fire on the wall made music that I found you.' I looked across the bar and I could see her reflection in the mirror and I said, 'That's great.' She was really dedicated because while she was working at this, she was looking for the right words, putting it together."

Although Eilleen was treated like one of the boys, they always took good care of her. Rick or Dave, who lived close by, generally walked her home after a gig. After a pool party during the summer, the flirtatious looks she had been exchanging with Mike Chabot turned to kisses and they started going out together. She might have been three years younger than Mike, but she was "serious about my career and my life. Men were always secondary. I never put a man first, ever."

"I'm not into how people look and she was a lot of fun to be with," says Chabot. "She had a great sense of humor—we clicked from that standpoint—we both liked music, played tennis a couple of times, then we hung out. It was nothing serious, a normal boyfriend-girlfriend thing, I bought a few things for her, but it only lasted a short time, just the summer. She was very, very energetic with regards to enjoying life; she knew what she wanted, that's for sure. Music was going to be her living, that was clear from day one.

I've played hockey with guys in the NHL, I've worked in business with people who are very successful, but not like her. She is probably the most driven soul I've ever met."

For her seventeenth birthday, Mike gave her a present that she still has today. "He gave me a black ledger and said, 'You've gotta stop collecting all your songs on loose pieces of paper. You should put them where you're not going to lose anything.' So I rewrote all of my songs into this ledger and I've kept that. I've been a little more organized from that point on."

Eilleen soon emerged as one of the most forceful personalities in the band. If they made a mistake, she let them know, no holding back. During one show Chabot hit the cymbal wrong and the stand crashed over, missing Eilleen by half an inch. She never missed a beat, kept right on singing, until the guitar solo. Then she turned round and yelled at him. Just as the solo finished, she turned back and came in note-perfect, right on cue. The audience never saw a thing.

She got her own back in October on Chabot's birthday. As a treat they let him play a drum solo while they brought a cake on-stage. Eilleen took the cake, went behind him, and pushed it right in his face. That was the signal for a cake fight. "We were not always the most professional," laughs Hartt, "but we liked to have fun." Unlike some of their contemporaries, they did not drink much and did not smoke pot. After shows at JP's, they would repair over the road to the Cosy Corner Café to eat and discuss any problems.

When trouble broke out, which it often did when drink took over the crowd, the boys protected her. One night at the Riv a serious bar fight broke out just as the band launched into Toronto's "Looking for Trouble." Unlike the Deep South of the United States, where the stage is often surrounded by chicken wire, the band had no protection, so the guitarists stood in front of their singer, using their C$1,500 instruments as shields, and, as the battle overflowed onto the stage, pushed the brawlers off with their feet. They never stopped playing.

On New Year's Eve 1982, Eilleen's voice completely gave out, and she could only manage two songs, one of which was "Auld Lang Syne." The boys went back to their oldest material, including some AC/DC songs, but nobody seemed to mind. By that stage it was already over for Longshot. They had decided to call it a day in the autumn, but agreed to honor their remaining commitments.

Longshot worked hard, perhaps too hard, for they seldom turned down a show. On the weekend of July 1, 1982, they picked up their gear from JP's, went down to Hollinger Park for a Battle of the Bands, and returned to JP's. The next day they played at a friend's wedding barbecue and ended up back at the park in the early evening. They played odd venues like a dance for a baseball team at La Ronde, the French cultural center, and the occasional bummer like the GV Hotel, where they earned less than the waitresses.

The problem was that, while Longshot was good, there was nowhere for them to go. In the year they were gigging, the furthest out of town they played was South Porcupine. It was a perennial problem, as John Emms recalls: "Not many bands in town lasted more than two years. Playing three weekends out of four you didn't have time to change the set list, so the audience got smaller and smaller. And if you went to Toronto you found out quick how you weren't as good as you thought you were. You would go see a band in a bar and these guys were schooled musicians and the drummer could play in time. That was an eye-opener."

It didn't help that Eilleen was still in high school and that the next set of decent gigs was a three-hour drive away in Sudbury or North Bay. But that wasn't a real problem, as Sharon would drive her daughter to the ends of the earth if she thought it was a step up the ladder. They talked about going on the road once Eilleen got out of school, but that was just talk. While the boys' ambitions ended at the city boundaries, Eilleen's did not. She was the one who left after a gig not in triumph but with the big black dog gnawing at her insides, "walking home alone at three A.M. with a rock in my pocket."

The experience of working in a rock band changed Eilleen's perceptions, shifting them away from country. She learned that there was more to performance than just singing. "I couldn't hide behind my guitar," she says. "I sensed a freedom that I'd never sensed before." It taught her how performance could be exhilarating, blow away the old fears, but at the same time it made her yearn for more.

"In the summer we were all booked up, so there was no point in leaving the area," says Hartt. "Why pay to go live somewhere else, when you can make better money at home? We talked to musicians that came in from out of town, making C$120 for the whole band to eat for a week. That's not a lot of money, you're not going to buy instruments, put money away for retirement on that. I never wanted to take that big risk of leaving. In the end, Eilleen was a lot more dedicated than the rest of us. We lacked ambition, but maybe because she went without when she was younger it didn't scare her to say, 'I can leave all this behind and work on my music, because this is what I want to do.' "

Longshot's final show at the Palmour Tavern on January 14, 1983, was not intended to be a permanent end. After eighteen months spending almost every night together the musicians needed a break, time apart. They settled into jobs and girlfriends and after a few months thought about starting up again. Hartt called Eilleen and asked if she wanted to come back. Even though the money would have been useful, Eilleen had seen their true colors. She said "No."

"We might have been the best band in Timmins, but that was Timmins, man," says Chabot, aptly summing up a band that might have done something. "My dream was never North Bay or Sudbury. It was pure outright fun for me. I did think about making a living at it, but drummers are a dime a dozen. When the band broke up, I joined a band in southern Ontario, gave it a shot, and it didn't work out. Eilleen went to a band down in Sudbury, but she was already looking beyond that."

Chapter Seven

THE WILDERNESS YEARS

AFTER GRADUATING from Timmins High in July 1983, Eilleen determined to expand her musical horizons. While Longshot had been a successful experiment, its ambition had been limited and she understood that no talent scout was going to discover her north of the Arctic watershed. For much of the next three years she spent her summers planting trees and her winters playing the Ontario club circuit, attempting to break into the business.

Musically she trod an uneasy path between country and rock. By the early 1980s, country music's flirtation with cocaine and outlaws had evaporated. Strings and spangles had reasserted their conservative sway. The radical limit of Nashville's ambitions was to achieve pop crossovers like Kenny Rogers and Dolly Parton's excruciating "Islands in the Stream." In the United States, while the corporate rock of Journey and Foreigner was challenged by British bands like the Police, Eurythmics, Culture Club, and Def Leppard, the real star of the era was Michael Jackson. Canada—and especially Timmins—was stuck firmly on the musical periphery. The advent of the video channel MuchMusic and FM radio showed just how much.

After the demise of Longshot, Eilleen was approached to join Flirt, a covers band operating out of Sudbury. Flirt's lead singer Diane Chase, who had decided to try her luck in the business down in Toronto, knew Eilleen from when they were children on the local talent circuit and recommended her for the job. Flirt traveled all over Ontario earning a reasonable way playing "rock, R&B, Top 40, whatever was making money at the time." Eilleen missed her graduation ceremony because she was on the road with them. Laura Surch saw them at a hotel in Blind River. "I managed to get my aunt to go into a hotel to see the band, which was a major deal," she says, "but it was just a job for Eilleen."

The more Eilleen sang around southern Ontario the more she realized how tough the competition was. To improve her range and power she took singing lessons from Toronto coach Ian Garrett. As she was living close to the breadline, she often didn't have the money to pay for her lessons, so as a trade, she cleaned Garrett's house. "He'd feed me once in a while too," she recalls. "From up in his studio I would look down on the corner outside his house where the taxis used to pick up and drop off the hookers. I thought, 'These girls are probably going home with something in their pocket,' though I would never have gone that far."

By the autumn of 1984, Eilleen had attracted the interest of Toronto-based producer/DJ Stan Campbell. In a Canadian *Country Music News* article Campbell enthused about his latest protégée. "Eilleen possesses a powerful voice with an impressive range. She has the necessary drive, ambition, and positive attitude to achieve her goals." Campbell was making an album with Tim Denis and drafted Eilleen in to sing backing vocals on "Heavy on the Sunshine." The following January, Campbell took her down to Nashville to record some demos.

The demo recordings cost C$10,000, which the Twains could ill afford. Sharon set about trying to raise some investment. "She called encouraging me to invest in Eilleen's career," says Jean-Paul Aubé, with a rueful smile. "She called more than once. She wanted money for Eilleen to live on while she got a portfolio together and developed contacts and connections. She didn't have an agent. I asked, 'How much will you need?' and she said C$25,000. I told her, 'I agree with you a thousand percent she has a lot of talent and she should be very successful. I'd love to be able to participate, but unfortunately I can't, as I've just taken on some fairly major commitments with McDonald's.' "

Sharon turned to northern Ontario's brightest—and only—country star. Mary Bailey lived in Kirkland Lake, a ninety-minute drive from Timmins. If Shania Twain's life can be likened to a modern Cinderella story, Mary is the fairy godmother—always there when she was needed. Mary had been successful in Canada, enjoying a run of country chart singles in 1976 and releasing two albums, *Mystery Girl* and *Think of Me*. She knew all about Eilleen.

"I was doing a show in Sudbury," she says, "and this little girl got up on the stage with a guitar and absolutely blew me away. She sang two songs, Willie Nelson's 'Blue Eyes Crying in the Rain' and Hank Williams's 'I'm So Lonesome I Could Cry.' Her voice reminded me of Tanya Tucker; it had strength and character to it, a lot of feeling. There was never a doubt in my mind that she had it; even at that young age she exuded a quiet confidence. Stars stand out."

Mary knew what it was like to be a child with a voice. Her middle-class parents had pushed her too, woken her in the middle of the night to sing at their parties. They drove her to talent contests as far afield as Windsor and Toronto, where she sang numbers by Jeanette Macdonald, Nelson Eddy, Mario Lanza, and the Ink Spots. She married young and had a family, but her ambitions did not wither with changing diapers. Her husband, Bob Kasner, "was totally and only into country music. So I listened to it, it grew on me, I grew to love it." Mary—or Eveline as she was known then—was ambitious and smart with it. She bought advertising downtime from local TV stations for next to nothing and used it to promote her records. Pretty, vivacious, and charming, Mary was an excellent networker who never forgot a face. She did well, but by 1985, her career was winding down and she was looking for a new challenge.

Sharon, ever mindful of her daughter's prospects, had kept in sporadic touch with Mary since '78. In the spring of 1985, she approached her again, ostensibly asking for advice on whether they had been overcharged for the Nashville demos. Mary listened to the tapes and told Sharon, "Yes, it was too much money," and how much they could have done it for, but all the while she spoke she was mesmerized by that reserved nineteen-year-old girl who sat in an armchair, silent while her mother did all the talking, but devouring every word.

"She sang a couple of songs that she had written," says Mary, "and I thought to myself, 'This kid is like nineteen years old, where does she get this? This is from a person who's lived sixty years.' Songs about being a woman in difficult situations, finding the best in a person, asking why are they staying in that relationship . . . pretty deep for a nineteen-year-old. No offense, but they haven't lived it and you don't believe that they think that deeply. But Eilleen could, she had an innate ability. She must have an old soul, for she always wrote beyond her years."

While Mary was impressed by the girl's talent, Bob was visibly blown away. Eventually, Sharon came to the crunch. Would Mary be interested in managing her daughter? "I had never managed anybody in my life," says Mary. "I managed my own career out of necessity, not choice. Bob and I talked to each other, and he said, 'She's a star, she deserves an opportunity.' "

Mary bought out Eilleen's contract with Stan Campbell and Eilleen moved into the Kasner home, a well-appointed wooden chalet with a stunning view over Kenogami Lake. For nine months she became a surrogate daughter, connecting with Mary in a way her two sons never could. While she was there, Eilleen enjoyed a quick fling with Bobby Kasner, which they tried very hard to keep secret from his mother, if not the prying eyes of his little brother. She was given her own room and helped around the house and kitchen. Mostly she played guitar and sang. She practiced every day for hours.

"She wouldn't just let her voice do it for her," says Mary. "You may be born with a talent to be able to sing, but ninety-five percent of us get by on that. She didn't, she perfected her craft. She listened to all her influences, especially Karen Carpenter. If you really listened to Karen she had this total control. Eilleen worked on that, learned to be able to control, how to use certain intonations to take the song further. She understood that the voice was an instrument, and how well she learned to play that instrument was how good her chances were. It's very rare finding people like that. Everybody wants to be a star but very few people want to do what's required . . . but she did it, in everything."

Just as Eveline Kasner was not the right name for a country singer, Mary knew Eilleen Twain did not cut it either. They discussed names for hours and eventually Mary suggested "Sophyah." She sent tapes to her contacts south of the border, including Ken Kragen, the manager of Kenny Rogers and Lionel Richie. The answers all came back the same: "Thanks, but no thanks." Mary and Bob never lost faith.

Toward the end of 1985, Mary took Eilleen down to Nashville to stay with her friend, record producer Tony Migliore. Fellow Canadian Kelita Haverland was cutting an album at Chelsea Studios and Tony drafted Eilleen in to sing backup. (When the album was released by RCA, the title track, "Too Hard to Handle," became a minor hit.) She wrote and demoed songs with songwriter Cyril Rawson, but after five months nobody had shown any interest, so she returned to Kirkland Lake to stay in the Kasner house. In order to raise extra money to finance the project, Mary went back to work, releasing a couple more singles.

There was a more fundamental problem. In 1985, country was so far from cool as to be beyond tepid. Eilleen did not want to sing country, she wanted to be a rocker. They began to argue, but Eilleen was not frightened of confronting her manager. After years of subsistence living, Eilleen had tasted middle-class luxury at Kirkland Lake, and while she liked it, that was not enough. Eilleen was not frightened of being poor. She had survived on mustard sandwiches in the past and, if she had to, would do so again. Once her mind was made up, the girl had a will of steel: She did not bend, she did not break, and she would not compromise. Certain that country was not the right route forward, Eilleen convinced Mary to let her front a rock band.

In September 1986, Rick Thompson had decided it was time to go to college to study music. The week before his audition with Humber College in Toronto, Eilleen called him up. "Listen, Big Bear, I've got a project going. I've got some musicians and we're going to get together in Kirkland Lake and I'd like you to come and play bass for me." Rick didn't hesitate for a moment.

The musical mainstay was keyboard player Eric Lambier, who, with his hair past his shoulders, looked like "a complete metalhead." Eric had two glass eyes—the result of a gunshot accident when he was a kid—but aside from needing some help to get behind his equipment, his handicap went unnoticed. The lineup was completed by Tom on guitar and Randy on drums (neither Rick nor Mary Bailey can remember their last names), both of whom had worked with Eric down in Toronto.

Eilleen lived with Mary while the band were in a second-floor flat in downtown Kirkland Lake, two blocks from the rehearsal studio, a converted changing room next to the hockey rinks. There was no wage, but Mary paid for rent, food, and the rehearsal space. Rick and Eric got up at 5:30 in the morning six days a week, even if it was forty below outside, grabbed some breakfast, and headed for the studio. When Eilleen walked in, the band was always ready to go. The music was a continuation of what Eilleen had been doing with Longshot and Flirt—production rock with a lot of Top 40 influence, nothing more experimental or out on the edge than a dance groove—except it was all original material. The cores of the songs originated from Eilleen, who threw ideas at Eric, which they then bounced back and forth. "They had a pretty good writing chemistry together," says Rick. "Because she is a singer, she likes to write with somebody who knows what they are doing with their instrument. She loves the tension of throwing ideas at people.

"There were times she'd run helter-skelter, she'd want to do so many things at one time. We'd go, 'Hang on, look at this, make it simpler,' but when she was running we couldn't pull her down if we wanted to. Harmonically Eric would have more ideas and say, 'That doesn't work.' She'd have to think about that for a little, so she'd clam up and put her pensive face on—I loved it when that would happen—and she'd come around after a while or she'd say, 'No, I want to try it my way.' Eilleen was the boss, she ran the show. She wasn't tough because we worked our asses off. It was one of the most productive times in my life. We came close to working up twenty tunes we could have played onstage—but we never got the chance."

After her brief dalliance with Bobby Kasner, Eilleen took up with Randy. "Eilleen was always cool with her boyfriends. She didn't change her 'one of the boys' attitude," says Rick. "Randy asked the rest of us in the group if it was okay if they had a relationship, which I thought was a very cool thing to do. He also said it didn't matter a hoot if we said, 'No way,' but they thought they'd be considerate and ask anyway." The band rapport was good. They enjoyed several parties in the flat. Rick remembers everybody watching the movie *This Is Spinal Tap;* the band all fell about laughing, while the nonmusicians sat there bemused, saying, "It's kinda funny, but we don't really get it."

After three chilly months in Kirkland Lake, Mary suggested the band move back down south and get ready to do some recording. In January, they moved to Orono, twenty miles east of Toronto, where Eric's mother had a tobacco farm, and set up their equipment in one of the drying rooms. They continued to rehearse and play for the odd visitor Eilleen or Mary invited out. They recorded a song, "The City," for a contest sponsored by Q107, the big local rock station. It made the final top twenty-five. Soon afterward, everything went pear-shaped.

The band hoped a record deal was imminent and kept asking about it. When nothing materialized they felt they were being kept in the dark about what was going on. The band seethed away until Randy announced, "That's it, it's finished." "We tried to keep the band going as a four-piece," says Rick, "but I kept getting, 'Rick, you sing all right, but you are no Eilleen Twain.' I absolutely didn't understand why the whole thing fell through, wasn't given much of an explanation, so I stayed angry at Eilleen for a while after that."

One of the reasons that no record deal materialized was that, by the end of the stay in Kirkland Lake, Mary and Eilleen were arguing constantly. "Eilleen and I always had little shouts," says Mary. "Some days we'd be diamonds, some days we'd be stones, it doesn't mean that we didn't love each other. She knew what she wanted, and worked toward it. I couldn't bring to the table where she wanted it to go: I was trying to make inroads in country, she was steering one way, I was steering another." Finally, after one argument, an exasperated Mary snapped, "If you don't want to sing country, what the hell can I do for you?" Eilleen left for Toronto and after the band imploded; they did not speak for nearly two years.

She had already found the man who was going to be instrumental in the next stage of her career. In the late summer of 1986, Mary had engineered a meeting between Eilleen and John Kim Bell, a half-Mohawk, half-American conductor. After a glittering career split between conducting Broadway musicals, symphonies, and ballets (he was the first Native to conduct a symphony orchestra), Bell had rediscovered his roots. He settled in Toronto and founded the Canadian Native Arts Foundation (soon renamed the National Aboriginal Achievement Foundation). The foundation was formed to help young Native people get a start in the arts. Mary was a friend of Gordon Burnett, a former president of the Canadian Country Music Association, whose Métis wife Suzanne was on John Kim's board of directors. After a couple of firm steers, John Kim drove down to the Burnetts' house in Welland, near Niagara Falls, to meet Eilleen.

"She had some sheet music for some pop tunes, so I played piano while she sang," says Bell. "I noticed that she had a very clear and strong voice, she had good control over it, very nice tone, and an extremely large range. She could sing Broadway torch songs, really sell a song, and she is capable of singing much more technically difficult, artistically difficult, and flamboyantly interesting songs than she now does for a living."

What also struck Bell was the girl's looks. "She was a very attractive young woman, not immediately sexy, because she was kind of small. She was very pretty, a natural beauty who didn't wear a lot of makeup. She had big poofy light strawberry hair that flew all over the place."

Bell was thirty-four, a big-city sophisticate whose tastes ran to high culture, good wine, and fancy foods. Here was this country girl from the forests of the frozen north, barely twenty-one, a jeans-and-sweats kid with no formal education to speak of. Not his type at all. Except he couldn't get her out of his head. He knew she had talent but he did not know what he could do for her. His foundation was just starting up and had no money and even less clout, yet Suzanne and Mary kept on phoning him, demanding, "What can we do to help Eilleen?" Eilleen, too, refused to take maybe for an answer and kept sending Bell the songs she was recording in Kirkland Lake.

After she fell out with Mary, Eilleen needed the help. She and Laura Surch, her old friend from Hanmer who was studying business administration, were living in a high-rise on Jane and Finch on the northwest side of Toronto. It was a dangerous part of town, a predominantly black slum area complete with shootings, prostitutes, drug dealers, and a plague of cockroaches. The girls were so broke they had no furniture. Eilleen slept on a mattress on the floor. Partly because he felt sorry for her—but mainly because he fancied her—Bell went to see her rehearse.

"I drove out to a barn out in the country east of Toronto to see her in some grunge band," he says of his trip to the tobacco farm in Orono. "She was never really satisfied with the band, she was always very precise, picky about everything. But I observed that she was a good singer, the best thing there. Of course, all the time I was going out to see her I was developing a relationship. I was obviously attracted to her and she liked me too."

It helped when the girls moved to the slightly more salubrious area of High Park on the corner of Indian Road and Howard Park, one block from Bell's home at 27 Indian Grove. She worked as a cashier in a little Zellars store in the nearby shopping center. A month later, she moved in. All the time she lived with John Kim she always had part-time jobs; she took a course at a computer school, which promptly hired her; she worked in a dry cleaner—anything to help pay her way. The rest of the time she concentrated on her career. She never stopped hustling. Professionally, she started to use the name Sophyah Twain.

It was an attraction of opposites. From the outside, it seemed a modern *Pygmalion*. He was Professor Henry Higgins to her Eliza Doolittle. From this northern waif he could create a five-star performer, and an elegant addition to any salon. John Kim was a "New York downtown kinda guy." She was a hard-cussin', tough-talkin' bushwoman from a blue-collar culture where you chain-smoked and drank your paycheck away on Friday nights (except Eilleen did not smoke and hardly drank, save for sharing the odd bottle of wine). At home they listened to a lot of classical music, jazz, and mainstream pop artists like David Foster, as well as black performers like Earth, Wind & Fire and Whitney Houston.

To her family, she was always "Leeni." John Kim preferred the pet names "Boobooeski, Boo, or Booboo," though he cannot remember where they came from. John Kim sometimes describes her as a "plucky kid," making her sound like some freckled brat from *Little House on the Prairie*.

Not that there was any doubt that Eilleen was beautiful, but you could see her roots in the way she walked: real fast, as if she were in a perpetual hurry to reach her destination, striding out at a bushman's pace, her arms swinging tight into her sides. A tough guy's walk, nothing feminine about it. Her buttocks never shimmied, never undulated with that Vegas strut that attracts men's gazes like hypnotized rabbits. There was nothing sophisticated about Eilleen or her wardrobe. She didn't have a lot of money, so tended toward the grunge look—velour pullovers, track pants, or jeans and heavy work shirts with tennis shoes in winter, shorts and T-shirts in summer. "She always wore pants rather than dresses," says Bell, "because her legs were short. High heels and nylons were not her style. When she dressed up she'd put on black pants, flats, and some nice sweater."

Her hair was always bushy, almost unkempt, and she had this habit of running her hands through it and shaking her head like a dog trying to shed fleas. John Kim found that funny and endearing. Men were drawn to her, but not because she was sensuous. She never flirted, appeared to have no concept of how sexy she could be.

"She had a perfectly shaped body with a flat washboard stomach," says Bell. "Yet there was always this reserve about her. Her sister Jill was older, kind of a sex kitten, attractive and effusive with her sensuality, the opposite to Eilleen, who suppressed it. She was quite well-endowed as a young woman, and because of that she was self-conscious. She didn't want guys ogling her breasts all the time, so she always wore things to try to minimize that. She wasn't shy and self-conscious in our relationship. We had a normal life that way, but as a person she was understated, shy, and innocent. She was very bright, able, and opinionated, she had thoughts about things. Okay, she wasn't going to discuss philosophy and Mahler, but she had insight into humanity, she was naturally a bright person."

However, try as they might, Eilleen and John Kim found it difficult to adapt to each other's lifestyles. Never comfortable in the city, she yearned for the forests and lakes. His idea of a vacation was visiting Italy or a Caribbean island; hers was to go to the bush. "One time we went up north of Timmins and rented a cabin, no TV, no running water," says John Kim. "She took me out into the bush to pick blueberries and I was hoping we weren't going to bump into a bear, as we couldn't outrun it. I had very expensive running shoes on, but the terrain was so tough with the rocks that jut out and point everywhere that my shoes were ruined. So that was our vacation, walking around out in the wilderness picking wild blueberries." John Kim did get to take her to Acapulco, where she was introduced to a major concert promoter from St. Louis. (Years later, Bell was able to tell his friend, "Do you remember Eilleen? Well, she's Shania Twain.") She turned down a trip to the Big Apple in favor of driving through Vermont to Cape Cod.

In January 1987, Selina Twain sent a box of frozen moose meat to Toronto. John Kim was not a big fan of moose, which is too chewy and rubbery for his palate. Eilleen stared out of the window for an hour. Then she went out into the backyard, where it was twenty below zero, cleared away the snow, and built a fire. Despite the freezing cold, she stuck the moose meat on a pointed stick, squatted down on her haunches "just like an Indian," and stayed there for the next two hours slowly rotating the meat.

One evening, they were dining out with John Kim's brother Kevin, a lawyer who lived upstairs, and his girlfriend. The conversation got increasingly loud and lively, which upset a customer at the next table. The man started mouthing abuse and eventually stomped over to their table. John Kim stood up to remonstrate. He only got as far as saying, "Excuse . . ." when the man picked up a glass of water and threw it. It missed him but hit Eilleen full in the face. Soaked and furious, she was stunned that her boyfriend did not immediately deck her assailant. Back home the bastard would have been spitting out teeth. "Aren't you going to do anything about that?" she demanded.

Eilleen was no doormat. She had a fiery temper and when things did not live up to her exacting standards she let the world know in no uncertain terms. Her emotional guard was always up, and if she loved John Kim, she could never quite come out and say it. In his turn, John Kim talks of their affair with a wistful, regretful air, as if their relationship existed in a different dimension. She owns a little piece of his heart, but he wonders, because he does not know, what, if any, place he has in hers.

"She was a sweet, warm-hearted kid," he says. "We had moments of tenderness. She had a sincerity about her, she could be scrappy, but she had a kind, soft side. There was also a rough edge around her. If she wanted something done a certain way and she didn't get it, she could become angry. I knew that side of her very well. She could be insistent, she could fly off the handle, she wanted what she wanted."

While it was the National Aboriginal Achievement Foundation that had brought them together, their Native roots were a mutual illusion. Although he was half Mohawk, John Kim was brought up in a predominantly white middle-class value system, while Eilleen, who was at most an eighth Native, and certainly did not look it, had a legal card and personal experience of Ojibwe traditions.

While Bell learned that Jerry was not her real dad, he chose not to question the assumption that her natural father was also Native. "She wanted me to believe that, as I was a Native person running a Native organization trying to promote young Natives. She was legally Native, culturally she was Native, and Native people accepted her. I guess she was sensitive about it, as the racism from the Native community toward whites can be horrible, too.

"We talked a lot about what I was trying to do. We exchanged views about what Nativeness was, what it should be, where we were going, and what we should do. We talked about how the culture was pretty dysfunctional and hurt, and it was going to be hard to ever fix it. Her view was different—'I know them, I worked with them,' she'd say to me."

In the beginning, Eilleen kept her relationship with Bell secret from her parents. To excuse her frequent presence at Indian Grove, she claimed she'd dropped by to use the phone. When the truth leaked out, Sharon and Jerry were not at all happy. Bell, in turn, was wary of Jerry, who seldom came to the city. In time, he got on pretty well with the family, especially the boys, Mark and Darryl (who still keep in touch). Jill's daughter Mandy would come to visit and be treated to the movies and lunches at the Spaghetti Factory.

Sharon was not convinced. She telephoned every day and visited Toronto regularly to push her daughter along. "Her mother thought that her living with me meant she was not pursuing her singing career," admits Bell. "She thought that, while I was helpful in a sense of refining her, I had no regard for her becoming a pop artist. That was all Sharon ever wanted. She was the driving force."

Sharon regularly phoned Mary Bailey, giving her updates and detailing her concerns over Eilleen's relationship with Bell. "To my mind, John believed more in himself than in her," says Mary, "and that's what bothered me when she was with him. He was a classical artist and if he had taken her into his environment, then I would have been fine with it. I think his intention was honorable, but it had to be under his conditions. He was the star of the show. And that frustrated me no end."

Certainly it would have been a big boost for Bell's foundation if he could discover a Native star. However, in 1987, he was the one with the career and the connections, the one who knew Leonard Bernstein and the people who made Broadway hum. Okay, so he was playing Pygmalion, but who was getting the benefit? Eilleen Twain. For her part, some of his friends dared suggest that she was using him as a meal ticket and a chance to climb up the ladder. "That's been the subject of speculation over time," he concedes. "She was seeking out people who could make her career and I was there at the right time."

Bell gave Eilleen opportunities to escape from the country straitjacket she felt her mother and Mary were pushing her into. She wanted to be a mainstream pop singer first, but if that failed, she told John Kim, "I'll get into country, and once I make it in there, I'll move into pop." It was a mutually convenient alliance. Bell did several things to push her career along. In a CBC documentary of 1986, he was filmed in his apartment playing the piano while she sang. There were no signs that she lived in the place and it looked as if he was just helping out a struggling young Native performer. Bell was hired to put on a Native talent show for Chief Walter Twinn's—a wealthy Native who later became a senator—fiftieth birthday party in Alberta. They rented an old fort in a suburb of Edmonton—real cowboy country—and Eilleen and John Kim flew out in the chief's private jet, where she did an hour's show wearing a tight leather outfit.

He did give her her biggest break to date when he staged his first big fundraiser for the National Aboriginal Achievement Foundation at the Roy Thomson Hall in Toronto on February 8, 1987. John hired Bernadette Peters, the movie and Broadway star, to sing with the Toronto Symphony Orchestra. He also put Eilleen and Miq'maq jazz guitarist Don Ross on the bill. Don and Eilleen did a duet, and then Eilleen performed with the Toronto Symphony.

"I had a nice dress made for her," says Bell. "We had a big wig made for her, so she had this big hair that went all the way down her back. She looked like Crystal Gayle. She only got a mild response; she sang very well, but she wasn't a performer. She didn't look at or talk to the audience because she was so scared." The newspaper reviewer for the *Toronto Star* was not so kind. Eilleen was furious, complaining to John Kim, "God damn it, look what he's saying here, I'll kick his ass!"

In one essential way, Mary's concerns about John Kim Bell were spot-on. While he recognized Eilleen's ability, fundamentally he despised pop music and would have preferred her to perform torch songs. He dismissed pop as unworthy of her talents and, by association, his. "Eilleen wanted to be a pop star and I was a serious musician," he concedes. "I have always felt pop stars get disproportionately paid for the talent they have. So while I wanted her to be successful, I didn't admire her goal."

While John Kim supported her and respected her efforts, he had seen hundreds of hopefuls queuing to be on the chorus lines of Broadway. He knew the odds. In the back of his mind was the ever-present thought: "Honey, how are you going to become a downtown Whitney Houston?" He did not believe in her chosen career path. One thing Eilleen has always demanded is that people close to her believe in her as much as she does.

By the autumn of 1987, the passion had seeped from their relationship and the differences that had once seemed so endearing were now widening the gap. "I enjoyed her company, we had some great times, I cared for her, I think she cared for me, but we were heading in two different directions," he concedes. He felt uncomfortable about the age difference and hovering unspoken was the knowledge that, when she was ready, Eilleen would up and leave. And his ego insisted that he had to be the one to make the break.

Fate dealt a tragic hand first. On the evening of Sunday, November 1, 1987, the telephone rang. It was the first of the two calls that changed the course of Eilleen Twain's life.

Chapter Eight

A WORLD TURNED UPSIDE-DOWN

IT WAS JUST ANOTHER normal Sunday evening in Indian Grove. Winter had not yet come to Toronto, but the thermometer was dropping fast. Inside it was safe, cozy, and comfortable, with a big fire that both lit and warmed the spacious first-floor sitting room. It had to be large to take the Steinway grand piano. There was a roll-top desk in the other corner, and a pair of couches flanking the fire-place.

John Kim and Eilleen were having a quiet night in, watching television. The routine was always the same; long ago they'd reached a compromise. Both watched *60 Minutes* and then *Murder, She Wrote*—Eilleen was a big fan of Angela Lansbury's detective show. She was curled up on a couch, snug in her sweatpants and baggy sweater. At moments like that she could forget the fissures in their relationship, pretend they did not exist for a few hours. When you have had nothing for so long, sometimes it is hard not to luxuriate in comfort like a cat.

The telephone rang. John Kim picked it up.

"You're John Kim Bell?" said a voice he didn't recognize.

"Yes."

"This is Selina Twain, Eilleen's grandmother," she continued in the same odd, stilted tones. A pause. "I'm calling to tell you that Sharon and Jerry have perished in an automobile accident."

Perhaps it was the formal way she spoke, but the blood drained out of John Kim's cheeks, the shock punching into his heart, sucking the heat out of the room. He stammered out, "Could you say that for me once again, please? I'm not sure I heard you correctly."

Over on the couch, Eilleen snapped upright, sensing something appalling, and called out, "What is it?"

"Sharon and Jerry have just perished in a car accident," repeated the voice. All Bell could do was ask, "Could you give me some more details?" as if knowing the facts could somehow make them recede back into the dream time. Eilleen was on her feet, standing by the phone, mouthing furiously, "What is it? What's happening?"

So he told her. He stood there with the receiver dangling useless in his hand, like a gun that had already fired its fatal charge and had no more use in it, told her both her parents were dead. She picked up the receiver in a daze, her grandmother talked, but all she heard were the voices in the background. Up in Timmins, Darryl, who had just come in, was having the news broken to him by his sister. The reaction was slowly sinking in, how her present had been shattered into the past, that in the future she was alone.

When she put the phone down, John Kim tried to comfort her, but she was beyond comforting. She ran into the bedroom crying hysterically, "Oh my God, my God," screaming from the depths of her soul. Eventually, she let him hold her as the tears that she never normally shed came pouring down. All night other calls came in from Timmins. One by one. All wanting to know what to do, sure that Leeni could somehow make it right again.

During the calls she was strong, regaining her composure because somebody had to. But once they ended she crumpled again. Tears and screams. Kevin's girlfriend, whom Eilleen hardly knew, came down to help. For hours she made endless cups of tea and rubbed the sobbing girl's back—rubbed her back because she was beyond words. The night passed like that: shudders, sobs, then screams as all the absolute certainties of Eilleen's life were dashed away. Jerry, the only father she had ever known, the one on whom they all relied. Gone. Her mother, who believed in her so unconditionally as to inspire belief in others. Gone. Lost in the pit of her despair, Eilleen Twain made her decision. There was no hiding from it. Deep inside she found and grasped the steel core at the center of her being.

When morning came she took back control. From now on, she was to be the rock on which the family rested. She had just turned twenty-two.

The snows of 1987 had come early to northern Ontario. It was frustrating for Jerry Twain. The tree-planting business was going well, he had new government contracts in the bag, and plans to expand, to move the office out of Montgomery Avenue. Winter made it progressively harder to supply the claim-staking camps.

On that Sunday morning, Jerry had to transport two of his Native workers beyond Wawa, where they would meet a helicopter that would drop them into the bush. As always, Sharon sat in the front of their Chevrolet Suburban, a nine-seater SUV, to keep him company. Mark, fourteen, scrambled into the back with the two Native workers. Darryl was supposed to go, too, but he had vanished. With time running out, Jerry asked his mother to make sure the boy was fed.

The last thing Jerry heard was the horn. He was driving along a bush road when they collided head-on with a logging truck. The Chevy was demolished. Jerry and Sharon were killed instantly. The two Natives were knocked out and Mark was thrown clear out of the back window, landing unconscious in a snow drift. He would have frozen to death if one of the workers had not regained consciousness in the ambulance and asked, "Hey, where's Mark?"

"What do you mean, Mark?" replied the paramedic, before explaining the Twains were dead. The ambulance turned back to the scene of the accident, and after a frantic search in the gathering dusk they found the boy. Mark survived, but he was traumatized by the accident. The "lanky, friendly, innocent boy" who John Kim Bell knew died in the crash.

But for a recent change in the law that restricted Sunday trucking on the highways of Ontario, the truck would never have been barreling along a narrow, untarmacked back road. "It shouldn't have happened" is what Shania has said in interviews. But it did and nothing was ever the same again.

The family went into a fugue state. "I called her," said Carrie Ann, who was about to turn twenty and was working in McDonald's. "I just remember pretty much saying what happened and hanging up the phone, and the next thing, it seemed that she was sort of there."

Down in Toronto, Eilleen knew she had to get back to Timmins. She had stepped out of herself and had to regain control. "I was in shock," she said. "The whole night I just cried, I was out of control, I was numb. I managed to get to my hometown for the funeral and once I was with my family, it made it a lot easier. But we were all lost. It was a terrible time."

Getting home was not easy. John Kim Bell had just bought a new Oldsmobile. The transmission went and he had to get it towed to a garage and rent another car. On the eight-hour trip north Eilleen said little and wept more, but inside where the numbness lay she began to wrest power over her emotions, preparing to bury them deep. The family needed her. Carrie Ann was the happy one, the one who never thought anything bad could happen. Jill had been gone ten years already, she had Mandy, a marriage in the cards, and she wore her emotions like a push-up bra. Mark was in the hospital. He was going to be okay, but God knew what the shock would do, and Darryl, poor confused Darryl, just thirteen, who had gone missing just before the family took off, had been fielded by his aunt Karen. He'd been damaged enough before he joined the family. Eilleen had been the leader, the one who held it together when Sharon had been too depressed to get out of bed. She knew she could do it again, but to do it she had to face sacrificing her dead mother's most cherished ambition, the one thing she had spent her whole life building: her career.

By the time she reached Timmins, Eilleen had made the decision. It was, she recalls, surprisingly easy. "After the accident happened, I had to consider quitting altogether. I was young, focused on the fact that I was going to be a singer, I was going to keep going until I had enough success so that I never had to worry about where my grocery money was coming from. When something like that happens to you, you don't have time to stop and think about it. It was so drastic that at the time I didn't care if I never sang again."

Once back home, Eilleen took charge. She organized the funeral within a few days, told everybody, "Okay, this is what we're going to do." She called Mary Bailey for the first time in two years. "Hello, it's Eilleen," she said, "my mom and dad are dead." Mary went to Timmins for the funeral, did all she could to help, but what could she do? What could anyone do?

Jerry and Sharon were buried in Timmins cemetery, their tombstone nothing fancy, reading simply, "Together Forever," one of many similar small memorials that line the graveyard. In Timmins, it was a three-day tragedy, for the Twains were not that well known. Helene Bolduc read about it in the *Daily Press* and thought, "Isn't it awful . . . the whole family, poor kids being orphaned." Dave Hartt could not attend the funeral, for he had just started a new job in the hospital and his boss refused to give him time off.

When the mourners had left, John Kim asked Eilleen what her plans were. "I'm going to stay and run my dad's company." She moved her stuff back home and within a few weeks of the funeral Bell ended their relationship. It had been on the wane for months, but the accident accelerated its demise. He tried to be calm and sensitive, telling her things weren't what they were, that maybe it was time for a change, but there can never be a right way of dumping your girlfriend after she has just been orphaned. There were no tears, just a cold anger in the way she took the news.

"Maybe she did feel that I was forsaking her when she didn't have any parents," he admits. "When I was breaking up she had an edge about it, an anger . . . I have always felt she never really forgave me for it."

Eilleen set about sorting out her parents' estate. Jerry had left much of his equipment in the bush, ready for the next planting season. She kept Karen on to fulfill all the winter mining contracts.

Kenny Derasp quit his road band and hurried to Timmins; arriving a week after the funeral, he helped run supplies out to the camps, for Gerry and Tim could not drive and were in shock. "I thought about keeping the business going," says Karen, "but I am only one person. I needed someone to go out in the bush and I couldn't handle it all by myself." The new tree-planting contracts were voided by Jerry's death and passed on to the next company in line. When she realized there was nothing left to keep going, Eilleen sold the business and all the equipment.

There was no will, so the family had to sort out the estate, which took time. Don Fraser and Jill went to Zudel's and asked if the Twains owed any money there. The staff were already devastated by the news and Paul Zudel told them everything was all paid up and then added, "That is one couple I'd have lent $50,000 to any time."

The process took its emotional toll on Eilleen. "For a time I wasn't even there anymore," she said. "Then slowly I found myself again. The fighter that I am, I was able to come to terms with what had happened; it was a saving grace which distracted me from grieving or feeling sorry for myself or being angry. I am good at moving on and forward and really meaning it, not burying it. I indulged myself in responsibility as opposed to grief. I was miserable but there was nothing I could do about it, so I didn't allow myself to grieve for almost a year. Before that, I went through some hard times."

For eight months after the accident, she was the leaning post just as Jerry had been, coping with all the responsibility, believing, pretending she could handle everything the world threw at her. As a reaction, on the weekends she threw herself into the Timmins party spirit; for the first time ever she went to clubs as a patron and not a performer. To anaesthetize her cares she frequently drank too much (and paid the price the next morning), dancing for hours with guys she met in the bars. "For a few months I was in party mode," she said. "I loved going out dancing; I'm not what you'd call a good dancer, but I loved being in a crowd and just letting go— usually with a few drinks inside me. I did a lot of that after my parents died. It was good therapy for me."

Dancing the blues away could only ever be a temporary, instant fix for her grief. Seeking solace, Eilleen drove out into the bush and trekked through the trees, remembering her parents, breathing in the stillness, hoping it might heal her. Sometimes she sang to herself. One plaintive melody came back time and time again. "I would go for long walks in the bush by myself with this song swimming around in my head," she said. "It was different. There was no chorus, no verse, just a thought." She sang it unaccompanied, a requiem for her parents. It was called "God Bless the Child."

One morning she woke up and the certainty had gone. With nobody else to turn to, she called Mary Bailey. "She said she didn't know what she was going to do," says Mary. "I told her, 'I know damn well what you're going to do, you're going to do what God gave you, and that's sing.' "

Chapter Nine

VIVA LAS VEGAS (MUSKOKA STYLE)

"I CAN'T DO IT," replied Eilleen, a break in her voice, "I've got responsibilities. I can't just go around getting gigs here or there or writing when I feel like it."

Mary promised to help her find work. She was doing some business at Deerhurst, a resort hotel in Huntsville, 145 miles north of Toronto, and suggested Eilleen come along for the ride. When they got there, she convinced the musical director Brian Ayres to give her protégée an audition. Auditions for the revue were usually held at night. Hilda Montgomery, half of Cherokee Rose, who were performing in the Green Room, had just taken her eleven o'clock break when she heard this voice emanating from the ballroom. "I just snuck in. I remember seeing this small person with a huge, beautiful voice singing a country song. She looked just really normal, relaxed, but I could tell she knew what she was doing. We would get so many singers who would come in and not be very good. Brian snapped her up and she started working almost immediately."

Fortunately, one of the two featured singers had just quit, so Eilleen was able to negotiate a contract that gave her enough to live on and support her family. She drove the two hundred and fifty miles north to Timmins, sold the house in Montgomery Avenue, and moved everybody down to Huntsville in June 1988. The family stayed in a condo on the property—Bill Waterhouse hated to see his entertainers homeless—until she found a small, run-down bungalow to rent out on Porcupine, fifteen miles from Huntsville, and bought a battered truck. Carrie Ann went to work at the Shoppers Drug Mart in town.

Their family life returned to a semblance of normality, but they were not so happy when the well ran dry. "She would bring these big jugs of drinking water from Deerhurst," said Carrie Ann. "We would all jump in her [truck] and go down to the river to bathe. We hated it." At the river, they filled five-gallon jugs to get enough water to flush the toilets and do the washing-up; laundry was sometimes done in the river.

Eilleen found a new boyfriend. Mike Taylor was a twenty-five-year-old accountant living in Mississauga, a suburb of Toronto. As he preferred the outside to the office, he had a cottage up in Burk's Falls. In late June, he was out on Horn Lake when he was introduced to Eilleen by a friend who worked at Deerhurst. Instantly smitten, he went to see her perform in the revue and then left a note on the windshield of her Jimmy pickup truck. They went out together for the next eight months, though their relationship was always overshadowed by the needs of the family.

Eilleen tried to be both mother and father—she insisted on screening Carrie Ann's boyfriends—but she wasn't Jerry. "She was really strict with us," says Mark Twain. "She was scared."

"Eilleen was forced to be a mother," says Mike. "Carrie Ann was very easygoing, never been a problem, the most levelheaded of the entire family. It was difficult with the boys. She has a low tolerance level, but under the circumstances she did an excellent job just being prepared to shack up with them all. I remember getting up in the morning and saying, 'What are we going to do today, Eilleen?' We'd look across the hall and there would be mountains of laundry and she would say, 'You know what I'm doing.' They were your typical teenagers. She did everything for them, cleaned the house, they didn't do any of their chores and she did all of them, at twenty-two years old. She could have a lot of fun and kick back, too, but she didn't have a lot of patience for the teenage way of life."

After the first shock of their parents' death and the move to Huntsville had worn off, Mark and Darryl started to spiral out of control. Eilleen realized that she could not do everything. Working nights six days a week was hard enough, but once she factored in rehearsals for a new show and demo time for her songs, there were scarcely enough hours left to run the household, let alone to give the boys any time.

"They were devastated," she candidly admitted. "I had so much sympathy for them, I grieved more for them than I did for myself. We didn't fight; it was very emotional, a tough, tragic time for all of us. Picking up the clothes in their rooms was the least of my worries. I was more worried about other things . . . drugs, alcohol, AIDS, pregnancy. I know I didn't do a great job, but I put every effort I had into it. If my parents had been alive and the boys had got into trouble, my parents would have been there to help. Big sister doesn't have the same impact. It's not the same."

Darryl had always had problems at school, now magnified by the sudden death of his adoptive parents. Eilleen was in a dilemma, for Carrie Ann could not be expected to babysit two teenage boys six nights a week. She decided to send Darryl to the Robert Land Academy in Wellandport (half an hour from Niagara Falls) at the beginning of the school year, while Mark went to Huntsville High. "It was a surprising move," says Mike. "It was all Eilleen's idea and it did make great sense. Eilleen knew she couldn't be a proper mother for a potentially delinquent kid. The idea is you put these troubled kids into a very strict environment where they are forced to come around and march to the beat of a different drum."

In Canada, boarding schools do not have the same social cachet as in England. Founded in 1978, the Robert Land Academy is a small (less than 150 pupils) single-sex boarding school run on military lines. It is the institution of last resort for many parents. The school prospectus claims to have "a record of making bad boys good. Virtually every cadet at Robert Land Academy has been in trouble with school authorities or the law; has a drug or alcohol problem; or is uncontrollable at home." It wasn't cheap (fees are currently C$30,000 a year) and at Deerhurst people wondered how Eilleen could afford the fees on her salary. Mike insists Eilleen used money left from her parents' estate and the insurance settlement from the logging truck company in the hope it was going to turn Darryl around.

Celia Finley, who worked in the wardrobe department, believes some of the fees were paid by the government. "Eilleen mentioned to me once that she tried to send them to military school and got Indian Affairs to pay for their tuition. She was an orphan with Native status who accessed all the resources she could from all levels of government. Through her relationship with Indian and Northern Affairs, she knew that there were, within any large organization, policies and procedures and funds available. She was a girl who always had a plan.

"She certainly gave me to understand that she was Native-born, she never mentioned anything about being adopted. I don't think she was consciously trying to hide anything. It was hard to hide anything with those two little buggers getting in her way. They were never anything but trouble."

To begin with, military school worked. "Darryl showed up after two weeks with his uniform on and his buzz cut," says Mike. "He was incredibly proud of what he was doing, he was getting good marks at the school. Mark thought, 'That looks cool, I want to try it,' and decided he wanted to go, too. It was his own decision."

Mark joined Robert Land the following September. His commitment level did not last much longer than his brother's, who had only survived six months. Darryl quickly fell afoul of the school's harsh regime, refused to compromise, and ran away. Mike remembers "picking him up several times in the middle of the night when he had run away from school." (He was fortunate. In 1998, two boys running away from the academy were killed by a train.) Early in 1989, Eilleen gave up the unequal struggle and Darryl went to live with Jill in New Liskeard. Mark's school career followed suit. The boys' behavior got no better.

"I got into trouble joy-riding in cars and ended up in a group home for troubled teenagers," Darryl told *The National Enquirer.*

"The two boys were troublemakers and Eilleen had to deal with that," says Dean Malton. "They were actually sweet kids, they just turned out a little bad because they lacked attention, and they had to deal with their parents' death. They'd get away with anything they possibly could behind her back, but in her presence they seemed to have pretty good respect for her, though I remember a few instances where she would tell them get ready for bed, and they wouldn't do it."

Late in 1988, using the rest of her parents' legacy, Eilleen bought a three-bedroom house in Melissa, a small hamlet five miles out of Huntsville. It cost C$80,000 but she had to spend C$12,000 digging a new well and when she sold it four years later, the property market had declined and she just about broke even. She had looked long and hard at another house way out of town, complete with barn and horse, but there were just too many potential problems. The house in Melissa had a small apartment in the basement she could rent out for added income. Eilleen was happiest out in the bush. Mike gave her a trailer hitch for her birthday so she could tow a boat with her truck and occasionally she used the Jimmy as a deadly weapon: "She would run down a partridge, throw it in the back, and take it home and cook it up for supper."

Her life was full of odd contrasts, one night all glitz and feathers, the next tramping through the snow in the dead of winter, gathering sticks and making a fire, while Sadie, the family German shepherd, dashed about. Eilleen loved Sadie—she'd leave the back door of the house open and the dog would come and go as she pleased. She had another dog, Roman, but he was killed by a neighbor's car. It must have seemed that trucks and winter took everything she loved, but by the time Mike came up on the weekend, the dog had beens buried. She might have hurt inside but she never showed a flicker of emotion, just got on with life.

There was a lighter side to Eilleen. Christmas '88 was a hoot, with all the family and Mike having a wild time out at the Melissa house. Sometimes on Saturday nights when the show was finished, she'd leap into her truck and head for Toronto. "She loved the idea of dressing up, of going out for dinner. I took her to a couple of Christmas parties, which she loved. We went to Vegas together, where she loved going to the shows. There was a little theater we went to where they have this thing when they shine the light on people and make them sing along to a song. They hit on her and she got up there and amazed the audience.

"One time she had a party at her house. There she was, running around, singing all over the place, having a big party, dancing and carrying on. She'd had a couple of drinks—though she never was a big drinker or into drugs or smoking, I don't ever remember her drunk—and then I saw the reality hit home . . . that she had these kids and the laundry to do the next day."

Mike and Eilleen split early in 1989. "We were certainly in love for a while," he says, before admitting, "There were times when things were fine, but she was tough. No question there. In the end, we were going in different directions. She wasn't ready to settle, she had her career, and she had to deal with the death of her parents. Eilleen basically tied herself up, forced herself to get on with life, and never had a chance to grieve properly. There wasn't a lot of sitting around the house crying. The reality is that teenagers at that age aren't thinking about their parents much anyway. Certainly they were upset, but it was not something that was talked about a lot. It wasn't something that was taboo, but they knew they had to get on with life."

In the Shania Twain legend, Deerhurst and its musical revue has been portrayed as a glittering Canadian clone of a Las Vegas resort hotel. Today that may be the case, but in 1988, Deerhurst was a very different animal, caught in the throes of change but still at its heart hokey, charming, and laid-back—occasionally to the point of insensibility.

Back in 1884, Charles Waterhouse, the son of a Yorkshire lawyer, answered a newspaper advertisement that promised opportunities farming in northern Ontario. It was a classic con. Young English gentlemen, scions of wealthy families who had more than their share of landowners, soldiers, and clergymen, were sent out to the dominions to create a new squirearchy. Except in Muskoka, there were trees as far as you could train a telescope, lakes everywhere else, voracious bugs, and the land was mainly rock on which no crop could grow. It was, however, stunningly beautiful.

As far back as the 1870s, people, mainly Americans, had been coming up to the Lake of Bays by train and steamer boat to idle away their summers hunting, fishing, or swimming. Charles Waterhouse bought four acres on Peninsula Lake for C$100 and, in 1896, built the Lodge, a wooden summer house of eighteen bedrooms, a dining room, a smoking lounge, and a veranda stretching its entire length. The investment was funded from the £5,000 his fiancée Hilda brought out from England, hidden in her corsets.

The hotel was a tremendous success; extra wooden bungalows were added and it was fully booked every summer, even through the depression years (helped by the tourist phenomenon created by the birth of the Dionne quintuplets up near North Bay). Charles was a genial host, behaving with perfect courtesy as if he were the lord of some grand English manor. Every winter, the Waterhouses headed back home, returning in early summer with their English cook, nanny, and servants. Their sons Gilbert and Maurice went to private school back home.

In 1925, Maurice took over (his brother had been killed in the Great War) and the business continued to tick over for the next four decades. Yet so much of it was keeping up appearances. Most years, they had to pawn the family silver to get enough cash to stock up with supplies for the summer. By 1972, Maurice's son Bill, the first to have been educated in Canada, might have been the heir to a delightful, if rather run-down, hotel, but in the words of a local resident he "didn't have a pot to piss in." Until 1972, there were only two phones at the resort and all the cooking was done on a huge wood-burning stove, dubbed the "Queen Mary" by the staff.

Bill was pretty canny. Prior to taking over Deerhurst Resort from his father, he had helped develop the Hidden Valley Ski Club. Recognizing that, in order to survive, Deerhurst had to become a year-round resort, Bill and his parents completely refurbished and

winterized the Lodge. One of his dreams was to have proper entertainment and, in 1980, he set about redesigning the Lodge, adding a
wing with a ballroom and connecting to the Four Winds Cottage,
which was converted into a discotheque. Wintering down in Florida
with his parents, he convinced Brian Ayres, a Canadian who was
working on a hotel show, to come north and run a musical variety
entertainment show in the summer. It went over so well that he
asked Brian to stay on and keep the show going all year round. Originally the manager of a rock band and a bass player who didn't
know anything about theater, Ayres became Director of Entertainment at Deerhurst.

The Lodge was the musical hub. Ayres worked his musicians
hard, making them jump from room to room until last call. The
ballroom became the permanent home for the revue, *Viva Vegas*.
The Cypress Lounge—also known as the Green Room—had
nightly entertainers performing four sets a night ranging from the
pop R&B of Cherokee Rose to the country of Silver and Degazio.
On weekends, the Four Winds featured a nine-piece rock band
belting out the standards of the day.

The *Viva Vegas* show was a wonderful illusion. The McIntyre
Theatre at Timmins High had infinitely better facilities. The ballroom was no theater, its acoustics were limited, and the guests sat
at long metal-and-pine trestle tables, craning their heads to see the
action. The stage—once it had seven musicians and a half a dozen
dancers on it—was cramped. The women's dressing room was so
crowded that some performers preferred to change in the ladies'
bathroom; the men had a curtained-off alcove at stage left. Everything about it—the music, the costumes, the dance routines—
should have been much too tacky for the clientele.

It never was. The show transcended the penny-pinching production values with its exuberance. The musicians and singers were
top-notch, the dancers gorgeous and together. In the darkness, nobody seemed to notice the carpet or the high-school-gym layout.
The show was as intimate as the resort. People loved it.

So did the performers, although the pay was not that great. Featured singers pulled in C$600–850 a week, while dancers were lucky if they made C$500. In 1985, the cast of the first *Vegas* revue had walked out en masse after a pay dispute. Mike Taylor remembers Eilleen earning about C$45,000 a year (C$850 a week). The whole show was done on the cheap. Celia Finley, a local housewife with limited theater experience and an ability to sew, was hired to design and make the costumes.

"Brian had all these ideas from the Vegas shows he'd seen and he wanted them translated into reality, but I never had a budget," laughs Celia. "We were talking shoestring here. Because he didn't come from a theater background, he didn't at first understand the need for a wardrobe mistress, costume storage, weekly cleaning. He'd bring back all these brochures from Vegas with all these ridiculous things on. I'd been to Vegas, I knew what these girls did: They came on, they strutted, they walked off; they didn't dance in the goddamned things. I had to guess about the costumes. He never told me they would be doing the splits or turn upside-down . . . and so the first night their tits would fall out."

The 1980s were great times for the staff at Deerhurst. Unlike most hotels, there were no rules about hanging out with the guests. "Here was this group of kids—mainly college and high-school dropouts—who'd found a reason to stay up here most of the year so they could ski, snowmobile, and booze cruise all year long," says Celia. "It went from endless summer to endless night. It was pretty lively. At the Four Winds, the band would play rock and roll until one in the morning and everybody would sit around and drink as much as they could until last call, when they ordered three drinks at once and sat there for another hour. After the bar closed, they moved off to the maître d's house in Hidden Valley until dawn. It was all pretty innocent until the cocaine era in the late 1980s, when a few people ran out of control."

For young performers, the *Vegas* revue offered the opportunity to stretch their talents and to try out new ideas. "If you had a good idea, Brian would use it," recalls Hilda Montgomery. "I grew up in the Bahamas idolizing Diana Ross and Brian said, 'Okay, we will do a Diana Ross section,' and it was wonderful. He worked with people and their talent and tried to bring the best out of them." The show lasted two hours, including a thirty-minute break, running Monday to Saturday, when there were two shows (except in weeks including holiday weekends, when it ran seven nights straight). Showtime was 8 P.M., but the dressing room would be crowded from 6:30.

From the day she arrived at Deerhurst, Eilleen understood that this was her finishing school, a place she could fill in the gaps of her stage education. She knew she could sing, but, despite Longshot, performance still unnerved her. Those years of singing in smoky bars to drunks had left her nervous about moving anywhere except behind the mike stand. Here she had to dance alongside girls who had been at dance class since they could put both legs into a leotard without falling over. She had to confront her long-standing shyness about her body and bared her navel for the first time— playing the Indian in the revue's Village People tribute.

"Her singing was so natural and free she was almost cavalier about it; it was a treat to sing with her," says Gilles Lanthier, who played keyboards, rhythm guitar, and sang. "The other aspects—the blocking, how many steps do you take, which foot do you start on, and partner work—she had to work harder on. When she first came here she was almost awkward—which is a kind word."

When she sang "Over the Rainbow," wearing a green dress so tight she could barely get in and out of it, it blew the audience away. "She sang the balls off that song," says John Kim Bell. "It is such a tremendous torch song, it really showed her talent, and you'd think, what's a kid like this doing here in this tacky little resort?" She and Gilles, who in those days looked uncannily like Lionel Richie, slipped into red satin catsuits for a blistering Motown medley—including Marvin Gaye and Tammi Terrell's "Ain't Nothin' Like the Real Thing" and "It Takes Two."

Although she could not dance as well as Lynn Hill, Karen Carrette, or Sherrie Higgins, Eilleen was determined to show off her best assets. Her hair had to be the way she wanted it and her clothes figure-hugging. "She was very particular to show off her great little figure," says Celia Finley. "She needed to offset the fact that she was short and it was easy to get lost in that sea of tall dancers. She had to stand out and insisted that everything had to be skintight and showed lots of décolletage. I remember making the alterations so they would be tight, tight, tight. You could never tell her that too tight was as bad as too loose."

On Friday and Saturday nights after the revue finished, she would join the rock band crowded onto the stage of the Four Winds. One of her standout numbers was Def Leppard's "Pour Some Sugar on Me." "She was a rock-and-roller when she was here," says Gilles. "We were a hot band and she sang stuff like Heart's 'Barracuda,' which is testing your vocal prowess."

By 1988, Deerhurst had grown from a small family operation to a huge employer running an enormous property—initially without a personnel officer. "It was a human resources nightmare," says Celia, who finally found a wardrobe mistress. She was a hippy relic from the Pacific Northwest of the United States who had somehow scammed herself full Canadian social security benefits. She often refused to help the girls fix their costumes unless they bought her a drink. One of the most powerful men in the resort was Michael Walker. Nominally the maître d', he became Bill Waterhouse's de facto second in command. He handpicked the staff that worked in the resort. Naturally they were very loyal to Michael.

"He was like a living god or something," says Celia, who does not mince her words. "The first time I had lunch with the cast I poked fun at him. One of them whispered to me, 'You mustn't ever criticize Michael.' He was a headwaiter, for Christ's sakes. Once new partners had bought in and wanted the hotel to be run differently, the party era was over."

Such chaos was not for Eileen Twain. Solitary by nature, now further confined by responsibility, she was not a party animal. Drugs did not interest her and she drank only to appear social. While to many Deerhurst was their life, a comfortable place to stay or to land in at the end of a career, to her it was just a staging post. For the first time in her life there was nobody there to back her up.

She saw all this potential around her just being wasted. So she went for it . . . and upset a lot of people in the process.

"Dressing rooms," says Celia Finley, "are inherently stressful places to be. Being cooped up in a small room with seven bitchy women, all of whom had egos the size of houses but barely a brain to click together between them . . . well, that was stressful."

The cozy bitchery of the dressing room was not for Eilleen. She played golf with Gilles and the girls a few times, as she was enthusiastic about learning it (the golf course, as men know, is an excellent place to do business). Deerhurst was only ever going to be a pit stop for Eilleen, a place to regroup until the boys were old enough to legally fend for themselves. Friendly and nonjudgmental Lynn Hill and Karen Carrette became her friends, but they had little in common. Eilleen's home situation and her ambitions made it hard to sit around with the other girls watching videos and gossiping. Particularly as, if she wasn't there, she was inevitably the subject of the gossip.

Eilleen made one early mistake that colored much of her two-year stay in Deerhurst: She had a fling with drummer Pierre le Gendre. Unfortunately, Pierre was also involved with Sherrie Higgins, one of the dancers. Higgins claims she came home early after a two-week vacation to surprise her boyfriend.

"When I opened the door," she told *The National Enquirer,* "my boyfriend and Shania were naked on the couch making love. And the horrible situation was made much worse because my mom was with me. Shania jumped up and grabbed a wrap—she was just crimson with embarrassment. I couldn't believe it. Here was the man I loved, naked with Eilleen. The house was in an uproar. I was crying my eyes out and my mom was screaming at my boyfriend and punching him. I called off our relationship right then and there."

When the allegations surfaced, Shania's only official retort was, "It has nothing to do with reality as I know it." Whatever the exact truth—the love lives of the Deerhurst entertainers could be as tangled as any episode of *Melrose Place*—Eilleen and Pierre soon split up. Because she had broken some of the unwritten rules of the resort, wittingly or not, Eilleen found herself ostracized.

In March 1989, Dean Malton arrived at Deerhurst to work as a sound technician. Although Dean was the son of comedian Wayne Malton, who headlined the show with his partner Mike Hamilton, he knew nothing about the internal politics. He came with no baggage. One night at 11:30, a week before he was to start work, there was a knock at his door. Eilleen was standing there with a bag of popcorn and a couple of movies she had rented. "Hey, how are you doing?" she asked. Dean, thinking, "God, I have this gorgeous woman standing at my door," invited her in.

They never got round to watching the movies, they just talked about music until dawn. Dean loved the Pretenders's *Get Closer* album; Eilleen hated Chrissie Hynde, complaining, "How can you listen to her, she can't sing!" She admired Mariah Carey, indeed anyone with a good voice, as if she already knew they were her competition for the future. It was the beginning of a close friendship. For the next eighteen months, whenever she wrote a new song, she'd call Dean, he'd demand to hear it and record it.

"Shortly after Eilleen and I started hanging out, one of the dancers came up to me and warned me, 'Dean, don't get involved with her, don't; you're going to get hurt.' That obviously had something to do with that whole fling that had happened with Pierre, but I didn't know that at the time.

"She was a great girl, really, she's just very driven," says Dean, who was never one of the party crowd at Deerhurst. "At the time a lot of people had something against her, probably because she had tunnel vision, she knew where she wanted to go, she knew that Deerhurst was not where she wanted to be in ten years, and that was taken as arrogance and ruthlessness.

"She wasn't into dolling herself up. She'd walk through the mall with her shoes untied. All the other girls would be coming into work with their makeup on, looking beautiful before they even got there. Eilleen would pull up with a bag over her shoulder, and walk in with her hair up, no makeup, nothing, she didn't really care what anybody else thought.

"She was fun, very family-oriented, she loved her animals. A perfect evening for Eilleen was to get home from work, put on her track pants, a big bulky sweater, and stand around the bonfire in the backyard with an acoustic guitar, singing songs or talking or whatever. She was very much a country girl, but when it comes to her music, and her lifestyle in general, she's certainly not this flower for everybody to just pick . . . she's not a prima donna in any way, but she's very driven and very focused, and what comes into her mind is what she says.

"I always felt that she was unhappy, somewhat jaded, by the fact that she was forced to come home and take care of her siblings. But she was never one to complain about anything, always kept it inside. If something was bothering her, she might say one sentence and then stop, or change the subject.

"When we sat around and talked, dreaming about being successful in the business, she'd get lost in another world thinking about it, yet her reality was stagnant. The fact that she was recording her songs was probably the only thing that kept her sane. The sadness I got from her came from a lot of different things; all she really wanted to do was to be liked by everybody and yet she wasn't, probably because her looks and her talent led to a lot of people being envious of her. And so she would spout off, but only in defense. Her parents dying made her that much more driven. All she ever wanted was to make it, to show her parents: 'Look, I did good.' So I don't think she felt she had to answer to anybody.

"I know I got wrapped up with her for a little bit," continues Dean. "How could I not be attracted to her? But it was that much more fired-up because we were being creative together. We were hanging out a good three months, nothing going on between us, and all of a sudden Paul was there. I never knew about Paul until he moved to town. Paul and Eilleen lived out at the house, and my girlfriend Julie Frick and I, we used to spend quite a bit of time up there, sit around the campfires listening to rock and roll."

Eilleen had turned to a handsome construction worker from her hometown. Paul Bolduc, a tall, dark French Canadian four years her junior, first met her in the bar of the Mattagami Hotel—the same bar where she used to perform as a child—in February 1988, when she was at home sorting out her parents' estate. After splitting from John Kim she needed a friend, and he offered to help in any way he could. He was struck enough to take her home to meet his mother, Helene, but as far as Helene was concerned that was all there was to it. Until awhile later, when Paul headed down to Huntsville to find work—including a stint as a bellhop at Deerhurst.

Eilleen's relationship with Paul worked very well. Sometimes in private she would refer to him as her "toy boy," but he was stable and loyal, a down-to-earth, beer-drinking, hardworking guy, intelligent but taciturn—just like Jerry had been. "Truly, I think she loved Paul," says Dean. "They made a great couple. He didn't talk a lot. She was in charge of the relationship and Paul was somewhat of a yes-man to her. He was not into confrontation, so if she was having one of her moods, Paul was not the one to start a fight, he'd just go along with whatever she was saying. She was moody, I can't lie about that. When she was off, she was off. If she was in a sniff, look out. But what woman doesn't? She was like every other woman I've ever known—they have days when they're kind of pissy and some days when they're not."

The other appeal Paul had was his family, which allowed Eilleen to be part of a secure, loving environment. Christmas and holidays reminded her of the old days. The Bolducs were a link to Timmins, to her roots. Eilleen struck up an instant and enduring friendship with Helene Bolduc, a clerical worker at Timmins Hospital. "We just seemed to have a lot to talk about," says Helene, "and we could go on in conversation for, you know, hours and hours. We would go for long walks. We always had good parties during the holidays—I have a sister that plays piano and guitar, and we just like to have a good time, a French Canadian good time. And my husband would make jokes, and he would say to Eilleen, 'One day when you become that superstar, I'll go drive your bus.' "

In the tight-knit community of Deerhurst, it was easy to upset people. The senior member of the *Viva Vegas* cast was Sammy Kelso, whose wife Mia worked the door of the ballroom. One night after she had been told not to let anybody else in to see the show,

Paul Bolduc rushed in at the last moment, and Mia told him he could not come in. Paul just snapped, "Don't be ridiculous," and walked past her. Mia got upset, Sammy yelled at Paul, which led to Eilleen losing her temper, and a major scene. Kelso never forgave her and has not had anything nice to say about her days at Deerhurst ever since.

For once, Eilleen's timing was spot-on. She had arrived on the cusp of a major change at Deerhurst. The storm clouds were gathering and she was able to take full advantage. In 1988, Bill Waterhouse finally sold out to Apotex, a major pharmaceutical company run by Dr. Barry Sherman, which invested C$100 million in the resort, expanding it to eight hundred acres with two golf courses. In a radical departure from the rustic wooden charm, they also embarked on an ambitious condo-building program, all marble and mod cons. They built a new pavilion that would house a bigger, more lavish entertainment. Apotex installed John Kotowski as the new general manager at Deerhurst. Born in Poland, Kotowski was an accountant in his mid-fifties who had helped broker the deal with Waterhouse. He was responsible for overseeing all the new building and development.

"Kotowski loved the entertainers," says Gilles Lanthier. "The two years he was there were the only times we got Christmas bonuses and we were the only ones who got them in the resort." He especially adored pretty girl-singers who flattered and flirted with him. Kotowski was no oil painting, sitting there at his table in the ballroom, short and squat, a benevolent bullfrog with a coronet of white hair talking with a thick Peter Lorre accent. He had a wide, homely face, blue eyes that existed only to twinkle, and a perennially beguiling smile. He was an old-fashioned charmer, a compulsive flirt, whose appeal was enhanced by the Polish fracture at the edge of his English.

Kotowski had a vision he was determined to carry through. There was talent at Deerhurst. Everyone said so. There were quality musicians on-site, choreographers, and different stages on which to perform. What better place to groom stars? What better atmosphere

to wine and dine record companies? Using an American sports anal-
ogy, it could become a farm team, spotting potential stars and developing, managing, and recording talent for the major leagues.

The man Kotowski brought in to get his fledglings out of the
Huntsville snow was producer Harry Hinde. Hinde, who started his
career in Detroit as Motown's only white record plugger, had enjoyed a reasonable level of success producing country artist Ronnie
Prophet. He had also found a girl called Phyllis Boats, changed her
name to Charity Brown, and made a successful album for A&M.
There is something faintly tragic about Harry. Like the hero of the
Woody Allen movie *Broadway Danny Rose*, he can spot the talent,
but is never able to capitalize before it turns to mist and slips out
of his hands.

Silver and Degazio became the first artists on the Deerhurst Entertainment roster. Mike's singing partner Rhonda Silver—though
they couldn't stand each other—was the first to spot the potential
in Kotowski. She was not the last. Michelle Marie Beer, the other
featured singer in *Viva Vegas*, also danced attendance. Kotowski
held the purse strings. Rhonda was the first to have John's ear; then
it was Eilleen.

Eilleen recognized where the power lay and set about charming
Kotowski. With youth, beauty, and talent on her side, she soon had
his attention. To onlookers the three singers resembled the Witches
of Eastwick, except that in this coven each was out for herself. "They
were all trying to get out of Kotowski what they could," says Dean
Malton. "And the fact that Eilleen got out of him what she could, and
they didn't, had plenty to do with the animosity between them."

"There were three of them," recalls Mike Degazio. He might have
been a beer-and-spuds local lad, but he ran a construction business
during the day and he, too, realized there were other advantages to
gain from cozying up to nice Mr. Kotowski. "He asked me if I would
start contracting, because he felt other companies coming in were
gouging him. I remember being in a studio down in Toronto recording with Rhonda and he came in and said he was all excited because
he'd just sold five buildings to some Hong Kong money. I was fairly

close to him on the business side, so I did end up spending quite a bit of time with him.

"Rhonda, Eilleen, and Michelle, all three of them were always around him . . . he'd buy them dinner, sit and chat, he was always chuckling and laughing, having a good time; there were rumors, of course . . . but I think he was harmless, he felt good about sitting out in public and having a talented, beautiful girl sitting down and having a glass of wine with him."

After Eilleen won over Kotowski, the rumor factory at Deerhurst went into overdrive. "She has a full-time condo on the property with a connecting door to his." "Her picture is on his bedside table." "He paid to have her teeth fixed." ("My husband paid to have her teeth done—he gave her a Hollywood smile," Mona Kotowski claimed in *The National Enquirer.*) Charges Shania Twain denies absolutely.

"There are stories of him spending money on her and other women as well," says Marg Reid, who worked in wardrobe. "There were all sorts of rumors about her new kitchen and her new well and the brothers' school fees." The rumor that Kotowski had bought Eilleen her truck started because the license plates on the brand new vans that he bought for the property were only one number different from Eilleen's Jimmy. Such gossip always follows the same formula. Old man with money/power plus pretty/ambitious young girl times innuendo must equal SEX.

Many who worked in Deerhurst back then say the same thing: "I heard she was sleeping with him, but . . ." and the "but" is that they have no evidence, no proof at all. For sure, after the show, she would come and sit at his table, chatting and flirting with him and his guests. So did the other girls, but nobody bitches about an also-ran the same way they do about an international superstar.

Although he has heard the stories, Mike Taylor does not believe them for a minute. He met Kotowski when he picked up Eilleen from his house in Mississauga to take her to buy some clothes for the show. "She was very open, didn't hide anything from me, and unless I was incredibly blind there was nothing happening that I was aware of," he says. "Kotowski had a lot of money and she knew it.

She was friendly with him because he did a lot of stuff for her to help get her career going. Nothing more than that. The gossip didn't annoy me, because I understood it . . . everybody loves to talk."

John Kotowski is not an easy man to find. He spends much of the year absent on business in Poland. He has had his share of harassment from the tabloids and is wary of saying anything about Eilleen Twain. His recall of events is not always accurate. He says he worked with her for four and a half years (when she only spent twenty-seven months at Deerhurst and he has not seen her since he left in March 1990), and that he fixed her an appearance on *The Tommy Hunter Show* (which never happened). He says the answer is straightforward—he paid her more money because she was worth it. He points out that Eilleen was friends with his wife and daughters, so there could be nothing improper in their relationship.

"I didn't have any scandals with her and vice versa and that is the way it is. Our relationship was strictly business," he says. "I singled out Eilleen because of her talent; I did see the future in her. Sure, I paid her more, and that's where the friction primarily was, because she was making more, much more, than anybody else. That's how I took care of things, paid her enough so she could support her two brothers and have a decent life. I took care of her because I saw an asset, I wanted her to be dressed beautifully, look beautiful . . . that is show business. I don't want to give any impression that I was doing something improperly or vice versa. I invested in talent."

Kotowski will not discuss the allegation that he paid for her to have her teeth fixed (though a former Deerhurst employee recalls him signing off on the payment). "I was no sugar daddy," he insists. "She was an employee of Deerhurst like Rhonda Silver and Mike Degazio. She was not satisfied when Rhonda got recorded first. I was paying her; the dresses I bought her, these things are part of the maintenance in recognition of her potential. I don't think she used me."

Lots of talented men, not just Mike Degazio and John Kim Bell, hung on Kotowski's words, laughed at his jokes, and got work out of him. But that was okay. Guys can do that sort of thing. It was business. Eilleen Twain was doing business, too.

Chapter Ten

A TASTE OF STARDOM

AS PART OF ITS NEW EXPANSION, Apotex decided to build the Pavilion, a huge complex with indoor tennis courts, a health spa, and a swimming pool. It also contained a big palladium show room, complete with terraced marble floors, and a pool in front of the stage, which was the size of a downtown theater. They needed a spectacular show to complement the space. Kotowski was not sure Brian Ayres was capable of putting it together.

Eilleen saw her opportunity and grabbed it with both hands. She told Kotowski: "I know somebody who will come up here, kick their ass, and make things happen."

John Kim Bell had the perfect credentials to impress Kotowski. He had started working on Broadway at eighteen, had conducted *A Chorus Line* and *On Your Toes*, collaborated with Gene Kelly, Vincent Price, Carol Lawrence, Sonny Bono, and the Bee Gees, and knew Leonard Bernstein. He had conducted the New York Philharmonic, the Toronto Symphony, and the Royal Philharmonic in London. Eilleen knew that he had grand plans for staging the National Aboriginal Achievement Awards on TV (which were first broadcast in 1994 and have since become an annual event), for they had talked about his ambitions many times. Above all, he was a professional who really understood production values. Eilleen was fed up with cheeseparing.

Eilleen and Kotowski took John Kim out to dinner and gave him the pitch. For him it was a no-brainer. How often do you get a chance to create a show from scratch with no apparent financial restrictions? Okay, so it went without saying who was going to be the star, but he knew she had the voice and he could fix any problems. It was a no-lose situation for Eilleen. She knew John would take the gig and that he would create a show that would make her shine. It was also a fair payback for the times he had supported her in Toronto. Sure she enjoyed the reversal in the balance of power, but Eilleen has always honored her debts. "She was friendly and nice to me," says Bell. "Considering the way I broke up with her she could have said 'piss off,' but she thought of me. It was very clever, because I really did take care to protect her and help her."

Bell's arrival in the summer of 1989 was akin to a giant meteorite crashing into Peninsula Lake. The fallout created a lot of bad feeling. Brian Ayres left and his assistant Lynn Foster resigned in disgust (though she came back a year later). For all his idiosyncrasies, Brian had been a popular guy. Because she had suggested John Kim, Eilleen was held responsible for his departure. "Of course, there were whispers and rumors," says Celia Finley. "To me, Eilleen always acted in a completely professional way. Sure she was looking out for number one, but when you are focused you have to be ruthless. This girl had a career she was serious about, so she wasn't going to drag her feet in the mud. Why wouldn't you take advantage of an opportunity like that, when you can see that all others around you are losing their heads, and if you keep yours it might pay off?

"Did she step over bodies? Absolutely. I was sorry for Brian because he had spent ten years building up an entertainment department . . . but he was a big boy and should have seen it coming. Brian's time was up. It was inevitable.

"Shania understood that the show needed to go to another level and helped convince the management to make her the star. Millions of dollars were being invested. That was a business decision. All these little twits in the dressing room can talk all they want, but the fact is any one of them would quite gladly have changed places with her."

Rehearsals for *A Touch of Broadway* started in July 1989, ten months before opening. The new cast members were on full wages, but only required to work in the day. As the old revue continued to play in the ballroom, those working in both were in effect pulling double shifts with no overtime. One day in August, Eilleen was rehearsing "La Vie en Rose" with Gilles Lanthier in a school out in Dwight. "Our producer wanted her to do it both in French and English, so we had to translate the French lyrics into English and I am fluent in both," says Gilles. "It was a beautiful summer day, we were sitting out back on the tennis courts with our guitars and I was in stitches, we came up with so many rhymes for rose—nose, panty hose, and every other possible idea—we were just having so much fun. She looked me in the eye that day and she said, 'Someday, I'm going to be there.' I didn't have any doubt . . . the only things that surprised me were how big and how quickly."

Viva Vegas employed up to seven musicians, eight dancers, and four principal performers, three technical people and a dresser/wardrobe mistress. The new show had a cast and crew of forty including thirteen dancers. One of the new employees was wardrobe assistant Marg Reid, who soon found herself working on the *Vegas* revue. Perhaps because of their shared love of the bush—Marg's husband now runs the largest dog sledding operation in Canada—or because she was a newcomer, she became friendly with Eilleen.

"She kept herself distanced from other people," says Marg. "I assumed that it was to do with what had gone on, the feeling people had about Brian leaving, but I think there is more to it than that. She did not make close friends because she's not a person to show her emotions. She was very quiet about things, she had her life and her direction."

Dancing and moving onstage were always the biggest problems Eilleen had at Deerhurst. Bell solved the problem by bringing in Sammy Vivarito, a former dancer and choreographer, to sort out the dance routines and give Eilleen some "real skills in moving." Sammy was only able to come up for a short period and Bell needed someone full-time, because "the kids had no discipline whatsoever, they weren't doing the same steps together." In came Aileen Sugano—another friend from Broadway—as the dance captain and resident choreographer. The tiny Japanese woman and Eilleen became fast friends and she set about turning the singer into an accomplished dancer.

By the autumn of 1989, Eilleen's schedule was shattering. In addition to giving seven shows a week, rehearsing *A Touch of Broadway*, and learning how to move and dance onstage, she was also preparing to demo songs for her first album. Even before he started recording Silver and Degazio, Harry knew that his next project must be Eilleen Twain. His wife saw her twice and announced she would be a superstar. He knew it too. "She had no fear, she had total confidence. She wasn't a great singer, she wasn't Barbra Streisand, Edith Piaf, or anything like. But she didn't sound like anybody else, she had her own style. I already saw the big star . . . I was crazy about her, the way she was there on that little stage . . . she was ready."

There were disagreements on the direction to take. "Offstage she was very quiet," says Harry. "If she didn't like something, she could give you a look, make a face. If you told her you were going to do something, and you didn't do it, then . . . look out. With me she never screamed and yelled, we disagreed on things, and we would discuss it to the point that sometimes we needed to take a breather, but that didn't last, in two hours everything would be okay again.

"She played me some ideas for songs; she had great ideas, great hooks, or ideas close to being a great hook. I wanted to take her pop-country with a little bit of edge on it, but she wanted to be a rocker. She told me she did country as a kid and at that time she didn't feel like doing it. I wanted to give her the benefit of the doubt and try those things. I was going to suggest bringing in Bob Ezrin, but I didn't think Bob would be receptive to the project. I didn't hear it going rock, really hard rock. It didn't feel right."

Eventually, Harry agreed to follow Eilleen's wishes and record rock songs. If those did not work out, they would go back and do it his way. He asked Paul Sabu, a talented young guitarist—"a cross between the guy from Kiss and Clapton, plus he had a little bit of punk"—to come up and write with Eilleen. They had first met in 1975 through R. Dean Taylor (who sang the hit "There's a Ghost in My House") and engineer Don Gootch. His plan was to "go down this path and change it gradually, and hopefully I would be able to get the type of songs and the direction I wanted."

"He [Harry] thought he could get a deal with A&M with her," says Paul Sabu. "I met her in Toronto and went up with her to the middle of nowhere. It kind of progressed. She was great and A&M really liked her and wanted to do a record. She had a lot of people kind of hanging on her I'm pretty sure she didn't want around. She had some pretty good reasons to really try.

"Working with Eilleen was easy because she was ambitious and willing to learn. When we started writing, she had no idea where she wanted it to go. There was no preconceived concept except she was always very focused on what she was doing," says Sabu. "She had this great voice, a sense of getting into a lyric and a huge desire to get out of Deerhurst."

Sabu and Eilleen hit it off right away. He was all California cool, swanning around in a full-length black leather coat, but he knew his stuff. "They got along," says Hinde. "They laughed a lot, the chemistry did work. They did enjoy each other's company, they definitely found a relationship together . . . but as far as I know, it was a working relationship." Kotowski mistrusted the flashy Sabu and complained to Harry Hinde that he would stab them in the back. Harry just thought he was jealous.

Sabu, who was paid C$15,000 for his time, remembers Eilleen as being a sweet, ambitious, talented girl desperate to break out of her small-town life and succeed at music. "It wasn't a Hollywood kind of recording studio," he said. "We had a cabin in the middle of nowhere. We were taking these eight-track tapes and carrying them around in the snow. It was way above the call of duty for that kind of stuff, but it was fun. I had never done that kind of stuff before."

The songwriting partnership worked, with ideas batted back and forth. Eilleen might come up with an idea, or a theme, and Paul would shorten the hook and make it grab the listener. When

Paul came up with hooks, she'd either tell him, "I don't like that," or "Yes, that's cool." Paul definitely added things, contributed a great deal. Most of the lyrics came from Eilleen, but her major problem was always in putting everything together musically.

Sabu flew up to Canada several times in the winter of 1989. As she was still doing the show at Deerhurst, he was given the use of a wooden cabin on the property (complete with all mod cons). Harry would drive up, drop by, and record the demos on a boom box. Some of the vocals were recorded in the sauna up by the Lodge by Dean Malton. If someone was using the lavatory, she couldn't record because of the background tinkle. They recorded the masters in Toronto at Gord Heins's apartment and two recording studios, Wellesley Sound and McClear Place, and bounced some of the sixteen-track tapes up to twenty-four- and thirty-two-track. Heins and Sabu played guitar; the bassists were Claude Desjardins (who also did the programming) and Bob Babbit. Eric Robertson was on keyboards and Barry Keane on drums.

Throughout the rehearsals for *A Touch of Broadway*, the relations between Eilleen and Michelle Marie became increasingly fraught. Recalls Dean Malton, who was doing the lights, "Michelle was always a little jaded because Eilleen had the torch songs, and she had to do the Ethel Merman numbers . . . and she was equally as good a singer. I remember her coming off and saying to Eilleen, 'Top that!' They were very professional. They would come out the door, big smiles on their faces, but as soon as they got off the stage it was pretty ugly. They were so at each other."

With two months to go, Michelle Marie was succeeded by Joni Wilson, a younger but equally feisty girl. Joni and Eilleen got on a bit better, but not much. John Kim gave Eilleen ballads and Joni the more comedic numbers—a wise decision, as Eilleen had little sense of comedy, but it infuriated her. "Joni," says Bell, "danced really well. There was this rivalry between them, tension all the time. And while Eilleen was a tough kid, if there was another tough one, it would hurt her feelings and she would shy away a little bit."

"There were diva conflicts, but none of it ever showed up onstage," agrees Gilles Lanthier. "In Eilleen's defense, Joni could be very difficult. It takes two to tango; it is not one person who is responsible for the problems and the conflict."

There were the odd nights when Eilleen, like any performer, missed shows, which meant the revue had to be rearranged. This led to more dressing-room bitching. Once, when they heard she was sick, one dancer cracked, "What she got, a hangnail?" Another night, Eilleen rushed in with two minutes to go, as she had been in Toronto recording and the traffic had been bad.

Eilleen also clashed with Mike Degazio in the Cyprus Lounge. As Degazio also played a rock and roll set in Steamers restaurant a mile away on the edge of the property, he always left his amplifier preset so he could walk in, plug in, and play. One night he came in to find Eilleen singing and playing the guitar, using his amp. He complained that she had used it without asking. "Okay," she said, "sorry." Degazio's story is that a few nights later, in he came and there she was doing the same thing. So he walked up and unplugged her.

"Maybe that's why when I asked her out to dinner one time she said no," says Degazio. "I never really got to know her that well; sometimes people's personalities clash. I have a hard time dealing with women being too dominant and thinking they can just say, 'Do this, do that.' "

While a few of the girls might have had problems with Eilleen, the musicians and the support staff seldom did. "I really liked her, she never did anything to me," says Marg. "I sat right beside her and I fixed her clothes. Some people can be mean, but I never found her high and mighty, she was always very appreciative of anything I would do."

With a budget of C$2 million, no expense was spared on *A Touch of Broadway*, quickly christened by Dean "A Touch of Bankruptcy"— a joke that stuck. The room looked fabulous, windows reaching up toward the sky almost to the ceilings, seating on terraced marble tiers, but it had not been designed as a theater. The acoustics never matched the ambience. The costumes cost C$50,000—including C$5,000 on a sequined dress for Eilleen's opening number. She made a show-stopping entrance at the back of the room, singing Bette Midler's "Wind Beneath My Wings," walking slowly past the tables, down the steps, and onto the stage. There were Stephen Sondheim numbers, Lionel Richie songs, and standards like "Over the Rainbow." Bell had two comedians write a skit on *Cats*. It was called *Dogs* and Eilleen played the French poodle. She sang "La Vie en Rose" with a microphone concealed in the rose in her hand.

"This show was very important for Eilleen for two reasons," says Bell. "One, it gave her a chance to refine her ability. I saw her go from the country bumpkin, always a great singer, to a kid who could look at you and flirt with you; that was more seductive, more sultry . . . and she learned how to dance. We gave her ambitious choreography, given that she was not a dancer at all. It wasn't just step to step, she was doing stuff all over the stage. We had her doing Gloria Estefan numbers, guys picked her up and carried her across the stage, and then she danced in formation, and she really came out, she grew as a performer. She had to work out. And she did because she was serious about it."

Nobody who saw *A Touch of Broadway* could doubt it: Eilleen Twain was a star. Except that, just as it seemed she had finally made it, everything fell apart.

While her songs were being demoed, Hinde had set about getting the other parts of the business sorted. Eilleen signed a producer's agreement with him on October 18, 1989. Photo sessions were commissioned and shot, including one with her posing in a deerskin bikini. Unlike Raquel Welch in *One Million Years BC*, she looks uncomfortable and forced. She also needed management. Anne Murray's manager, Leonard Rambeaux, was invited to the resort for a weekend with his family and was suitably impressed by her performance. Leonard agreed to manage her—provided she had a record deal.

That proved to be the sticking point. A&M were heavily courted, especially after the Silver and Degazio album did well enough to be nominated for a Juno. At the Juno awards show in March 1990, Kotowski met Gary Hubbard, the record company's vice president of finance, and invited him to have dinner and see the show the next time he was visiting his cottage in Huntsville. When he did, Eilleen sat down at the table and had dessert. "Harry had told me all about Eilleen Twain. She was a talent even in those days," he says. While Gary liked what he saw, the record company's A&R men were less impressed (talent scouts hate being pointed in the right direction by bean counters). "Granted she sang Broadway numbers, but they couldn't see beyond that," says Hubbard. "They didn't like the tracks Harry did with her either. A&M don't like to be reminded that Eilleen Twain and Shania Twain are the same girl."

The demos were indeed worlds apart from the sequined sophistication of Deerhurst. The best song was "Send It with Love," about the death of her parents, in which the anguish in the vocal is all too apparent. The other songs are, in the main, raw and raucous, with Eilleen's voice fighting the guitar, not surfing over it. She had grown up on Dolly Parton, Stevie Wonder, Karen Carpenter, and Elton John, not on Janis Joplin and Grace Slick . . . and it showed. The sound was also out of date, harking back to the early 1980s. Tastes had changed. Pat Benatar's career was long on the slide, Heart had peaked. Mariah Carey and Whitney Houston were what record companies wanted to hear. Eilleen singing "Wild and Wicked" was not.

Even as the rejection slips piled up, Harry was not too worried. He hoped he could get Kotowski to pay for the demos next time and maybe the girl would listen and they could do some country-pop. Unfortunately, Deerhurst was tumbling into a financial black hole. In the context of a C$100 million development and C$2 million on *A Touch of Broadway*, Kotowski's plans to spend C$50,000 launching the career of a girl singer were no big deal. However, the massive cost overruns on the Pavilion—budgeted at C$8 million, it ended up costing three times that—coincided with some serious changes in the economy. Deerhurst was hit by a sharp left and right: cash flow and recession. By May 1990, when *A Touch of Broadway* premiered, the resort was in considerable financial difficulty.

Building the Pavilion had been a black comedy. When the walls were all up it was discovered that a huge crane had been left in the middle of the show room, so they had to be knocked down again. For some reason, perhaps because it looked good on paper, it was decided to double up the new show room by having the pool in front of the stage. John Kim Bell ordered a fly system and moving lights from Italy. That was the easy part. The stage, though twenty meters wide, was not nearly deep enough to accommodate the sets and props. So a hydraulic stage had to be installed. It rolled majestically out over the pool and snapped up into place. This took forty minutes and it weighed tons. There was no loading dock to bring in sets of any size. When Bell announced he needed to cut a hole in the wall, John Kotowski went crazy.

"How am I going to get things in and out?" demanded Bell.

"Well, take them in the front door."

"You can't take in a thirty-foot-high Statue of Liberty through a pedestrian door. It's got to be loaded in, and you've got to have hydraulics."

"I'll be goddamned if you're going to cut a hole in that wall." A week later, Bell told a crew to cut the hole he needed and never informed Kotowski about it.

The condo developments that had seemed such a good idea suddenly ran into bureaucratic problems. "It was a hot potato seller," says Mike Degazio. "Everybody wanted one. All you had to do was put ten percent down and Deerhurst would build you a condo. As soon as you were issued an MCC [Muskoka Condominium Corporation] number, you had to pay the balance." The Ontario government was so stretched in issuing the MCC numbers that a massive backlog built up. Having built dozens of condos, the resort was unable to get the balance owing to them, but still had to pay interest on outstanding loans.

In March, Kotowski pulled the plug on Eilleen. There was no more money to spend on recording sessions and making videos. Naturally, she went ballistic, stormed into his office and was there for forty minutes. This was betrayal. What about all those promises? But there was nothing he could do. Kotowski acknowledges that the last time he saw Eilleen, "we parted in a cold way." Apotex brought in

Canadian Pacific Hotels to run Deerhurst. Shortly after the new management was brought in, Kotowski moved on. He left the resort and the country because he "got involved with medicine in Poland."

Eilleen turned to one person who had never let her down. Mary Bailey had told Eilleen that if and when she wanted to make a country record, Mary would do whatever it took, pay whatever it cost, to make it happen. "Out of the blue she called me and said that she'd given a lot of thought to it, she was ready to make records and do country music. Was I interested in helping her out?" says Mary. "I really struggled with it. But I also knew that she's a great talent. So I had no choice."

Mary swung into action. Once again, she bailed Eilleen out. She bought back the publishing, management, and recording contracts from Deerhurst Entertainment for C$5,000. Harry Hinde called Craig Baxter, the financial controller of Apotex, begging him not to sell her contract. Baxter told him, "Harry, you're just whistling in the wind. Forget this girl, you know we've got to cut our losses and run." Harry had invested a great deal of his time and money in the recordings. He had paid Sabu C$15,000 and spent a further C$16,000 on recording studio bills, and was left with tapes that he couldn't get arrested with. Eilleen called him once, four weeks after it fell apart. The next thing he heard she was in Nashville. The big one had gotten away.

Canadian Pacific, which knew how to run a resort hotel, wanted to use the Pavilion showroom for conferences and business functions. After discussions to take *A Touch of Broadway* to a Toronto theater foundered, they decided to close it down at the end of the summer season. It had been brave—or rash—to believe that the resort could expect to fill a five-hundred-seater show room three hundred nights a year. The show only ran for five months.

"The show was good, the location was wrong," says Gilles. "The room was beautiful, but acoustically terrible. Too much marble and brass, the ceilings were way too high. It was very high-tech with posh, elaborate sets and a huge budget, but it was Muskoka and a tourist area. In the city it would have been a hit."

Many of the dancers and musicians, including Gilles and Lynn

Hill, went back to the ballroom in the Lodge and quickly pulled together a new revue, which is running to this day. Others, including Rhonda and Eilleen, did not have their contracts renewed. Mike Degazio stayed on singing with Christina Taylor (now his wife and a successful gospel songwriter). During that last summer, Eilleen sometimes sang with them as part of a trio in the Green Room. "It always was a fun room; it was so jammed, I don't know why the floor didn't cave in," says Mike. "We did some country stuff, three-part vocals, it was just brilliant. Essentially they wanted Chris and I to back up what Eilleen was doing, which was fine, though what we ended up doing was I got to sing the lead vocal while they did the harmonies. Those two dealt with each other the most, so there was never really any friction there, because my wife is so easygoing. Eilleen was the boss, Chris was the one holding it all together musically. I just kinda floated along, playing acoustic guitar."

To have the cup of stardom so close to their lips that they can taste it and then dashed away is a blow from which some performers never recover. Not Eilleen. She never was a quitter.

In many ways, her last few months at Deerhurst were her happiest. The boys had finished with school and there was nothing left she could do to keep them off their chosen paths. Her contract with the resort was coming to an end, and with it her responsibilities. For the first time in years she was free to concentrate on what she had to do. The experiment in rock had failed, so it was time to let Mary have her head. Finally, Eilleen had the perfect showcase. She looked exquisite and she sounded exquisite. Throughout the summer, Mary was inviting record companies to come and see her.

She left the resort in September 1990. After her last performance on a Saturday night, she asked Marg Reid if she'd come to brunch the next morning. "I turned up," says Marg, "and it was just she and I. She'd been there two years and I felt bad that I was the only one she'd invited. I still feel sad about that today."

Eilleen didn't. This time she knew she was going places. In those last weeks, a big fish from Nashville had seen her . . . and bitten.

And she had found her new name.

Chapter Eleven

STATE OF THE COUNTRY

DICK FRANK HAS BEEN AN ATTORNEY in Nashville "forever," if not quite as long as his family has been in Tennessee. One ancestor fought under Andrew "Old Hickory" Jackson, giving the British army a bloody nose at New Orleans in January 1815. He is an old-fashioned gentleman lawyer, reeking of Southern courtesy, behind which hides a sharp, no-nonsense business brain, who does not like the way lawyers shop for record deals in the modern business. His credentials are golden. He was at the first board meeting of the CMA (Country Music Association) back in 1958, when they spent the whole time arguing exactly what country music was (he says, "I know there is one unbreakable rule in the Country Music Association, it was adopted at the second board meeting—no one will try to define country music") and has represented Roy Orbison, Acuff-Rose, Don Williams, and Don Everly.

Dick never charged Mary Bailey for his first job, a minor dispute over the ownership of some master tapes. She appreciated his efforts and used to call in to see him whenever she was passing through town. In the summer of 1990, she phoned, inviting Dick up to Canada to see Rhonda Silver and Eilleen perform.

"I thought it was a really good trip for my wife and I, someone to pay our way and bring us up to Ontario," says Dick. "I've always liked Toronto, so we flew up for the weekend in August, had dinner on the first night, listened to one of the acts, very talented club singer. Lovely girl, nice voice, but lacked in my judgment that little magic ingredient. So the next day we drove up to Deerhurst."

At that point Dick had not heard any of Eileen's tapes. That Saturday night he went to see the late show of *A Touch of Broadway*. "When she stepped out onstage she owned it," he says. "I've seen that on a very few occasions—Nat Cole could do it, Lena Horne could do it, Sinatra could do it—and I have trouble thinking of any other artist that projected a personality through an entire venue. For one of her numbers she came out in a black dress with a red rose, singing in faultless French. You know what a dinner theater is at eleven o'clock at night—dishes clashing, drunks talking. You could have heard a feather fall. So after the show we got together and on due consideration I said yes, I would like very much to work with her, because she had more natural talent than I had ever personally experienced before."

Dean Malton, who wanted to be a record producer, was recruited to demo some country songs. When it came to making music away from the show, a lot of the rivalries were forgotten. Dean has an "album's worth of stuff that I did with Rhonda that Eileen sang background on" and another tape with Joni singing Eileen's songs. "Eileen was always very open with her advice; she wasn't the type to keep it all in and not share any of her ideas with anybody. I was dabbling in singing when I first met her," says Dean. "She told me, 'Whenever I'm in the car, whenever I'm listening to the radio, I never sing the melody, I always try to harmonize with it, and that's how you get good at singing harmony.' I started doing that, and to this day I still do."

The first three country songs were recorded one Sunday evening when the Pavilion was dark. The musicians (Dean on bass, Pierre le Gendre on drums, Glenn Bladon on guitars, and Pete Pereira on piano) set up the band room while Eileen was miked up in a "really great-sounding stairwell." They sat down, arranged and recorded three songs live: "Diamond in the Dark" and "Love in My Pocket" were simple, no-frills country weepies, while "Go and Be Gone" was rockier. Eilleen's voice rings with a sincerity that was lacking in many of the sessions she did with Harry and Paul Sabu. Mary obviously liked what she heard, because Dean was paid a couple of hundred dollars to record four more tracks. Retiring to his basement with a drum machine, Glenn, and keyboard player George Guerrette, he produced "Lay Down Your Arms," "I've Seen Better Days," (lyrically a real kitchen-sink melodrama with added vibrato), the jaunty "If I Were You," and "I Thought I Left the Storm." The songs may appear somewhat clichéd, but in country if the heart rings true all is forgiven. The way things turned out, none of the basement tapes would have disgraced Eilleen's first Nashville album.

Satisfied that she was heading in the right direction, Mary set about investing in her protégée. "My dad was making his money and my mom was spending it on this dream," says her son, Robert Kasner. "Everything had to be perfect before she went out with Shania."

Back in Nashville, Dick played the basement tape to Norro Wilson, whom he had known since the producer had worked in the mailroom at Acuff-Rose. Wilson has played most of the roles available on Music Row: performer, songwriter (he cowrote Charlie Rich's international hit "(Did You Happen to See) The Most Beautiful Girl in the World" with Billy Sherrill), record company executive (head of A&R for Warner Brothers), and producer. A genial warm bear of a man with a dry, self-deprecating humor, he has proved capable of straddling the changes in Nashville style and fortune. He has produced veterans like George Jones and Tammy Wynette as successfully as new country divas like Sara Evans and Mindy McCready. In 1991, he was coproducing Sammy Kershaw with Mercury Records A&R executive Buddy Cannon.

Dick wanted to sign Eilleen to Mercury, which was a subsidiary of the Dutch multinational Polygram. Mercury was on a roll with artists like the Kentucky Headhunters, but they were seriously short on superstars. Dick reasoned that, while they had great distribution and a far better international setup than most US companies, they needed Eilleen as much as she needed them.

"Dick Frank called me over to his office. I listened to this tape

she'd done in a basement in Canada and I could hear her voice tex-
ture. Then he showed me a picture—and she is *so* ugly," jokes Wilson. Eilleen flew down to Nashville and immediately hit it off with
the producer. They went into Fireside Studios and demoed three
songs. Eilleen was acutely nervous, faced with a recording session
that could prove to be her last chance, but as ever she kept her
feelings hidden. Sensing her anxiety, Wilson determined to relax
her and set about cracking jokes, the way Jerry used to.

"She has a great sense of humor, she likes jokes and laughs and
laughs—whether they are clean or dirty," he recalls. "I told her, 'I already know you're good. I can hear that. I want to try a few things
with you, see what suits you best.' I only had a budget of $1,500
and we did three songs, including 'You Lay a Whole Lotta Love on
Me,' which I'd recorded with Con Hunley when I was at Warners.
On that budget I didn't have time to nitpick, but the feel was great."

Looking for feedback, Wilson played the tape to Buddy Cannon,
who loved it and immediately took it off to his boss, Harold Shedd.
Shedd liked what he heard so much that when Eilleen met him he
flipped, thumped himself on the chest, and announced, "I want."

"I thought she was a star when I heard her," says Shedd. "She
wasn't the greatest singer I'd ever heard, but she had a uniqueness
about what she did. I've produced twelve of the biggest acts in
country music, so I kind of felt she might be one of those acts."

The deal Dick negotiated was pretty standard for the time: five
albums at a royalty rate rising to 14 percent. "It had a number of
special provisions, but it was not what I would call a monster contract." The advance for the first album was only $20,000. Harold
Shedd made two further suggestions: that he should produce her
debut album and that she should find another name. Eilleen Twain
simply did not cut it.

Eilleen and Mary had discussed a better stage name many times.
The singer was determined to stick with Twain to honor the memory of her parents and she already knew what she wanted to be
called. *A Touch of Broadway* had employed a head wardrobe mistress and four more dressers. One of the dressers who worked for

Eilleen and Joni Wilson was called Shania (neither Marg, Joni, nor John Kim Bell can remember her last name). The girl told them she was an Ojibwe who had been adopted soon after her birth and that her name meant "on my way." Marg Reid, who worked alongside her, is not so sure about that. "I believe it might not have been a Native name at all."

There is a continuing confusion about what "Shania" means and if indeed it is an Ojibwe word or phrase at all. The language is dying out, not helped by the many different dialects and regional words. Mary Bailey did some research and came up with the alternative meaning "silver," while "zhu-ni-ya"—an Ojibwe word from Northern Minnesota—best translates as "money." There is no mispronounced or misheard phrase in either Ojibwe or Cree that comes close to meaning "on my way." Yet the legend of her name continues to be repeated in the media to this day and will doubtless provide the obituary headline when Shania eventually passes on.

So Eilleen became Shania Twain. It was a good choice, easy to remember, both exotic and instantly familiar. Shania hinted at the exotic, showed the Native Canadian in her, and it trips off the tongue easily in a chant. Twain had a resonance all its own. Mark Twain was the pseudonym of writer Samuel Clemens, who, in his masterpieces *The Adventures of Tom Sawyer* and its sequel *The Adventures of Huckleberry Finn*, had chronicled nineteenth-century Southern life both exquisitely and humorously. Shania Twain is the sort of name a country singer should have.

Country and western music is as American as apple pie, woven deep into the fabric of the nation's mythology. It is also a totally artificial creation. During the 1930s, two distinct musical forms, Appalachian mountain music and western swing, were melded together by Hollywood, neatly sanitized, and packaged with a cowboy hat sitting on top, a maraschino cherry with a wide brim. That cornpone image made by the movies has meant that country music has always been a bit of a joke to the rest of the world, its musical value confined to a ghetto—if a ghetto can consist of wide-open spaces. Outside of its core market, country was never cool for more than ten minutes. How can a redneck be cool contrasted with a jive-talking, hip-waggling dude from Harlem?

What is often forgotten under a sea of bad jokes about Trigger and Dolly Parton's breasts is that country and the blues woven together created rock and roll. "It's the backbone of American music— blues and country, 'cause country and western and blues are right there together, just that close, and gospel. Everything else comes from that," says soul singer Rufus Thomas in Peter Guralnick's seminal book *Lost Highway*.

The traditional home of hillbilly and bluegrass music lay in the Great Smoky Mountains of Tennessee and North Carolina and the Blue Ridge range. Both are part of the Appalachians, a natural barrier separating the East Coast of the United States from the fertile plains of the Midwest. In 1750, the Cumberland Gap was discovered and Scots laborers, Irish weavers, runaway slaves, and indentured servants (both black and white) poured through the natural gateway to settle the cheap land available in Kentucky and Tennessee. The whites carried their fiddles, mandolins, and lutes, their Celtic jigs and reels, and songs dating back to Elizabethan England. The blacks brought their five-string banjos, adapted from the longnecked lutes of West Africa. The two cultures swapped musical ideas back and forth and the geographical and cultural isolation of the mountain hillbillies spawned a unique fiddle and banjo sound.

Although their records sold from day one, the music industry regarded both white and black country music with ill-disguised contempt. The blues, slave music from the plantations of the South, was labeled "race music," while the white string bands were "hillbilly"—an implied slur that still stands today. In his 1979 biography of Jimmie Rodgers, Nolan Porterfield memorably describes how the New York–centric business viewed country as "a sort of backward, ugly, show-biz stepchild that refused to go to school and learn from its betters, but could not be locked up in the back room." In many ways its attitude was not very different in 1990.

In 1924, Charlie Poole and the North Carolina Ramblers sold one hundred thousand copies of "Don't Let Your Deal Go Down," while Vernon Dalhart, a failed light-opera singer, sold a million copies of "The Prisoner Song/Wreck of the Old 97." Those songs are still country standards. The original string bands concentrated on fast and furious instrumentals. The Carter Family changed that. A. P. Carter was a fiddle player from Virginia who soaked up traditional Appalachian songs at his mother's knee and spent his life searching out new material. His wife Sara played banjo and autoharp, while her cousin Maybelle (who married A.P.'s brother Ezra) developed a unique guitar style. However, it was not instrumental prowess that turned them into major stars, but their blend of tight harmonies. Vocal harmonies have been an essential ingredient of country ever since. By the end of the 1920s, the Carter Family was a major act, creating a dynasty that, notwithstanding multiple divorces, has spanned three generations. Maybelle's daughter June married the original man in black, Johnny Cash, while June's daughter from her first marriage is Carlene Carter.

The first country superstar was Jimmie Rodgers—also known as the Singing Brakeman and the Blue Yodeler. Diagnosed with tuberculosis, his disease exacerbated by poverty and the itinerant life, Jimmie cut just 110 sides in less than five years before literally drowning in his own blood in 1933. In his lifetime, he sold twelve million records, an incredible figure considering his brief career spanned the years of the Great Depression. Nolan Porterfield wrote of Rodgers that he "couldn't read a note, keep time, play the 'right' chords or write lyrics that fit. All he could do was to reach the hearts of millions of people around the world and lift them up. They listened and understood."

When Rodgers was recording, there were few musical barriers. Louis Armstrong played trumpet on "Blue Yodel No. 9." Jimmie was one of the first to use a Hawaiian guitar. The Hawaiians played seated, with their guitars laid horizontally, the strings raised with no frets so they could run a steel bar rather than fingers up and down the neck. The instrument was later electrified, and in the 1950s, pedals were added to create the pedal steel guitar, which, along with the dobro, gave country its most distinctive instrumental sound, the melodic sob, the catch in the throat that mimics the human voice crying.

Western swing originated further south and further west, pioneered by the much married, never fully reformed boozer and fiddle player Bob Wills. His Texas Playboys were a big band (from twelve to twenty-two strong) featuring brass in addition to banjos, fiddles, and guitars, playing good-time dance music and Texas two-steps punctuated by Wills' high-pitched shouts of "Ah haaa" when they were really cooking, alongside songs like "San Antonio Rose" and "Faded Love." Although he recorded some bluegrass and yodeling numbers, Wills always insisted his band was closer to Dixieland and the big-band jazz of Glenn Miller and Benny Goodman than to country, sometimes fighting with the audience to prove his point.

Inspired by the commercial success of Rodgers and Wills, the movie business fell in love with the image of the Wild West. Hollywood turned Gene Autry, Tex Ritter, and Roy Rogers, who had begun their careers as Jimmie copycats, into Singing Cowboys. They dressed in glittery suits, run up by Nudie's of Hollywood, that would have lasted about a minute out on the range. The magic of the movies spread the cowboy image and the syrupy songs they sang worldwide.

Radio, the other booming mass media, saw the appeal of country early. WLS Chicago put their *National Barn Dance* on the airwaves in 1924. A year later, WSM Nashville came up with the *Grand Ole Opry*, a weekly live concert, which is still running (though the venues have gotten bigger). As the home of the Opry, Nashville soon appropriated for itself the position of the *de facto* HQ of country music. It has been setting the agenda ever since. Acting out of the purest commercial motives, Nashville became an anchor on country music, a self-appointed censor of what is acceptable and what is not, channeling once rebellious music into vinyl jars labeled "prude plus added family values" or "for Godfearing folk only." Fortunately, while the contents are often filled with sanctimonious bullshit leavened with hypocrisy (country singers are just as prone to sup to excess at the table of stardom as their pop colleagues), every so often they turn out to contain pure moonshine. The greatest stars have been those who broke the mold and fought against the respectable straitjacket of Nashville.

Country's greatest rebel, a legend in his own lifetime, was Hank Williams. He drank and pilled himself to death at twenty-nine, leaving a legacy of 170 songs, including classics like "I'm So Lonesome I Could Cry," "Jambalaya," "You Win Again," and "Your Cheatin' Heart." Born in poverty in rural Alabama with a spine defect that left him in constant pain, Williams sang songs that reflected the realities of working-class life. Hank's Joes survived in dead-end jobs, waiting to drink the weekly paycheck away, and lived their lives down at the honky-tonks and bars, full of petty infidelities and discarded dreams. His concerts were rambling, lethal affairs, pumped along by his band the Drifting Cowboys, who had no need of a drummer. To the establishment, Williams was a serious threat. They despised his thick hillbilly accent and his contempt for money, the fact that he drank too much, swallowed pills by the handful, played with guns, destroyed hotel rooms, and threw dollar bills out of the car window at passersby. Williams was in conflict with life itself, enjoying rock and roll excess while Aerosmith were still in diapers. He wowed the audiences on the Opry—being called back for six encores on his first appearance—but eventually they told him to come back once he was sober. He never did.

Williams focused country songwriting back on its core audience, telling tales they could understand. Lyrics have always been very important in country music. They allowed Kitty Wells, the first, and for a long time only, female country star, to tear off her apron and tell the guys to stop crying in their beer. The 1950s were a boom time for country—half of Decca's and Columbia's sales were rooted in country music. Singers like Hank Thompson, Eddy Arnold, and the Louvin Brothers toured constantly, building up a solid circuit that financed careers for the next four decades. Slim Whitman, a second-rate yodeler, became a bigger star outside the United States than in it.

The advent of rock and roll changed country. Rockabilly and

skiffle borrowed from it, but catered to a new group. Teenagers do not exist in country music, where you are a man with attendant responsibilities—workin', cheatin', and drinkin'—or you are a woman who falls in love, has to look after the kids, and then worries about her husband's cheatin' and drinkin'. Faced with the Red Indians of rock, country circled the wagons and retreated behind them, cutting off the exchange of musical ideas with outsiders and breeding only with its own. Occasionally, bright stars like Patsy Cline might shoot up before—if they survived—falling back carefully to the hayride and country fair circuit.

Country songs worked in the pop world, but not if they were perceived as country. The song that allowed Tom Jones to make the great leap to international stardom was not "It's Not Unusual" but "Green Green Grass of Home," a classic country weepy. His manager, Gordon Mills, understood that you could take country songs, arrange the hell out of them, sell millions, but you must never admit where they came from. Country music's greatest strength has always lain in the songs—and maybe the high lonesome wail of a pedal steel in full flow—and the connection that the songs give to their listeners. Rock stars like Gram Parsons understood that; so did the Eagles and Linda Ronstadt, but to stay country was just not cool.

The genre has produced stellar talents: songwriters like Dolly Parton plus underrated geniuses like Guy Clark, Billy Joe Shaver, and Townes Van Zandt; great voices like George Jones, Tammy Wynette, and Loretta Lynn; dark, brooding characters in Merle Haggard and Johnny Cash. There were bursts of beards and dope credibility in the late 1970s, fronted by Waylon Jennings's and Willie Nelson's Outlaw movement, but in general, Nashville's attitudes toward women and blacks were perceived as Neanderthal and its political views to the right of conservative. But there was money to be made and a machine to be fed. A singer who joined the treadmill, worked hard, and paid their dues could see a twenty-year career beckoning. Country music was profitable for the multinational record companies—and the stars who made it—because the market was defined. Recording budgets were set low and touring was expected. It did not cost a great deal to launch an artist. This did allow for careers to be built slowly.

By the mid-1980s, country music appeared to be in a parlous state, its traditions corrupted by the electronic age, turned to saccharine by an overdose of strings and sequins. In 1985, *The New York Times* declared the traditional Nashville sound virtually dead—at about the same time as Hollywood decreed the western movie a defunct art form. (Hollywood's attempt to cash in on the Urban Cowboy boom of the early 1980s was a disaster.) Both forgot that country, like the cowboy, is an integral part of American mythology. Those were the dark years before the dawn.

Seven years later, the sales of one country singer accounted for 9 percent of EMI Music's $2 billion global turnover. Garth Brooks spearheaded a national resurgence in country music. In two years, he sold over thirty-five million albums, outstripping Michael Jackson, Madonna, and Whitney Houston. His second and third albums—*No Fences* and *Ropin' the Wind*—both sold over ten million copies, phenomenal figures for any artist, but unprecedented for a country act.

Garth Brooks was a most unlikely superstar. He was pudgy, with a tendency to overindulge in junk food; he always wore a cowboy hat, primarily to hide his thinning hair. But he could communicate direct to the heartland. Sure, he had a voice that could reach deep inside, but he wasn't a grab-you-by-the-heart-and-squeeze-until-you-can't-cry-another-tear communicator like Jimmie or Hank. Garth was a marketing genius. He understood how the business worked.

By copying George Strait's cowboy image, whether by accident or deliberate design, Garth placed himself in the center of a conservative musical tradition and its attendant audience, to which he added a mixture of natural charisma coupled with rock showmanship. Initially rejected by every label in town, Brooks's eponymous debut album, released in April 1989, was no overnight success. His first single, "Much Too Young (To Feel This Damn Old)" scraped into the top ten, after Garth and his manager Bob Doyle had driven his battered pickup truck to promote it at any radio station that would let them in the front door. The next three singles were all country number ones.

Garth worked hard to keep his success (his album sales now exceed one hundred million). And once he made it, he did not cut himself off from the fans who put him there. One night in Texas, the show finished at eleven and he was still there at 6:30 in the morning, signing autographs and talking to the fans. One of his most endearing qualities, along with his impeccable Southern manners, was a seemingly compulsive desire to reveal his personal life, whether it be telling the world about his infidelities or outing his sister on prime-time television. As ever with Garth, there was another, more calculated side to it. "I made a conscious decision to tell the truth," he said, "for what the media finds out is ten times worse than what you tell them."

It was in his live shows that Brooks broke most radically with Nashville traditions. A fanatical Kiss fan in his teenage years, he imported standard ideas from rock concerts—wireless microphones and instruments, pyrotechnics, varilights—and gave high-energy performances that rivaled Bruce Springsteen at his peak. Garth possessed that unique ability—much coveted by political demagogues and preachers—to mold the mundane into something very special, to absorb the energy of the crowd and throw it back at them tenfold. New converts to country were impressed.

By the time he released *No Fences* in 1990, Brooks was one of Nashville's leading lights. What nobody expected was that the album would crash into the pop charts at number one, instantly placing Garth in the national spotlight. He was fortunate in that the *Billboard* charts had just gone over to SoundScan, a system that for the first time reflected real record sales. For a long time, country had been selling more records than were showing up in the charts; SoundScan counted more accurate sales figures from mass-merchandise stores in nonurban parts of the United States. Wal-Mart stores in the Midwest and South had always sold a lot of country records, but for the first time the media realized how many.

Nashville's boom was aided because American pop music had

temporarily lost its center. By fragmenting into subgenres like rap, heavy metal, and grunge, radio had created a generation gap that effectively alienated the baby boomers, the one audience with money to spend. They had grown up listening to melodic rock, exemplified by the singer-songwriters and California sound of the Eagles, and found it again on country stations, listening to new stars like Garth, Clint Black, Randy Travis, Wynonna Judd, and Reba McEntire. They could hear the words, it was well sung, played, and produced, and with families to feed, they were also prepared to buy into the stability it promised.

"If it's the role of alternative music to be breaking the boundaries, to challenge the status quo, Nashville represented a contrasting force," said Bernie Leadon, a founding member of the Eagles turned Nashville record producer. "My teenage son liked rap: It's angry, it's a voice crying out, 'We don't give a shit, there is no hope, so we're going to burn it all down.' Country also talks about societal breakdown, always has done, but it upholds family values, is supportive of centrist policies, about people who have the guts to get up and go to work. They'll buy a car because they expect to keep up the payments. Both rap and country are handling reality, but country does buy into the American dream, coupled with the work ethic. Life's hard but life's good."

Nashville became a boomtown, with record companies and songwriters sprinting in from Los Angeles, signing up the office space and anything that sang in a cowboy hat. In 1992, country acts accounted for some 20 percent of all record sales in the United States, $4 billion worth. In 1985, only sixteen country albums went gold (over five hundred thousand copies sold). In 1991, thirty-three went gold and another thirty-five platinum (over one million copies sold).

In the first flush of its Garth Brooks–driven success, with new country radio stations opening up in Northern cities like Boston, country music appeared to have the world at its mercy. Instead of becoming more daring, encouraging artists who wanted to break boundaries, who sought success across the ocean rather than north of the Mason-Dixon line, Nashville turned in on itself. "There is a tendency with money in the air to go straight for the format," said Bernie Leadon sadly. "The new labels came in and said 'Give me a Brooks, an Alan Jackson, a George Strait,' they were more worried about covering bases with existing proven acts than developing new ones."

To break new acts, Nashville found itself in thrall to country radio programmers, just as the corporate rock of the 1980s had been to FM radio, where the unspoken commandment was "Thou shalt play Led Zeppelin, preferably 'Stairway to Heaven,' once every hour." Radio stations have never been in the business of selling music. They sell advertising, and to do that, they want more listeners than anyone else in town. They find a niche and—as long as it's working—stick with it. They do not like change. The power of country radio over record sales meant that country artists had to first break through radio by sounding like someone else, sell tons of albums, and only then develop a distinctive sound. While a premium was placed on talent, a general lack of offensiveness to twenty-six hundred radio programmers was equally important.

This is the opposite of pop and rock, where artists break through by being different, even visionary. This may involve being offensive, as with the Sex Pistols and Eminem, but the rock business long ago realized that upsetting Mom and Dad is a surefire route to success— provided the world knows how upset Mom and Dad are. Country had taken the opposite tack, being deliberately folksy, down-home, and cozy. Its very appeal could also become very boring very quickly.

MTV had broken the rock radio stranglehold. By the mid-1980s the video channel had redefined rock and roll, brought in a whole tranche of new acts where the look counted as much as the music. The two country music video channels—CMT and TNT—had not had the visual impact of MTV. Their programming was conservative. Visually, new country was just old country sung by younger guys in bigger hats and tighter jeans. Shania Twain was to change that.

Chapter Twelve

MUSIC ROWS

HAVING HAROLD SHEDD PRODUCE her debut album should
have been a great move for Shania Twain. It was a fairly common
practice in Nashville, allowing the executive a bonus, in the form of
producer's points, if the record was a hit. Having the boss behind
the desk meant he should really get behind the album with marketing and promotion. Harold also had a proven track record. He
had produced Alabama's groundbreaking crossover hits, albums
that sold in the millions where previously a country hit notched up
only two hundred thousand sales. He had enjoyed great success
with songwriter K. T. Oslin. And he was on a run at Mercury, having signed the Kentucky Headhunters, Sammy Kershaw, and Toby
Keith. Just prior to going into the studio with Shania, he finished
the biggest hit of his career—Billy Ray Cyrus's "Achy Breaky
Heart" and its accompanying album, *Some Gave All*, which went
on to sell ten million copies. Because Shania had struck up such a
good rapport with Norro Wilson, it was agreed that he and Shedd
were to share the production duties and the points.

A year after leaving Deerhurst, Eilleen had a new name and an
American contract with a happening Nashville label (considered
very prestigious in Canada). Her debut album was about to be
recorded by two of Music Row's most successful producers. She
moved to Tennessee with Paul Bolduc, rented a small apartment in

the Landings off Elliston Place, bought an old car, and started to hone her best songs in preparation for the record. Next stop Hitsville.

Unfortunately, Nashville does not work like fairy tales, where talent and beauty will eventually be recognized wherever they hide. It is packed full of great singers, red-hot musicians, and accomplished songwriters who have never had a break and may never get one. Like any entertainment industry Mecca, it is ridden with gossip, jealousy, half-forgotten feuds, and the exploitation of the wannabes by the kingpins. It is a town where music is a commodity, a product that can and will be manufactured and molded to suit the demands of the consumer. The country music establishment had ways of doing things, rules to be obeyed and dues to be paid. Shania knew none of them.

"I had gone to Nashville before with Mary Bailey and Stan Campbell, but that didn't work. The first couple of times I didn't really have anything to do, I was just this young girl people were trying to change," says Shania. Her preconceptions of what Nashville was were based on the music she had listened to as a child—at a time when much of the music had been edgy and Outlaws were the rage.

"We're talking Dolly Parton," she says, "we're talking about Tammy Wynette—how many times was she divorced and married?—we're talking Johnny Paycheck's 'Take This Job and Shove It,' Willie Nelson smoking pot, and Waylon Jennings with all his drinking and the coke. This was not Pleasantville. We were talking about people who lived coarse and tough lives, we're not talking about saints here. I grew up listening to that music, so when I went to Nashville I had these lyric ideas, I was in your face. I didn't realize what had happened to country music since I was a kid. It had definitely turned into Pleasantville.

"I had no perception of what Nashville was all about. I'd been there a few times, but I'm a Canadian from northern Ontario, what do I know? I didn't understand the structure that existed in Nashville. I have realized that it is a very successful structure, since it works very well for a lot of people. But I questioned it for myself and it wasn't for me. I was a square peg in a round hole."

It was the musical assembly line that really got to her. Writers scheduled sessions like doctor's appointments, got together from nine to five, with a break for lunch, to write songs tailored for country radio. She did forge a partnership of sorts with Kent Robbins, who had written dozens of hits for the Judds, John Anderson, and Ronnie Milsap. Together they wrote "God Ain't Gonna Getcha for That," but it was a professional, not a magical, relationship.

"I wrote with a few people, but it didn't work out, so the songs I came to Nashville with ended up on *The Woman in Me*. I let myself be a product," admits Shania, "but I questioned everything—I was a hick from the sticks with not a hell of a lot of diplomacy. I didn't fit. I would stay up all night, eat junk food, write songs, get on the microphone. They didn't want to know about my songs. They weren't really taken seriously, because I was a nobody and I was new in town. I knew that I had better keep my ears and eyes open and learn, and I planned on basically evolving over time."

As Shedd and Wilson prepped the recording sessions—the budget was around $125,000, standard for a country debut—they shopped around Music Row for songs, corralling material from established writers like Gretchen Peters, Skip Ewing, Mike Reid, and Kent Robbins, and hit upon Tony Haselden and Stan Munsey's "What Made You Say That." Shania soon realized that they were not interested in recording any of her material. Mary rushed into action like a bear defending her cub. "I was determined to get them to record her songs," she says, "because I knew she had something. Even if it was getting a writer to help tweak them, she deserved that, she had worked hard for it." She pushed so hard that on several occasions it was Shania who reined her in, saying, "Mary, forget it, let's just get out of here." Mary was rocking the boat and in Nashville that was not what women did.

"Most people don't know how it worked in Nashville. The people who ran the record label chose the songs," says Norro Wilson, who eventually agreed to let her cut "God Ain't Gonna Getcha for That." "Her songs were not bad and most singers who come to town, their songs aren't worth a flip. We didn't show enough attention to her songs, as we were looking for what we thought was right for the label."

Harold Shedd is both more defensive and certain. "She didn't have anything song-wise that would contribute to an album. She didn't have them finished. We did what we thought were the most commercial songs that related to that first project. We cut a couple of her songs, but she was not the writer that she is now, and she would not have been that writer had she not met Mutt Lange."

The recording sessions at Music Mill Studios were not especially comfortable for Shania. "I would have preferred Norro to do more of the album because he and Eilleen had a real good chemistry, which was not entirely true of Harold," says Dick Frank, choosing his words carefully. "I smoke a pipe and have for many years, and I've found that that kind of smoke does not affect my ears."

Shedd might have had the ears, but with his success came the certainty that he knew he was right. He was a Georgia boy, born right on the Alabama state line, and beneath his executive veneer lurked some old-fashioned attitudes, particularly toward women. In the studio, he was the boss, and if the girls didn't like it their options were to retire to the kitchen . . . or the bedroom. Harold was a physical person who liked to touch, and not always in a paternal manner. This was anathema to Shania, who is not a touchy-feely person and was not prepared to reciprocate.

"She knew how to keep men at arm's length when they needed to be, but didn't offend them, she's very cool like that," says Norro Wilson, who had done his best to make sure Shania had settled in town. He phoned her regularly and took her, as his guest, to the annual BMI country awards dinner.

Two of the songs on Wilson's demo tape, including "You Lay a Whole Lotta Love on Me," were upgraded for the album. For the rest, it was primarily Shedd's call and Shania soon learned it was best to stay out of the studio except when she was needed to sing. The producers tried everything to make a radio-friendly record. The musicians were top-notch—drummer Larrie Londin had played with Elvis, the Everlys, and Chet Atkins; guitarist Reggie

Young with Waylon Jennings, Jimmy Buffett, and Johnny Cash. The material incorporated all the usual Nashville elements: up-tempo numbers contrasted with ballads, all suffused with a pop-country sheen, showcasing Shania's vocal skills.

As the recording sessions were underway, Mercury Nashville underwent serious restructuring. Out shopping for labels—a surefire way to boost market share—Polygram had bought Motown and A&M Records. As country music was booming, A&M decided to establish a presence in Nashville. Harold Shedd was to head up A&M, while Luke Lewis came in as president of Mercury Nashville. The idea came from Polygram boss Alain Levy to pair a record man (Lewis) with a creative force (Shedd). The formula had worked well in the past—but not in this case. The situation was complicated because, although Lewis was the president of the label, Harold Shedd did not have to answer to him.

When the news came through, Shania and Mary were worried. New chiefs often ignore their predecessor's projects. In fact, the appointment of Luke Lewis was one of the most important events in Shania's Nashville career. "The making of that record was troubling for her in a lot of different ways, some musical, some personal—which I'd rather not speak to because I wasn't there," says Lewis diplomatically. "She and Harold clashed, especially during the recording process. We had some pretty straight-up conversations about the political climate. She wasn't pissing me off and she sensed that right away." The upshot was that Lewis, Shania, and Mary forged the start of a close working relationship.

Like Shania, Lewis was a Nashville outsider. He loved country music passionately, but understood that the world did not end at Highway 40. Born and raised in south Florida, Luke's teenage buddy was country rock legend Gram Parsons. "I loved him," says Lewis. "Musically he took me here. I wouldn't have ended up here without him. Like a lot of artists, he had to embellish; he'd sing Scottish folk ballads and claim he wrote them, puff-yourself-up shit, when he actually had it anyway." Luke can recall the first record he bought (Guy Mitchell's 1956 hit "Singing the Blues") and was once the only white face at a James Brown concert. After serving as an army journalist in Vietnam, Luke worked for a Tennessee record distributor and then as an editor on *Record World* magazine before landing a job in sales, promotion, and marketing with CBS, helping acts like Michael Jackson, Bruce Springsteen, Cyndi Lauper, and Men at Work to rule the charts. He ended up as New England regional manager, before being poached by MCA in Los Angeles as vice president of sales and marketing in 1988. Two years later, he was promoted to be vice president and general manager of its Uni Distribution at a time when Bobby Brown, Tom Petty, and the Fine Young Cannibals were at their peak.

Although his experience was in the nuts and bolts of the industry, Lewis yearned to run his own label. When he was offered the opportunity at Mercury Nashville, he leaped at it. What he brought to the table was the knowledge of how to maximize marketing and sales on a national, not just a regional, basis. He thought big and he thought outside the box. If Michael Jackson, a black artist, could sell over forty million copies of *Thriller*, why couldn't a country act? Luke also had a different philosophy about recording—he believed the artist should be able to choose, not the head-office hats.

"Mercury changed quite a bit with Luke, and that was fortunate for everybody there, because he gave Shania freedom," says John Grady, then senior vice president of sales, marketing, and promotion. "At that point, I don't believe any of the other companies in town would have done that. He had the vision and the guts to do that, to say, 'Go make your record and bring it back and we'll listen to it and we'll take it from there.' "

Unfortunately, that attitude was too late to help *Shania Twain*, which was released in April 1993. It is easy to judge it against what was to come, but the truth is there was nothing special about it. It sounded okay, a bit bland and obvious, but the songs were flabby, missing any killer hooks, and the vocals, though technically fine, were lacking in self-belief. Lyrically the songs were equally predictable. A cheated, put-upon wife in "When He Leaves You," a lament about the decline in good ole country values ("There Goes the Neighborhood"), lots of "lyin' " and/or "cryin' " set next to "Oh my God, I'm so lucky that this wonderful guy walked into my life" themes. At least in "God Ain't Gonna Getcha for That" Shania broke the mold by buying the beer and delivering the pickup lines. The best song, by a mile, was the bouncy opener, "What Made You Say That." *Shania Twain* was not a bad record, it just wasn't very good. Worse, it was boring.

Perversely, although the songs on her debut offered little insight into what was going on inside Shania's head, the original album sleeve is a stunning photograph that really does capture her very essence. The photograph shows her standing in the snow, on a chill day where the deep blue of the sky diffuses over the snow. She is dressed in a fringed buckskin jacket with a fur collar and fur moccasins—a deliberate visual play on her Native heritage. To her left, standing motionless, is Cane, a large gray timber wolf. A fire smolders in front, but they both look straight ahead, two pairs of bright unblinking eyes staring into some future that only they know. It is a most unlikely image for a country singer and the stronger for it. It really is her, the great outdoors, the fire . . . and the wolf. Both aloof, both alone, but standing together, alert and aware. She is the wolf, and the wolf is her. Her very soul manifested in animal form. This is not an entirely fanciful notion.

"She's always been different," says Mary Bailey. "I'd sit and look at her and she always reminded me of a wolf, always very aware of everything, but always standing back. A wolf stays back among the trees and never gets right into it and she's like that, always aware, always back. There is an aloofness, a shyness about her, but she is always totally aware."

In Timmins, the shooting of the album cover was a big deal— local girl makes an album for an American record label. The session was shot out near Kamiskoka. Shania was in her element; she trekked out to scout the location wearing her grandfather's old snowshoes, and built the fire herself. The Native Canadian/woodland warrior theme was continued in her first record company biography.

What now seems strange was how the video for her first single, "What Made You Say That," completely contradicted the intrepid snow maiden image. Mercury had reservations about shooting a video at all, arguing that CMT (Country Music Television) did not affect sales, but Mary convinced them to fund it. Shania sat down with director Steven Goldman and came up with a script that involved her cavorting around a Florida beach with a bare-chested male model. The tenuous musical link was that the song contained steel drums.

"I thought I was going to have the freedom to be myself," she said, "to have control over my image and the way I portrayed myself and my music. It didn't turn out to be that way, but I was sort of like, well, if I can't have any control, then what am I doing here at all? I felt I should be myself, ignore the warnings and go with it."

The video cost $40,000, a mid-range budget at the time, which required Montreal-born Goldman to scout the locations, take her shopping, and even pin her clothes. Both he and Shania were determined to get away from the expected image. There was to be no dressing in a Daisy Duke ensemble. Shania had a very clear idea of how she wanted to represent herself, contemporary and modern, because that was the way she saw her image heading. The radical move was when she danced around showing her bare stomach. Wearing a bare-midriff outfit—though no belly button could be glimpsed—and going braless under a tight evening gown was, she contends, the bravest thing she had ever done. Although very tame compared to what was to come later, in 1993, female country singers did not behave in such a wanton manner. The video raised a few eyebrows.

"I was warned by my label there might be repercussions. They didn't come out and say, 'No, you can't.' It was more like, 'We're kind of advising against that. This could be the end of your career. It might not work.' And I didn't care, really."

"That video was Eilleen's idea," says Mary, "and Steven Goldman allowed her the opportunity of being who she was. It was great. It wasn't bold, it was just sensuous, and that's what she is. Do you know what it did? It excited people. They were saying, 'Hey, Nashville isn't the bales of hay and the straw, it's not that tarty look.' It turned her into a nineties woman."

Although the video attracted media interest, CMT initially refused to play it and the song stalled in the country charts at fifty-five. Mary was furious, berating the record company. "It was a hit song, it got up the charts. Why didn't it fly? But they [Mercury] had other irons in the fire, they couldn't commit to making that song what it should have been. I was very unhappy, because I think it deserved more."

Luke Lewis agrees: "We put the record out and we actually had a hit—that we missed. Faulty promotion, I call it. It became a top ten record in about half a dozen cities. It was a bit white bread, but so is most country, and hits have broken out of there before. It was a hit record, but we couldn't get it through the system. It was bad timing, faulty planning. I wasn't paying attention to radio; when they tightened their playlist, I put the record out right in the middle of it. I didn't know what the fuck I was doing."

Touring has long been considered the mainstay of country music, so much so that an entire twenty-year career can be spun off a couple of hits. It costs a lot of money to tour an act from scratch, money that the record company has to provide. For a newcomer, the established route was to start as the opening act and work your way up the bill. The difficulty was, to get the opening slot, you had to bring something to the party—like interest from radio. If you couldn't get on radio . . . you couldn't get on the tours. Vicious circle.

Another of Lewis's bright ideas to break out of Nashville thinking was the Triple Play Tour. It was conceived during a brainstorming session with Ron Baird of CAA (Creative Artists Agency), who had just opened the Nashville branch of the most powerful agency in Hollywood and was looking to make his mark. (He signed Shania in 1992, saying, "Mary brought Shania into my office, and she had the characteristics and attributes of a star.") The idea was to give live exposure to young acts, thus forcing radio to pay attention.

With three new acts they wanted to push—Toby Keith, John Brannen, and Shania—Mercury agreed to underwrite the costs. Baird booked a sixteen-date tour in markets (Louisville, Dallas) where they had significant country radio stations. The gigs were in small clubs with a $10 ceiling on the ticket price. Each act did a twenty-minute set and had to use Toby Keith's backing band. The theory had worked in the rock market, but Triple Play died. "It was one of the hardest projects we'd done because nobody had heard of any of these acts, and nobody cared," says Baird. "So we had to kind of push and jam and cram. We didn't even take a commission on it, there was so little money."

The situation was further complicated when Keith's "Should've Been a Cowboy" was a bona fide radio hit, eventually reaching number one. The tour did nothing for Brannen, while Shania held her own. "It gave me a vision of her potential," says Baird. "She was fine given the circumstances, working with a band that wasn't hers. She did very respectably and everyone liked her. She made a good impression on the audience and on the radio people." Which, as radio was not all over her songs like a rash, means it achieved almost nothing. "I think the video has more to do with her success than the tour did," adds Baird. "The video aspect of that first album was probably more significant than anything else. It established her sexiness, and beauty, and it clearly established her belly button! It was unheard-of in country music. Sexiness was discouraged because women fans would be intimidated."

The video for "What Made You Say That" proved to Shania that being young, sassy, and sexy worked, that she did not have to conform to Nashville's ideas of the correct feminine image. In sharp contrast to their Nashville bosses, CMT Europe loved the clip and showed it so much that for a couple of weeks it was their number one high-rotation play. It was different enough that it attracted attention from two major players who were not country fans. The first was actor-director, sometime Hollywood bad boy, and the first Mr. Madonna, Sean Penn.

Sean Penn had just branched out into directing movies and wanted to expand his skills in videos. He had completed one for David Crosby and his agent suggested he look at two other CAA clients, Susie Bogguss and Shania Twain. Choosing Shania was easy. His agent contacted Mary, suggesting that he direct Shania's second video. Shania was literally "jumping up and down" when she heard the news. One Sunday night she called Retta Harvey at home and said, "Sean Penn's in town, and you've got to come and meet us at the office." The three all looked at his showreel, discussed his ideas, and then they went out for a drink.

"We closed the bar," says Retta, now senior director of video production. "Shania was drinking, but not to excess, but he was quite drunk. Sean was very quiet and reserved until he had a couple of cocktails and then he was like your best friend. By the end of the evening he was telling everyone in the bar jokes and doing imitations and was just a very entertaining man."

At one point in the evening, when Shania had gone to the bathroom, Sean, who at the time was separated from actress Robin Wright (whom he later married), leaned over and asked, "So, is she serious with this guy?"

"Well, she's been living with him for years, I think it's pretty serious," said Retta. "Anyway, I don't know if that's an appropriate situation for us to be talking about here. I think that's between you and Shania." Any half-hearted flirting Sean did that evening was ignored by Shania, who showed no interest. Or perhaps she did not notice, because later, when Retta told her the story, she gasped, "What, he said what?" and burst out laughing.

All the time Shania lived in Nashville, industry bigwigs hit on her with three-chord regularity. Many artists in her position would have leaped at the chance of a dalliance, however brief, with a member of the Hollywood elite. Penn certainly had connections. The stakes were the highest she had ever played for, yet she turned them all down. What, one wonders, would the Deerhurst gossips have made of that?

"Dance with the One That Brought You" was shot in May. Penn brought in burly character actor Charles Durning, a veteran of countless movies, including *Tootsie* and *The Sting*, to play the character of Good-time Charlie. Set in an old-fashioned barn dance, the video reeked of nostalgia. Penn was impressed enough by Shania to suggest she try acting. Despite being much more traditional, the song made it no higher in the charts. The final single, "You Lay a Whole Lotta Love on Me," featured a straightforward big-hair video, but by that stage the album was dead.

First time out, *Shania Twain* sold around one hundred thousand copies. It did especially well in Seattle, Denver, Salt Lake City, and Minneapolis, strong but not traditional country markets (perhaps they related to the snow better than the arid plains of Texas). Worryingly, it did nothing in Canada. Well enough for a debut—halve those sales and she would have been shopping for another deal— but disappointing.

In Nashville reality, Mary Bailey's contacts, so impressive in northern Ontario, could not guarantee Shania overnight success. Her tough, no-compromise attitude had hit a brick wall of indifference. Nashville was a good ole boys' town; they ran it and it was their way or the highway. "How far can you fight?" recalls Mary with a weary sigh. "Realistically, artists are a dime a dozen. A record executive has got five hundred artists walking through his door. They misunderstand that there are artists who truly have something to say, who have a business sense as well, who say, 'Look, if you allow me this opportunity, I think that I can . . .' They think you have developed an attitude. I didn't have the reputation of being the sweetest little girl on the block. But I had to; I'd rather them hate me and love her."

Mary realized that for Shania to command the promotional backup to take her to the next level, she had to command some extra clout . . . and that she didn't have it. At times she thought, "Am I the only one that believes? Can she be who I know she can be?" As it became apparent that the album was not going to catch, the doors slammed shut and Mary spent more and more of her family's money to keep the show going.

Not sharing her problems was a mistake that was eventually to cost her dearly. However, it was Mary who took the first telephone call from the man who was to change Shania Twain's life way beyond the extent of her dreams.

Chapter Thirteen

THE SVENGALI FROM SOUTH AFRICA

ALTHOUGH THEY GREW UP DECADES, hemispheres, and continents apart, there are many uncanny similarities between Mutt Lange and Shania Twain's musical backgrounds. Both grew up in places that were far beyond the known periphery of the music business, both were marked out from their peers by an obsessive determination to learn their craft, and the type of music they heard as children was straight-ahead commercial pop.

Robert John Lange was born in Mufilira, Northern Rhodesia (now Zambia), on November 11, 1948, the second of three boys. Mufilira is a mining town on the Congo border, right in the center of the Copperbelt, the richest seam of copper ore in the world. His South African–born father, Ivan Guy Lange, was a mining engineer—not a suit and tie office manager, more a pickax and shovel guy, a foreman in charge of teams of native workers—a reclusive man happiest on his own. In contrast, his mother Elizabeth (née von Wartenburg) was a very cultured, sophisticated woman who came from a landed family in Germany. Their marriage ended in divorce before Mutt turned fifteen.

The three Lange boys, Peter, John, and Bill, enjoyed a comfortable colonial upbringing, but far from the verandaed luxury of Happy Valley. There was domestic help, but not hot and cold running servants, as the Langes were at the lower end of the expat social scale.

While the white population was able to support a string of social and sports clubs, it could not support a segregated high school in every town. From the age of eleven, the Lange boys were sent away to boarding school, paid for by the government. John followed Peter to Guinea Fowl, in Gwelo, Southern Rhodesia (now Gweru in Zimbabwe). The school was in a converted RAAF training barracks from the Second World War. Pupils' movements were controlled by a blast of the air raid siren.

Another student at Guinea Fowl was Johan du Plooy, now a doctor living in Canada, who played in the cricket team with John Lange. "He was one of the opening bowlers," he says, "and I was the wicket keeper. He was a good all-round sportsman. He played rugby as well, but I don't recall him being into music at all. He was a quiet guy, always humble, friendly enough, he was never a big deal, never a bully. I got to know him better after I moved to Belfast High School."

During the early sixties, the political situation in Southeast Africa became increasingly unstable. The federation of Rhodesia and Nyasaland was always opposed by nationalists arguing that it existed only to serve the economic interests of the white population in Southern Rhodesia. Violent unrest led to its dissolution in 1963, with the two northern territories becoming independent as Zambia and Malawi. Zambia's leader, Kenneth Kaunda, had his own agenda for the copper profits, and the whites in Southern Rhodesia became increasingly militant in their refusal to accept black majority rule. By the time Ian Smith made his unilateral declaration of independence in 1965, the mining industry was in turmoil. By then the splintered Lange family had returned to South Africa. In 1963, Ivan Lange had a new job as a mine manager in Klerksdorp, sixty-five miles southwest of Johannesburg, and as a divorced man needed to send his sons away to complete their education.

Belfast High was in South Africa, situated on the High Veldt of the Northern Transvaal, halfway between Pretoria and the Mozambique border. Du Plooy's parents had sent him there to learn Afrikaans and he never understood why John Lange ended up there.

It was a state-funded, coeducational boarding school that took in teenagers from all over Africa. The boys loathed it. According to du Plooy, "It was extremely rigid, unbending, cold, isolated, it wasn't a pretty place, it felt to me like a prison." At Guinea Fowl, the educational system was English in origin and relatively liberal. At Belfast, it was Dutch Calvinist, intent on rigidly following the repressive Christian Nationalist Education policies of the apartheid government. Discipline was all, and fun—unless it involved maiming other boys on the rugby field—was unhealthy. "Although we had girls at the school, we weren't even allowed to hold their hands," says du Plooy. "During school break the girls would go to one side, the boys to the other. We weren't allowed to mix except at specially organized social evenings where they kept us all indoors and watched us like hawks. Radios were not allowed in the school.

"John hated Belfast High. If any of us could have got out of there we would. At one stage I wanted to run away and he did, too. We discussed it but, of course, we never did."

Due in part to the regard South African education authorities had for Rhodesian educational standards, John Lange was placed in a grade where he was one of the oldest in his year. He was average academically and a reasonable sportsman, but he didn't enjoy the team sports because they were compulsory. Even then he knew he wanted to be a musician. A pop musician. There he was at fifteen, blond hair cut so short it could only hint at curls, fair-skinned freckled face, practicing his guitar and telling his friends, "I'm going to be involved in music," to which they all went, "Oh yeah, right."

He struck up a close friendship with James Borthwick, a year ahead academically but one day younger. James was already a five-year veteran, as he'd been packed off to Belfast soon after his mother died in 1958. "Mutt and I quickly discovered a mutual interest in music," he recalls. "In 1963, there was a school band, but only instrumental, that played at debating evenings and behind the screen before the movie in the school hall on Friday nights. We played piano, trumpet, T-box bass, and drums . . . which were military drums placed upside down on the floor, and a cymbal hung from a science lab retort stand. By the time Mutt had arrived, I had graduated from T-box bass to drums.

"The advent of the Merseybeat sound inevitably led us to the vocal, three guitar, and drums format and so I left the dance band and formed up with Mutt on rhythm guitar, Roland Deale on lead guitar, and Sydney Baker on bass. At first we were a bit shy to try singing and so played Shadows tunes and other guitar instrumental stuff. A favorite was 'The Rise and Fall of Flingel Bunt,' in which Mutt played a mean lead guitar!"

Over the next two years, the band went through frequent name and personnel changes. "In those days of schoolboy bands, finding a name came before even learning the songs," says Borthwick. It was John Lange who decreed that everybody should have nicknames. It was his friend Vernon "Bird" Loker who first coined the nickname "puppy" for him, because "he was always ragged looking, like a dog." "Puppy" Lange accepted his name for a while before he decided it wasn't rock and roll enough and, in typical self-deprecating style, altered it to "Mutt," which stuck. He was in good company. His younger brother Bill ended up as "Slug"—apparently because he was pudgy, slow, and laid-back— Raymond Arenstein became "Compost," and Borthwick, the third in a line of James Hamilton Borthwicks, was "Junior."

The first band was called the Renegades and then it was the Phantoms, and within a year after the first of many lineup changes, the Comanches. Johan du Plooy joined first on piano and then on rhythm guitar. "John was never going to be the lead singer," he recalls, "he didn't have a good voice at all. Even back then he was more interested in making music itself than performing; he didn't want to be the star."

"The Comanches went through quite a few permutations," says Borthwick. "Even in such a restricted environment, it was extraordinary how many allegiances were regularly being broken and reformed." In 1965, the band rechristened itself as the Visions, with Robert John "Mutt" Lange on lead guitar, Vernon "Bird" Loker on rhythm, Raymond "Compost" Arenstein on bass, and James Borthwick on drums.

"It was as the Visions that Mutt and my friendship intensified," says Borthwick, who disagrees with Johan's memory of Mutt's vocal prowess. "Central to our musical tastes and ambitions was vocal harmony, and Mutt and I had voices that blended perfectly. The rough, gravelly voice he later became known for was only cultivated in the seventies. Mutt had an excellent voice and ear for harmony, and notwithstanding his tireless capacity for working hard on the songs we sang, and the fact that none of us could read music, he was without question a natural musician. Even in those early days, we would spend hours and hours practicing in his room, perfecting our blending of voices. We chose songs that put this to good effect, rarely singing songs that required a lead singer. Like every other schoolboy band of the time, we were convinced that we were going to hit the big time . . . as soon as we could afford the gear."

They played pop hits by the Swinging Blue Jeans, the Searchers, the Everly Brothers, the Who, Herman's Hermits, the Beach Boys, the Hollies, Wayne Fontana and the Mindbenders, the Yardbirds, the Byrds, the Zombies, Brian Poole and the Tremeloes, and Manfred Mann (an expat South African). Despite their radio ban, the school did allow the band to practice and even to play at school functions. Dancing, however, was not permitted.

"There was another Belfast institution that had some bearing on Mutt's perfectionism," says James, ". . . the school cadet band, which was very prestigious as it had, against all odds, won many competitions. It wasn't easy to get in. I auditioned as a bugle player in 1961 and became a drummer in 1964. Mutt joined in 1965 and played the tenor drum, which involved a lot of twirling and flash. What was significant about this band was the bandmaster. Although he knew very little about music, he was a slave driver: We practiced for hours and hours, through freezing winter, before school, during breaks, and after school hours. We were also expected to attend a band camp during our vacation. All of us learned, albeit forcibly, how to work as a team and what it meant to strive for perfection."

During the school holidays, Mutt often traveled from Klerksdorp to Johannesburg to stay with his aunt, who lived in a grand old house in the very upmarket suburb of Houghton. She was a wealthy widow and something of an eccentric. Her husband had been an executive of the giant Anglo-American Corporation. She drove around town in an old Rover packed full of her dogs, of various shapes and sizes, who had scratched the wood and paintwork to smithereens. In her lounge was an old Steinway grand piano, which Mutt would tinker on. Mutt was always experimenting with music. One morning when staying in Klerksdorp, James Borthwick woke to hear his friend playing "Little Red Rooster" on his dad's cello.

In Johannesburg, James and Mutt spent their evenings at the movies or devouring whatever local bands were on offer, traveling by bus and foot to dances, concerts, and "battle of the bands" competitions. None of the bands they saw—Dickie Loader and the Blue Jeans, the Staccatos, the Four Dukes, Bill Kimber and the Couriers, the Bats, Royal Showband, Gene Rockwell and the Falcons, the Bow Street Runners, Thyne Eak, Birds of a Feather, Group 66—meant anything outside of a South African music scene contracting in increasing isolation. That didn't worry the boys, who avidly studied their musical techniques, admired and coveted their instruments and equipment, and dreamed their dreams for the future.

Their dreams had a slight hiccup in 1965, when James and Johan du Plooy matriculated, while Mutt had to endure another year of school. At that time there was a draft system in South Africa and 90 percent of white males ended up having to serve nine months in the military. The trick was to get a job before being called up, because the law required an employer to pay in full for that nine months so you would be discharged with a tidy sum in your bank account.

Which is exactly what Mutt did. After graduating from Belfast at the end of 1966, he landed a job as bank clerk and was called up in April 1967. While his contemporaries in America and Europe were sampling the delights of the Summer of Love, Mutt was serving as a medic in the South African army. When he was discharged early the following year, Mutt set about fulfilling his ambition. He spent his accumulated pay on "a magnificent Fender bass amplifier and Fender Precision bass guitar" and moved into a boarding house in Kensington, Johannesburg, with his brothers, Peter and Bill. The room he had could hardly contain the new equipment.

Meanwhile, James Borthwick had landed a job at the South African Broadcasting Corporation as a sound engineer on a radio station. When Mutt came to visit him in the studio, his eyes lit up; he realized that was what he wanted to do. Somehow the former bank clerk managed to convince Dave Gooden, who owned Sono-vision studios, that he was the right man for the job of apprentice sound engineer. Perhaps Gooden recognized a kindred spirit, as he had gone out on a limb and built the studio himself. When Mutt joined the studio, the staff consisted of Dave, his sister, who was the secretary/typist, and a delivery man with a bicycle. It was later to expand to a huge double-story business with all the latest state-of-the-art sound equipment.

While Mutt was being apprenticed, James had quit SABC to study for an economics and accounting degree. He formed a band with guitarist Steve McNamara, who was doing an arts degree. Mutt was impressed with his guitar-playing and on a few occasions they played gigs in Johannesburg with Mutt on bass. In 1969, during the university vacation, Mutt and James recorded a demo in Sonovision studios.

"Mutt would literally press the 'record' button and run around into the studio, pick up his guitar, and sing. All the tracks were his own compositions, except one song which we wrote together. It took us days overlaying my acoustic guitar, his bass, and both our voices, overtracking harmonies. Mutt already had a sense of perfection. By now he had made some contacts in the local recording industry and persuaded someone in Gallo's to listen to our efforts. They were knocked out by what they heard and immediately offered us a recording contract under the unfortunate name of Sound Reason.

"Everything was done in such a rush and we were so enamored by the whole affair, we didn't stop to think. Steve McNamara was drafted into the group as a third member, although he didn't do

much on that album. The arrangements were done by someone
who, although an excellent musician in his own right, had no affinity for the songs, and the result was a disaster. I think it was a lesson
to Mutt to never again rush into things. But he never gave up and
continued being positive in spite of virtually no sales."

Mutt's ambitions remained undimmed. He dreamed of making
it overseas. Almost four decades later it is hard to explain just how
radical, nay inconceivable, an ambition this was. The local record
business was no more than a cottage industry, which grew more insular as the outside world slowly showed its disapproval of the
apartheid regime.

The only pop music Mutt heard in his youth was international,
hits with strong hooks and melodies that stuck in the head. There
wasn't much else out there. In the mining towns of Northern
Rhodesia there were no radio stations, so music came from what
records the expat community brought with them—and their tastes
were often suspect. Long before he heard Elvis for the first time,
little Mutt listened to Slim Whitman, and has loved him ever since.
In the mid-fifties, the Florida-born country singer, with extra added
yodel, was hugely successful with hits including "Rose Marie," "Indian Love Call," and "Serenade." Somehow, Slim touched a chord
right across Africa. Nigerian superstar King Sunny Ade has described Whitman as one of his earliest influences and his band line-
ups invariably include a pedal steel guitar.

While the guitar is ubiquitous across the continent, it is unlikely
Mutt was exposed to much black African music as child. Musicians
as accomplished as the Zimbabwean Thomas Mapfumo learned
their trade playing covers of the Beatles, Sinatra, and Presley. The
record bars were colorful places where the local artists' records
were pressed by the dozen, with covers made from wallpaper off-
cuts, but not places where a young white boy would hang out.

In South Africa, the music scene was even more segregated. "The
black music scene was traditional, not so vibrant as the unique
sounds you hear coming out today," says Geoff Williams. "It hadn't
evolved back then. There was interest in soul music, some great jazz,

and a lot of traditional township music. We weren't really exposed to each other's music. White audiences had vastly different tastes." There was no television and the state-run radio stations played the international hits (alongside middle-of-the-road covers by bland white pop "stars" like Gê Korsten, as tasteless as they were talentless). Anything more left-field could only be found in specialist import shops in big cities. Jimi Hendrix's *Electric Ladyland* was a proscribed text, featuring a black guitarist and an album cover displaying topless women of all races. It hit every puritan button available.

"The scene was so restrictive," says Ralph Simon, "with three million whites who didn't get involved in black music. As a white kid, you didn't hear much black music unless you looked for it. The Beatles were allowed on the radio until John Lennon made the pronouncement that they were bigger than Jesus; then all their stuff was banned. When you took a record to radio you had to take the lyrics, and if they didn't pass muster with the censors at the SABC then you couldn't get the record played."

South Africa's hippie revolution, such as it was, came late, but bands like the psychedelic pioneers Freedom's Children, Abstract Truth, and Rhodesia's Otis Waygood Blues Band did manage to emulate their English and American idols. Acid trips, pot smoking, communes in the country, and long, drug-fueled, and (sometimes) inspired jam sessions—often with black musicians like the legendary and exquisite sax player Kippie Moeketsi—were part of the scene. In its context, it was wild, and by 1970, the government was stomping on longhaired deviants with boots, scissors, and military call-up papers.

After Sound Reason folded, Mutt immersed himself at Sonovision, working on radio soap operas and jingles for ad agencies. Jingles only lasted fifteen seconds and nobody cared much how they sounded—except Mutt, who was obsessed with getting the right drum sounds. He set about forming a new band called Hocus. James Borthwick had just switched to studying for an arts degree when Mutt presented him with an ultimatum. "He told me he had musicians lined up for a new project he was working on and it was now or never. I told him, 'I still have a lot of thinking to do' and that was it—our paths split. I went back to university, though Steve quit his course to follow Mutt. I still saw him on occasion, but since I was no longer part of his ambition, our friendship cooled."

Geoff Williams got a call to be the drummer. He was reluctant to go to an audition, but when he did he was knocked out. "He was already Mutt when I met him," says Williams, "so there we were— Mutt and Geoff. I thought, 'Hell, these guys are really talented.' I was asked to join and within a matter of months we were full-time. We weren't commercial, but to secure a gig and get some money, we did a crash course learning hits. Mutt was always the driving force. When I first joined we had a lead singer, Colin, but Mutt was a far better vocalist than he was. From when we turned professional Mutt was more or less the lead singer. We cut back to a trio with Steve McNamara on guitar and had to keep it very tight."

After Johan du Plooy went to do his military service, he had lost touch with Mutt. In 1969, while working as a medical rep, he attended a trade fair in Johannesburg. There, playing in a small tent off the main area, was a three-piece band called Hocus. The bass player, who had sandy hair down to his shoulders, looked very familiar. It was Mutt. "He always knew exactly what he wanted and he worked for it," says Johan. "It didn't happen by accident."

In 1970, Mutt quit Sonovision and the band rented a house on a fifty-acre plot near Mulders Drift, fifteen miles from Johannesburg. Their gear was permanently set up in the lounge and each had his own bedroom. Getting it together in the country was not an excuse for Hocus to smoke bales of pot and drink themselves silly. They might have had long hair, but that was as far as the rebellion went. "Hocus was an extremely clean band," says Williams. "Mutt and I used to have a few beers, but he didn't ever smoke and after he became a vegetarian he didn't even have a beer."

The band survived on a tight budget; their live work was supplemented by jingles for soap powder or soup cans. Mutt would write it, the band would rehearse it, and then they'd drive into town to record it. Mutt was obsessed with getting their sound right and they rehearsed for hour after hour. "He wasn't a raging dictator. Everyone did their own self-development on their instruments, Mutt more so than anyone. He was incredible; after a full day's rehearsal you could hear him doing scales in his room and he'd have the music out, getting into some new scale, trying out a new finger grip, writing something."

"Some people get born with talent, but he wasn't a born musician. He worked helluva hard at crafting his profession, he listened and he learned and he practiced. His voice was so versatile. He had a kind of Van Morrison/John Fogerty voice: strong, forceful, and quite distinctive. Mutt liked those big voice people, but he also had a breathy voice, full of little breathy bits and nasal intonations. If you listen to Bryan Adams, Def Leppard, and Shania, they all have very similar intonations in their voice and I'm sure that Mutt imparted it."

Mutt was always trying to get the sound and balance right. Miking up was primitive, if it happened at all, though they always tried to put a mike in the bass drum. Otherwise everything was balanced by ear. Mutt could never stand too much volume, so Hocus toned down. They were fanatical about hearing what was going on. While their songs were tightly constructed and disciplined, with no freak-out guitar solos—Mutt hated showing off and would never hurtle around the stage—they still flowed. At the spine of every song were the bass and drums. Once organ player Alan Goldswain and singer Stevie van Kerken joined from the Music Corporation, Hocus could specialize in another of Mutt's great loves, vocal harmonies.

The Johannesburg music scene only consisted of a few small clubs, so Hocus lived vicariously through imported music magazines and albums. When *Melody Maker* arrived from England, they devoured every word. Reading the gigs pages was the equivalent of a refugee from behind the Iron Curtain staring in the window of a department store. "Elton John had just started up and we'd see he was at the Roundhouse, Atomic Rooster was here, the Strawbs were there, the Moody Blues were doing a tour. We were astonished because there were huge name bands just on a little strip ad in the corner." While many of his contemporaries would have been

using the gatefold sleeve of the first Crosby, Stills, and Nash album
for cleaning grass and rolling joints, Mutt digested every word on it.
He knew which studio it was recorded at, where the mix was done,
where it was mastered, who the backing singers were, what session
musicians were hot. They talked about such minutiae all day—
except when they were rehearsing.

Musically, their major influence was American West Coast
country rock as pioneered by the Byrds, Poco, the Flying Burrito
Brothers, and the Eagles. British acts like Elton John, Emerson Lake
and Palmer, Free, Rod Argent, and King Crimson were also important. "Mutt and I always had a penchant for the country music of
groups like Buffalo Springfield and Poco, which we regarded as our
ideal band," says James Borthwick. "But we knew that their music
had a limited following in the broader scheme of things, and we
only had two voices." Although they never recorded an album,
Hocus had a Top 10 hit in Rhodesia with "Roll Me Over," while
"River Roll" picked up radio play in South Africa the next year.

Mutt called record companies in the States, who were impressed
enough with the five songs that were completed to want to talk of a
deal once their album was finished. It never was. By 1971, the band
had grown to a six-piece, all pulling in different directions. Mutt had
started to get some freelance production work. He and Stevie
(whom he had known since they were four) had become an item
and she was one of the country's most in-demand backing singers.
He started to see a bigger picture than a run-down farmhouse on
the outskirts of Johannesburg. Hocus split in November 1971. Their
last gig was in Pretoria. Mutt and Stevie married the next day, and
Geoff was their best man.

More important was Mutt's burgeoning business relationship
with Clive Calder (born December 13, 1946), who had, coinciden-
tally, just formed two record and entertainment companies. With
his partner Ralph Simon (born December 7, 1946), he set up
Sagittarius Promotions, which was involved in artist management
and promoting shows at the Electric Circus in Johannesburg, while
Clive Calder Productions was involved with production and song

publishing. Clive was a live wire, a skinny blond guy, a fine crick-
eter who played the piano, and while he loved music, he was always more interested in the business side. He was *Billboard*'s South
African correspondent, then hooked a job as an A&R manager at
EMI Records. After an eye-opening trip overseas, he decided he
knew how to make records and how to break them, too. Like all
great managers, Clive could talk the talk. He told Otis Waygood,
"I'm going to turn you into the biggest thing South Africa has ever
seen," produced their first album in two days, and then hyped the
hell out of their first tour, reaching small towns whose longest-
haired inhabitants had previously always been goats. Clive also produced two albums *(Astra* and *Galactic Vibes)* with the acid-astral
rockers Freedom's Children, sometimes described, by nostalgic
South African rock critics, as "the best band the world never
heard." (Stevie van Kerken had sung on their first album.)

In Mutt Lange, Calder recognized he had stumbled upon a large
uncut diamond. At a time when all around him were crumbling,
Mutt held firm to his belief systems. He started to produce local
artists—some of whom were also managed by Clive—and had instant success with Jessica Jones, whose "Sunday, Monday, Tuesday"
was a South African number one in 1972, while "Waikiki Man" was
a chart topper in New Zealand and Rhodesia. He also worked with
Richard Jon Smith, the first black singer to make an impact with all
sections of the community. Mutt's other specialty was rerecording
international hits for local compilation albums.

"Mutt was very well known as this budding engineer who could
always come up with a snappy jingle," says Ralph Simon. "He always had that bent and flair for coming up with very good hooks
and melodies. He studied the charts and those records that had
commercial success. In a small market like South Africa, you had to
be very derivative. We put out an album called *The Greatest Hits of
Johnny Nash* and Mutt would play and sing on every track; *The
Greatest Hits of the Troggs,* and he'd sound like Reg Presley. He
knew how to be a human jukebox."

Even then, working with primitive equipment, Mutt knew what

he wanted and how to get it. The fundamentals of his technique and approach were the same back then. "I was always amazed at his absolute focus and passion . . . he was like a single clear thought, but always relaxed," recalls Paul Wright, who worked as an engineer at Sonovision with Mutt. "This came out strong in those early days of multitrack recording. While most people were putting lots of layers down and then 'fixing it in the mix,' Mutt would know *exactly* what picture he was creating right from the start. I also recall his comments making me aware of just how important the bass guitar is in the scheme of things. If you can sort of imagine all those harmonies building up out of the bass line . . . great things happen."

In South Africa, Calder and Simon's interests stretched beyond pop and psychedelic rock bands. By February 1972, they had concluded recording, management, and publishing deals with most of the top black acts south of the equator. The idea, spearheaded by white Afro-rock group Hawk, and black soul acts the Miracle and the Triangle, was to look to the international market. Calder was ahead of his time, for the real interest in "world music" did not take off for another decade. While local audiences enjoyed this multiracial approach, the authorities did not. As government crackdowns effectively destroyed the local rock scene and sanctions made it very difficult to sell records abroad, Calder and Simon made the decision to leave South Africa for London. From being sharks in a small pond they found themselves just another piece of bait, bluffing furiously to make their way. However, Clive Calder was a born predator, supremely capable of triumphing in the global music business.

By 2000, Clive Calder's Zomba Group was the largest independent music firm in the world. Still privately owned, its annual sales topped $1.2 billion. Jive Records, home to Britney Spears, the Backstreet Boys, R Kelly, *NSYNC, Billy Ocean, Steps, A Tribe Called Quest, and Groove Armada, had a phenomenal 7.16 percent share of the market. Zomba was an interconnected web of fifty companies spanning eight divisions: records, music publishing, production, music libraries, record/software distribution and export, film/TV music, recording studios, and instrument hire companies.

In June 2002, Calder sold Zomba to BMG Records, the music division of German media conglomerate Bertelsmann AG, for a cool $3 billion. BMG had acquired a 25 percent stake in Zomba's music publishing division in 1991, and in 1996, 20 percent of its record division. Showing just how shrewd a businessman he is, Calder forced the German corporation to exercise its option to buy Zomba just six months before it expired. At the time its market share had declined to 3.4 percent.

Yet without Mutt Lange, that multibillion-dollar payday might never have happened. Everything that made Zomba great, they were doing in South Africa thirty years ago, albeit in microcosm.

"Mutt was very instrumental in the rise and rise of Zomba," acknowledges Ralph Simon. "He played a major role in the growth of it. Clive and I had both come from a music and music publishing, live entertainment background. We always felt we had the ability to develop a business that had the various legs of publishing, a record company, a music studio, and a live business."

In early 1974, Mutt left for London with Stevie. They were signed to a singles deal by Phil Carson at Atlantic Records and while he cut a couple of sides, nothing seemed to happen. To make ends meet, the couple sang backing vocals for Arthur Brown. Clive and Ralph arrived the next year, having landed Richard Jon Smith a deal with Polydor. After they had Mutt produce Smith, they started pushing him hard. "It was largely an attempt to get Mutt some work when the Atlantic deal didn't come together," says Simon, "which led to the whole notion of managing producers—which we were the first to do."

In the days of punk and Rock Against Racism benefits, being a white South African required a lot of explaining in the English music scene. Nobody knew that in the early years, Zomba was kept afloat by laundering money for the ANC. Funds were invested in the company in England, and Zomba in turn arranged for envelopes stuffed with cash to be tossed over the fence of a convent in a Johannesburg suburb.

"Mutt was the only thing Clive had, he managed him as an

artist as well," says Nigel Grainge, the head of A&R at Phonogram who, in 1975, gave Mutt the first City Boy album to produce. Over the next two years, he also did albums for Graham Parker and the Rumour and displaced country rockers Clover (whose lead singer was Huey Lewis), while at the fledgling Virgin Records, Simon Draper had Mutt produce the Motors, whose "Airport" was a big hit single. Simon Draper recalls, "These two rubes turned up. They were throwing their weight around and they wanted to be record producers. Unfortunately they were very uncool, slightly off the pace." Mutt's big breakthrough came from Grainge, who had signed the Boomtown Rats to his new Ensign label in late 1976.

Grainge liked Mutt because he, too, was a record nut, a compulsive collector, a real fan. When he was in South Africa, he had devoured every scrap of information available on album sleeves and that desire to know everything has never left him. "Most record producers are closeted in a studio and not aware of what is going on outside; very few of them take the time to discover what they are competing with," says Grainge. "They are usually a year behind everybody else. Mutt always wanted to know what was happening. He'd make lists and say, 'Come on, Nige, what shall I get?' One of the reasons we got on so well was that he reacted so well to all the obscure stuff I was into. He loved bands like Spirit and Quicksilver Messenger Service, all those classic American acts of the late sixties, and would always look for that kind of vibe. Even in 1975, there would still be a huge slew of obscure stuff that would come through Warners and Columbia that would be exciting. Steely Dan were just being launched."

That is one of the secrets of Lange's success. He listens to music all the time, to all music, to pop, rock, country, heavy metal, AOR, reggae, soul, folk, teeny bop, rap, and punk, judging it on musical merits overlaid by a sound commercial ear. Because he is not bound by genre he is able to cross over, taking bits with him to sprinkle into the mix like fairy dust. Mutt's early successes came with bands where he harnessed the collective energy and created a distinctive sound—but always with a commercial edge and melodic heart.

With his help, the Rats, a ragged bunch of Dublin protopunks, became regular chart toppers. Their first meeting was not a success, as
Bob Geldof recalls in his autobiography *Is That It?*:

"Chris [Hill] and Nigel introduced us to Mutt Lange, a brilliant
record producer who was then relatively unknown, but who has
gone on to become one of the most successful in the world. We
played for him at Chessington. 'What do you think?' the Ensign
man asked him hopefully. 'I think they're terrible,' he replied, in his
clipped South African accent. 'What on earth do you expect me to
do with this lot? I really would rather not get involved.'

"They took him to see us perform and he changed his mind.
One week into recording at Dieter Dirk's studio in Stommeln, just
outside Cologne, we began to wish that Mutt had stuck to his first
instinct. Robert John Lange was a martinet. He was a perfectionist
who drove others as hard as he drove himself. We had made our
demo tapes in a little studio owned by Eamonn Andrews in
Dublin. The whole thing had taken a couple of hours. We just ran
through the songs a few times and picked the best version. With
Mutt, the recording lasted eight weeks. We did seventy-eight takes
alone for 'Lookin' After Number One.'

"We had in our brief two-hour experience in the studio played
together as if it were a live performance. Now we were required to
create a layered production with each instrument playing on its own
away from the others. The sound had to be broken into its compo-
nent parts in order to give the producer greater control in the final
stages of mixing the instruments together. It caused us enormous
initial difficulties. For the first time we actually heard ourselves in-
dividually, and we were embarrassed because some of us were playing completely different chords to the others. We had been playing
these mistakes live for months. We lived in an apartment connected
to the studio and often worked from 10 A.M. through to 2 A.M.
Mutt was obsessive about detail and would spend hours going over
and over the same thing until in the end we lost the feel of it. We
felt inadequate, the more so because Mutt himself was a brilliant
musician and was impatient with our fumbling.

" 'Hit it harder, hit it harder, Johnny,' he would call through at Fingers pounding the keyboard. 'Harder, Pete, it's not coming through.' In the end Pete's fingers were raw with playing. Mutt was a bass player himself and, unintentionally, he kept belittling Pete's ability. 'That's no good. You're not playing it properly. It goes like this.' Then he would play it and completely outclass Pete."

The Boomtown Rats were also a big break for Calder and Simon, as Grainge recalls: "I knew nothing about publishing when the Rats deal had been done and when we were talking to Mutt, Clive then asked Fachtna O'Kelly, the Rats' manager, what they were going to do with their publishing. They didn't really know, so Clive offered to set up their own publishing company through Zomba, which he did for a handling percentage. Smart. We never made a penny out of the Rats because of the structure of our deal and he built his empire on them without the outlay of a penny."

Steve Brown, now a successful record producer, worked as a tape operator and engineer for Phonogram in the late seventies. He worked with Mutt on recordings with City Boy, the Rats, and Graham Parker. Frequently Steve was close to tears from sheer exhaustion. "If I hadn't have worked with him," says Brown, "I'd have doubted myself when I got into sessions where things aren't going well and you, the producer, have to pull them together. He was a big disciplinarian, which I liked. If you are going to call a recording session, you are there before it starts, to get your bits and pieces together. It's a business, not a coke-snorting, booze-drinking madness."

As Lange never took drugs or drank, there were some tense moments during the Graham Parker sessions when some of the musicians were way gone on amphetamines. During the recording sessions for the second Rats album, *A Tonic for the Troops*, Brown recalls Mutt insisted on a minimum six hours' sleep a night, but "He'd still be awake two hours before anyone else. Then he would put on his track suit, eat some breakfast or energy food, and go out running for at least five miles, come back, eat some more food, shower, and go to the control room half an hour before anybody else. He was a vegetarian. In terms of discipline he was way out of his time. We never talked religion, but I would imagine there is some force that drives him on. He had a very disciplined lifestyle."

He drove musicians hard. Says Brown: "City Boy were post punk, good players, they wrote pretty good songs, and he stretched them as far as they could go. We'd do sixteen hours a day, six days a week. It wasn't clinical—we were going for performance, but performance goes with feel. Mutt is into feel. It's not just getting the notes right, it's getting the feel too. Mutt is totally soulful. As an engineer, I was waiting for the performance so we could move on to the next thing. Steve Broughton was doing a guitar part. He did it for about three hours and I saw him performing his heart out, doing what I thought he would never achieve. He looked up at Mutt and Mutt wasn't looking at him, so he looked over at me and I went 'Yes,' gave him the thumbs up. Mutt gave me such a look and said, 'No.' It took another four hours to get the thing right."

Yet however hard he pushed the artist, Lange pushed himself harder. Many nights he sent the band home, and while the engineer hit the buttons he went out into the studio and replaced the instruments and the backing vocals himself. He stood behind the mike, cupped his hand behind his ear, like some ageing folksinger, to get the tuning just right, and when he sang he literally threw his body at the microphone, giving a virtuoso performance nobody ever saw. "He is not a great musician," says Brown, "but he is very competent and he has a great deal of feel. What he loses on the technical side he gains on the feel and soulfulness. His feel for backing vocals was totally amazing, which manifested itself on all the Def Leppard records."

If genius always requires 90 percent perspiration, Mutt insists on delivering 98 percent. For all his success, he is aware of his limitations. As he once explained to Helene Bolduc, it does not come naturally to him, and it never has. While David Foster can go and work on a project for a month and he's done, to achieve the same result Mutt knows it will take four months and that he will have to work harder. But because he's a perfectionist he will stick to it until he gets there. All it takes is time and focus.

Before the advent of computerized mixing desks in the late seventies, the producer's job was still considered by many to be to
transfer a live performance onto vinyl. Lange looked beyond that
and technology caught up with his vision. He and Geldof argued a
great deal as Mutt started dissecting songs, taking the melody and
saying, "We must change those two notes because it is derogatory
to the scan of the song." If he lost the argument with Geldof, which
did happen, Mutt employed his final weapon: He sulked.

"If a producer is sulking you are not going to get much work
done, so you might as well try and get where he's coming from,"
says Brown. "Bob used to say, 'The guy sulks and I can't stand it.'
And Bob was a champion sulker of his own."

Lange was not available to produce the Boomtown Rats' biggest
hit, "I Don't Like Mondays," although he did the rest of the recording for their third album, *The Fine Art of Surfacing.* Then he switched
musical genres to Aussie hard rockers AC/DC. For their second outing together, Lange had to help them overcome the seemingly in-
surmountable loss of original lead singer Bon Scott. *Back in Black*
went to number one in the United States and Australia, eventually
selling nineteen million copies. "He really can hear it," says Ralph
Simon. "He evolved the way Brian Johnson sang after Bon Scott
died. They made four albums together and he brought a tacit commercial edge to them, added backing vocals, which really lifted the
broader acceptability of the new heavy metal." Mutt was a hard
taskmaster, but an adept at creating diamonds from chaos. Few men
could have salvaged Def Leppard not once but twice.

Lange's production on *High 'n' Dry* in 1981 set the band up in
America, but during the recording of their follow-up, *Pyromania,*
guitarist Pete Willis was grappling with a drinking problem. He
kept appearing at the studio either drunk or not at all. "On the
road, there is a semi excuse for getting kinda crazy, because it is not
a natural way to live," said singer Joe Elliot. "Then Pete started acting like that in a fixed place—in the recording studio. He pitched
up to play a guitar solo drunk; if he'd had the guitar on backwards
it would have sounded as good. Mutt just bawled him out, told

him not to come back to the studio until he got his act together. Basically he never came back."

The huge momentum that *Pyromania* created appeared lost on New Year's Eve 1984, when drummer Rick Allen lost his left arm in a car crash. In December 1986, during the *Hysteria* recording sessions, Mutt too crashed his car. He was on his way to the studio on the outskirts of Hilversum, Holland. It was first thing in the morning, it had been raining; he skidded on the brick cobbled road and smashed his knee on the dashboard.

"Knowing Mutt," says Rick Allen, "he was probably thinking about music and forgot he was driving. He hurt his knee very badly and was in hospital for three weeks. All the time he was there he kept demanding keyboards, and drum machines were sent in so he could keep working."

Once, during those same sessions, Mutt left the control room to relieve himself. Elliot, scarcely the most accomplished musician, picked up a guitar and began to fool around. Mutt came back in and announced, "That's the best hook I've heard in five years." The hook became the chorus for "Pour Some Sugar on Me," the album's anthem. *Hysteria* sold over fifteen million copies. "It became the most important song on the record," says Elliot. "And it was done almost by accident. Had he not gone for a piss . . ."

Ralph Simon believes Mutt's influence on Def Leppard was greater than its members ever realized. "Having come from the background of being a sonic constructor and knowing how he heard the end sonic architecture, Mutt knew exactly what he had to do. He would either sing the parts or the backing vocals and if you listen to Joe Elliott—who could never really sing properly—and then early Mutt work, Mutt's phrasing punctuated everything he did."

"Mutt wanted to compete with Michael Jackson, get our songs played on Top 40 radio," says Rick Allen. "He helped us create this sound that was very polished, very appealing. It could cross over into more of a pop market, but it still had the guitars. Because it was so appealing we couldn't get away from that sound . . . so we stuck with it.

"I miss working with Mutt. He always knew what he wanted, though at times his perfectionism drove us crazy. It was our problem, because it showed us we weren't as good as we thought we were. Over a relatively short space of time we had to improve tenfold. We couldn't keep up with him."

Lange had a fanatical attention to details. In the days before CDs, the final step in making an album was the cutting. As you got toward the center and the grooves got closer together, the sound quality decreased, so it was important to push the levels back up. "When I was cutting *Hysteria* to vinyl, Mutt would send the album up one track at a time and get that absolutely right," says Steve Brown. "Mutt notices everything and he wants it spot on. Side one, track one, and then he would send up track two. That had to run right, with the right space in between tracks and the right EQ. That happened twice a day. The album was done after six days; most took one or two at the outside. It made a bit of vinyl perfect."

The success of Def Leppard and AC/DC showed that Lange had the right ears for the lucrative American market. His work with Foreigner on *4* was an exhausting process, as his collaborator Thomas Dolby recalls. Mutt was never far from music. His idea of relaxation was sitting cross-legged on the bed of his Manhattan hotel suite "doing pitch-perfect covers of Van Morrison songs."

Says Dolby, "You play something over and over and think you've nailed it. And Mutt says, 'That was great, man, but in the fifteenth bar, the third note was a hair early.' And you say, 'Okay, you want me to punch in?' And in his sweetest South African accent, he goes, 'No, just take it from the top.' You might end up playing the same part a hundred and fifty times. After a while, it can drive you crazy.

"Mutt is aware of the precise placement of every single note in every single track," he says. "At the same time, he can sit back in his chair and listen to the record like he's a nineteen-year-old fan hearing it for the first time. That's an incredible skill, and one that results in hit records."

The Cars wanted the same gloss that turned Foreigner into an

FM radio staple. Like Mutt, their leader, Ric Ocasek, was a stickler for getting it just so, and hang the time and the expense. Mutt, despite his painstaking approach, did bring his projects in on budget, whereas the Americans were profligate with studio time. The recording process was so intense, Mutt almost had a breakdown—and he never worked with the band again. "Mutt's a definite stickler for feel," said keyboard player Greg Hawkes. "He'd sit there with somebody for hours working on a part, and only looking for the feel. If he didn't hear the feel, it wasn't down on tape. Mutt would always refer to the demos and say, 'You've got to have the feel of this,' or, 'This doesn't have the feel of the demo—do it again.' That's the point of creativity, it's always trying to get that feel."

It was Mutt who insisted that "Drive" was a hit. "It was a simple song, direct. I thought it was kinda weird for a single," admitted Ocasek. "It was all two, three chords and droning; the subject matter was kind of depressing. But Mutt always said, 'It's a big single.' And I always went, 'Sure.' " "Drive" was a worldwide smash in 1984, and the following year, it was used so effectively during the Live Aid concert that it still tugs at people's consciences today.

Mutt had strong views on lyrics. "Lyrically, negativity wasn't in Mutt's vocabulary," recalls Joe Elliot, whose songs took on a darker tone when they stopped working with him. "Mutt's got absolutely no shame about being a commercial record producer. Lyrics are secondary. Mutt would say, 'When it comes to writing lyrics, it doesn't matter whether they're good or bad. They just have to be memorable.' Sometimes I'd play him personal stuff, and he'd go, 'I really like that.' Then we'd play it in the studio, and he'd object. He'd say, 'As your friend, I like it. But it's not pop, and it's not going to sell, so shut it.' "

Ric Ocasek also disagreed with Mutt's views on words. "I think it's still a kind of poetry, or some sort of poetic form with music," says Ocasek. "Mutt Lange used to say, 'Nobody ever listens to the lyrics anyway, so who gives a shit?' I like Mutt, but he just has firm beliefs about things like that."

In his songwriting, Mutt returns time and again to the same

sources for inspiration. One particular favorite is B. W. "Buckwheat" Stevenson's "My Maria," a US Top 10 hit in 1973. (Stevenson, a Texan equally at home singing country, blues, and rock, died in 1988 following heart surgery. He was thirty-nine.) "Mutt always goes back to B. W. Stevenson because he feels that the melodic integrity of the pop hook was what fed his muse," says Ralph. "He uses a lot of hits from the late sixties and early seventies as a touchstone and reference point, as guidelines for how he should meld someone. He knows how to construct a song that has the common touch."

Working with Mutt was an exhausting, long-winded process. The perfection he sought was time-consuming and could be bad for band morale. Stars used to being cheered every time they stumble up the fretboard do not like being told to do it again and again. And again. Few acts could face a third album with Mutt unless commercial sense triumphed over ego (AC/DC managed four albums). The Rats constantly tried to escape. Def Leppard started *Hysteria* with Jim Steinman and continued with Nigel Green before they realized how much they needed Mutt.

In 1989, Bryan Adams was going nowhere. The Vancouver-born rocker had spent two fruitless years trying to follow up the disappointing *Into the Fire*, and sessions with Steve Lillywhite and Bob Clearmountain had to be scrapped. He started working with Lange. "Mutt's a lovely guy," said Adams. "I've got nothing but fantastic things to say about him. He really pulled me out of a rut. I'll be forever indebted to him.

"Let's be honest: Mutt could work with my mom and have a hit record. We come from similar backgrounds and with similar musical interests. When we first started writing together, it was obvious that we were going to make a good record together . . . the fact that we've carried on since that is due to the fact that we've had some great moments making music, not to mention a few dodgy Indian curries!"

The two of them hit it off, established a method of working together that neither had ever had before and that Lange was later to refine to perfection with Shania. Lange forced Adams to rethink his whole modus operandi. "He made me realize there really were no rules, and that a song just has to have something special, no matter what it is—that you have to come up with it, make it work, stretch it, rip it apart, strip it down, take its clothes off, and see how it looks. One of us would come in with an idea for a song, and we'd try and set up some sort of structure for it, then puzzle over it for a while, try and come up with a middle eight; then he'd come up with some genius rhythm thing for it, and we'd go back and listen to that, then realize the verse wasn't very good; so we'd erase that, rewrite the verse—it was unbelievable!

"He'd take old songs that Jim Vallance and I had written, which I thought were quite cohesive, and he'd listen to the chorus and say, 'That chorus is quite a good verse.' I've never met anyone like it in my life. He really is an all-encompassing producer: He writes, arranges, sings, plays. There were times when we were working around three in the morning, and I'd go, 'Look, I can't sit here any longer,' and he'd say, 'Okay man, see ya later.' So I'd go off to bed, wake up around ten or eleven, go back to the studio, and he'd still be there—and not only had he not gone to sleep, he'd also sussed out the problem we'd had the night before!"

That cut both ways. After their first collaboration, Mutt swore he would never work with Bryan again. At times, Bryan's working habits drove him so crazy he had to go out in the woods and take a walk around the house. If Mutt, with his obsessive approach, couldn't take it, it must have been bad. However, they did end up doing songs on two more albums.

Their major songwriting collaboration was "(Everything I Do) I Do It for You," used on the soundtrack for the movie *Robin Hood: Prince of Thieves*. It topped the UK singles charts for fifteen interminable weeks in 1991 and sold millions. *Waking Up the Neighbours* was a massive hit, another ten million seller. There were criticisms— Adams was not a big fan of Mutt's trademark layered backing vocals and Joe Elliot dared to suggest it was just a Def Leppard album with a different vocalist. (He later apologized.) In the early nineties, Lange also collaborated with power balladeer Michael Bolton, cowriting the hits "Said I Loved You But I Lied" and "Can I Touch You . . . There?" and producing the album *One Thing*. In December 1993, the month he married Eileen Twain, Lange had three songs simultaneously in the Top 10 of the US Top 100 singles chart—"Please Forgive Me" (Bryan Adams); "All for Love" (Bryan Adams, Rod Stewart, and Sting), from *The Three Musketeers* soundtrack; and "I Said I Loved You . . . But I Lied."

He appeared to be at the height of his profession. In fact, his greatest triumph was still to come, and from the most unlikely source: country music. During his career, Lange had dabbled in country—recording albums with Clover (who later metamorphosed into Huey Lewis and the News) and the Outlaws—without much success. "Mutt was always a closet country picker," says Rick Allen. "If you take the distorted guitars off 'Armageddon It,' it's definitely a country tune."

By 1993, Lange was ready for another challenge. The Garth Brooks explosion had shown that Nashville had the power to shift millions of units, but their sound was still outdated and thin compared to what he could deliver.

Chapter Fourteen

A SPIRITUAL MAN

MUTT LANGE'S LOVE LIFE was nowhere near as successful as his recording career. It was remarkable primarily because all the women he married or became seriously involved with continued to adore him long after they broke up. They also ended up as friends with each other, perhaps because they realized that any long-term relationship with him was doomed. Mutt was a serial monogamist, yet his one true love, the only mistress who could always captivate him and take him away, was his Muse.

He was a difficult man to be married to, charming and attentive when his attention was focused on the girl, but impossible to distract once he entered the recording studio. In there, time, life, and love receded into mist. In *Is That It?*, Bob Geldof suggests that Mutt's tyrannical producing on their first album was partly due to the strain of the breakup of his marriage to Stevie. In the only extant picture of Hocus, one can see Stevie resting her hand on his knee, staring straight at the camera with a proprietorial intensity while Mutt has just the tips of his fingers on her wrist and the skewed look of a man who would rather be somewhere else. During the recording of the Rats' third album, "A Swedish girl was always in the studio with him," says Nigel Grainge, "probably because he spent so much time in the studio it was the only time to keep up with him. He pretty much ignored her."

Mutt's second wife, Olga, was quite different from Stevie—a definite case of opposites attracting. Despite her name and Scandinavian ancestry, her upbringing and accent were cut glass, upper class, English. Olga was a stunningly pretty blonde, a former model always surrounded by a cloud of gorgeous women. "She was a party girl, into the club scene, very high-spirited, and shared his passion for all things Indian," says Alison Green, an American music business lawyer, who met them both at a party in their house at 4 Fernshaw Close in Chelsea. "She loved to throw dinner parties, she had like a salon, the Gertrude Stein of rock and roll. She bonded with all the bands he produced, she was a people magnet, the most outgoing girl you could ever meet. She and Mutt were complete polar opposites."

On the rare occasions when he was present at his wife's parties, Mutt was excellent company. Conversationally he had a wide range of interests—everything from gardening, high culture, ballet, and painting to sport, especially rugby and soccer, and geopolitics—and was a polite listener. "He was a really nice guy, very quiet, very mellow," says Alison. "I don't think he had an evil bone in his body. His biggest single vice was being a workaholic, so focused that the world ceased to exist. His work habits were legendary. He'd disappear for days on end, lock himself in the studio, sleep on the floor until he was physically ready to drop."

In 1980, when Mutt was working with Foreigner on 4, he was poised to become one of the biggest producers in the world. While he was raking in the money, there was such demand for his services that he would go sequentially from album to album. When he eventually finished a project and had driven himself to the point of exhaustion, he and Olga headed off on vacation, where he recharged his batteries before throwing himself into the next one. By the mid-eighties, despite the all-night parties, rock and roll widowhood had palled on Olga, who reluctantly called time on a marriage that was no longer a marriage. "Olga was devastated by the breakup," says Alison, "she was crazy about Mutt, she adored him, she really, really loved this guy. But as time wore on she recognized this wasn't a phase, it was a lifestyle, ingrained in his personality, and it just wasn't going to change. She wanted kids, somebody to share her life with."

Money was never an issue to Mutt. After he and Olga split, he bought a mansion in Surrey. He decided to build a shrine outside his bedroom window. Unfortunately, there was a three-hundred-year-old oak in the way. He paid thousands of pounds to have the oak moved and replanted. He gave Olga the house in Chelsea, never abandoned her, and supported her financially without a quibble. Clichéd as it sounds, he has remained friends with all his exes, helping Stevie emotionally when she went through problems, giving her a song to record on her solo album, which was released by Silvertone (part of Zomba). After their divorce, Olga discovered a rock band, Romeo's Daughter. They were signed to Jive, their publishing went to Zomba, and Mutt produced their first album, keeping it all in the family (and their bank account if it had proved to be successful).

Although he has worked for years with bands who were devotees of sex, drugs, and rock and roll, Lange was never interested. After "workaholic," the word that describes him best is "spiritual." It comes up again and again. "He was very spiritual and, for all his fame and fortune, very humble," says Alison Green. "They had a meditation room in their house, but what was so cool about Mutt and Olga's marriage was that he never expected her to follow his beliefs. They shared this bond, but with Olga it was more fashion; she found her own way to follow, while with Mutt it was more in his heart. To him it was the core of his being."

Olga's interest in Indian mysticism was more social than spiritual. She regularly invited some of the biggest names in rock with their wives and partners—including Mick Jones of Foreigner and Chris Squire from Yes—to parties attended by the trendy mystic of the day. One particular favorite was a guru who, according to one party regular, "was more Essex than Indian. I doubt he'd ever even been out East. We all had to sit in a circle chanting "Guru Dave, Guru Dave" over and over again and it was so ludicrous I had to stop myself laughing. (Years later I learned we were all supposed to be chanting 'Guru Dev, Guru Dev.') Dave might not have been very spiritually enlightening but he was very good at extracting donations. Mutt was very seldom there as he never got back from the studio until six in the morning, and I often wondered what it was that kept them together."

Recording studios are inherently stressful places, cocoons fueled by artificial light and air, where the body's natural rhythms soon become reversed and daylight, unless it is dawn, becomes an enemy. Mutt Lange has a unique reputation in the business for remaining calm and composed. He is an ascetic amidst excess, a monk among the mayhem. Those who have worked with him knew he was a vegetarian and an exercise fiend who did not drink alcohol, smoke, or take drugs. Most did not inquire further and Mutt never volunteered much. Steve Brown assumed that because he didn't eat eggs he must have had an allergy to them. Mutt chose never to correct him. However, for those who are interested, Mutt Lange has a great impact on their lives . . . and not because of his musical abilities.

"Mutt has had a guru in India for thirty years to whom he has always been very spiritually devoted," says Ralph Simon. "He never did want to be in the limelight. Sometimes it's almost as if he is using his spiritual path to take him through to the end result. For him the path he follows is in trying to construct some kind of 'happiness shrapnel,' musical pieces that have an enormous impact globally. The impact of his songs is far greater than many political leaders."

He does not preach or proselytize but leads by example. Three members of Def Leppard, a band who have had more than their fair share of rock and roll excess leading directly to tragedy, are now vegans. Guitarist Phil Collen was the first, while Rick Allen and Vivian Campbell have now followed suit. Collen has also been heavily influenced by Indian spirituality and the laws of karma, though he never says which path he follows. Allen, having fought a long battle against tequila and cocaine, has now found his own spiritual peace.

"I'd been heading that way ever since I met Mutt," acknowledges the drummer. "For years I knew that might be an answer, but instead I was attracted to the polar opposite—here's a bottle, here's a mirror—constantly banging my head against the wall, hurting myself. I realized that I had to find my spiritual side, a cleaner way of life. It works for me. It's a purely personal thing."

It is hard to find anybody who will say a bad, or indeed any, word about Lange. The word friends and ex-wives use to describe their feelings for him is inevitably the same: "love." He is, and wishes to remain, an intensely private person.

Bryan Adams has said a little. For years, Bryan suffered with facial skin problems and he had given up eating red meat. Following Mutt's example, he stopped eating anything with a face, no chicken, no fish, and no eggs. He also started to explore Lange's spiritual path. "He improved my spiritual life. I'm not incredibly religious or spiritual, but I learned a lot of ways from him, the laws of karma. I read books on his path and it's very interesting."

It would be easy to dismiss this as another musician's fad, a twelve-step program for the spiritually disenfranchised. Except Mutt Lange has been following the same path since 1970. Even as a teenager at Belfast High he was interested in metaphysical matters. "John had none of that anger you often get with teens," says Johan du Plooy. "He was so busy with sport and music that he didn't have time to be idle and angry. There were people who had that anger, but he was a gentle young guy, well liked and respectable."

The catalyst was the arrival of John Savage-Reid, a charismatic boy who lived in the Sudan, nicknamed "the Camel," and a committed Baptist called Brian Gurney. Says du Plooy, "The extent of my faith at the time was if you were nice to Granny, kind to the cat, then you'd go to heaven, and here were these young guys who actually believed, really believed. It was the first time we'd ever really been exposed to Christianity. We got a group together, John, me, and a guy named Spooky—David Spour. We'd spend weekends at Spooky's farm outside of Belfast, have these heavy discussions about religion, and play with his monkey, which would run up if you put sugar in the tea cup. John was a very strong Christian at a time when we were being exposed to different philosophies. There weren't many of us and the rest of the school ignored it completely. How much it influenced Mutt's later life I don't know, but it certainly did mine."

The second and most radical stage of Mutt's spiritual development happened in 1970 when he was living in the farmhouse with Geoff Williams and Steve McNamara. "Hocus had a recess over a long weekend and the three of us went our separate ways to catch up on personal things," says Geoff. "It was over that weekend that Steve was exposed to the path. On his return, he told us all about this Eastern philosophy. It was very strict, no stimulant substances, no alcohol, not eating anything living at all. Fish, eggs, both would be the taking of a life. Mutt and I were a bit skeptical, but we all had a live and let live attitude."

Mutt didn't follow McNamara immediately, for he is a man who takes his time before committing himself to a cause. When he did, at the end of the year, he did so absolutely. "Mutt is an all-or-nothing guy," says Williams. "He does not profess to be something and have a T-bone steak for his birthday. I would put money on it that Mutt has not had a drop of alcohol in the last thirty years. It didn't cause any open friction or animosity; everybody was most tolerant. Mutt is very private and once he decided it was right for him, he never tried to convert other people. He did pass the odd comment sometimes. If I was cooking a piece of steak in the pan, he might walk past and go 'moo.' "

The path that Mutt follows is called Radhasoami Satsang. It was founded by Shiv Dayal Singh in the Punjab in 1861, a breakaway from Sikhism, which was in a state of turmoil after the Sikh kingdom had been defeated by the British. Sikhism, too, had been born during a time of chaos. In the early sixteenth century, as the Muslims were establishing military supremacy in Northern India, Nanak, the son of a Hindu merchant in Lahore, had a vision of God's presence while bathing in a river. According to legend, after a full day of silence, he pronounced, "There is no Hindu and no Musselman [Muslim]." Shrewdly, he adopted a unique garb that combined both Hindu and

Muslim features, notably the turban. The faith he developed was eclectic, stressing the unity of God and brotherhood of man. From Islam came the concept of a single creator called the True Name and the futility of idol worship. From Hinduism he took the ideas of karma, reincarnation, and the ultimate unreality of the world, while utterly rejecting the caste system. Sikhs believe spiritual release can only be obtained by taming the ego through devotional singing, constant recitation of the divine name, meditation, and service. Nanak also emphasized the unique role of the guru (teacher) as essential in leading people to find God.

Nanak was succeeded by nine further gurus, the tenth of whom, Gobind Singh, turned his teachings on their head. In 1699, he founded the Khalsa, the Community of the Pure, and turned the Sikhs into warrior priests. After Gobind Singh's assassination, the Adi Granth (the collected writings of Nanak) was declared to be the guru. No further human gurus were allowed. As warriors, the Sikhs fought the Muslims, eventually ruling most of the Punjab before losing two wars to the British.

Radhasoami Satsang went back to the earliest tenets of Sikhism—vegetarianism, abstinence from stimulants, and repeating the name of God—and the teachings of medieval, often rebel and unorthodox, Indian "saints." Primarily, it was a modern manifestation of Sant Mat (Path of the Masters), a philosophical school that some claim dates back to the dawn of recorded history and that stresses the importance of listening to inner sound. Most radically, it was led by a living guru, as practitioners are initiated by a master who has reputedly already made the inner journey.

The idea of the path of sound and light is universal. Versions can be found in many of the world's major religions, including Christianity—it is referred to in St. John's Gospel. Sant Mat practitioners try to merge their soul with a "true" and "pure" God, minus the beliefs, practices, and rules that make up most organized religions. They believe it to be a scientific method of entering the kingdom of heaven while living in the here and now. They hate being described as a "religion" or, even worse, a "cult."

The meditation technique requires acute concentration on a point behind and between the eyebrows, called the ajna chakra ("seat of the soul"), considered a gateway into the human soul. The senses are withdrawn and "collected" at this point. At worst, practitioners claim that this meditation clears up the clutter of everyday life; at best, it leads to contact with the true God and finding the true self, which in turn leads to wisdom, unconditional love, fearlessness, connectedness, bliss, and spiritual immortality. (And in Mutt Lange's case, marriage to one of the most desired women on the planet and a fortune running into hundred of millions.)

Radhasoami Satsang came to the West in the early twentieth century. Kirpal Singh was the first Sant (Perfect Living Master) to visit the United States, in 1955, and later founded his own independent organization, Ruhani Satsang. It is now known as the Science of Spirituality/Sawan Kirpal Ruhani Mission, whose current head is Rajinder Singh, fifty-four, who was an electronic engineer and researcher at AT&T until he was selected as the organization's new leader by his own spiritual teacher, Darshan Singh. Unlike many similar sects, it does not encourage active recruitment and proselytization. As Mutt did, people discover it through word of mouth or educational seminars publicized on the alternative spirituality circuit.

While a man's religion should be allowed to remain a personal matter, the problem is that when Shiv Dayal Singh announced that there were once more living gurus, he declared open season. Anybody with a few acolytes could anoint themselves a guru and command absolute obedience from their followers. Scattered around the world there are currently over one hundred different groups that follow parts of the Radhasoami tradition.

In 2000, tabloid newspapers in America and Britain attempted to link Mutt and Shania with a controversial Sant Mat offshoot led by Thakar Singh, which has many followers in Germany and Switzerland. While Thakar claims to follow the path of Kirpal Singh, he split from Kirpal's designated successor, Darshan Singh (whom Mutt continued to follow), in the late seventies and set up his own sect.

Mutt Lange is not a follower of Thakar Singh. He meditates and exercises regularly, sticks to his vegetarian diet, eschews alcohol and drugs, and keeps a regular journal. He may have practiced sexual abstinence in the past, but he has also been married three times with various girlfriends in between. "I never heard Olga complain about that," laughs Alison Green. "If they had no sex it was because Mutt was never home." While there is a delicious irony in the idea of the man married to an international sex symbol refraining from sex with her, both his and Shania's friends always laughed at the idea that their relationship was platonic, long before they learned she was pregnant.

There must also be a shadow cast by Mutt's beliefs. He may be gentle and charming, but by his very nature he is a controller. People who are drawn to him are then attracted by his beliefs. Both Mary Bailey and Shania now follow the same path.

Just because he does not appear to have any enemies in a business that enjoys enmity does not mean Lange is a pushover. "Mutt was never a guy to suffer fools, he wasn't a guy to suck up," says Alison Green. "He picked business managers who were really tough and totally insulated him from anything he didn't want to deal with. One way he could stay really nice was by putting up this protective zone. Clive Calder was tough . . . like steel would break on that guy. Mutt was his cash cow and Clive wasn't letting anyone interfere with that relationship. Clive took care of business beautifully and Mutt did what Mutt wanted, which was to create with absolutely no interference . . . and they all got exceedingly rich."

It is much easier to be a nice guy if you have one of the record industry's hard men in your corner. For years, Mutt was represented by Zomba, headed by Clive Calder, a notoriously tough negotiator who gives no quarter in his deals. "He's legendary for being hard," says British record company executive Dave Bates, who has known Calder for over twenty-five years. "Some people might say he's too hard, but it's his money, his expertise, and their choice. If you get involved with Clive and he really believes in you, you've got every chance of success. He's not a charity; he's a business that happens to work in music."

Mutt's exact relationship with the Zomba group is a source of much speculation. Because it was a private company, nobody knew who had a piece of it. Industry observers are convinced that Mutt must have owned a percentage of the corporation he did so much to build. Ralph Simon, who surely knew when he split with Calder after a dispute over business ethics in 1990, is noncommittal, saying, "I think it extremely unlikely that Calder would give Mutt any interest in the Zomba structure. The avaricious nature of what Zomba became in the 1990s is the complete antithesis of what Mutt is."

In 1993, Mutt Lange was one of the most private, but powerful, men in the music business, with fast-track access to all the movers and shakers who mattered, and was very capable of using his clout to get his own way. He was quite prepared to give Shania Twain what she had always wanted, but much of it, initially, would have to be on his terms.

Chapter Fifteen

ENTER PRINCE CHARMING

THE LEGEND IS SIMPLE. It was a coup de foudre, love at first digital glimpse. Mutt saw Shania's video and fell in love with her. He knew he had to have her, so he pursued her until he did. In riding to the rescue, Prince Charming turned her career from squatting in the basement to owning the castle.

According to Shania, they met because "David Rose, who worked at A&M in London, would give Mutt new stuff coming in and my CD and video package was one of them. Mutt was very intrigued. He loved my voice, loved my story, he liked my video, too, but more than anything my story drew him to me." Another version is that when he was working in his studio, Mutt liked to watch Country Music Television and saw the video. Everything about the clip that had upset the programmers in the States had the opposite effect on Lange. He fell for Shania big time and when he subsequently listened to the album, he felt she had a voice.

He was certainly struck enough to set about breaking his cardinal patterns. Mutt, who had not worked with a woman singer successfully since Jessica Jones, actively set out to pursue an unknown artist. He hadn't done that for years. He hadn't broken a new act since Def Leppard. As one of the top producers on the planet with combined album sales well over the one hundred million mark, he commanded a royalty of 5 percent and an advance running into six

figures. Only established acts could afford him. Nashville was probably the only recording center in the world where his name meant
next to nothing. The first time he called and spoke to Mary Bailey
she thought he was an overenthusiastic fan.

"It came through a business source that there was a fellow who
wanted an autograph and so we signed a picture," chuckles Mary.
Shania signed it but left the "e" off Lange. Over in England, Mutt
called the office and went into charm offensive. "I got a phone call
from Mutt. I knew he had something to do with the music business, but I had no idea he was a producer, I just thought he was a
guy with a strange name. Anyway I had a conversation and he was
just so wonderful to talk to. We started conversing back and forth
and it was quite a while before I got Eilleen and Mutt to actually
have a conversation. I kept saying to Eilleen, 'You have to phone
this guy,' and she was saying, 'Later I'll get around to it.' "

The clincher came when Mary mentioned to Luke Lewis that
this English producer was calling up and seemed interested in Shania. Lewis, one of the few people in town who knew just how important Lange was, was knocked out. When Shania eventually
phoned him from her apartment she had no idea who he was, just
that he was this Brit Mary was insisting she talk to. His first question to her was: "Do you write?" This sounded great because she
was fed up with fighting the Nashville system of getting as many
different songwriters on an album as possible—lots of pie for
everyone.

"Yes," she replied hesitantly.

"Can I hear something?"

"Okay," she said, "I'll send you a tape."

"No," came the firm reply, "I want to hear something right now,
sing some stuff for me."

Bizarre though the request sounded, it was music to her ears.
None of this "let's schedule a songwriting session a week from Tuesday." This was organic, a creative spark from a guy four thousand
miles away. Shania propped the phone receiver on the pillow of her
couch, pulled out her guitar, and started playing songs, her songs.

She played "Raining on Our Love" and "Whose Bed Have Your Boots Been Under?", "This Man of Mine," and "Home Ain't Where the Heart Is (Anymore)." Each time she finished she waited for his response; each time he said he loved it and asked why it had not been recorded. Playfully she asked what he was working on and so he sang her what was to become Michael Bolton's "I Said I Loved You But I Lied."

Everything Mutt said was what she wanted to hear. He praised her voice, but obliquely criticized her first album. "The way you're singing right now," he said, "even though it's over the phone, that's the voice I've heard bits and pieces of. That's how you should be sounding all the time. If you're doing your own stuff, you'll be able to get that."

By the end of that first conversation they agreed to start writing songs together, sending packages back and forth by Federal Express, singing and chatting over the phone. "I didn't know who he was," insisted Shania, "just this guy with a weird name. I trusted him because he played me some music of his on the phone; there was a musical trust and a bond there before anything else. I love our relationship and the way it all started, it was so real, based on no inhibitions. I was not intimidated by who he was."

At the time Lange was recording with Michael Bolton and writing with Bryan Adams. Bolton recalls: "I had never seen Mutt like that before. He was as focused on Shania as he was on his work. He just had an instinct that she was it for him." When Mutt learned that Shania would be appearing at Fan Fair in June, he convinced Adams, who loathes country music, to make the trip to Nashville with him. He told Shania he was thinking of coming down "with Bryan" and asked, "Why don't you come and meet me?"

"He figures I know who he's talking about," said Shania, "then he starts talking about things referring to Bryan Adams music and I said, 'Can you hold on a second,' went over to the record collection, and I had bought *Waking Up the Neighbours*. I pulled it out and there is his name on the back. I didn't say anything, acted like I'd known all the time, but I was so embarrassed."

The international Country Music Fan Fair convention takes place every June in the Tennessee State Fairgrounds. It is unique in the music industry in that it allows twenty-five thousand fans an opportunity to actually meet, chat, collect autographs, and maybe even have photos taken with their favorite stars. There are parties galore and concerts in which even the biggest names perform a few numbers. The price the fans have to pay is hours queuing for everything from autographs to food and toilets as well as sky-high souvenir sales. For record companies, it is a cost-efficient way of introducing new acts to a committed audience.

Nobody paid much attention to Shania Twain at Fan Fair '93. Her record company was far more interested in Billy Ray Cyrus, whose cloying, irritating, but infectious "Achy Breaky Heart" had become an international hit. Then Mutt Lange turned up backstage with Bryan Adams. As Adams was pumping the flesh, Mutt, who loathes such things, shrank into the canvas. His eyes kept searching the crowd, looking for one person. Shania came in and had Mutt pointed out to her. He was not what she expected: "tall, thin, blue eyes, blond with long curly hair, so neat looking."

Shania is not physically spontaneous—"I'm not a huggy touchy person, which in America can be seen as quite odd"—but the moment she saw him, she ran straight over and hugged him, enveloping him in a cloak of her arms as if she had recognized the missing part of her soul and was not prepared to let it go ever again. Giddy, she rushed over to Mary, saying, "Come here, come here, this is Mutt." Mary, too, was captivated. So was Mercury, once they realized that Mutt was serious about working with Shania and indeed that he was going to stay in Nashville and write with her for the next two weeks.

By that point Mutt's interest in Shania was more than just a professional crush. He was seriously smitten. Sitting in the back of the limo taking Bryan and him back from Fan Fair, he raved about her. Sure, he hadn't been 100 percent convinced by her singing live, but that was something that could be fixed in the studio. The problem, he told Bryan again and again, was that she had a fiancé.

"I can see that might be a problem," said Adams dryly. "Let's see.

On the one hand . . . carpenter. On the other hand . . . world famous record producer. World famous record producer. Carpenter. Yes . . . tough call."

Shania was smitten in a different way. She maintains that she had no romantic interest in Mutt before they met—"I didn't expect him to look the way he does," she admits. "I thought he was fat, I pictured him as this workaholic, I figured he probably sat down all the time, an overweight guy with long graying black hair in a ponytail"—but he had already reached her in a way Paul never could. Music had always been, will always be, more important to her than sex. "I didn't fall in love right off the bat, it took about . . . a month," she laughs. Those first weeks in Nashville they didn't do much writing, just swapped stories and laughed a lot. For Shania it was a revelation. She had never met a man like him before. Here was this guy—okay, so he was older, but he never held it over her the way John Kim had; okay, he was rich and powerful, but she already knew people like that and how to play them. But she couldn't play Mutt because he didn't abuse that power. Instead he teased her just like Jerry used to, christened her "Woody" because "I had short bangs when I met him and he thought I looked like Woody Woodpecker."

Just as he had with Bryan Adams, Mutt turned the way Shania thought about her songs upside down and round about, made her look at them in a different way. First he told her, "We need to go into your catalog. I want to know what you've been writing, then we'll go from there." He showed her how verses could become choruses, choruses become hooks. He told her, "No, that lyric's not quite there yet." Her lyrics moved from the generic to the personal. Instead of resorting to cliché, she came over sassy, teasing, but self-contained and strong—the antithesis of the Nashville woman in song but spot-on in terms of nineties reality. Mutt believed that titles were an important part of the happiness shrapnel. They could color the flavor of the song; one word could make a difference. Changing "This Man of Mine" to "Any Man of Mine" altered the entire sexual dynamic (though only two lines of Shania's original lyrics survived the Mutt recording process). The singer was now in control, no longer passive. So simple to see. So difficult to do.

Bailey describes Mutt as "a gentle soul" and you don't get many of them in the music business. He was so calm, so comfortable, at ease with himself, but there was nothing weak about him, nothing that could be pushed aside like yesterday's man. The absolute calm he radiated came from power. Shania knew, as women always do, that he was attracted to her, but he didn't make any sudden lunges, or indeed any sexual moves at all. Men had never acted like that with Shania, so it intrigued her all the more. She connected with Mutt on nonphysical planes, musical and spiritual. It sounds trite, but sex was irrelevant.

"No, I wasn't surprised when they became romantically involved," says Mary, who also became infected by Mutt's beliefs. "Because they were so compatible artistically. With Mutt, his personality, his kindness, and his warmth, it was probably a very natural progression. So it didn't surprise me and I don't think it did change the basis of our relationship."

Others might disagree. Mutt is an all-or-nothing guy. Along with an intense love, he brought the ability to make things happen. Not just total financial security for several lifetimes, but serious business connections. Access to the best studios, to the best musicians, the best lawyers. Fine, Jive was not going to take over her contract, as their expertise was in teen pop and rap/R&B, but they knew all the people who could make things happen outside of the country market. Once she had Mutt, Shania's need for Mary began to evaporate.

What moved Mutt and Shania from the professional to the personal was a writing trip they took to Europe. He suggested she come over on the Concorde, but Shania had never heard of it, did not know there was such a thing as a supersonic airliner. They disappeared inside his home to write and then went on to Spain, Italy, and Paris. "We pretty much wrote almost all of the album before we even revealed our feelings to each other at all. Which wasn't long," said Shania. "I've always been that way. I've never, ever, ever let a guy know the way I felt about him until I know. Because I'm just never a fool for that. I don't know whether I'm just really old-fashioned that way or what. But I always felt there's no point making a fool of yourself."

Shania has said repeatedly, "We were meant to be together," but the actual moment of revelation came one day in Spain. "We just hugged. We'd hugged before. I mean, good-bye, at the airport. But that time we didn't let go for the longest time. It was so intense, I thought: 'I really don't want to let go of this person.' At that moment we knew we had a lot to talk about.

"It wasn't a kiss. It wasn't like a very sexual moment or a passionate moment, it wasn't. It was a very sweet, honest moment." For Shania that was it. From that moment on it was all cut and dried. "Looking at him the day I fell in love and looking at him the day before? Two different things.

"The most special moment we had together was when I got back from telling my family about my new relationship and how serious it was. When I met up with Mutt I felt like my heart was going to beat out of my chest. He felt the same way, and we were like, 'Oh, we can never be apart again.' I just never felt such a strong connection before. I felt like I'd been away from him for ten years, but it had only been two weeks."

Before she could commit to Mutt, Shania had to tidy up a few loose ends, one of whom was her fiancé. Unable to find regular work in Nashville, Paul Bolduc had returned to Timmins. In August, Shania went up for a visit and broke it off. Paul was very upset, but he knew that to Shania the music had always and would always come first. He could not compete. "They split up, stayed friends, and he understood," says Helene Bolduc. "Not because he wanted it, of course; it's always hard to go through leaving somebody you've been with, but he totally understood the love she had for the music and he had a lot to learn about it. He couldn't do what this guy [Mutt] could, and she loved to be with the person that just heard and saw her for what she was."

After Paul and Eilleen split, Dean Malton used to see him at the

Cottage, a bar in Huntsville. "He didn't show it if he was upset. He didn't run away from Huntsville, go hide anywhere. He was back in town doing his thing, and hanging out on weekends in the bar. Paul had a good circle of friends, and being a very good-looking guy he moved on relatively quickly."

For Paul, the wounds were still raw on September 21 when Shania came back to Timmins to play a gig in the gymnasium of Theriault École Secondaire (the French high school right next door to her alma mater). Mutt came along to mix the sound. For Timmins, the show was a major deal. "We were so proud that someone actually had an album out on a major label and they would come back and play," says John Emms, who reviewed the show for the Timmins *Daily Press*. To Emms's ears, the band was not up to scratch, better than Longshot, but not up to the standard of platinum Canadian artists like Tom Cochrane or Bruce Cockburn. (Mysteriously, the first four paragraphs of his review were never published.) It must have felt the same to both Shania and Mutt. Aside from TV appearances and a handful of showcases, she did not give another live concert for almost five years.

"We were all hoping for the best, but the first few songs, Shania was beside herself with nerves," says Emms. "I could hear the mistakes, I could hear the fluffs. But once the nerves went she was out front and she was shaking it. In the end, it was triumphant and everyone was ecstatic. Even though the band didn't play that well, it was a wonderful evening, everyone was happy."

Once she had relaxed, Shania remembered where she was. In Timmins, she was still Eilleen who had nothing to prove. Graciously she announced, "I'm always going to be grateful to J.P. Aubé for giving me the opportunity to have my first professional job at the Escapade Hotel." The crowd cheered; J.P. squirmed in his seat with pleasure.

After the show, J.P. and his wife hosted a party for the band at their house. When Mutt arrived, he promptly took his shoes off at the door, very much the custom in Northern Ontario. He charmed Charmaine by immediately noticing and then asking informed

Eilleen at six. Her first school photo.
(DON FRASER)

The Twains in 1973. Left to right: (back) Carrie
Ann, Eilleen, Jill, (front) Mark. (DON FRASER)

Grandma Eileen Morrison's house in Hoyle. Sharon and her daughters lived here after Clarence Edwards left. (ROBIN EGGAR)

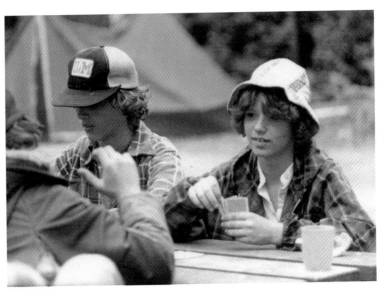

Playing euchre on a camping trip to Halfway Lake Provincial Park with Pinecrest Public School, Hanmer, June 1979. (TED EVANS)

Jerry and Sharon bought this house on Montgomery Avenue, in Timmins, in 1981. The top floor was rented out. Eilleen and Carrie Ann slept in the basement. (ROBIN EGGAR)

Downtown Timmins. Wednesday night is still talent night in the Maple Leaf Hotel (right). Back in the '80s, Eilleen Twain would bring her guitar and sing at the venue—sometimes she even won. (ROBIN EGGAR)

Mary Bailey in her heyday as a Canadian country star. Mary first saw Eilleen sing when she was eleven, and was to be her guide, mentor, and support for many years. (REDFERNS)

Viva Vegas. Eilleen singing at Deerhurst in 1988.

(MIKE TAYLOR)

Eilleen with her then boyfriend Mike Taylor during
a trip to Las Vegas, 1988. (MIKE TAYLOR)

"I need bigger hair!" Eilleen in the bathroom of her
house in Melissa, Christmas 1988. (MIKE TAYLOR)

Mutt Lange in his band Hocus in South Africa in 1971. Clockwise from top left: Alan Goldswain, Geoff Williams, Mutt Lange, Stevie van Kerken, Steve McNamara. (GEOFF WILLIAMS)

Shania and Mutt cut the cake at their wedding. (AMERICAN MEDIA)

The Queen of Country meets the Prince of Wales at Party in the Park, July 5, 1998. Shania's clothes were still being fitted in the car on the way to the event. (THE PRESS ASSOCIATION LTD.)

Shania the rock goddess performing in New York. (EBET ROBERTS/REDFERNS)

questions about her collection of abstract paintings. "Mutt is a very interesting guy, very calm, a person with no airs and no pretensions, very sincere, attentive, and considerate," says J.P. "It was just before they got married and they were very comfortable with each other."

Six weeks later, Mutt invited Shania to Paris, where he was recording with Bryan Adams. He told her: "I know I'll be working in the studio and I'm not going to have the time to be with you very much, but I want you to be able to enjoy Paris, so I want you to invite your sisters along, too."

Shania stayed in a hotel just off the Champs Elysées. The night after she arrived Mutt proposed on bended knee, presenting her with a 2.5 carat ring. It was three o'clock in the morning and he had just come back from the studio. What Shania didn't know was that she had unwittingly brought her own engagement ring over with her. Mutt had told her, "Listen, someone's going to bring you a small package. There's a video in there that I've got to see. Could you bring it with you when you come to Paris? And don't lose it!" and oblivious to the obvious, Shania merely nodded okay and brought the package along with her. "I knew something was coming," said Shania later, "because he had invited my sisters. He wanted them to be there for that moment."

"I didn't have to actually convince him about marriage, but for him it was a big, big step," she admits. "Mutt hadn't been married in so many years and he was never getting married again. In his mind, he was well mature, well past the stage of the novelty of marriage. Then I come along and there was no avoiding it. We were just so obviously destined to be together."

Jill and Carrie Ann were worried, telling her, "You just met this guy, you can't get married." It was so out of character for their cool, calculating sister. She was the one who always looked but never leaped, the one who kept her head when all around were swooning. Mutt was the only man she'd ever been with who was more centered than she was. Although he only influenced by example, they could see subtle changes in her. Doubtless, as family members always are when confronted with the whiff of cult, they were concerned about his allegiance to Sant Mat. On the plus side, he was good looking, charming, and fabulously wealthy, so maybe Leeni had finally met her true match . . . and anyway it would take a meteorite strike to change her focus.

Shania and Mutt were married at Deerhurst on December 28, 1993. It was a small ceremony, family and close friends only. Helene and Larry Bolduc were invited but chose not to attend. "I did it for Paul, I didn't want to hurt his feelings, I knew he still cared more than just being friends with her," says Helene. "Everything was really fresh, and still a little bit raw. Eilleen understood my position very well. She said, 'I would love to have you there, I will miss you if you're not there, but it's up to you.' I thought of her all day."

It was a formal affair. The bride wore white, a low-cut dress with a halter top, long white gloves stretching above the elbow, and a floor-length train cascading from the floral band in her hair. Mutt, a good head taller than his new bride, wore a tuxedo with a traditional pleated shirt complete with wing collar, studs, and a pair of white roses in his buttonhole, and his hair was on his shoulders. Jill's daughter Mandy was the maid of honor and her little cousin Jarret the ring bearer. The wedding cake was a classic three-tier affair and the picture of them cutting it shows Mutt beaming out to the world while his new bride looks up at her Prince Charming in absolute adoration. Those watching remarked that they had never seen Eilleen look so happy.

For the first time in her life, Eilleen Twain understood what it meant to be free of financial worries. She could, perhaps, have let her dreams pass on down the river, but she still believed, as she always has, in her destiny. She had always accepted it without qualm if people wished to invest their money in her talent, for that was her due, but the idea of being a kept woman filled her with horror. More than ever she was determined to play the new hand she had been dealt, to break the bank, and to prove the doubters wrong.

For their honeymoon, the Langes set about recording the most expensive album in the history of Nashville.

Chapter Sixteen

THE GREAT NASHVILLE BANK ROBBERY

ALTHOUGH OTHER NASHVILLE FOLK have their doubts, Mary Bailey insists that Mercury would have made a second album with Shania whatever. She does admit: "Having a proven producer with an unbelievable track record, who's expressed interest in a new talent, absolutely brought credibility to the team. I was very comfortable with Eilleen being with him, knowing that they started writing with a purpose, a purpose of an album. As a manager I'm totally going to support that. Number two, it allowed her the opportunity of being relaxed and finally having someone who was on the same wavelength. For me, it was finding someone who believed in her as much as I did."

Luke Lewis was ecstatic at the idea of a Lange/Twain collaboration from the get-go. "I was completely out of my mind excited about it," he says. "The guy had written a zillion killer songs. I came from a rock and roll space and it didn't scare me. Our initial conversations were about the budget, because he was wanting to spend— for what was going on here at the time—an extraordinary amount of money on the record."

The average budget for a Nashville album was $125–150,000, and Mutt hadn't done anything that cheap since 1976. Despite his track record, he had never made a country hit. The simmering differences between Shedd and Lewis boiled over into war. Shedd liked to point out that Billy Ray Cyrus's debut (admittedly recorded with his backing band) had only cost $65,000, and the figures that were being batted about for Shania were closer to $400,000.

"Harold didn't want to do the album, I mean at all," says Luke. "He didn't want to sign off on the budget. I was working in this precarious position with him, with my bosses trying to keep us at peace with each other. We were at each other's throats, we had completely different philosophies. Not to slight Harold, but he didn't get Shania. To my mind, Norro Wilson and Buddy Cannon— who doesn't get enough credit around here at all—those were the guys who heard something special in her voice and personality."

Mutt, doubtless after much consultation with Clive Calder and Steven Howard at Zomba, solved the problem by making Lewis an offer he would be daft to refuse. "Mutt said he would cover everything over two hundred grand," says Lewis. "Him and her—she was definitely involved—made a really righteous move which took me out of the line of fire politically, allowed them to do it, and spoke to their own belief in what they were doing." Those who know Zomba's deals doubt that Mutt would have financed the recording out of his own pocket unless he got a higher royalty than his usual 5 percent. He probably ended up with 6 to 7 percent, rising with increased sales. The cost of *The Woman in Me* has been variously estimated as anywhere up to a million dollars, though its eventual cost was closer to $750,000. If Mutt had been charging his full commercial rate, it would have been far higher.

It was a masterstroke, in one move sidelining old Nashville, while ensuring that the new guy, Lewis, was utterly committed to the project. He had to make it happen—provided, of course, that Mutt and Shania came up with a halfway decent record. *The Woman in Me* was much, much better than that.

"Mutt Lange studies whatever he's going to go after," grins session drummer Paul Leim. "He was coming into town for the first time, and he knew every musician he wanted, just like the notes he wanted and the licks he heard. This was like a bank robbery, planned from the very beginning. He came to Nashville, robbed the bank, and took all the money. It was great."

Paul Leim is the only musician to have played on the first three Shania Twain albums. He played on about half of the first album, all of *The Woman in Me,* and for *Come On Over* was promoted to be session leader. "On the first record she was another hopeful. She's a beautiful young woman, but it wasn't quite different enough to me," recalls Leim, who had relocated from Los Angeles in 1989. "The tunes that they had were good songs, and they could or could not have been a hit on anybody, and they just happened to not be on her. The most successful artists I've worked with, like Lionel Richie and Amy Grant, who have been the most focused on what it is they're doing, are the ones that write their own material. When it starts coming from the heart, that's when it really starts making a difference."

In Los Angeles, Leim was used to working with producers who thought nothing of spending three days to get a single part sounding right. In Nashville, due to a combination of budget and tradition, the emphasis was on speed and feel. Top session musicians were given their head. "Normally we make up our own parts," says Joe Chemay, who played bass on *Come On Over.* "We make a living being spontaneous, throwing ideas out constantly. We listen to something, everybody just goes on and plays it, everybody listens to each other, and you just go on until the producer is satisfied. Then in the mix the producer would discard what he did not want."

What Mutt required was the opposite. As a sonic architect, he carried the complete picture for every song in his head, but required the players to listen to everybody else, so that the songs were interwoven from the roots up. "If this was a hundred years ago, Mutt Lange would be Beethoven," says Leim, shaking his head with admiration. "He hears it all in his head, he hears every guitar, he hears every bass note, every vocal. He is the one responsible for making hit songs, regardless of what it takes. It doesn't matter if it takes a day, an hour, or a week."

For the *Woman in Me* sessions at Sound Stage Studios, Mutt set aside one full day for each backing track—a long time by Nashville standards, where session musicians expect to lay down three tracks a day. After he had finished his eleven days with Shania, Leim went back to Sound Stage to record with Linda Davis. During a break he popped in to see how Mutt was getting on. Mutt asked him, "So what have you got done?"

"Oh, we got one," replied the drummer.

"You've got one what?"

"We've got a track."

"It's only eleven thirty in the morning," exclaimed Lange. "How do you do that? How can you get what you want in that amount of time?"

(The answer is that John Guess, the highly successful producer of Davis's album, *Shoot for the Moon*, had a different approach. The album came out in 1994, a year ahead of Shania's. It was a good record, full of sharp, questioning songs, but it did not even go gold. *The Woman in Me* sold twelve million copies.)

Mutt had already done his research. When the session leader, guitarist Larry Byrom (once of Steppenwolf), recommended the best players in town, Mutt knew the names and work of everyone suggested, and many of those he finally chose—like Leim—had experience playing pop. Bassist Dave Hungate was a founding member of the million-selling corporate rockers Toto, pianist Matt Rollings had played with Lyle Lovett, and guitarist Dann Huff had almost cracked it with country rock band Giant. On top of that pop-flavored rhythm section, Mutt added the solid country roots of guitarists Brent Rowan and Brent Mason, and fiddlers Joe Spivey and Rob Hajacos, while much of the pedal steel work came from John Hughey. Hughey is a legend in his own right, having given Conway Twitty's songs their distinctive sound and toured with Loretta Lynn and Vince Gill.

Sessions began every day at 10 A.M. Mutt assembled his core musicians, played them his demo, and discussed what he wanted. Sometimes, if he needed early input, he telephoned and played ideas over the phone. (Leim recalls: "The first time I ever heard the line 'when I have a bad hair day' [from "Any Man of Mine"] was Mutt singing to me over the telephone from England. He was con-

cerned, asking me, 'What do you think of that line?' ") In the studio, those musicians who used charts made notes. During the first
run-throughs, he might ask the electric and acoustic guitars to play
specific figures, get the bass and drums to play exactly the way he
wanted. Moving on to the verse, he would stop and start, then explain in specific terms the way he wanted it. Once the basic track
was down the real work began: replacing everything.

For Mutt, everything starts from drums and bass. So Leim went
back into the studio until the drum track was spot-on, while the
other musicians rehearsed their parts. That might take until 8 P.M.
When the bass part was being replaced, the bass player listened only
to the drum track. Says Leim, "Mutt's specific all the way down to
when the bass cuts off. The bass should not be playing when the
snare drum is hitting. We are talking in terms of milliseconds, but it
cleans up the track." That attention to detail was carried on to every
aspect of the recording process.

In the studio, Mutt has no sense of time passing; he is so focused
he doesn't know if it's ten in the morning or ten at night. It nearly
finished off fiddle player Rob Hajacos during "If It Don't Take
Two." Mutt had him in the studio for two hours, correcting everything. The third beat of the second bar on the first verse, the second
upbeat of the eighth bar, he knew each one, had it marked in his
mind, and knew when it was right. During one break, Mutt heard a
groan from the studio and asked offhandedly, "Is there anything
else?" Rob replied, "Have you ever stood for two and a half hours
and held a fiddle under your neck? I can't move my head." Mutt
was horrified and immediately called a break, asking Rob, "Can we
get you something to eat, can we get you a drink . . . ?"

Like film directors, record producers can all too easily become
tyrants. Not all the musicians, used to the easygoing approach of
Nashville producers, could cope with Mutt's demands. In Music
City, they call it "burning the bees." Leim, who was used to such
demands in Los Angeles, says, "With Lionel Richie, we cut 'Truly'
for three days, and 'Stuck on You' for three days. And to me, 'Stuck
on You' sounded the same three days later as it did the first time

we ran it down. But they'd heard something else and it was my job to get whatever it is they wanted. Some of the guys from here said, 'I just can't take that pace, I can't do it over and over and over again, it's done.' I'm sorry, but if the guys were getting frustrated because he sees the vision and they're not able to capture that, then they are in the wrong."

Mutt never raised his voice, he was always reasonable, polite, and nice with it. He could always coax one more performance out of his musicians, saying to Leim, "That was a wonderful performance, that was great, but can we do it one more time and just keep the hi-hat closed just a little bit?"

"That's why I'm saying he heard everything in his head," says the drummer, "and if anything distracted him away from what he wanted to hear at that time, he noticed. If you listen to his records, if you listen very specifically, you will hear a fiddle for a second, then it will go away, and then all of a sudden there's a line on an acoustic guitar, and then that would go away, and it will be this Duane Eddy electric guitar part. And then that will go away and go back to the fiddle."

"(If You're Not in It for Love) I'm Outta Here!" begins with a scream of sheer frustration. Legend has it that it was Leim, brought to the end of his tether by Mutt's demands. Not so, he laughs. "Larry Byrom was supposed to start the song with the guitar riff and kept trying to get it right. He would stop, and say, 'Wait a second, here we go.' I'm trying to keep the energy going and when you concentrate that hard you're totally focused and he stops again . . . and again. I was like, 'We've got to do this, we've got to do this now!' I just lost it, I screamed, 'Aaargh.' So then I went, 'Three, four, five,' I don't even know why I started on three . . . so Larry started at that count of five when there's not five beats in a bar anyway. And Mutt left that on the record!" At the end of "No One Needs to Know," Leim quipped, "Here's your record, boss." Mutt left that on, too.

"My family is Leim, it's German, right?" says Leim. "Mutt paid me the biggest compliment I've ever had. I'm not patting myself on the back. We cut this track and he said, 'Bloody amazing,' and I went, 'What?' and he was just listening down the drums. He said, 'German precision and American feel.' He couldn't have said anything that made me feel any better than that, it was awesome. He made me feel like a million bucks, he's a wonderful guy. And a lot of rock producers, and pop artists I worked with in the eighties—whose names will remain unmentioned—are not nice at all."

While it was the Mutt Lange Show, Shania had a tremendous amount of input; she was in the studio all day, every day, six days a week. There was no antsy behavior, no disappearing off shopping or hanging around doing her makeup. She sang every pass every time, giving full-on guide vocals to every backing track. He treated her the same as every other musician, except occasionally when they got into arguments over vocal parts.

"I think you ought to sing it like this," said Mutt, to which she might reply, "Yes, but I feel that if the words are more intimate I ought to be more like this." Then they would start what Leim calls this "'Oh honey' thing . . . with Mutt saying, 'Well, honey, I think it ought to be,' or 'Sweetkins, I think it ought to be' and 'Sugar baby, why don't you try it like . . .' Mutt is very demanding at what he wants, but in such a gentlemanly fashion, you can't get mad at him."

The final vocals were all recorded up at ARP Track Productions in St. Anne des Lacs, near Montreal, Quebec. If Shania paints with words and melodies, Mutt paints with sound. He got to work, deconstructing every instrument on every track bar by bar and putting it back again triple-tracked, sonically enhanced. At one level it is a purely artificial construct, but stitched back together and placed in its correct position in that extraordinary mélange that he calls a song, it sounds anything but. Shania's albums crackle with an almost metaphysical energy, just as Michael Jackson's did when Quincy Jones was behind the control panel.

Each melodic hook was accentuated by leaving an infinitesimal space around it and every bass drum beat punched like Mike Tyson. All the vocals, but especially the harmonies, are classic Mutt, multi-layered so that it appears one voice is singing with the force of a choir of angels. He employed the same technique on the strings, stacking fiddles so they sounded both like a fuller, richer solo instrument and a full orchestra. Second-guessing the arrangement is as effective as bottling clouds—one moment there is a soaring pedal steel riff, and when you expect it to come again, he unleashes a guitar solo that would have a Def Leppard fan shaking his mane in approval.

The album was mixed at Le Studio in Morin Heights, Quebec. Tragically, Le Studio's engineer Lynn Peterzell died of a heart attack soon after the record was finished in October 1994. When Mutt finally pronounced the record finished, the Mercury Nashville execs flew in to listen to a playback. As dusk approached, Shania covered up her nervousness in her usual way: She fired up a chainsaw, gathered enough logs, and lit a roaring fire.

The Woman in Me was, and still is, a groundbreaking album. That in itself was not enough. Every musical genre is full of great records that millions do not know exist. Some, like the extraordinary *The Velvet Underground and Nico*, initially reviled and a commercial disaster, hang around long enough to be regarded as among the most influential albums of all time. Country music has long had a habit of ignoring exquisite gems—Guy Clark's almost perfect *Old No. 1* and anything Gram Parsons ever recorded—because they were too different. In 1994, *The Woman in Me* sounded unlike anything else. And Mercury had to sell it.

Internal reaction was not universally euphoric. "I was taken aback," admits John Grady. "I knew it was tremendous music; I didn't know if it would fit. Fortunately I've had a history in the more successful companies I've worked for of having to deal with records that didn't fit." The then head of promotion didn't hear it at all, and suggested to Lewis it needed to be sent back and remixed. Many of his staff were scared to death by it. "We can't understand the record," they whined, "it's too pop, it's so obvious." (In a sense they were right, because when Shania's songs were played on the radio they stood out a mile, popping, fizzing, making other productions sound flat by comparison.) Lewis countered by hiring promo men who had worked pop radio.

Luke was convinced. When he called Alain Levy, the big boss at Polygram, and told him, "I'm going to spend an out of the ordinary amount of money chasing this thing because I believe," Levy, who had liked seeing ten million Billy Ray Cyrus records come out of nowhere and who knew just what Mutt Lange could do, turned him loose. With a release date of February 7, 1995, there wasn't a lot of time to spare. Most of the money went to radio promotion, with a disproportionate (for Nashville) amount on videos and photo sessions. Initially the marketing plan went badly awry.

The first hiccup occurred in Cowboys, a Nashville line-dancing club. At the time, country dance clubs were really happening and the idea was to launch "Any Man of Mine" through the clubs. Luke took a rough mix to the DJ at Cowboys and asked him to play it so he could gauge the reaction. It was a fiasco. "I don't dance—not country dance—so I walked into it cold," he laughs. "The problem is in the way the song is structured. It starts out as a line-dance riff and then it turns into a two-step riff. People started the song doing a line-dance and then it runs into this two-step when you don't have a partner. What a dumb-ass thing. It wouldn't have occurred to me in a hundred years."

It was decided to hold "Any Man" and go with "Whose Bed Have Your Boots Been Under?" "'Boots' was a little more formulaic and it didn't have that 'Pour Some Sugar on Me' guitar riff that made radio programmers crazy." The first video, made in England, featuring a pair of animated boots, was too clever by half. The decision was made to junk it, and instead, Mary convinced Mercury to employ the services of a man who knew how to bring out the best in beautiful women.

As an actor, John Derek enjoyed only fleeting success; as a lover, he had a far better track record, numbering Jane Fonda and Brigitte Bardot among his conquests and Linda Evans and Bo "10" Derek among his wives. Derek was an autocrat who knew what image he wanted to achieve and, like Mutt, he was married to a much younger woman. At their first meeting Derek took one look at Shania and announced, "Somebody get me a knife. I've got to cut that nose off!"

and wanted to back out of the project. Bo, who had bonded with Shania immediately, convinced him to come back on board.

Derek took control, spiriting Shania to California to shoot on his property, where she did some very sexy photo sessions that were used to good effect. He stamped a specific image on the album cover artwork and the Christmas promotional calendar that was sent out to radio stations, retailers, and the media. Mercury also used the shots in an advertisement in *Sports Illustrated*'s college basketball preview issue, which, while it might not have been a traditional country market, certainly raised more than flickers of interest.

John also shot the videos for both "Boots" and "Any Man of Mine." Looking at them, it's hard to know what the fuss was about. "Boots" is set in a diner where Shania sashays around in a backless, clinging burgundy dress, flirting with a bunch of central casting rednecks, who ignore her. These scenes are cut with sequences of her playing a guitar and singing, wearing a sleeveless waistcoat that ends above her midriff. At no point can you see the belly button that was about to become so famous that a comic later quipped it should have its own agent.

"Any Man of Mine" really caught the imagination. The scenes of Shania in a field wearing tight jeans and a blatantly bare midriff were shot separately by director Charley Rendazzo and spliced together with Derek's sequences that showed Shania metamorphosing from cowgirl to society sophisticate. Again, scarcely taboo-shattering . . . but very sexy.

Shania called the shots in terms of what she wanted to wear and how she wanted to be presented physically. "For the country music image, it was definitely different and sexier. I came to Nashville with a certain amount of naïveté," said Shania. Being Canadian, she was more aware that there was life outside country. Back home she had watched MuchMusic, listened to other musical genres, and took all that into account. "I wasn't really aware that I was being that controversial, until people started to say 'Your image is too sexy,' and that I was going to be intimidating to women. I said, 'Are you crazy! Everybody shows their midriff, just relax. I'm young, I want to enjoy that. I'm a woman and I want to enjoy it now, while I can.' I was just lucky that somehow it clicked and it worked."

If Shania knew exactly what she was doing, there was still that risk that CMT might simply ignore her. They tried. Says Lewis, "I never had a moment when I choked and thought, put on some clothes, girl. It did occur to CMT. I hate to bash them, but the truth is they had a committee out there that decided that her videos were . . . not suitable. They can absolutely take no credit for breaking Shania Twain, they were not supportive. Okay, they have been since—but at the beginning it was pulling teeth, one of the biggest pockets of resistance we ever met. It was frustrating; they were playing everything and suddenly went shy on us."

While MTV and VH-1 have had a radical effect on rock and pop music, CMT and TNN have been much less influential on country music sales. "There's a lot of people in this community," agrees Retta Harvey, "who still don't feel that video is a viable form of exposing an artist and getting an artist to sell. I don't think CMT on its own has definitely broken an act. Shania has helped them more than they've helped Shania. She's certainly brought in a hell of a lot more viewers than they had." Videos helped cement Shania's image as somebody new and exciting, but first Mercury had to generate interest.

The key to turning "Boots" into a hit was radio play. Lewis knew that if he didn't get the first record away the whole album could be lost—and maybe his career with it. The six markets that had gone with the first album all played it. It wasn't the first Shania Twain record for those markets, it was the next one. That was enough to get a low chart placing on January 14, 1995, but the twitchy promo men were being proved right, as other major stations were reluctant to follow suit. The record began to lose momentum, the chart position slipped. As it was on the verge of being lost for good, Luke "went to the wall": He pounded on the amenable stations to keep with it. "Go with me on this," he implored them, "long enough to see what reaction we get from the public." They did, and suddenly the public got it, calling in, wanting to hear it . . . and buy it, too. The record climbed to eleven, although there were still radio stations that never played it at all.

"I'm not sure without those six markets it would have made it," admits Lewis. "It is a very unusual thing in country music, as the programmers are in lockstep and they all play the same records every week or they don't play them, and there are very few regional breakouts—in fact, I can't think of one since. 'Boots' was a much bigger hit than anybody remembers. It sold a half million records very quickly on its own. By then we all knew 'Any Man of Mine' was the one that was going to blow it wide open."

At CBS, Luke had seen the way Frank Dileo, the head of promotion, had stacked the singles off *Thriller* (later, he went on to manage Michael Jackson). Before one had reached the top of the charts he started the next one off by releasing it to radio. "Any Man of Mine" debuted on May 13, and after some stress-inducing staggers of its own, climbed all the way to the top, spending twenty weeks in the charts. Long before it was cold, "The Woman in Me" was out, soon followed by "(If You're Not in It for Love) I'm Outta Here!," which also made it to number one. In 1996, "You Win My Love" and then "No One Needs to Know" both went to the very top. Eight singles were released from the album, unheard of in Nashville. This tactic might have pissed off country radio programmers, who liked having to play the same records for months, but it helped to build, then maintain, momentum. "For me that wasn't out of the ordinary at all," says Lewis. "It was pop rules. There are differences in marketing country, but not really; you get records in the stores, get them on the radio, get them exposed in the press, and you put them on the road—which was the one thing we didn't do."

With radio firmly onside, the visual impact of Shania's videos kicked in and the album started to sell by the truckload. Whenever the mold is broken, rumors of skulduggery follow as close behind as shadows. On Music Row, stories circulated that the sales had been boosted by the carpetbaggers (Lange and Lewis) using dirty pop tricks, buying thousands of records and then storing them in a warehouse while the album shot up the charts. "They said Mutt and I went out and bought the first 250,000 records. I wish I knew how to be that manipulative," Lewis grins. "Actually I do know how . . . but not to that scale."

Such sales manipulation is much harder to achieve in America than in Britain and much less common. In the United Kingdom, it has generally been confined to hyping the sales of singles. Prior to 1991, the US album charts were notoriously easy to rig, but the arrival of SoundScan had made it far tougher. To make enough of a chart impact, an album needed fifty thousand added sales (half the original pressing of one hundred thousand), which would have been prohibitively expensive. "The story is unbelievable," says Larry le Blanc, *Billboard*'s Canadian correspondent. "Most record stores in the States don't carry a lot of country music product; most country records are sold through chains like Wal-Mart, which only stock a few copies. If you had one or two chains reporting that they had sold thousands, SoundScan would ask how come it is not selling through Wal-Mart. They would have noticed really quickly and they were looking for that stuff. Secondly, there wouldn't have been enough of a shipment out there for him to buy out."

The sales of hit records generally resemble the screen of an EKG machine, or the stock market on a volatile day, up and down all the time. Blips occur between single releases or TV appearances. What still stuns John Grady was the way *The Woman in Me* displayed a steady rise. The record never went back, it just kept going up all the way until Christmas, when the market got so inflated it had to go down a bit.

"I was asked, 'What was the single most important thing you did in this?' " says Grady. "The answer was: I never ran out of the record. I didn't get in its way. It was its own vehicle, a living being. It didn't sell because of a marketing plan, or anybody's tremendous idea out of here." Lewis, aware that he is being watched over his shoulder by Clive Calder, who knows all about making hit records happen, says succinctly, "If I can take credit for anything in this whole process it's that I didn't fuck it up."

The next step was to hire a band and go on the road. This

threatened some logistical problems. Mary Bailey had her Nashville office in a converted apartment on 20th and Grand, and as the record picked up momentum, her staff increased and became stretched and stressed. Mutt and Shania were living fifteen hundred miles away on his three-thousand-acre estate on Blue Mountain Road outside St. Regis Falls in upper New York state, part recording studio, part guesthouse. To play the songs to Mutt's exacting standards required more than turning up and plugging in. Hiring musicians who lived in New York made it easier for him to supervise rehearsals.

The first musician to answer the small classified ad in Albany's *Metroland* was guitarist David Malachowski, a graduate of Boston's Berklee College of Music who had toured with Janie Fricke and John Michael Montgomery. Mutt and Shania checked him out at a small club gig in Burlington, Vermont, and a few days later he found a message on his answering machine: "Hello, David, this is Mutt Lange calling. I'd like to talk to you about putting a band together . . ."

Malachowski reeled off an impressive list of names: bassist Graham Maby had been at the nucleus of Joe Jackson's band for years, while drummer Gary Burke and Allison Cornell (fiddle, keyboards) were also Jackson veterans; guitarist Shane Fontayne had toured with Lone Justice, Peter Gabriel, and Bruce Springsteen. They passed the first test. "I know Shane, he worked with me on a Bryan Adams album," said Mutt; then he paused. "Why don't you put the band together?"

On June 14, Mutt, who drove up from Michael Bolton's house in Connecticut, and Shania, who flew in from England, arrived at Sweetfish recording studios in Argyle, New York. The band, augmented by Marc Muller (pedal steel) and Phil Skyler (keyboards), began to play. "Mutt sits near the far wall and leans forward, putting his head close to his knees, to listen," writes Malachowski in his Internet diary. "Shania sits facing us, on a stool. We perform 'Any Man of Mine' first and really hammer it. When we finish, Shania gets near hysterical, laughing with delight. 'That was great! Those guys in Nashville, they can't rock out,' at that moment, I knew we had the gig."

Next up was "Boots," which had Shania giggling at the nifty end-
ing, and then "The Woman in Me," where she got serious and delivered "a devastating, emotional take of the song." At the end she said,
"Terrific, great, you play very well together." They chatted for a
while, discussed plans to open a tour, when Shania prophesied, "I'm
never gonna win any awards."

With Shania's old Kirkland Lake colleague Eric Lambier replacing Skyler, and the addition of a couple of Nashville musicians,
Randy Thomas and Dan Shaefer, that was to be the core of her live
musicians for the next eighteen months. Within a fortnight, Shania
was in the United Kingdom, playing a series of small promotional
gigs in London, Manchester, and Glasgow. At the time they made
little impact, but have now reached legendary status with the
media, who claim to have been there in sufficient numbers to fill
an arena. It is indicative of Shania's international ambitions that, at
a time when she was on the cusp of her American breakthrough,
she was prepared to go abroad.

Once back in the States, Shania shuttled between major TV
shows, *The Tonight Show* with Jay Leno and *Live! with Regis and
Kathie Lee*. Plans were discussed for the band to rehearse up at the
studio during the autumn prior to going on tour the following January. On August 30, she and the band performed at a Mercury
showcase for radio program directors at the Ritz Carlton in Laguna
Beach, California. Luke Lewis got up to introduce the act and announced, "Shania has just turned down a lucrative tour with
Wynonna to concentrate on her next album . . ."

Perhaps that was not the most tactful way to break it to the musicians. Had he had any hair left, Ron Baird at CAA would have
torn it out months before. From the moment "Boots" started picking up play, his phone had been ringing, and with each week the
offers increased: club dates, support slots, one-off country fairs. By
the summer he had great offers for Shania to open, from both Neal
McCoy and Wynonna. He told Mary that Wynonna was offering
$15,000 a show. Mary turned it down flat, told him that in a year
she would be earning $100,000. "I've never said 'no' more times in

my life than with Shania Twain," says Baird. "She could have played anywhere, everywhere. We didn't turn down tens of thousands, we turned down millions of dollars. Shania always had in her mind that she didn't want to tour until, when she went up onstage, every song she played was a hit song. She was betting on her career and this was an extraordinarily risky way to do it."

Naturally, her refusal to tour was sneered at by Music Row. This proved she was just a producer's puppet, she couldn't sing live, and probably hadn't sung on the album in the first place. At Mercury they knew differently, for Shania, Mary, and Mutt had told them directly, "Do you want us to work up a tour? Or do you want us to make up another record? Which one?"

That was easy. Record companies do not make money out of touring. It also gave Shania and Mutt the chance to confront a more serious problem: what to do about Mary?

Chapter Seventeen

GOOD-BYE, OLD FRIEND

THE VERY THING that had made Mary such a good manager for Shania was also her greatest weakness: Mary had believed in Shania when she was still Eilleen, when nobody else did. When money was tight and they had to share hotel rooms, it was Mary who slept on the floor so that Shania could get a good night's sleep. It was not a take-take relationship, because Mary gave willingly. Her Achilles's heel was that she loved Shania too much.

"She was like my daughter—I never had one," says Mary. "And I just believed in her so much, and so I just wanted her to be the best. Probably that parent thing, you know: You want to go to the ends of the earth? Count me in, I'm going with you. I just was so proud of her, I loved being with her, taking her somewhere and having her walk into the room, knowing that she's just carried herself and presented herself so well; I was never embarrassed by her."

Most daughters grow up and leave home. She and Shania had argued, but that was normal, natural. She forgot, or chose to forget, that Shania had left her twice before, only to come back when she needed help. But that is what daughters do, so naturally it can be forgiven, if not quite forgotten. Now things were going so well, Mary reasoned, there was no need for Shania to leave again. It was Shania, Mary, Mutt, and now Luke Lewis, the Four Musketeers versus Music Row.

Mary adored Mutt Lange; indeed, she still does. Mutt never preaches, he leads by example. Mary was almost as captivated by his inner strength as Shania. Willingly she became a vegan and began to study the same spiritual path. As sales for *The Woman in Me* built, it quickly became apparent that here was a monster record by an artist with a green record-company boss and an inexperienced manager. The opportunities to blow it grew every day. The person in the weakest position financially and logistically was Mary.

To begin with, she did not have time to notice. The management office on 20th and Grand was soon under telephone siege. When a record explodes out of nowhere, attention focuses squarely on the manager. Yesterday nobody returned her calls. Today every media outlet, every TV and radio station, every promoter, every backstreet T-shirt manufacturer and two-bit hustle merchant hit the phone. Of course, Mercury and CAA were fielding most of the traffic, but in the end every decision that might fill Shania's diary had to be okayed by Mary. Musicians had to be booked and confirmed, their travel arrangements sorted. Mary hired Gillie Crowder—an expat Brit who had worked for concert promoter Harvey Goldsmith on tours for Queen, Elton John, and Bob Dylan—and Julie Kerr to run the Nashville office, and her eldest son Bobby helped out. Up in Toronto, she employed Patty Lou Andrews, the daughter of an old friend, to deal with press and promotion inquiries. The office was so cramped that Mary's bedroom and bathroom were soon invaded by boxes. Gillie could never start her day's work until the phones stopped ringing at 6 P.M.

Although Shania was living in St. Regis Falls, she was not content to let it all happen for her. Every Tuesday morning at nine (Nashville time), no matter where they all were, there was a conference call between Mary, Gillie, Patty Lou, and Shania. The call lasted until every item of importance had been discussed. While Shania had strong opinions on what she should or shouldn't do, she was also perfectly amenable to discussion and could be persuaded to change her mind. Once committed, she never gave less than 100 percent. "Shania is perhaps the most professional and the hardest-working of all the artists I've worked with," says Gillie. "When she was working on the road, she was never demanding, as long as she had her vegan food."

Mary had cash-flow problems. Suddenly she was running an office, paying three salaries, flying between Nashville, Canada, and upstate New York. Money was pouring out with none coming in. Royalties on record sales, songwriter's royalties, and performance fees are accounted twice a year (usually December 31 and June 30) and monies owed may not be paid for up to a further ninety days. Furthermore, much of Shania's first royalty check from Mercury would have been eaten up paying back the advances she had received on the first album. Mary knew that she would have more than enough to cover her overheads by the end of September, but that did not solve the short-term crisis. Traditionally, an artist with sales momentum goes on tour to generate cash flow. Shania was not going on the road.

Partly due to the poverty of her upbringing, Shania could never feel secure until she was financially secure in her own right, no longer reliant on a husband or a manager. (She has admitted that she didn't feel fully comfortable in her relationship with Lange until she had achieved her own financial success. "There was no way I was going to enjoy life beyond my own personal means," she says. "He thought it was ridiculous. But I worked my butt off, and now I'm independent financially.") In fact, because she was married to Mutt, Shania had no money worries and could afford to wait for the royalty check. Mary could not. Bob Kasner had bankrolled the operation for a long time, but now it was placing considerable strain on the family finances.

Mary was inexperienced. She did not know the movers and shakers, the people who can settle problems with a click of their fingers. As far as touring went, she was a tyro. Soon after the CMA Awards in October 1995, Shania told Mary she should consider getting a partner who would concentrate on that side of the business. Mary agreed to try, though Gillie, who did know about it, told her she could learn that side of the business quick enough. Good tour managers are not cheap, but they are always available. Mary looked around but found nobody who she felt could be trusted with Shania's career.

"I know I needed to take it to the next level," says Mary. "I only had so much experience and so many contacts. I did try and find comanagers, they were just not there, and I had a lot of disappointments. No matter where I went to find support it just didn't happen. It was frustrating. I never told Eilleen those things; maybe I should have, but I kept everything inside, because I felt she had enough on her plate trying to make records, she didn't need to hear my problems."

Mary had lost the ability to communicate directly with her artist. "She was halfway around the world, or I was up in Kirkland Lake, and we're trying to make things happen. I was so concentrated that our communication started to fade. So instead of us talking with each other, we ended up talking through others. Once you do that, it's over." In business, as in love, when that spark goes, it is hard to rekindle.

Over at Mercury, Luke Lewis had established a personal relationship with Mutt and Shania independent of Mary (Luke is the only other person to call her "Woody"). "I had a good relationship with Mary Bailey," says Lewis. "I didn't have a beef with her at all, we worked really well together; we had our squabbles, the normal record-company management shit. I felt like Shania did, that as supportive and as big a vision as Mary had, she didn't have the experience. We knew she had to go on the road and that she had to start working international." He pauses and then cuts right to the heart of the matter. "Neither Mary nor I knew how to do either one of those things, that was a flat fact. Somebody had to jump in—I guess one of us had to go." However, it is generally the case in the music business that the head of the record company is both more important and more powerful than the artist's manager.

The tension increased. After Mary heard that Shania had publicly discussed asking a third party to act as her manager, on a salary plus bonus basis, she exploded. She sent a legal letter warning her off such a course of action, alleging "tortious interference" (suggesting that she was trying to make a new contract while already under contract to Mary Bailey Management). As he had acted for both parties, Dick Frank refused to get involved, thereby cutting himself out of some substantial legal fees. By this stage, the only solution was to sit down face-to-face and see whether the situation could be resolved.

In December 1995, Shania fired Mary. Mary will not discuss the circumstances. From that moment Mary was out of the loop. After she was fired, Big Bob Kasner went incandescent and vowed to use every penny he owned if it was needed to get what he thought was owed to her. Mary did not have the heart for a long drawn-out battle. As she says, their relationship "was never about money." To her, it would have been airing the family secrets to the world.

Mary did eventually receive money from the record sales of both *The Woman in Me* and *Come On Over*. She has now reached a full and final financial settlement running into millions of dollars.

At the 1996 Canadian Country Music Awards, Mary was presented with the Manager of the Year award. Mainly out of bravado, she took on a couple of new clients, including Joni Wilson from *A Touch of Broadway*, but her heart was no longer in it. It is difficult to step back to earth when you have ridden a comet. A year later, she quit management altogether. "My life deteriorated," she acknowledges, "because even when I was here [at home], I wasn't here. I lost many things that are really valuable to me." The fallout almost destroyed her marriage. She and Bob split up for a while, but have since been reconciled. Unlike his wife, Bob cannot forgive Shania. At the slightest mention of "Eilleen," his face goes absolutely still, his body rigid, and he retreats inside a bushman's silence that speaks bibles. Mary has found solace in her faith and refuses to dwell on the negatives, rationalizing that while Mutt took something valuable from her, he gave her back something worth much more.

She insists that she now bears Shania no ill will, that it was all for the best. At the time, she admits, she felt hurt, but as she now says, "Perhaps she had more common sense than I had. They had to do it. Sometimes when the party's over, the party's over." Yet when she says those things a shadow of darker memories flickers behind her eyes. It still hurts, because it was so personal. She loved . . . and however much she rationalizes it, she cannot help but feel that she was betrayed.

To Mary, Shania is still the daughter she never had, though she now sees that so many of Shania's strengths—the focus, the determination, the sometimes humorless pursuit of a goal and a ruthlessness in obtaining it—are more usually perceived as male characteristics. "We all have weaknesses," she says, "yet I have no idea what hers are, because I never saw any. She's so very strong in many, many ways. It's the wolf in her. In the end," says Mary, "you live with the choices you make."

Was Shania right to fire Mary? The people now around her obviously thought so. Luke Lewis admits he "wasn't particularly upset," while Ron Baird adds: "It was an appropriate point in her life and career to go to a world-class manager. She needed to have someone who had a perspective that was as big or bigger than hers. There was no way that Mary could have that, because she never had that experience." By December 1995, doubtless in part caused by the steady drip-drip of doubts being poured into Shania's ears, the rot had set in. Other managers have been incorporated into a larger setup, but that would not have worked. Mary cared too much. She was always professional, but to her it was personal. To Shania, it was business first.

Such things are seldom handled well. Shania Twain was thirty years old, she had been trying to make it forever, and now that she had it within her grasp, she was not going to let emotion stand in her way.

As she has always done, Shania moved on. She had too much to do to worry. "Change is normal," she said when asked about Bailey. "I like to go forward. I'm not a stand-still kind of person. I don't get caught in the comfort zone." In the short term, Shania determined to manage herself with the aid of her New York assistant, Sheri

Thorn, with Patty Lou Andrews doing press, all overseen by advice from Mutt and Zomba. It worked fine as far as Mercury was concerned. "I was concerned about her not having a manager for a while," says Lewis, "but as it turned out, it brought the three of us closer together. We started talking even more together, so we never felt out of touch. I was able to translate her concerns to the staff."

Because she was not touring, Shania's videos had taken on an increased importance and so did their budgets. It was the only way for anybody to get a glimpse of what she was like, and how she was as a performer. She took it seriously. "Most artists," says Retta Harvey, "the less time they can spend doing a video the better. They look at it more as an annoyance, and not a means to an end. They're greedier, they'll only go two or three hours into it, where Shania's like, 'I will sit here and I will watch, I want to make sure that everything is done the way we need it to get done.' " It took five hours to fit Shania into her skintight bell-bottom pants for "(If You're Not in It for Love) I'm Outta Here!" During the shoot for "You Win My Love," the crew were all flagging by hour twenty-two. That was the point at which Shania announced, "Let's do this one more little thing, I think it will look really cool," and started to do a series of somersaults, cartwheels, and backflips in front of a gigantic black-and-white checkered flag.

For the third single, "The Woman in Me," Luke Lewis, who had been impressed by Billy Ray's clip shot at the Grand Canyon and need something to placate Polygram's international companies, shocked Retta Harvey by asking her, "Where can we go that is completely distinctive, some place that's larger than life, that you have never seen before in a country video?" It was a rhetorical question, as he then announced, "You go to the pyramids." The shoot was indeed exotic, with Shania filmed in the oldest mosque in Cairo, in an ancient tomb, and riding a horse across the desert "dodging pyramids," wearing a flowing white veil. Despite its lavish appearance, the budget was relatively low—only $150,000—because director Markus Blunder had shot in Egypt before.

The three-day shoot was grueling. In July, the daytime temperatures can reach 120 degrees. Shania had to be up at 3 A.M. so she'd be made-up and ready when dawn broke at 5:30 A.M. Shooting continued all day until the sun set at 9 P.M. Mary Bailey was knocked over by a wild horse and ended up with a badly infected elbow. On set, Shania could not eat any of the food. Every day, the crew had chicken kebabs and she had to make do with plain rice and bottled water. Fortunately, the Indian restaurant in the hotel knew how to do vegetable curries. There were more than a few cultural differences, as Shania wrote in a diary for *Country Weekly*. "All these women were around me. They were in black, I was in white. In Western culture, white is always the sign of innocence. In Egypt, white is considered a flamboyant color, whereas black is a humble color. We did some magnificent scenes with the women. They were wonderful. If my shawl was to come off, or if I took it off for a second, the women would run up to me like mothers and cover my shoulders for me . . . The mystery of the place just got to me. I got choked up for a bit while we were doing a take."

She continued to do showcase gigs, award shows, and TV shows (*The David Letterman Show* twice in six months), using the core of musicians assembled by Dave Malachowski. Her insistence on playing live might not have impressed the folks in Nashville, but at the *Billboard* Music Awards on December 6, 1995, they had Tina Turner swaying and grooving in the aisles. At the American Music Awards in Los Angeles (January 30, 1996), the host, Sinbad, complimented Dave: "You guys are bad, you're the only ones playing live and you're bad!"

By the time Fan Fair 1996 rolled around, Shania was the biggest country star in America. Mindful of how important it was to silence the doubters, the eleven-piece band rehearsed their five-song set at Soundcheck in Nashville. On Tuesday, June 11, Sammy Kershaw introduced Shania and her band. As she was about to lead off into "Any Man of Mine," her earphone monitors packed up and she was unable to hear what any of her musicians were playing. Roadies scurried around trying to sort out the problem but as Fan Fair operates on a tight schedule, with no more than five-minute gaps between acts, Shania realized that she would have to put up or walk off. Quitting was not an option, so she went ahead performing the short set without monitors. It went okay, especially under the circumstances, but it was not the triumph everyone had hoped for.

Videos and TV shows might have put her face and her songs out to a huge audience, but they do not connect with fans in the way personal appearances do. At Fan Fair 1995 (where she gave a short three-song set), the queues for Shania's booth stretched way back. While most artists give up two hours at the most, Shania spent a minimum of four and never cut her line off. Like Garth Brooks, she stayed there until everyone got their moment with her. For disabled fans, she gave extra time; she stood up, walked in front of her table, and addressed them straight, eye to eye, treating them as individuals, not objects of pity. On those days, it was not the fans who caught the edge of her tongue but industry people who believed there was more important flesh to press.

On September 21, 1995, Shania performed "The Woman in Me," backed by the Vancouver Symphony Orchestra, at the opening of General Motors Place, a giant shopping mall. Twenty-five thousand fans went berserk. Seeing that success, Mercury (Luke Lewis gives the credit to John Grady) suggested that she make a personal appearance at the Mall of America in Minneapolis.

It was a calculated gamble; PAs, especially in the middle of winter, can fall flat. Minneapolis was her biggest market. On February 10, 1996, the main atrium was packed out; over twenty thousand came to see Shania. She had not intended to sing, but did a couple of a cappella numbers. The experiment was later repeated at an outdoor mall in Dallas, to over thirty thousand fans. Both times she signed autographs for hours, talked to the fans, and posed for photos with them without ever complaining. Every person who came to the front of the line had her photo taken with Shania by a member of the Mercury staff. That was PR at its purest, reaching directly to the heartland. Such gracious behavior has a long-lasting effect. It helps create loyalty that can last forever.

It was a marketing coup that spread Shania way beyond the

country market, positioning her for a crossover into pop. In 1987, Debbie Gibson had been introduced to the teen market by touring and playing in shopping malls. Her records had then exploded up the pop charts. To launch *Come On Over*, the mall signings were hyped up into Fan Appreciation Days, and Shania went back to Minnesota, Dallas, Toronto, and Calgary. A year later, Jive Records, part of Zomba, followed a similar blueprint when breaking Britney Spears. Were they copying Shania's success? Or had they had input into the idea in the first place?

Shania works like she walks. Fast. She becomes absolutely focused on what she is doing, to the exclusion of all else. People working with her are expected to do the same and if she does not complain, she sees no reason why they should either. Nor does she stop to air-kiss and pass the time of day, for that is wasted time. In an industry where backslapping and brownnosing are essential social graces, such behavior can be perceived as cold and snobbish.

Luke Lewis believes she is misunderstood. "I've never met an artist who worked harder than her. Ever. She never misses a beat, to the extent that some people think she is cold and standoffish, because they get around her when she is hyper-focused. She is not going to stop and pat somebody on the back, especially cohorts. Label people had to get used to the idea that she wasn't going to stop. As a result, some people have the impression she is icy or cold, which is not fair."

By Christmas 1996, *The Woman in Me* had sold over ten million copies, overtaking *Patsy Cline's Greatest Hits* to become the biggest-selling record by a female country singer ever. Shania had also surprised the business by appointing her new manager. Looking after her own affairs was only ever a temporary option. She had been looking for the right professional heavyweight management company for a year. Shania had been courted assiduously by most of the industry's major players, including Bryan Adams's manager, Bruce Allan. (Adams says that at times he wishes he had never helped Mutt meet Shania, as the producer is always too tied up with her records to make time to write with him!) Her choice was a man who had never had any dealings with Nashville. However, Jon Landau did manage Bruce Springsteen, one of the most respected artists in America, and had done so for over twenty years.

Starting out as a journalist, Landau entered music business legend when, in 1974, he penned the line: "I saw rock and roll's future and its name is Bruce Springsteen." He started coproducing Bruce's albums the following year and became his manager officially in 1977. Landau and his business partner, Barbara Carr (a former Columbia record executive who is married to Landau's journalist buddy Dave Marsh), have built up a formidable reputation as serious movers and shakers in the industry. They are artist builders and supporters, not manipulators out for a quick kill. Their experience with Springsteen's heroic touring schedule and the worldwide success of *Born to Run* gave them the international nous and infrastructure Shania needed to get to the next level.

It was Shania who approached Jon Landau Management, probably on the recommendation of Clive Calder. (Zomba had administered Springsteen's song catalog outside the States for some years.) "I approached them because they had international experience, which not a lot of management does, because not a lot of artists are interested in being international. They had maintained success and integrity with a class act," said Shania. "The reason I chose Jon is that he was very receptive to the direction I was already headed. I wasn't interested in somebody who was going to reinvent my career. He was willing to join, as opposed to take over. There was a mutual respect that I appreciated."

For Landau it presented an interesting challenge, taking on an artist who had already sold ten million albums. He likened it to jumping onto "the middle of a fast-moving train." He never dreamed how fast and far the train would go. To start with, Shania needed career guidance in a medium that Mutt Lange could not provide. During 1996, her past had come back to haunt her. Following close in its wake, scenting blood, came the tabloid hounds.

Chapter Eighteen

BAD BLOOD (AND TABLOID HACKS)

LIKE EVERYTHING IN LIFE, stardom has a downside. The longer you're up there, the easier it becomes, but at the beginning it is emotionally exhausting, equal parts exhilaration and fear. The early days of celebrity are also the times of fraud. While the star has all the trappings of celebrity, the money isn't there; they inhabit a film set—it looks wonderful, but there is no substance behind the front. The fear lurks behind the designer shoulder pads, whispering in the ear: "This could all end tomorrow."

Once you become a star, your greatest ally flips overnight and becomes your enemy. Once you had time on your side, now you have none. No time at all, because everyone wants a piece of you. Every TV chat show, every radio DJ, every magazine with a circulation higher than zero demands a piece of your life as if it were their constitutional right. In America, the celebrity culture no longer allows for privacy. Public face in public place equals public property. Success begets jealousy. Overnight success begets a spawn of green-eyed monsters with honey on their lips, poison on their breath, and talons dipped in venom. A new star needs help from people who've walked down the street before and can see where the puddles end and the sewer begins. Shania had none of that. Sure, she had heavy-weight supporters, like her super-rich, super-successful husband and the boss of her record company, but in Nashville they were both

outsiders, too. To Music Row minds they weren't real country people . . . and neither was Shania. To their minds she hadn't paid her
dues, hadn't waited her turn. She had not toured. Knocking about
bars and country fairs when she was scarcely big enough to hold her
guitar did not count. She broke all the rules that had been set up to
keep country pure (and a few people very rich). She didn't live in
town, she didn't hang with and kiss up to the right people, attend
the right functions, she didn't spread the wealth by covering lots of
different songs, she flaunted her body, she was too sexy. (One must
never forget that Nashville is a deeply conservative town; its biggest
industry is not country music but printing bibles.) What really ran-
kled was that Shania had been proved right.

"Mutt and Shania don't pay songwriters here," says Sandy Neese,
then senior vice president of publicity at Mercury. "No matter what
anybody else tells you, that's not popular, because nobody else in
town has a piece of them. They were totally self-sufficient. If you're
part of the Nashville community, you know the songwriters and the
publishers, the producers and all those people, are going to vote for
you. And then she didn't tour right away. You've got to be out there
touring to be Entertainer of the Year, that's part of the total package."

Nashville chose to teach Shania a lesson by ignoring her. Despite the success of *The Woman in Me*, she did not win anything at
the 1995 CMA Awards. In 1996, after having sold nine million
copies, it was the same story. Three nominations and . . . nothing.
No album of the year, not female singer, not even video of the year
as a consolation. (Shania might have revolutionized country video,
but the award went to Junior Brown's "My Wife Thinks You're
Dead.") She finally received her first CMA Award, Entertainer of
the Year, in 1999. She also won the International Award, which for
some reason does not appear on the CMA Awards list. Apparently
the CMA does not believe albums bought in Paris, France, count as
much as those bought in Paris, Texas.

"In a sense, she was never embraced here," says Luke Lewis.
"There is a carpetbagger thing in the South. I came here from California and some people thought I was going to Californicate the

place. I am a bit abrasive and brash and not very good at politicking and we didn't get recognized here, truthfully, until she had won some BMI writer awards, which you earn and they are not political. Finally she wins Entertainer of the Year—thirty million records later. I don't think she was bitter about it, though she and I have laughed about how naïve we were and also how jumpy that we were going to step on a landmine somewhere. We knew we were in a minefield, but we didn't know where any of the mines were—it's that sort of town. I guess we were running so fast we missed most of them."

There is an old industry cliché that runs, "Where there's a hit, there's a writ." In today's celebrity-obsessed world, it has a further twist. "Where there's a hit there'll be a hack digging in the dirt." In America, the real muck-digging is left to tabloid newspapers, and in 1996, Shania was only just starting to blip on the radar of *The National Enquirer*, the *Globe*, and the *Star*. The country press preferred to operate by innuendo. As the Milli Vanilli saga was still fresh in people's minds, that was the best place to start. In 1989, Rob Pilatus and Fabrice Morvan, two pretty-boy disco singers, had enjoyed a worldwide smash with "Girl You Know It's True" and collared the Grammy for Best New Artist. Then their German producer, Frank Farian, revealed that they had never been in his recording studio. The boys were stripped of their awards and cast into outer darkness (Pilatus eventually committed suicide in 1998). Mutt Lange, who was a similar Svengali target, stayed resolutely silent, which fueled the rumors.

"The press," recalls Sandy Neese, "was trying to hint,' . . . well, he's a tremendous producer, she can't sing, she didn't really write these songs, he did,' and bait her into performing. Her whole reason for not performing at that point was she didn't have enough songs to do a full set. She was the number one artist in the format, so it wasn't like she was going to go out and open for somebody so people would stop writing about her. Then it became an issue: 'She's not touring because she can't cut it.' I'm sure there were lots of times when she was really hurt."

One of the most-quoted, and, to be fair, wittiest putdowns, came from Steve Earle (an extremely talented singer/songwriter who all but squandered his career on drugs and booze) when he ad-libbed in an interview: "It doesn't take a rocket scientist to figure it out. She's America's best-paid lap-dancer." Shania had waited and struggled for too long to let such sticks and stones goad her. But the whispering campaign did arouse interest in her past.

On April 5, 1996, her image took a major knock. The unlikely source was the Timmins *Daily Press*, which opened a sensational front-page article with these hard-hitting words: "The *Daily Press* has learnt that Twain has woven a tapestry of half-truths and outright lies in her climb to the top of the country charts." The nub of the story was that Regina Nutbrown, her paternal grandmother, claimed that, since she had got famous, she had ignored her relatives. "All she talks about is this Indian man," Regina told the paper. "But what about her real father? What about us? I wrote about a year ago, but once she started going good, she never wrote. I wish she would. I don't know what's happened to her."

For a small-town newspaper to attack its most famous daughter so openly guaranteed international coverage. The country music press who, star divorces and booze and drug addictions notwithstanding, make a big deal about roots, tradition, and family values, promptly came over all sniffy. It was not that big a deal. Complaints that stars ignore their relatives are as regular as a new moon and about as interesting: There will always be another one along soon. The revelations about her bloodline were more interesting. So Clarence was her biological father, not Jerry, and there was the damaging suggestion that she had lied about having Native blood to advance her career.

The irony, which might have amused Jerry, who had endured enough prejudice in his lifetime, was that while a Native Canadian country singer was exotic news, an Irish Canadian country singer was not. Not telling the world that Jerry was her adoptive father was hardly criminal fraud. The media like things simple. Trying to explain the complexities of her family background to interviewers with the attention span of a sound bite was too difficult. (Most still do not know Clarence is not Jill's father, nor that Darryl is actually Jerry's nephew.) It was no big secret; some of her friends knew, some did not. Children do not run around telling all and sundry they are adopted. They want to belong, not to be different.

Did Shania deliberately pretend to be Native to arouse interest? Nashville had made a meal of her heritage. Yet when she was recording with Harry Hinde, she had infuriated him by refusing to exploit it. With John Kim Bell she was billing herself as a Native singer. Bell knew that Jerry was not her father, but says he was very surprised to learn that she might have no Native blood at all. Ever since the story broke, Shania has maintained a consistent line. Sharon told her the Edwardses had Native blood. Why should she not believe her?

In the final analysis, emotional truth must win over literal truth. As a child, Shania desperately wanted to believe that she was part Native. Sharon did too. Shania once told May Thompson, "I don't know why, but my mother always wanted to be around the Indians." She was five when Jerry came into her life; she had no memory of Clarence, except in the quarrels that stalked her nightmares. Her grandmother Eileen died when she was seven and the only living relative she knew was her Uncle Don. Along came the Twains, who loved her unconditionally, and she loved them back. Small wonder she wanted to belong, to really belong. She loved and admired Jerry. She wanted to be his daughter, if not by blood then by word and by deed. When she had refused to change the Twain name, it was *his* memory she was honoring.

Dick Frank, her former lawyer, put his finger on the crux when he said, "It was very upsetting to her. She looked upon [Jerry] as her father, and she was very proud of her Ojibwe heritage. Her biological father had [left] her mother very early. Eilleen has just drawn a curtain over that part of her life. I think it was terribly painful to have that curtain ripped open. I think she felt that it dishonored her father who raised her and sought to diminish his role as a father."

The controversy also affected the Twains, who had endured a miserable time since Jerry's death. They were just recovering from a double tragedy. Tim Twain had died of leukemia in July 1994. He was only thirty-six. Gerry passed away a year later, diagnosed with cancer but finally succumbing to pneumonia. Attacked in her hometown, the one place she felt secure, Shania went on the offensive, issuing this statement:

I've never had a relationship with my biological father, Clarence Edwards. From about the age of two years old, my mother and Clarence were separated. Soon after, Jerry assumed the role of being our father from that day forward, even though it wasn't until a few years later that my mother and Clarence actually divorced and she and Jerry married. My father Jerry then legally adopted us and to this day remains the only father I have ever known; emotionally or in any other way. He was the only one who was there for me on a daily basis, through thick and through thin, until he died in 1987 in the car accident that also killed my mother.

Although I was briefly introduced to Clarence a couple of times in my teen years, I never knew him growing up. My mother did not deprive us of the knowledge of his existence. She let us know where he lived, what he did for a living, a little about his family background, and that there was some Indian heritage in his family. That's what I was raised to believe and know from her to be true.

I never deliberately avoided contact with the Edwards family, but my father Jerry's parents loved us as though we were their very own grandchildren and we were equally accepted by his other relatives. That's the family we belonged to. It was my Gramma Selina who made my stage clothes when I was a kid. It was my Grandpa Gerry who spent hours with me in the woods teaching me to track rabbits and telling me all his bush stories. It was on the Mattagami reserve that I spent many summer weekends playing with my cousins. Therefore, I never felt the need to seek the love or support of another family, because I had it from the Twains.

I don't know how much Indian blood I actually have in me, but as the adopted daughter of my father Jerry, I became legally registered as fifty percent North American Indian. Being raised by a full-blooded Indian and being part of his family and their culture from a young age is all I've ever known.

That heritage is my heart and my soul, and I'm very proud of it.

Faced with that, the newspaper caved in and issued a front-page retraction, waffling about "a misunderstanding" and finishing off: "the *Daily Press* sincerely regrets any suggestion that Ms. Twain lied."

While the fuss went on and commentators, both white and Native, pontificated, nobody bothered to ask the Ojibwe at Mattagami what they thought. "When the fuss broke, we never questioned her for a minute," says Willis McKay. "I was on the phone to her in the States and I said that there was never any question about her roots. In the days that she was around here, she mingled with everybody and everybody accepted her as a Native person, regardless of whether she was white or not."

Legally, too, Shania was laughing. "I remember we had one problem with immigration when she was coming back in from Canada," says Dick Frank. "We had to go into action through Washington, but happily she is a registered Ojibwe. The Ojibwe nation originally populated both sides of what later became the Canadian/US border. Under our Native American laws, Ojibwe are citizens of both countries. It made it very simple."

That should have been that. But it had opened up the whole can of Chapleau worms. Now the tabloids knew where to go if they needed some dirt on Shania. In 1996, all the juice they needed was being supplied by Mark and Darryl.

The boys had a bad reputation in Huntsville. "They were troublemakers, delinquents, into petty theft," recalls one girl who knew them. "They were basically partyers and while I don't think they would have hurt anybody, they were teenage boys causing a ruckus for something to do." One day, Celia Finley was driving along Main Street heading out of town. "Mark Twain ran over this little puppy. And they both stood there staring at it. I stopped on the other side of the road, got a blanket from my car, and got the puppy onto it and I gave it to them and said 'You go straight to the vet's with this dog.' "

In such a small community, such behavior will not be tolerated for long, no matter who your sister is. On New Year's Eve 1995, the pair were pulled over on suspicion of driving a stolen car and Mark refused to give a breath test. On January 5, they both pleaded guilty to impaired driving and taking a vehicle without consent, were fined, and had their licenses suspended. On May 6, 1996, Mark was in trouble again. He was drinking with his girlfriend at Deerhurst and kicked up a fuss when the bartender refused to serve him any more. The row spilled over into the parking lot, he smashed the window in his girlfriend's car, and when the cops were called he swung his backpack at a policeman and hit him in the face with it. He was charged with assaulting an officer.

Two weeks later, Mark was arrested again, along with his brother and two friends, Darrell Stock and Paul Bartz. At 4:30 on the morning of Monday, May 20, police were called to the Festing Toyota dealership on Centre Street in Huntsville after a neighbor was woken by the noise of the men trying to steal cars. Three vehicles were damaged before the four were caught leaving the area. All four were charged with theft over $5,000 and possession of burglary tools. Darryl, Stock, and Bartz were released on bail on Tuesday and, after a court hearing, given suspended sentences. For Mark, the consequences were far more serious. On June 5, he was sentenced to six months in jail. After his release, the brothers took the hint and left Huntsville.

The media jumped all over the story, which was embarrassing for Shania. While she was livid in private, her public comments have remained consistently sanguine. "I have two naughty younger brothers," she said in 1999. "They are doing okay right now; they have stayed out of trouble. It's not an excuse, but when my parents were killed it completely wrecked them and getting into trouble was part of that."

To Shania, keeping the family together is still as important as it was in November 1987, or further back in the days when the heating was turned off and there was only bread goulash to eat. In private, she worries about the boys, where they are and what they're doing. She tells friends, "Darryl will be Darryl and Mark will be Mark," meaning "It doesn't matter what I do, nothing has changed. They have to learn for themselves, they have to be responsible for their own lives." Darryl has tried her patience many times, but she remains faithful to him, because she hopes that one day he will grow up and become a man.

Another savage attack on Shania came in June 1997 with the publication of Laurence Leamer's book *Three Chords and the Truth*. In it, he suggested that Shania's story was "a brilliant reconstruction . . . a virtual past," that she had made up or exaggerated the poverty of her childhood to give herself a real good country image. Leamer's target was not specifically Shania, for he took on the whole country music industry, raking over bodies and spraying good old-fashioned vitriol over icons like Wynonna, Vince Gill, and Reba McEntire. In the reviews and publicity surrounding the book, Shania was scarcely mentioned. Leamer had fastened on minor inaccuracies and inconsistencies in her interviews and from that determined her whole story was a pack of lies. He was wrong, which went a long way to undermining his whole thesis. Jenny Bohler, Reba McEntire's spokesman, dismissed the book, which never sold well, with "I think a better title would be *Three Chords and Half-Truths.*"

After *Come On Over* went nuclear and Shania crossed over into pop, the tabloid hacks returned to the forest of northern Ontario in force. Chapleau was invaded by journalists from the *Enquirer,* the *Globe,* and *Star* looking for some dirt and offering hard cash for it. Clarence did eventually speak to the *Enquirer,* but refused payment. His comments—compared to those of his relatives—were innocuous, but sounded as if they were forced tabloid-speak. "Shania's my daughter, and I'm very proud of her. But it breaks my heart that she's cut me off. If she would just call me and say, 'I love you, Dad,' that would be priceless to me." Since a photographer staked out his camp and snapped him urinating off the front porch, he has refused to say anything at all. Other members of the family were more forthcoming, especially if they had been bought a few drinks. After years of frustration and hurt festering away, the stories that poured out about Sharon were not kind, but nor did they reflect well upon the Edwards clan—except Clarence.

Goaded into replying by the revelations, Shania stated in interviews that she had only met her father very few times, that he never contributed financially to her upbringing, and that when he tried to call her after Sharon and Jerry were killed he was "inebriated." All true, but to the Edwardses she sounded so unforgiving. The family had their own perspective.

In 1972, Clarence settled down with Shirley Caby, two years his senior. Under Shirley's influence he tried to reestablish contact with his daughters. The initial catalyst was his mother, Regina Nutbrown. "My mother always liked my grandmother," agrees Shania. "She wanted me to know her and so I met her. My grandmother was a really lovely lady but it was her who pulled a fast one and invited Clarence. I didn't know he was coming. She just wanted us to know each other. It was not unreasonable and she was getting a little bit older then. I understood that so I wasn't upset or anything. My mother had never raised us to hate him.

"I met Clarence for the first time that I was old enough to remember when I was thirteen. By the time you are thirteen you are old enough, you know who you are and who you want in your life."

There were other meetings during her teenage years, but the problem was that every time Shania saw him or his family, something went wrong. Basically Sharon and the Edwards clan hated each other. When Eilleen was seventeen, she and Sharon were passing through Chapleau and stayed the night at Desi Edwards's house. Clarence chose to stay away; his elder brother did not. Gordon turned up drunk as a skunk and proceeded to tell Sharon what he thought of the way she had treated his brother. "I said what I had to say to her," he says. "I said, 'I know you like a book, don't bullshit me,' told her that she hated my brother so much because he left her, she'd put poison in the girls' heads. I don't think Eilleen was too impressed with me, probably thought, 'There's another uncle, there's another drunk,' but that's the way it was for me in those days."

"Clarence loved his daughters," insists Lori Edwards. "He wanted to be involved with both of them, but she was so obsessed with him that he wasn't going to. She poisoned them against him. He told me when he was leaving my dad's place, 'Do you know what it feels like to be crazy? You feel like you are wearing a baseball cap and you have that tightness around your brain.' He had that for a long time."

After Sharon and Jerry were killed, Clarence's mother did make some effort to forge a reconciliation. (She was no sweetheart. In 1971, Harold was told by a doctor in Sault Sainte Marie that he would die within six months if he didn't quit drinking. On hearing the news, Regina walked out and moved in with another man, whom she later married. Harold drank himself to death within a few months.) "Her grandmother would come to town once in a while for shopping," says Helene Bolduc, "and she would call Eilleen and say, 'Do you want to meet me for lunch? I'll be in Timmins.' They would have lunch together. I think the grandmother really wanted the father and the daughter to become close and it just wasn't realistic. That happened a couple of times a year, maybe four or five in all."

Encouraged by his mother, Clarence phoned Eilleen every few months. He was reaching out to her with no ulterior motive. The problem was that the only way he could pluck up the courage to call her was to reach for the bottle first. That did not make for much meaningful dialogue. "After my parents died he would call and he would be drunk and that turned me right off," says Shania. "I said to him, 'Please don't call me again if you can't call sober.' I felt a bit bad afterwards because, looking at it from his point of view, he has two daughters who he never knew, he probably has a lot of regrets. Maybe he didn't have the courage to call sober and he wanted to reach out to us. He knew we didn't have parents. He was probably feeling for us. Perhaps I should have been more understanding, but I was just going through too much stress."

"She had a lot of mixed feelings about him," says Helene. "I think at one time she would have liked to get to know him, and she did have a lot of respect for her grandmother. But after all this stuff in the paper, she thought, 'What is happening?' "

Shania's reaction to the stories in the *Daily Press* was natural enough. She considered that Regina, and by implication her father, had betrayed her again. Life was too short and she was too busy to spend time mending fences that appeared irretrievably broken. "The whole thing with the Edwards family is incredible," she says. "I may get my musical talent from that family, but how could they feel abandoned, or whatever words they use, because I never knew them. I met the family a couple of times throughout my life. I've kept a distance ever since and that is the way it is." When Regina died in 1998, she did not acknowledge it in any way, did not attend the funeral or send a card or flowers. Naturally, this incensed the family again.

One catalyst came after Shania was interviewed on *The Oprah Winfrey Show*. Clarence sat drinking in the bar of the Sportsman Hotel, watching. "He was here when she told Oprah her dad was an Ojibwe Indian," says Lori Edwards, who was working behind the bar. "Clarence never said a word but he was weeping. A while later he dropped six pictures of Shania and him on the bar, saying, 'Let her deny this.' "

One of the photographs was of Clarence standing next to Eilleen and Carrie Ann. She is wearing a yellow gown and about to attend her prom night at Pinecrest in 1979. "You see that dress?" said Shirley. "Well, we bought that dress." This tallies with Shania's comment: "The very first time I remember meeting him very briefly was when I was thirteen." Another time Shirley says she and Clarence took the girls clothes shopping and they all went out for a very civilized supper. Sharon offered to put them up for the night, made up a bed in the living room with pillows and blankets. In the middle of the night they were woken up by Sharon attacking them, kicking, punching, and screaming abuse. Shirley, who is not a physically aggressive person, stood up and told her, "You cannot do this to him anymore," and they left the house at four in the morning. Another time, according to Shirley, they took the girls to supper and Eilleen ended up having a major row with her mother, screaming, "Shut your mouth, mind your own business."

The tabloid stories presented Clarence as an innocent party and Sharon as a loony nutcase. Kenny Derasp, who lived with the Twains in Hanmer, recalls matters very differently. "Sharon talked about him a couple of times and had nothing good to say about him. I was there one time when he turned up in town and he called Sharon, wanting to see the girls, and she was really upset. She spoke to the kids, who totally refused to see him, they wanted nothing to do with him. I read the stuff the tabloids printed about Sharon: One said she was a crazy woman, one said she was an alcoholic.

"There is no way that woman could have been an alcoholic. I've tossed a few beers back with Jerry, but Sharon seldom drank at all. There was no alcohol abuse in the family." Smoking was a different matter. "The store was a mile away, and if Jerry was out in the car, I could see her start to get fidgety when she was down to half a pack. She knew it would take fifteen minutes to walk there and twenty to walk back, so she started to get very raggy, scared she was going to be running out. Sharon was really passionate. She was quite excitable, we had a lot of laughs together."

A few years ago at a family Thanksgiving dinner, Clarence got a little tanked. After a couple of drinks he turned to Lori's mother and said, "At least you have your kids." Lori said to him, "Clarence, it is not necessarily all your fault that you don't have them."

Except that in the end it is. Clarence made his choice when he abandoned his family and disappeared for six months. Probably he did contribute more than his daughters ever knew, but at that moment he opted out of their lives. If Eilleen had not grown up to be Shania Twain, perhaps they might have reached an understanding. But because she is a star, every time she does anything, it is another wound, another reminder of how he failed as her father.

He lives thirty miles out of town in his bush camp, living off his railroad pension. He has no phone but he has a generator, a four-wheel-drive, a Skidoo for winter; he hunts and fishes and does not drink so much anymore. He has thrown in the towel and accepted that his daughter wants nothing to do with him. He says of her, "She's written me off. What can I do?" He could have cashed in on her fame, sold his story, but he will not do that, for he doesn't want to torment her any further. In his way, he is an honorable man.

When Timmins held its Shania Twain Day in 1996, he and Shirley attended, staying right at the back so she did not have to see him. When other members of the family tried to make him go and say hello, he refused to move. All he said was, "She knows who I am."

Chapter Nineteen

COME ON OVER ... AND OVER AGAIN

SHANIA HAD BEEN WORKING on the songs for her third album for years. In early 1996, she was playing early versions of "Rock This Country!" and "Black Eyes, Blue Tears" to Sandy Neese. She wrote the words to "You've Got a Way" upstairs in Michael Bolton's house in New Jersey, when Mutt was working with the crooner back in 1994.

Once she started working with Mutt, Shania had to learn a new means of writing. He was as interested in her half-formed snatches of melody and phrase as he was in complete songs like "When," a clever reworking of old clichés into a new hit that was composed while driving in the car with Mutt. By the time they reached their destination two hours later, the job was done.

Shania has refined her techniques over the years. Everywhere she goes, she carries a notebook and usually a small tape machine or minidisc recorder to sing down snatches of melody ideas. "We write everywhere," she says. "When we're driving to the grocery store we write. Sometimes I come up with a melody when we're in the car and if I didn't bring the tape deck, I have to sing it all the way home so I don't forget it. When I get home I run up to the tape deck to record it." Her notebook is full of jottings, a word or a phrase that stuck in her memory the moment it was uttered. "It's the way she does it," says Helene Bolduc. "When people are talking, she's always observing and listening and trying to pick up on something to write a song. She's always scribbling away. And when she's ready to write songs, she'll get ideas from the book or maybe she can pick up a title from it."

The lyrics on *Come On Over* were clever and sassy, managing to sound more intimate than they really are. They had moved on from the previous album and a long way from the standard country formula. "It's basically my personality coming out in my lyrics," says Shania. "My husband is partly responsible for that, he encourages it in me. I haven't always been brave enough to say some of the things I've said through my songs. I'll show him a song and he'll say, 'You've got to say it like it is. Be yourself. So come up with all these lyrics that are fun and independent.'

"Writing's like coloring. Kids like to color. They don't have a reason to color—they just like it. They have no inhibitions. They are totally open to being creative. That's how I feel about songwriting. It's a chance to just create without inhibitions." Shania's writing is much like her personality she writes as she speaks. When she first wrote songs, the process was an escape in itself; part of her did not care if nobody ever heard them. "I never wanted anyone to hear things unfinished," she recalled. "My mother used to try so hard to catch me songwriting and I would just get so mad at her. I'd take my guitar and I'd go write out in the bush somewhere. That's the way I was.

"I'm not really sure why I was so guarded about that sort of thing. Even today when I warm up vocally I have to make sure there's nobody around or I just cannot relax, I can't do it. I've always had a real shyness and lack of confidence in myself musically and it's very strange, that. I mean, when it comes to stage, I've learned to jump into another skin, but when it comes to something intimate like to just sit down and sing something to someone, it's very awkward."

Lyrically and thematically, Shania and Mutt are united in that they are determined to accentuate the positive. Just drawing on Shania's personal history would provide enough material to drown a listener in their own tears, but even her most heartfelt songs, like

"God Bless the Child" and "Send It with Love," do not strip her soul naked, lay her past out on the train tracks, the way Alanis Morissette's songs do. Such songs do exist in Shania's vaults, but that is where she intends them to stay, unheard even by her husband, which may be a pity. "There are some things I won't want to share," she says. "I'm not that dramatic, I don't feel the need to communicate my innermost feelings—and people wouldn't get it, so what's the point? I only want to release music that people relate to. I write a lot of music I don't share, for the same reason people have diaries. It's not a creative thing. It's therapeutic."

Just because she is married to Mutt does not make it any easier to pitch song ideas. He is always so busy that timing is everything. "He has his own projects and he's not always with me. Actually he's not with me that often," she says. "We have to be together for more than one week to really get writing. It's impossible not to see each other for a whole month then get together for five or six days and expect to write anything. We're together and we don't have to plan when we are going to write. We write best when we are sitting around relaxed and almost bored. Then we'll start. It's quite fun. It's relaxed, there's nothing contrived and it's really natural. If anything, when you know each other so well, there are fewer inhibitions, because I would be afraid to reveal so much to someone else.

"Our writing styles complement each other. We both come from different places. Lyrically we think differently enough to make it interesting. He's the type of guy who almost never puts the guitar down. He's always got it on him, he walks around with it. He's great on the guitar and while I write on the guitar as well, I'm not a great player. The up-tempo ones come from him most of the time, but we bank our ideas. When he's writing music, I'll ask him, 'Who's that for?' If it's not for somebody specific I might say, 'I like that, maybe we should do it on our next album.' If it's for somebody specific I'll let it be."

As with its predecessor, the song titles on *Come On Over* were snappy captions, taglines, and manifestos in their own right. Exclamation marks were scattered like confetti over "Whatever You Do!

Don't!" and "Man! I Feel Like a Woman!," while the bracketed titles returned in "I'm Holdin' on to Love (To Save My Life)" and "Don't Be Stupid (You Know I Love You)." The "(You Know I Love You)" part of the title was added later by Mutt, a neat twist turning reprimand into reassurance. Such puns and gentle double entendres have long been part of the Lange repertoire—Bryan Adams's "The Only Thing I Like on You Is Me" is an earlier example. "He was always the master of the double entendre; if ever there is some kind of sexual ambiguity in the lyric, it's down to Mutt," says Ralph Simon, who believes his lyrical influence is much underrated.

The original title of "Love Gets Me Every Time" was "Gol' Darn Gone and Done It" which cracked Mutt up when he first heard it. It was changed because the record company were worried that radio DJs would trip up pronouncing the tongue-twisting words. At times, the songs come perilously close to carbon dating themselves. "I'm Holdin' on to Love" is packed full of knowing references to psychics, the Internet, Dr. Ruth, and psychiatrists, while "That Don't Impress Me Much," with its famous nod to Brad Pitt, loses its impact if you don't find the Hollywood star du jour sexy in the first place. The words to "You're Still the One" are autobiographical, an oblique look at her relationship with Mutt and "the nice feeling that we've made it against all odds." "If You Wanna Touch Her, Ask!" and "Black Eyes, Blue Tears" are as close as Shania ever gets to overt feminist statements. The former is about respecting women's personal space and is a definitive slap in the face at gropers—something she had personal experience with back at school. "Black Eyes" issues a manifesto on domestic abuse less dramatic than Garth Brooks's "The Thunder Rolls," although cynics might argue about the merits of or hidden meanings behind the words "I'd rather die standing than live on my knees, begging please . . ."

When the time came to record, Shania and Mutt resolved to take their pop-country to its fullest extent. Most country albums are around the twelve-song, forty-minute mark. They determined to record sixteen songs with nearly an hour of music. "When we decided to put the band together," says Paul Leim, who was appointed session leader, "Mutt phoned and played every song for me over the phone, just him singing and playing guitar. It took most of the evening. He called back about an hour later and started talking about players, asked me about this one and that one. Then he called me back and told me who he wanted."

Joe Chemay, who had played with the Beach Boys, Pink Floyd, and Leon Russell, took over bass duties, while the guitar parts were divided up between Biff Watson, Dann Huff, and Brent Mason. Pedal steel duties were split between John Hughey, Paul Franklin, and Bruce Bouton, while fiddlers Rob Hajacos and Joe Spivey were augmented by Larry Franklin and Stuart Duncan.

For the sessions at Masterfonics Tracking Room in Nashville, Mutt had even more specific ideas on how he wished the songs to sound. This time there were no budgetary restraints and he determined the record would take as long as he thought necessary. "On the first record he wasn't that specific, because he felt under a time constraint," says Leim. "In my opinion, it's a little bit more Nashville, you can hear the players contributing a little more. He said it was frustrating to him to have to finish it so fast, but I love that album, it really sounds like what we cut. The next one obviously sounds like what we cut, but he took it to another level of perfection . . . But once again, the proof was in the pudding; there's a fine line between perfection and soulfulness, which is what he tries to find. Mutt brought a whole new level of professionalism and expertise to this town."

Once again, Shania was in the studio adding her vocals to every pass, every take on the backing tracks. One day, Mercury had scheduled some interviews, and Shania was really pissed off that she had to do them while the band was recording. She came back into the session and apologized, "I hate it when they schedule something like that when I'm trying to work." She hated it because it interfered with the creative process and she wanted to be part of that.

"Mutt thinks more along the line of production than I do," she says. "When we're writing a song, we might throw ideas out. I might say, 'This would be great with a fiddle,' or he will say, 'This is the type of guitar sound we should go for on this song.' We'll talk through stuff like that during the songwriting process, but it isn't until you get in the studio that you start experimenting with it. You don't always know what your best points are and what your weak points are. It's hard for a singer to be objective about herself. A good producer knows what those elements are. I know what sound I want, but he's the producer. I don't go into the studio to tweak the guitar sound for ten hours. I can't even be interested in that, but I can tell him creatively what I want."

There is a trick with empty plastic bottles where you hold it behind your neck, tilt your head to one side, and then pull hard on the bottle, which cracks, sounding like you have broken your neck. One session, Dann Huff was out in the hall drinking from a plastic bottle of Evian water and decided to treat the film crew chronicling the recording process to his performance. Dann sat just behind Mutt in camera shot. As he started massaging his neck, Leim called, "Dann, what's wrong with your neck?" Mutt looked around as Dann replied, "I don't know." Crack! While the sound was more of a dull crunch, it got a big laugh from everybody. A few moments later, Mutt, who had been bursting to speak, announced, "You know, if that had had a little more highs on it, it would have sounded more like you were really popping your neck." Paul laughed, "Listen, he's producing the joke." Mutt went bright red to increased laughter.

For the musicians, the routine was the same: sixteen tracks, sixteen days, starting at 10 A.M. and finishing whenever. "I was aware of Mutt, but I had never worked with him," laughs Joe Chemay. "I didn't know that everything I had heard was actually true. He's such a perfectionist and likes to go over it so many times. But after working with him, I realize why he does that. He's working out the arrangement the whole day, he is concerned with perfection, but that's his method of getting every note exactly the way he wants it.

"It wasn't hard at all. Sometimes it can be when you have somebody making you play a certain way, but Mutt is such a gentleman that I was happy to do whatever he asked. He knows exactly what he wants. Not by the brand of guitar, but by sound. When he put the call out, he just said bring everything you have. I have seven or eight basses that travel with me in a trunk, and we went through and listened to all of them. At the beginning of each song, if the one I picked didn't sound exactly the way he wanted, he'd ask to try a different one."

Mutt did let the musicians add their own touches. He knew that he wanted Joe to play fretless bass on "You've Got a Way," but other than that he let him have his head. "We cut that all day with just a trio," says Chemay, "just drums, bass, and acoustic guitar. The fretless bass allowed me to slide and make gradual note and pitch changes. I had quite a lot of input on that song.

"Mutt's arrangements separate all the instruments nicely; the song will play along and there will be a steel part, and at that point everything drops away from it. It's not clashing with anything else. It sounds like you can mix it with a yardstick, push everything up, and instruments would pop in at the right times without actually having to mix them."

In fact, it is the mixing process where Mutt's record budgets soar, when he insists that that separation Chemay talks about is absolute. The biggest sonic change in the recording process on *Come On Over* was in Mutt's use of Pro Tools, a computer program that enabled him to bring his perpetual search for perfection one step closer. If the advent of digital recording technology and computerized mixing desks changed the way records were made, Pro Tools changed the way songs were edited.

In the analog days, when everything was recorded on magnetic tape, moving a guitar riff to another part of the song was laborious; it had to be rerecorded from the master tape onto half-inch tape and then "spun in," literally cut into position by hand. It was so hard to get absolutely right that generally it was quicker to get the musician back in, except that a "perfect moment" cannot always be recreated to order. Using Pro Tools, the only limitations were the size of the hard drive and the extent of the producer's patience. With Mutt, patience has never been an issue.

Pro Tools is a software program that edits songs the way a word-processing program does words. Chunks of music ranging in size from a full string section to a half note on the hi-hat can be cut or copied and then pasted wherever the producer wants. If the bass guitar and the bass drum were absolutely together for nine notes, but out by a millisecond on the tenth, the mistake can be fixed. Once the producer has the performance he wants, he can move it half note by half note until it is precisely the way it should be. And in the exact part of the song it should be. Vocals, too, can be differentiated, fixed differently, backing vocals enhanced again and again until they sound like choirs of angels; a note that's a touch flat can be tweaked, but the better the original recording, the less obvious the tweak. Mutt's production on *Come On Over* was cutting-edge, and the credit "All Programming, Pro Tools, Sequencing & Editing and that extra Swedish Swing: The Excellent Olle Romo" says it all.

However, Hal aside, computers have no soul. While Pro Tools can varnish the sound, it still cannot turn wood into platinum. In the end, it comes back to moments of magic; the original song and the playing still have to be there. At the base of all Mutt's best work, for all his nit-picking, lies soul.

The album's full-scale romantic ballad was "From This Moment On." The genesis of the song was anything but romantic. Shania was curled up on the sofa while Mutt was busy watching Inter Milan playing soccer on the satellite channel. Shania started scribbling away and then disappeared into the kitchen to grab her guitar and finish the job. She never did find out who won, but she came back with a powerhouse ballad she thought perfect for Celine Dion. As the pair developed the song, they realized it worked best as a duet. Shania's first choice for a partner was Elton John. Instead of bringing in an established country superstar, they chose Bryan White, a twenty-two-year-old from West Virginia, who had been making waves without cracking the top echelon.

White leaped at the opportunity. He traveled up to the Langes' home in New York. "I'd never actually collaborated, as far as a duet, with anybody before," he said, "so it became a lot of fun. They let me do exactly what I wanted to do, and I think we blended real well together. I got to work out all kinds of different arrangement things with them. I say 'them' a lot because I think of it as not only working with Shania but also with Mutt, who's so much a part of her sound. They were always both there. Basically, a lot of her [vocal] part was already down when I arrived. That meant I, mostly, did my part to her track because she had already finished. Vocally, it was extremely challenging. That's what made it so interesting and fun."

Shania later described Bryan as having "the best male voice in country music. Beyond country music! He's an excellent singer. So he needed to be on this record, because the song soars. It demands that. It demands dynamics." Bryan's is the only vocal on the album not sung by Shania or Mutt.

When it came time to promote the album, the success of her Fan Appreciation days encouraged Shania to repeat the experience. On November 4, 1997, she returned to the Mall of America. The lines started forming at 6:30 A.M. and twenty thousand fans turned up to welcome her back. On November 9, she took over Santa Claus's North Pole area at the Southcentre Mall in Calgary, Alberta, the heartland of Canadian country music. Twenty-seven thousand people showed up to see the singer, who, dressed in black pants, matching crop-shirt baring her belly button, and a baby blue jacket, did not hide behind security. When she was asked to wave to some fans not in the autograph line, she marched to the front of the stage and climbed on top of a speaker. Several times she walked into the crowd to greet a fan in a wheelchair, she picked up babies like an aspiring presidential candidate, hugged children, and posed for photos. When the scheduled end of the autograph session approached with thousands of fans still in line, Shania—who did not take a single break—insisted on staying until everyone got their autograph.

The marketing was carried out very differently in the United States and the rest of the world. While Europe went straight for the pop market, America chose to break *Come On Over* out of country and then cross over. "Love Gets Me Every Time" roared to the top of the country charts, quickly followed by "Don't Be Stupid," which made it into the Top 10. Mercury then stacked a series of album tracks one after the other. By Christmas, some country stations were playing fifteen songs off the album.

The crossover single was always intended to be the third release, "You're Still the One." It took off like a scalded cat. At one point her record was being played on five different radio formats: Country, Regular Adult Contemporary, Hot Adult Contemporary, Pop, and CHR (Contemporary Hit Radio). Some of the country stations got very pissy; Shania was hot and they wanted to be the only wavelength in town playing her records.

"All of a sudden they wanted to own her, wanted to be the only one that's bringing you Shania Twain," says John Grady. "The record came out of Nashville, on a Nashville label, so the country stations got very proprietary. Suddenly we were fighting a war at radio, and they made threats about her music, they made threats about all of our music."

Taking Shania off the playlist would have been cutting off their noses, but boycotting less popular Mercury products could have had serious consequences for the label. Lewis and Grady held their nerve and stuck to their position as the record raced to the top of every chart available. Once the record had crossed over, there was little country radio could do except keep on playing it. Eventually, there were to be nine singles released off *Come On Over* and the album sold over twenty million copies in the United States. (Technically, there were ten singles released—"I'm Holdin' on to Love" was released to radio stations without any video or promotion whatsoever and was not available to music buyers. Mercury did this so that Shania could tie Janet Jackson's record of ten tracks released as singles.) In May 1998, Polygram sold out to Universal. It made no difference to the album, which kept on selling. Mutt and Shania did have a long chat with the new big boss, Doug Morris, and explained that they were happy with Mercury Nashville, who continued to work the record.

From the outset, Mercury knew video was going to be an essential part of that crossover. The country feel was dumped from the beginning as Shania was determined to go glamorous, whether it was classical sophistication ("From This Moment On"), flirting with half-naked hunks in moody black and white ("You're Still the One"), or playing the cabaret decadent in top hat and gloves ("Man! I Feel Like a Woman!").

"In the early days she always had a say in how she looked, in terms of clothing and hairstyle and makeup," says Retta Harvey. "And it just got progressively more so, because she knew who she was, and how she wanted to be presented as a performer. Now when we do videos, she's pretty much running the show, she's figuring out who she wants. She's calling the directors, she's dealing with the ideas with them directly, and I'm basically here to make sure it's all taken care of, financially and contractually. I handle all the nightmare phone calls."

The average video budget was $350–400,000. "You're Still the One" was the most expensive. It was shot in Malibu, and bad weather required an extra day's shooting, which kicked the budget over the half million mark. Half the cost of each video is recoupable against her royalties; the other 50 percent is considered a company marketing expense.

"Shania knows that half of it is her money, she wants to get it right, and she's a perfectionist, so she's going to do it till it's done. She's a trouper. We've had times where we've shot twenty-two, twenty-three hours, because she wants to make sure it's done properly." The killer video was "That Don't Impress Me Much," where Shania, wearing a somewhat improbable fake leopardskin ensemble, hitches across the Mojave desert, turning down a series of lifts from increasingly more gorgeous guys riding Harleys, Jeeps, and stallions. It was a camp classic that programmers, VJs, and viewers adored. The work of a woman who knew how to exploit the medium to the full.

That only left Shania two worlds to conquer. The stage . . . and the rest of the planet.

Chapter Twenty

ON THE ROAD (AT LAST)

SHANIA TWAIN'S COME ON OVER TOUR began at the Sudbury Community Arena on Friday May 29, 1998. The day before, when everyone else was worrying themselves into a frenzy, Shania drove out to Hanmer. She stopped by Proulx Court, took a stroll along the trail she once walked to go skating on Onwatin Lake, and on a whim dropped in on her old school, Redwood Acres. It was lunchtime and she happily chatted to the stunned kids and had her photograph taken.

The night of the show, Shania was the calmest person backstage. She went through a meet and greet ritual, shaking hands with contest winners and well-wishers, and found time to talk with her old friends in her dressing room. On the second night, Lynn Bond, who had come to see her backstage, managed to lose her tickets on her way back to her seat. During the show Shania announced, "Lynn, did you find your seat?" Despite all the palaver, she had taken in the information that her childhood friend was in a state.

In the minds of the media and the Nashville music industry, Shania's refusal to go on the road had taken on a ridiculous significance. She had always known that she could deliver live, but being Shania she had left nothing to chance. Failure was not an option. To Shania, record sales were just numbers, not personal like the Fan Appreciation days. "I haven't had the opportunity to feel the audi-

ence's response," she said. "There's a void for me and I want to see
people respond to my music, live. Just to get out there and just, I
don't know, vent. Just get out there and physically put myself into
my music . . . I can't wait for it."

Once she had made the decision not to go out until she could
headline, Shania started formulating the plans for her stage show.
She drew on everything she had learned. The big Pink Floyd and
Rush shows she had loved as a teenager, the pure showbiz Vegas
glitz that Deerhurst had hinted at, the touches of intimacy that
were so important to a country audience. Aware that if she used
too many hydraulic sets and special effects the critics would once
again accuse her of hiding behind technology, she resolved to focus
on "lights, sound, and performance."

In 1996, on a promotional trip to New York, she described her
show to Sandy Neese, telling her, "I don't want it to be about special
effects. I want it to be a big party, I want the audience to be as involved in it, have as much fun as we are onstage, I want a band that's
energetic and works as hard as I do. I want to do something for the
hungry in every city. I want to bring on the local choir, I want to
bring somebody up from the audience who can sing . . . if somebody
had given me a chance like that to get up onstage and sing when I
was a kid . . . well, I'm going to do that."

Just as she does with her videos, Shania came up with the basic
concepts for the show and then found the best men to sculpt them
in reality. Jon Landau, who loves to get involved in conceptual
planning, was an essential sounding board. Along with Jon came
another Springsteen veteran, tour director George Travis. Travis's
last three projects had been world tours for Bruce, Madonna, and
Mariah Carey, representing a wide cross-section of diva demands,
complex staging, and sheer stamina. "George is a remarkable fellow," says Ron Baird. "His whole job was to translate into reality her
visions, desires, and direction, and sometimes to tell her, 'There's no
way to do that.' I think he did a spectacular job." Shania spared no
expense and gave him carte blanche to hire the best, most experienced people. The show used the very latest technology, revolving

treadmills; the video screen was a prototype built in China, all state-of-the-art equipment. She and the band might have been big-stage virgins, but the guys behind the scenes knew how to make the Pope rock.

In today's marketplace, the most successful concert tours are no longer just about the music. They have to be an event, a spectacle, part Broadway show, part theme-park ride, a combination of high energy and effects that assaults the eyes as well as the ears. However, while constant touring is an integral part of country music, the live shows have remained traditional, visually as dull as dishwater—grizzled old cowpoke in hat, jeans, and cowboy boots stands still and plays dang well. Shania was determined that her live band break the mold.

The trick was to keep the country sound, but present it as if it was something new. The players had to be accomplished, versatile musicians capable of playing the complex song arrangements, but also had to look young, cool, and funky. "I can't have anyone in the band who doesn't have my energy," said Shania, explaining her choices. "I don't want people who have been on the road for years and are just doing it in order to do it. And I like a clean band. I don't like drugs. I don't like alcohol. I like to have clean-living people around me."

After he had finished remixing *Come On Over* for Europe, and Shania took off to promote it, Mutt took on the role of musical director. He only kept two musicians from the *Woman in Me* days: pedal steel guitarist Marc Muller and fiddle player Allison Cornell. From Nashville's young scene he recruited guitarist Brent (B. B.) Barcus and drummer J. D. Blair. Blair was a six-foot-tall black guy in wraparound shades and dreadlocks who looked like he had stepped off a street corner in Compton. His résumé was equally impressive, mixing up funk with Bootsy Collins, gospel with Take 6, Lyle Lovett's Large Band, and Shelby Lynne's R&B-flavored country. There were two Australian expats who had fetched up in Tennessee: guitarist Randall Waller, the joker in the pack, and bassist Andy Cichon, once a member of Oz hard rockers Rose Tattoo.

By late January 1998, Mutt's attempts to find a keyboard player who could double on percussion and accordion and sing high had floundered. B.B. recommended Hardy Hemphill, with whom he had played behind Steven Curtis Chapman. Hardy was cooking dinner at home when he had a call suggesting he learn "You're Still the One" fast and get out to Los Angeles even quicker. After borrowing a friend's CD and spending an intensive day rehearsing, he was invited to play with Shania on Jay Leno's Super Bowl show two days later. Fiddler Cory Churko, a native of Moose Jaw, Saskatchewan, who also played guitar, mandolin, keyboards, and percussion and sang, quit his job as a computer animator to enlist.

The final recruit on fiddle was Roddy Chiong. In February 1998, Chiong, who also acts and had appeared as a Chinese hitman in Mel Gibson's violent thriller *Payback*, was at loose ends when he got a message to call Brent Barcus. Roddy was not too enthused when B.B. talked about a possible country gig he had, saying, "Do they know that I'm an Asian guy with long hair? I don't like to play fiddle music too much. More rock kind of stuff." When the name Shania Twain came up, he blanked it. Something nagged at him all night, so the next morning he looked her name up on the Internet. Minutes later he was back on the phone to Brent. Then he rushed out, bought two of Shania's albums, and spent the next two weeks practicing the songs.

In March, Roddy flew to Albany, where George Travis picked him up for the three-hour drive to the studio in St. Regis Falls. "When we arrived at the very large house," writes Chiong on his website, "I said hello to everyone and we started playing right away. I almost didn't have time to be nervous. There was a very pleasant man at the front of the room telling us what to do and he was obviously the leader. I didn't know who he was—which ended up working to my advantage because it was Mutt Lange, Shania's husband. The first song we played was 'Don't Be Stupid.' This was fine by me, because I had practiced that one the most. But I was in for a surprise—the version that we were going to play was a new version called the 'international' version, which would require me to relearn the song in a slightly different way. Slightly enough to mess up my whole audition (so I thought)! Incredibly, the power went out and nothing was working, so everybody took a thirty-minute break—just enough time for me to figure out the new parts! It went smoothly, and we continued to play most of the songs from the album.

"My playing seemed to be up to what they were looking for, and next Shania wanted to know if I could sing. We were just about to get started on that, but something in me felt like I wasn't quite ready and I needed some time to warm up, so I asked if I could have five minutes. Incredibly again, a one-hour lunch break ended up being called! There was no way that I was going to pig out on lunch and then try to sing. So, I went into the exercise room, jumped on the stationary bike and did some easy pedaling while warming up my voice and learning the harmony parts to the song 'No One Needs to Know.' Well, that one hour did the trick because when Shania and I got together, my voice was there where it needed to be."

Chiong was hired. His first gig was the *Divas Live* show on VH-1, after which the band settled down to five weeks of intensive show rehearsals in Lake Placid. Apart from J.D., all of the musicians wore microphone headsets, allowing them the freedom to roam the stage while re-creating the complex vocal harmonies on the albums. For Mutt, the sound was everything. Early in rehearsals it became apparent that the complexities of his arrangements made mixing the front-of-house sound too much for one man.

"Due to the sheer number of inputs and the fact that we are trying to duplicate the record mixes as close as we can, it was decided that we needed another sound engineer," explained John Kerns, another Springsteen alumnus, the engineer who started the tour. "The show is pretty hectic because there are so many cues—about fifteen to twenty per song for each of us." His coengineer was Nigel Green, who has mixed a large amount of Mutt's studio work. Green concentrated on Shania's vocals, while the second engineer provided a series of sub-mixes that were then placed in and out of the overall balance. Despite press stories that he was attending the World Cup finals in France, Mutt was omnipresent in the first days of the tour, adding little tweaks, minuscule touches on faders in a series of last-minute adjustments. Once it was up and running to his satisfaction, Mutt left the tour. There are too many variables in live shows for his comfort.

After a month, Shania invited Ron Baird, Luke Lewis, and other key Nashville personnel up to Lake Placid. Ron, who had had the hottest act in country on his books for six years and not earned a penny, was nervous. "I was curious," he says. "I didn't know how good it was going to be. She did a dress rehearsal for twenty people in this arena, and it was fantastic, so much better than I could have ever hoped for. In thirty years I've seen thousands of shows, but clearly from the very beginning this was one of the very best shows I've ever seen."

The first casualty of playing to an audience of thirty thousand is intimacy. The first fifty rows have a great time, but to those at the back, up close to heaven, the figures leaping around the stage might as well be matchstick men cavorting in hell, while the sound in the worst aircraft hangars can be better in the parking lot. Giant video screens and Mutt's painstaking rehearsals solved some of those problems, but not the physical one. Fans come to see live shows because they want to—or imagine they might be able to—touch the star.

During *A Touch of Broadway*, when Shania had entered the hall from the back of the audience, the effect was always electric. On tour, as the band struck up the opening chords of "Man! I Feel Like a Woman," she was silhouetted against a waterfall of tumbling fireworks, borne to the stage on a platform, a queen sitting on her throne, but a queen who reached out to touch her subjects as she passed. Some nights she walked through the crowd, or leaned down off the runway signing autographs as she sang, collecting flowers and gifts, acknowledging the giver without missing a beat. Before the third number, "You Win My Love," she stood behind a giant yellow spotlight and swung it into the audience, eventually focusing on the very worst row of seats in the auditorium. The folks caught in the beam were then invited down to take new seats in the front row. It was a trick Garth Brooks had used, but its effect was the same—she won their love. At other predetermined points throughout the concert, Shania invited little kids or fans up to sing with her—something that did not always work musically. The intimacy of watching her face in close-up on the big screen was magnified, as one could see how her gaze rose and fell, focusing once in a while on a particular person, accompanying a shy smile with a tiny wave of the fingers.

The show blurred the country boundaries from the start. Shania wore tight outfits, revealing her world-famous midriff for at least half the set, tirelessly working the stage from side to side, from back to front. For the quick changes before "Black Eyes, Blue Tears" and "From This Moment On," Helene was waiting in a booth just off the side of the stage. "We had it all down pat," she says, "because we had a minute and twenty-eight seconds to do it." The musicians all wore skintight T-shirts or vests—except the "Groove Regulator," J. D. Blair, in his outsize headphones and ski goggles—displaying buff muscles, tight buns, and firm abs, not a paunch or a piece of denim in sight. Musically, the show bore as much relationship to country music as the Police did to reggae: The instruments were familiar, but the groove was pure pop. The final number, "Rock This Country," did Def Leppard proud, complete with guitar posturing and pyros going off in all directions.

At the climax of Marc Muller's juddering lap steel solo on "(If You're Not in It for Love) I'm Outta Here!," Shania stood on top of a giant bass drum and with a flash of smoke disappeared down it. Moments later, she appeared in the middle of the auditorium, being carried back through the crowds to finish the song. Michael Jackson employed a similar magic stunt on his Bad Tour and the reaction from the crowd was always the same—how did she do that?

Away from performances, Shania's relationship with her musicians was friendly but distant. "Before every show we would do a vocal warm-up," recalls Marc Muller, "usually the gospel vocal breakdown on 'God Bless the Child.' Then Hardy, the appointed band preacher, would say a prayer asking for a great performance and continued band unity. Then we'd all say a huge *'Amen!'* and go to our spots offstage and wait for the lights to go down." There were practical jokes played onstage. Allison Cornell got her own back on Shania one night by "making a rude picture pop out of the Polaroid camera when she thought I'd just photographed her with a fan."

Once the business was over, Shania headed for her bus, while the band, who were only allowed alcohol after the show was over, headed for their own. Shania's bus was custom-made. It cost a million dollars, complete with a cinema, a media room with a state-of-the-art communications system so she could do interviews when traveling, a fully stocked kitchen, plus a bedroom, bathroom, and kitchenette at the back for her assistant. Shania's bedroom, complete with a large fixed bed, en suite toilet, and hot shower, was at the front of the bus, away from the noise of the motor and the pumps. The only personal security Shania would allow on the bus was her German shepherd Tim (named after her hometown, Timmins), a trained guard dog fiercely loyal to the mistress who issued all his commands in German.

Just before midnight one Sunday night, Helene Bolduc had returned home after an exhausting twelve-hour shift in the Emergency Room at Timmins and District Hospital. The phone rang. It was Shania saying, "Are you ready to come on the road with me? It's my first tour and I'd really love to have somebody personal with me on the bus; you and Larry would be great." Larry, who was driving for Sears, came in at three and saw Helene sitting on the floor. Once he realized that nobody was sick, he blurted out, "We're going on the road, all this getting the tour ready, I just had this gut feeling she was going to ask us."

So Helene, who admits she "didn't know a thing about anything," went on the road with her as her personal assistant. "I was in for a lot of surprises. I took care of the bus. Larry was driving it, but he was driving at night when we were both sleeping, and then in the morning he'd park that bus at the next venue and go to sleep in a hotel room.

"She wanted a bus on the road so she would have her own home, her own setup the way she wanted it. If she was on the bus, she was not disturbed, because everybody had to come through me. If she was sleeping, I wouldn't disturb her for anything. The minute she had one foot out of that bus, everybody wanted her, it's like 'Shania, Shania, Shania,' a thousand times in a few hours. She was not having an easy life. And I think when she got tired, she was even worse. A few times I'd have snapped. She never did, she won't."

Once a day, Helene and Shania sat down to go through the stacks of requests that had built up. "She'd do interviews, a whole ton of things, unbelievable, nobody knows what a star has to do. Some days I would just look at her and I'd say, 'Why do you bother going through all this?' On the day of the show she would do a sound check at five o'clock. Then she would have to get made-up to do television interviews, sometimes as many as five. There were nights when it all got too much and she said, 'Helene, I don't want to do this,' and vented her frustration." The meditation techniques that Mutt uses have never been so effective for Shania. She is too impatient when things do not happen easily or the way she wants them to.

After Mutt went back to the studio, they would talk on the phone every day for hours. She had hoped to write some songs on the road, but there was hardly enough time for that. "After the show we left immediately, and she would just shower, get into her PJs, and then we'd just talk, not about the show. I'd talk about the family, the cottage, talk about anything else and that would unwind her."

Helene's role was mother as well as confidant. One of her most difficult jobs was making sure that Shania ate enough—her high-octane performance burned thousands of calories that her vegan diet did not easily replace. "Sometimes she would feel weak or tired, and I'd tell her, 'You've got to eat more,' I'd make her shakes in the morning, rich with cream, because she could use the calories. I'd leave food everywhere, so if she was hungry, it was there to snack on. Every night I'd make her meals. Before a performance she didn't want anything heavy, just a lot of vegetables, soups, and stir-fries with tofu in them."

Shania's diet contains no meat, no fish, no eggs. Wherever she travels, a blender goes with her so she can make fruit and vegetable drinks. Her concert rider is spartan in its simplicity. In her dressing room she required "Six large ripe California oranges suitable for juicing, six lemons, three papayas, three mangoes, eighteen apples, six bananas, one pineapple, one cantaloupe, one honeydew melon, one small watermelon, ten pounds carrots, three medium beets, two bunches celery, three heads broccoli, quarter pound ginger root . . . and a kettle for boiling water." Other requirements included salt-and-vinegar potato chips, two packages of Mori-Nu Silken Style Soft Tofu, orange cheese popcorn, assorted herbal teas, twenty-four small bottles of spring water (at room temperature), twelve cans of Diet Coke, six cans of ginger ale (Canada Dry if available), and six cans of orange soda. If Helene was not preparing her vegan dinner, it had to be cleared with the road manager in advance. Pasta dishes had to be cooked from angel hair pasta made without eggs. Desserts, cobblers, and cakes had to be eggless, as did the dozen homemade cookies and muffins demanded. Shania has a sweet tooth and likes her candy as much as salt and vinegar–flavored potato chips.

Shania's greatest extravagance was bringing her horse Dancer on tour. Dancer, an Andalusian purebred, had his own special trailer, and Shania took off on him at every opportunity. That put her personal injury insurance premiums sky-high. "He's my knight, beautiful, regal, with a very powerful high action," she enthused. "Dancer has had special training, on his passage and gait and all that special stuff. He's a ballet dancer, very muscular and strong with a swan neck. He gets frothy at the mouth and very excited. He's great fun to ride, but quite intimidating."

Helene instructed Shania from the get-go to tell her if she wasn't up to the job. Her worst blunder came toward the end of the tour, when Shania was flying to Europe for the Party in the Park and the concerts in the United Kingdom and Dublin. It was right after Shania's show in Timmins, and everybody was all over the place in the post-gig euphoria. Her wardrobe was shipped with all the equipment. The problem was that she was meeting Prince

Charles and didn't have a thing to wear. Instead of chilling out, Shania had to buy a suitable outfit—everything she liked was either too long or didn't fit right. Jan Stabile and Barbara Carr, from the management office, were frantically sewing, hemming, and making the outfit as they drove in the car to meet the Prince. "I was supposed to think of those things for her, and I goofed there," says Helene. "She never said a word about it, nothing."

Shania is a perfectionist who demands the same standards from those who work for her. When she makes decisions, she expects action right away, but throughout the tour Helene never saw her lose her cool. When she got angry she bit her lip and then quietly told the management what had to be changed. Her brother Darryl was originally employed as a pyrotechnics assistant on the show, but once his behavior became unacceptable—turning up late or not at all and then reminding his colleagues of who he was—he was warned and finally fired.

In the twenty-three-song set, the high point for musical drama was "God Bless the Child." Shania was joined onstage by a local choir. Beefed up by dramatic tympani and extra verses, the song was moody and powerful, so very different from the gentle, heart-tugging a cappella version on the record. This was swiftly followed by a clip of Shania as a child, which in turn introduced a performance by a youngster with enough talent to win a local talent show or radio competition. To some, it was a twee interlude that sat uncomfortably next to the navel-baring rock that went before and after. To others, it was the one point at which she revealed her intimate feelings.

Giving a child an opportunity to sing onstage with her is one of Shania's ways of giving back. She was given chances when she was a kid, so this was payback time. Lightning can strike twice. One young girl who won the local radio contest to duet with Shania was Avril Lavigne. Shania remembers her well because of the long blond hair that cascades below her waist and because Lavigne also hails from a small town in Ontario (Napanee, population five thousand). Avril had a big voice and she was already singing at country music fairs all over the province. By the age of seventeen she had reinvented herself as a streetwise skater punk chick. Her first single, "Complicated," became the American summer anthem of 2002 and subsequently an international hit. Avril's debut album, *Let Go*, went to the top of the album charts and stayed there for over a year. It has now sold more than seven million copies in the United States and the same again around the world.

Shania does not often wear her emotions on her sleeve, but the way she talks about child hunger should silence the cynics. It comes from her guts, from a physical memory of the time when her stomach was empty. To help assuage that emptiness she has given hundreds of thousands of dollars away. The royalties from "God Bless the Child" are split between two organizations—Second Harvest Kid's Café in the United States and the Canadian Living Foundation, who are also given a portion of all proceeds from T-shirt, calendar, and poster sales. In the States, the money she has raised has helped launch twenty-two separate Kid's Café programs. In addition, she donates tickets to every concert so local food banks can run raffles, while a donation is also given to a specific local charity. In Timmins, the money went to Mattagami First Nation, the local food banks, and the hospital. In Europe, she donated to the War Child fund for Kosovar children.

"A lot of stars support different charities," she explains, "but only a few deal with poorer families and underprivileged people. One reason that I contribute so publicly is to raise awareness. Only a relatively small part of society can really understand what it means to be truly poor, when you can't afford the most basic things . . . Other charities are fine, but they often don't deal with people who are in a really needy situation. And I know from personal experience what it means to be poor. I was one of those people who couldn't afford basic essentials. People who are well-off don't know what it's like. They can be ignorant of the fact that there are people out there who are really hungry. Food is one thing you can't get by without and there are a lot of people who can't afford it."

"I was that hungry kid," she explains. "My goal is to save kids the humiliation, the anguish of feeling inferior." Backstage, before and after every performance, Shania worked her way through a line of dozens of well-wishers, including sick children and terminally ill fans. "A lot of artists [wouldn't meet with a dying fan], and I can understand why," she says. "But I've been through enough in my life that I can relate to people very well. I'm not tough. I'm strong. And I think there's a very big difference."

On May 11, 1999, the day of her show at Fiddler's Green Amphitheatre in Englewood, Colorado, Shania paid an unannounced visit, with no media publicity, to the hospital where five high-school pupils were still recovering from the appalling massacre at Columbine High School three weeks earlier. She had decided to make the visit when she learned that one of the wounded, a student who had hung from a second-floor window during the shooting, was a huge fan of hers. The kids screamed with delight when they saw her, and Shania gave each of them a signed photo and a portable CD player. When questioned about her visit later, all she would say as she fought back tears was, "Well, you do what you can."

The tour was a triumph, elevating her from country star to pop superstar without missing a beat. Between May 29, 1998, and December 5, 1999, Shania Twain played 164 shows in five countries (primarily the United States and Canada; she also gave seven concerts in Australia, three in the United Kingdom, and one in Ireland) to over 2.5 million people. The tour grossed $86 million, the highest-grossing country tour in history (Garth Brooks actually played to more people, but pegged his ticket prices to $19.50). Only the Rolling Stones were a bigger draw.

Not bad for a little girl who, when she started to perform around Sudbury, had to be forced onto the stage . . . and who had often left it in tears.

Chapter Twenty-One

SHANIA TWAIN SUPERSTAR

IN JANUARY 1998, Shania Twain was a huge star in the States, fif-teen million albums big and rising. But she was a country star, and if record companies know one thing, it is that country doesn't sell in Europe. Capitol had spent a ton of money to make Garth Brooks's *In Pieces* a hit album, but none of his succeeding records had broken the Top 10. Country has to be sold as something, as anything, else.

Being part of a niche market was not on Shania's agenda. She was determined that with *Come On Over* she would become an interna-tional star and that she would do whatever was necessary to achieve that. On January 3, she arrived in London to stay in the Milestone, a small, discreet hotel on Kensington High Street, a low-key beginning to one of the most effective marketing campaigns in recent times.

"Not a lot of American artists are interested in being interna-tional. I am," she said without any trace of bravado or arrogance. It was a simple statement of intent. At that point, *Come On Over* had sold about ten thousand copies, all imports, to die-hard country fans in the United Kingdom. "I am Canadian. A lot of Canadian acts have had success in Europe first, so I am acutely aware of the rest of the world." Twenty-four months later, the album had sold a further three million copies in Britain, thirty million around the world, and Shania was a bona fide pop superstar, the C word forgotten, mixed out of her résumé as adroitly as the fiddles out of the European mixes.

Shania was always different from the usual American country stars. There was a formality, a cool reserve about her; she spoke softly in an accent that did not spit grits and chitlins. Her handshake was just that: a nod of her head preceded a slight pressure on fingers and palm, then quick release. No fake bonhomie, no air hugs or multiple air kisses. Shania preferred to keep her distance. What struck audiences was how poised, how pretty, and—when she stood up— how petite Shania was. Instead of the usual cowboy chic and big hair, she wore a beige sleeveless high-necked ribbed sweater that accentuated her figure but focused attention on her face, with its perfect cheekbones and flawed nose. She was gorgeous, but real, a woman of thirty-two with a true *Angela's Ashes* life behind her, not some teenager mouthing Spice Girls sound bites. The hunger that blazed in her belonged to an aspirant, not a woman who had no need to work again. She had control, power, and money . . . and one thing was quite clear: It was not enough.

In a different era, *The Woman in Me* might have gone international. As one might expect, it did brilliantly in Canada, selling 1.8 million copies (it is now double diamond, selling over two million), and it went platinum in Australia. "The pattern was to get a crossover hit in America before we took it international," says Luke Lewis. "Billy Ray Cyrus did that with 'Achy Breaky Heart,' which went pop over here before it went overseas." Lewis believed he could break out with the title track, "a ballad which everybody over there was hollering for," which is why he sent Shania to shoot the video in Egypt. It didn't happen. "I don't think they felt it was right," he admits, "which left Mutt and me frustrated out of our brains."

Luke's enthusiasm did get to David Munns in London. Munns, who was Polygram's head of international, got Shania and saw the potential. On July 5, 1995, she made a short promotional tour of Britain playing lunchtime gigs at three small clubs—the Renfrew Ferry in Glasgow, La Gitaine in Manchester, and Venom in London. The reaction was positive, but building a buzz involved interesting the media. They were not that interested. As the record continued to sell in the States, Munns refused to give up. What the record company had to do was not so much think outside the box as chuck it away and build a new one.

In September 1996, Munns contacted Richard Beck at LD Publicity. LD is one of the most well-respected PR companies in Europe, whose client list has included the Rolling Stones, Tina Turner, Peter Gabriel, and Janet Jackson. Once again, interest was hard to arouse, though they managed to book her a slot on the major prime-time TV show *The Des O'Connor Show.* Just prior to coming in, Shania had to return to Canada for major surgery on her wisdom teeth and the show was pulled. Soon after, she appointed Jon Landau Management and Munns decided to wait until there was a new album.

Once a record goes multiplatinum in the States, there is a great deal of pressure on the overseas companies to duplicate that success. However, many American artists are not prepared to devote the energy and the time necessary and cannot be bothered to tailor their sound and image to the demands of an international market. Mutt and Shania were.

After *Come On Over* was completed and delivered to Mercury Nashville, Mutt spent the next four months remixing 70 percent of the album. This involved diluting or removing the twang elements. On "You're Still the One," the obvious fiddle and pedal steel parts were cut right back and the pop elements of the song brought to the forefront, and it is one second shorter. The running order was also resequenced: the United States version began with "Man! I Feel Like a Woman!," the international with "You're Still the One."

Great Britain is still considered the tastemaker for Europe. Germany may be a bigger market, but Britain has a national media—newspapers, music and style magazines, radio and TV stations—that reaches the whole country in one hit and prides itself on spotting and selling trends. While over the last decade the singles charts have changed to reflect saturation marketing campaigns—records regularly enter the charts at number one and sink almost as quickly—there is still a prestige to getting a UK hit.

David Munns hired LD Publicity, and they set out to formulate a radical campaign. "All the press photos were of her with a horse and it was so country," says Richard Beck. "From the start I refused to do country media, because I knew they would buy her record anyway. Luckily I was backed by the label and by Shania herself." The American artwork, all bleached out and flying hair, was rejected, and George Holz did a new photo session. The new cover was very simple—Shania, head turned toward the camera, with disheveled hair, a half smile, and a bare shoulder—and very effective. Hinting that coming on over might be very rewarding, it was sexy, but not overt.

"David Munns gave us carte blanche to do what we wanted on the act," says Beck, "so we went all out. She had been marketed as a country act in the past, so the first thing I suggested to set her aside from the country thing was doing interviews with *FHM* and, for credibility, *The Times*." Beck had already confirmed the photo session with *FHM* before he had met Shania. At the time the magazine, while an important player, was not the lads' mags market leader, selling some three hundred thousand copies an issue. Its content—a mixture of sexy photo shoots and irreverent, nudge-wink articles on sports, beer, and sex ("The World's Sexiest Women" leading into "How to Tell If You Have Genital Herpes")—was nowhere near Shania's American profile. Fortunately, she agreed to do it.

For Beck, the *FHM* session with Barry Hollywood was nerve-racking. The results exceeded all expectations. Shania came out looking beautiful in a bustier and a white suit, showing cleavage but not leg. Everybody loved the shots. *FHM* ran an eight-page feature and a poster campaign on London buses. Shania had Polygram buy the rest and they were used as press shots for the European campaign. "In Europe, the pictures made her mainstream." (In America, fans do not like them at all, calling them the "Frozen Shania Pics" because she never smiles.) "People would look at her. From being a country girl she became this sexy diva," says Beck, who credits the *FHM* session, *The National Lottery Show*, and *The Box* with being the three factors that helped her crack Britain.

Shania had made her own personal impact on the promotion campaign. On January 8, the record company had hosted a party for her at Alberta's, a chic bar over the Alberta Ferretti showroom at 205–206 Sloane Street, London. A true professional, Shania worked the room, speaking to every media person—TV, radio, and press—no matter how small. She was particularly charming to Richard Park at Capital Radio (the most important independent radio station in London). Within a few days, "You're Still the One" was on heavy rotation at Capital.

The BBC's *National Lottery Show*, which regularly pulls in twelve million viewers, desperate to discover whether they have become millionaires, is a great place to showcase a new single. Shania's performance on Valentine's Day had its problems. She was singing live to a backing track, and after three run-throughs announced, "I'm not happy with the sound I'm getting in my ears." The management called Mutt, who had stayed in the hotel, and sent a car to pick him up. The sound engineer, who was getting very twitchy, almost had heart failure when Mutt walked in. Any union regulations were forgotten as Mutt spoke to Shania over the talkback. Within thirty seconds, she was happy with the sound and did a perfect take. Whether this was his magic touch or the placebo effect, Mutt never said.

The Box is a cable TV show in which the viewers dial up and request the video they want to see. It is the most-watched satellite music program in the United Kingdom, with six times the viewers of MTV. More importantly it has a very young demographic; it is the channel the kids watch, and they are the people who still buy singles. "You're Still the One" was an instant favorite, quickly getting two thousand requests a day. The song entered the charts at number ten on February 28, 1998.

Two days after *The National Lottery Show*, Shania flew to Austria on a two-week promotional tour of Europe designed to follow the template that had been set in Britain—glamour, credibility, and selective amnesia when it came to the C word. After a week in Germany, Switzerland, and Scandinavia, she flew into Edinburgh, where she got into a Mercedes minivan and spent the next two days crossing the United Kingdom. The first day they visited Glasgow, Newcastle, and Manchester; the next took in Birmingham, Bristol, and London; then she took the Eurostar to Paris and did further promotional work in France, Italy, and Spain. The routine was the same: Starting at 8 A.M., she visited local radio and TV stations for interviews, accompanied by a local journalist who would interview her in the bus between venues. Aside from one impromptu walkabout at Watford Gap service station to buy some new videos to watch on the bus, Shania was on the go all day, doing phone interviews until she reached the hotel late at night.

"There was never a moan, she would do whatever was necessary to break this record," says Beck. "This was an artist who had incredible success in America. *Come On Over* was at two on the *Billboard* chart and she was in the back of a bus schlepping it out like any other band in a transit van. She is the most professional artist I have ever worked with. Her regime, her lifestyle, her work ethic are stronger."

It was a low-key affair, high on work-rate and low on drama. Her entourage was never more than four people: Barbara Carr and Jan Stabile from Jon Landau Management, Cyril Lanoir to do hair and makeup, and Beck. To begin with, the national record companies were surprised, and a little put out, by some of her requests. Breaking long-established traditions, she did not like to be met at the airport with all the attendant fuss and would sometimes decline meetings with company personnel, reasoning they would be more productive in their offices than at her hotel. Her strict vegan diet made the ubiquitous record company dinners an ordeal. When she is on show and working, Shania does not like eating and talking at the same time, so she started to eat in her room first and then would just pick at the dinners. At the end of every trip, Shania sent a personal signed thank-you letter to the major executives of each record company. In a business where thank-yous are generally perfunctory, such small courtesies are major motivators.

During the two years that she was promoting *Come On Over*, as well as making her first-ever concert tour, Shania made nine promotional trips to Europe, unprecedented for an artist of her stature. In April 1998, she flew down to Australia to do the TV show *Hey Hey Saturday*. As her appearance was also tied in with the Australian Grand Prix, sixty thousand people turned up. That kicked the record into the stratosphere Down Under. In Europe, Germany was the first territory to rack up the hits, followed eventually by the rest of the continent.

Even as she got bigger and bigger, Shania stuck to one rule: no bodyguards. Valuing her privacy, she realized that having personal security men draws attention. When she was staying in London, Shania often went out shopping in Kensington High Street, horse-riding around Rotten Row, or walking in Hyde Park all by herself, dressing down, perhaps by pulling a hood over her head. She bought an Aga and kitchen equipment for the new house in Switzerland at Smallbone & Co. on the Fulham Road and nobody recognized her—partly, perhaps, because she is so petite that people, expecting a larger-than-life star, simply look over her head, but as much because she walks very fast. Because she does not expect to be recognized, she is not.

Most evenings, Shania retired to her room to eat and be alone. When the party went out to dinner—the Bombay Brasserie is a particular favorite in London—she would first reflect on the day's business and discuss the forthcoming schedule. She loved to talk about her family and get into passionate discussions, for she has firmly held opinions about most things and can get loud when expressing them.

When she laughs it can still a busy hotel lobby, as Richard Beck recalls: "We had an ongoing joke. I'd always told her, 'I don't do bags and beans,' and, of course, one day in Cologne I had done both. She buzzed my hotel room and asked me to come downstairs, where she said to me, 'I'm really unhappy with the air-conditioning level in my room.' As I walked away to sort it out, she started laughing with that laugh that stopped everybody in the foyer and said, 'Get back here, I'm only joking.' Silly things, slapstick things, make her laugh. And when she laughs it is funny because she is so loud."

For all the smiles, Shania does not like doing promotion—she would much rather be writing songs or performing. She regards it as a necessary evil, provided it has a specific point. (In February 2000, a headline spot at the Brit Awards was turned down because she felt that the album had already peaked and she would only be doing it as a vanity exercise. She also canceled promotion tours to France, Germany, and Asia.) By the end of 1999, there were times when, behind her eyes, one could see the bone-dead tiredness that stars get when the promotion treadmill has run one single, one video, one interview too far. She felt as if her past was another country that had been invaded too many times. On those occasions she might have to be psyched up, but she never threw prima donna tantrums, regarding that as unprofessional. When she does an interview, she gives it her full attention. In return, those working for her are expected to measure up to her work ethic. She dislikes press conferences, as there is no one-on-one contact, but her major bugbear is television.

"I really don't like television, it makes me nervous," she says. "TV is restricting. Someone else is in charge. I have no control." Not being in control always worries Shania, and when things go wrong, the warning signs are easily recognized: a thin-lipped nonsmile interspersed with swear words. Once Shania unleashes four-letter words, it is a sure giveaway, for she seldom swears.

"Anything to do with production, sound, or visuals is monitored and controlled," says Beck. "All I know is that there are no ifs and buts. Shania and Mutt know how they want to present something and that is how it has to be done. There is no room for the label to change or deviate from that at all."

The only blip that marred the effortless rise and rise of Shania Twain was the release in 1999 of the tracks that she had recorded with Paul Sabu and Harry Hinde in Deerhurst ten years earlier. The album was originally released over the Internet and then marketed in the United States by Jomato Records on CD as *Beginnings 1989–90* by Eilleen "Shania" Twain. (In Europe, it was repackaged with a sexy cover as *Wild and Wicked*.) Shania was not impressed. "I don't mind listening to my old stuff, but it annoys me that people make money out of that," she said. "If I met that person, I would slap their face, it is so rude. I feel like I've been betrayed by a fellow music person."

The recordings were very poor quality, taken from an old tape and cleaned up. The mix was shoddy and most of the songs are simply not very good. The cover of Cher's "Half Breed" is excruciating. On the US sleeve, the credits for the musicians are inaccurate. The record also stated that "A significant portion of the proceeds from the sale of this recording is being donated to Make-A-Wish Foundation and Second Harvest/Kid's Café." Those may be Shania's favorite charities, but they have yet to receive any money, probably because Jomato has filed for protection from bankruptcy under Chapter 11 in the United States.

To cap it all, from the first release of the record, Harry Hinde has been in dispute with Jomato and Paul Sabu. Harry's lawyer claims that "Harry Hinde owns all the rights, title, and interest in the masters and has never assigned these rights to any other party. If something has been done with these tapes, it is not with his permission." Sabu, however, has alleged that he owns the copyright and half the publishing. For its part, Jomato claims it thoroughly vetted its legal status with the recordings, and the record company boss, John Edwards, says, "We licensed this from Harry Hinde and Paul Sabu in April 1999."

The murky path of the *Beginnings* album has continued on. Paul Sabu believes it has sold up to seven million albums around the world—which is most unlikely—but whatever he claims, he has yet to be paid. "When *Beginnings* came out, it was surrounded by really weird happenings," he told *The Toronto Globe and Mail* in December 2001. "On the album I'm credited as cowriter for all the songs. When I went to get paid for my work, I found out that some-how . . . I was no longer the songwriter of record. To date I've never been paid for any of my work, or for publishing or songwriter's royalties, nothing."

After trying to sell his master tapes to Universal and Shania without any success, Harry Hinde decided to finally finish the record he had started in 1989. In February 2001, after raising some C$200,000 from, among others, John Kotowski's son-in-law Walter Haidasz, he set about remixing sixteen tracks at East Iris Studios in Nashville.

Along with the tapes, Harry had kept Eilleen's original handwritten notes in which she specified her favorite vocal tracks and he tried, wherever possible, to incorporate her ten-year-old desires.

"When I was sitting there listening to her bare voice through the speakers, people were standing outside the door," says Hinde. "They knew the voice but it was so different. When they came in and found out it was Eilleen they were a little bit shocked. They liked it as much as the stuff she is doing now and the smiles on their faces when they heard her singing "The Heart Is Blind" were just amazing. I figured I'm not going to play around with this, I'm just going to do the best possible mix I can.

"I left in some technical glitches because that's the way she sounded at that time and this has value as a document of her singing. I was advised to clean it all up, but I just took out the pops and hiss that comes with age to a tape. I redid only one track ["The Heart is Blind"], which isn't on the album."

In North America, *The Complete Limelight Sessions* (with six more tracks than *Beginnings)* by Eilleen Shania Twain was released on Limelight Records in October 2001 (February 2002 in Europe). *Limelight* was distributed by Koch Records, a leading independent label specializing in rap, cowboy country, and Bob the Builder. The album never broke on mainstream country radio. Its first single, "The Heart Is Blind," started well, but ran into problems after Thanksgiving. Harry talks darkly about pressure being applied to radio stations, who were subtly reminded at the highest level that there was a new Shania album due out within the year. They suddenly lost interest.

The Complete Limelight Sessions sounds a lot better than *Beginnings*. Of course, it's unfair to compare it with what came later but it still falls short of being a valued musical artifact. It is hampered both in the original choice of material and its modern commercial intentions. Caught between hard rock and soft country-at-a-pinch ballads, Eilleen never sounds relaxed. The most effective track by a disco mile is the very rare "It's Alright (Mother Presents Harder Deeper Mix)." After being given a seven-and-a-half-minute club treatment by "The Mixers" (Paul "PJ" Jenkins, Tim "Drik" Schoeps, and Elisha Hoffman) and Guido O, the track earned rave reviews in dance magazines for "its sexy and mysterious vocalist" and made it onto *Billboard*'s Top 20 Dance Tracks. Unfortunately for Harry, there was not enough money left to release it commercially. As ever, his timing was imperfect.

There will always be interest in an artist's early work, but total sales of *The Complete Limelight Sessions* stalled at around eighty thousand (sales of the *Shania Twain* album are now close to two million). "I hope Shania likes what I've done. I think she will," Harry said when the album was first released. He then refused to let the album be released as a cheap special to the Wal-Mart rackers at the same time as *Up!* hit the stores.

As ever for Harry there has been a scorpion's sting in the tale. In May 2005 he was contemplating legal action against Koch Records, which claimed to have spent more money promoting *The Complete Limelight Sessions* than the album had earned. Earlier in the year Paul Sabu had once again licensed his *Beginnings* demo tapes for a few thousand dollars. Harry seems doomed to never make any money from discovering a genuine superstar.

In his own way, he is an honorable man who has only ever wanted to do right by his one-time protégée. "I tried to play fair, to stay true to what Eilleen and I were trying to create back in Deerhurst," he says sadly. "Of course I'd like to have made a few bucks but I always took the high road. Everyone thinks I'm a millionaire— they have no idea. I feel such a fool." Shania, however, will remain unimpressed.

When the third single, "From This Moment On," was released in November 1998, *Come On Over* was already a platinum album (three hundred thousand) in the United Kingdom, a bigger hit than many had thought possible. In 1999, Shania's profile reached new heights. When she flew in for the première of *Notting Hill* in April ("You've Got a Way" was played over the closing credits but was never released as a single, as Mutt did not want it to be), Julia Roberts, a big country fan who was briefly married to Lyle Lovett, specifically asked to meet her. After a series of negotiations—Julia's agents wanted to meet in a private room—they met up at the cinema and chatted for a long time. At the same time, there was talk of Boyzone star Ronan Keating doing a duet with Shania, but nothing ever came of it.

"From This Moment On" pushed sales to a new level, but the killer was "That Don't Impress Me Much," complete with tongue-in-cheek video. The song, released in June 1999, spread all over Europe like a summer rash. When Shania performed at Capital Radio's Party in the Park on July 4, 1999, that was the song that had them rocking, the number that had all the headline writers punning away. On September 1, 1999, eighteen months after it was released, *Come On Over* finally made it to the top of the British album charts. It remained there for the next sixteen weeks.

The album sold over two million copies in Canada; helped by astute marketing and the use of special mixes, it even cracked the French Canadian market in Quebec. It went multiplatinum in Germany. In Australia, after the longest stay in the Top Ten since ARIA began compiling charts in 1983, it has become one of only a dozen albums to have sold over one million copies. In 1999, Shania's sales accounted for 10 percent of Universal Music's global sales. By the turn of the millennium, Shania had achieved an almost unique cross-section of the audience. She had the adult market that buys albums and the kids—young girls from eleven to fourteen who adored her image, indeed wanted to be like her—that buy the singles. Her music, in very much the same way that Michael Jackson's once did, engages children on a fundamental level. They don't care about the subtext of the words, they just love the songs and the way she looks. To the late teens and early twenties she was certainly not credible, as far from hip as can be, but that has never been her—or indeed Mutt's—market. Their happiness shrapnel is now embedded the world over.

Chapter Twenty-Two

THE CHÂTEAU

EARLY IN 1999, Shania and Luke Lewis were getting into their stretch limo following an awards show in Canada. She was wearing a sheath dress so tight that she could barely move her legs, let alone walk in it. Luke let her in first and as she went to sit down, the leather seats and the slick dress material combined to create perpetual motion. She scooted the length of the car and landed flat on her backside. Luke's immediate reaction was to crack up laughing. Mid-howl he checked himself, for he realized this had become a defining moment. How would Shania react? There comes a point at which a star turns into a prima donna, a diva into a demon. To them such things are not funny. Not funny at all.

Shania lay in the back of the limo, legs akimbo, in a most undignified heap . . . and roared with laughter. "What I am living right now is probably the lightest time in my whole life," she has said. "I don't take myself too seriously, but I take my music too seriously. I never have lived a normal life. I never will, I guess."

She can still laugh at herself, still finds the idea of what she has become faintly ludicrous. It helped when *The National Enquirer* printed a story that after her concert in Timmins on July 1, 1999, she had rekindled her affair with Paul Bolduc, offered him a job driving her bus, and caused him to split up with the mother of his two children. When Helene read the story, she couldn't tell Paul what was in it because she was laughing too hard. So did Shania whenever the subject was raised.

She didn't laugh so much when Darryl sold a story about the Lange Christmas celebrations to the *Enquirer*. The story the magazine splashed on can be best summarized as follows: no meat, no booze, no sex, Indian cult with dead dodgy leader brainwashes superstar. "Family members are deeply worried," Darryl told the tabloid. "We're afraid that Shania has been dominated by the cult and has become like a robot, following their extreme beliefs. Mutt calls all the shots—and Shania follows along. Shania is not the same—and it's all because of that weird Sant Mat cult."

Although the "robot" sound bite was to haunt Shania for the next few years, the story was all smoke and shadows. The link with the branch of Sant Mat led by the highly questionable Thakar Singh was intriguing but irrelevant, as Mutt and Shania are not among his followers. Darryl wasn't so much worried about his sister as he was angry . . . and broke. He had traveled to Switzerland with a deal already agreed with the *Enquirer*, who even supplied him with a camera.

What hurt Shania was the betrayal. She had invested so much in setting up the Christmas gathering, inviting over all her family. Mutt's brother Bill flew in from South Africa with his wife and daughter. "I'm going to have a great Christmas," she had said the preceding October. "I'm staying home. I could make a lot doing a show, but how much money does one person need? I'm bringing my whole family out to Switzerland; they have never been there. I'm so excited. For New Year's I'm going to build a campfire in our yard, stare at the Alps, and set off some fireworks." They did all that. Everyone had a great time . . . until March, when the story broke. Mutt, who cherishes his anonymity, was particularly upset and took a long time to forgive Darryl.

Such is the price of fame. It was one of the reasons Mutt and Shania had moved to Switzerland in the first place. By the end of 1997, neither was enjoying living in upstate New York. Mutt missed England. He missed sports. Ice hockey, baseball, and basketball were cold comfort for a man weaned on rugby, cricket, and above all, soccer. Mutt loves watching soccer matches—during the late eighties, when enjoying a weekend break from recording in New York, he thought nothing of taking a Concorde flight home, watching either Spurs or Watford play, and catching the plane back the next day. "He loves all sport," says Shania. "He loves to talk about soccer and, like any good wife would, I listen to his soccer stories. He's very funny, he watched Manchester United all the time because a great friend of his would die for the team. He doesn't follow specific teams anymore, he loves players. He watches the game very closely. Being from South Africa, he watches all their rugby games." Mutt is also "an avid gardener; it is one of his passions" and found the lack of variety in plants and flowers frustrating.

The Langes did their best to belong in upstate New York, making substantial charitable contributions to the local volunteer fire department, schools, and woodlot operators. For much of the year, St. Regis Falls is a small tight-knit community, but it does attract thousands of vacationers and weekenders. As a result, Shania felt under constant scrutiny. "If I wanted to go to the mall and do my Christmas shopping, I couldn't do that anymore. It is not being recognized that bothers me. I don't find that obtrusive, but in the States people can get so assertive, like it is their right to talk to me, and they make a loud thing about it which causes a whole fuss. I hate that. I don't want to be treated like a star, I want to be like everybody else."

The final nail came after Mutt fell afoul of the local environmental policies. Although he owned three thousand acres, he was not allowed to make any changes that might affect the welfare of the local wildlife without permission. "He didn't damage anything," says Helene Bolduc, "he just made it more beautiful, it didn't stop the animals from going to drink anywhere, do anything." The existing building was little more than a lodge attached to a studio and he wanted to build a bigger house. Permission was refused to do the building work and despite employing lawyers to sort the regulations out, Mutt was not prepared to fight it out in the courts with all the unwelcome publicity that would bring. Instead, he decided to leave the States.

Mutt asked Shania, "Do you want to be living like this?" and they got to talking about where they'd like to spend the rest of their lives, a place where they could have more privacy, a garden, access to lots of soccer games, and generally live among people who were not as enamored with fame. They considered moving up to Montreal, but the top rate tax bracket in Canada was too high for such a high-earning couple to consider. Mutt wanted to be in Europe. Switzerland became the ideal compromise, for the Swiss make a virtue of ignoring celebrity.

When the Langes first started looking for a place, they didn't really know what they wanted. "We just decided to look in Switzerland," Shania says. "We did narrow it down to the Vaud region because we like it. They grow palm trees there. It's very temperate. And, of course, we're right in the Alps. I really missed the snow. So that made it special for us."

During the summer of 1998, when Shania was on tour, the Langes quietly left St. Regis Falls and moved to a château in the Vaud canton just between Vevey and Montreux, less than sixty miles from Geneva. Le château de Sully has been described variously as having a hundred rooms and costing millions. It doesn't and it didn't (locals estimate the cost at around £5 million). It is difficult for foreigners to get permission to buy a house in Switzerland. (Tina Turner rents her house in Zurich and their near neighbor Phil Collins, although married to a local girl, had to wait three years before he was officially allowed to buy.) Because he was planning to build a recording studio and bring artists into the country, Mutt was considered to be a special case.

"We weren't looking for a place that big, but you are very restricted as to what you can buy," says Shania. The original house was designed and built in 1882 by the Geneva architect Emile Reverdon for Baron Bertrand de Boucheporn, whose family had fled France during the Revolution. Intended as the permanent residence of the Baron and his family, it was designed as much for comfort as for show, far closer to a mansion than a drafty old castle (a real old-fashioned castle, La Tour-de-Peilz, is a few minutes' drive away).

The house was officially designated a "château" in 1929 when its new owner, Zürich industrialist Wilhelm Escher, had it redesigned by local architect Ferdinand Kurz. The spectacular Byzantine swimming pool in the basement was transformed into an auditorium, an annex was added to the east, a porch to the north, and a semisunken swimming pool to the west. The house then went through a succession of owners, including a company that sold off much of the estate, the writer Joseph Kessel, Liliane Borle, and then a public utility company.

Stories of the château's massive size—even after it was downsized to a mere forty-six rooms—have always amused Shania. "It doesn't have anywhere near any of those numbers. It has six bedrooms, one kitchen, a library, TV room, a study, and there's also a living room off the lounge. That's it actually. It's not that different from your average big house. It's not like Versailles. I think all of the châteaux in this region have an interesting history. But there's nothing particularly special about ours. It's just a big house with a great view and French architecture from the 1800s."

So what Mutt and Shania own is a big, but not massive, house with an imposing entrance hall and plenty of spare bedrooms. It is private, visible from a boat on the lake but not the road, yet not secluded. It has its own recording studio, Sully Sound, and an attached farm—where Shania's horses live in a giant barn better appointed than many a home—surrounded by a few acres of land. The view from the front looks over wine terraces that run down toward Lake Geneva. At the bottom of the terraces is the soccer field belonging to the high school and gym complex right next door, a series of modern concrete buildings well masked by trees.

Until July 1999, Shania had never spent more than a few weeks at the château. The previous Christmas, she had only a ten-day break between tour dates and New Year's Eve was spent onstage in Phoenix. Although she and Mutt had been married almost six years, they had never spent huge blocks of time together and never in a place that was truly their home. The union of two such formidable work ethics had been hard to schedule; they talked every day for hours, but that is not the same thing as being in the same space.

There were times in the early days of their marriage when the gossips insisted she had only married him as a career move. If that was ever true the doubts are long gone, for Mutt has a unique ability to make people love him. One of Shania's most treasured possessions is the rough draft of their wedding vows complete with all their scribbles. "I've kept the draft and I've kept the actual vows," she laughs. Mutt's other relationships ended because he was never there, and eventually, love was not enough. For much of their marriage, Shania was never there either, but what they shared was more than physical love. "A lot of the time," she said, "it's true, he's not there and I'm not there. But the largest chunks of time we've been apart are over. I will never leave home for such a great length of time again; it's my reward. The key for him and I is that we share something so intimate and so unique in our music. It is something we're always going to have, it's not ever going to go away. It's not like a relationship where what we have most in common is our love of tennis and if one of us decided they don't like tennis, there goes the relationship.

"There were two years of me being away a lot and I hated it," Shania has admitted, denying the industry gossips who claimed her marriage was in trouble. "I don't want to do that again, so we won't do that again. We got through it, and we're closer than ever."

With some relief, Shania disappeared off the bottom of the celebrity radar screen for nearly two years. Her time out of the spotlight allowed her to reconnect with Mutt, though it took time to get used to each other. "We're taking it slow, we're living together for the first time almost in seven years," she told BBC 2 DJ Bob Harris at the 2000 CMA Awards. "We eat lunch together, we eat dinner together, we take weekends off, and we're having a life and making a record all at the same time.

"It was so great to be together again. It was as if there was a time lapse from the time we got married to then, and we hadn't had a chance to get as close as we wanted. It was like being married for the first time, like a honeymoon period again. Now we can spend weeks together without any outside contact.

"I needed a break, physically and mentally. In Switzerland, people are calm and discreet. They might say hi or give me a smile, but they're not jumping up and down or shaking. I don't feel like a star there. I feel normal. I needed to leave behind the whole 'Shania' thing and be myself. I finally settled into my house, I got my wardrobe organized. I put up my work clothes into a separate closet and pulled out all the simple clothes I like to wear every day. I got back into cooking, gardening, and then we did all the things we love: hiking in the mountains, riding horses, skiing. Our favorite thing is to ski all day and then come home for a fondue. For the first time in my life, I was just resting."

For Shania, the hardest part has been learning "how to chill. My husband is a great chiller. When he works, it is extremely intense, but he knows how to relax, to kick back, to be a couch potato all day. I can't do that. I can handle sitting and watching a movie, but I'm not going to sit down for another hour and just flick through the TV channels. I have to be in the kitchen making something. I love to cook when I'm at home during the day. It is relaxing, therapeutic, and I am doing something."

Although, like Mutt, she prefers not to discuss it, Shania has been following the path of Radhasoami Satsang for some years. She tries to meditate for two and a half hours each day, but when she's on the road she can usually only manage to squeeze in five-minute bursts in the car. "I have always been searching for more than organized religion," she says. "I believe there can only be one God, but there are so many religions and each one thinks they have got the only answer. But if they have all these different gods how can that be?

"Even as a small child, I realized something was not right here. I thought, 'How come there are so many Santa Clauses? They can't be everywhere at once!' and I was always searching for the answer. I spent my whole youth trying to figure out who's got the right god and I was never satisfied with any one religion's explanation. When I discovered this particular spiritual path, I felt very in tune with it because what I learned was to understand and respect everyone's perspective. It's all about understanding that there is only one God, finding that in yourself, and really making a conscious decision to live a clean-living life—which I always did anyway.

"I have always been an optimistic person and this path is all about that. It's about trying to accept the bad things in your life, accept them as lessons, things you have to go through in order to grow, looking inside yourself in order to find the true spiritual you. It is nothing complicated, not even a religion, it's just really an understanding. It was natural for me to give up meat and live a gentler way of life."

Even before she made that decision, Mutt had never put any pressure on her to stop eating meat. After she started reading and learning more about it, she, too, decided it was a waste to kill an animal when she physically didn't need to eat it to survive. She cooks with tofu, masses of fresh fruit and vegetables ("I'm a chopper not a slicer"), and the many new cheeses she has discovered in Switzerland. Vacherin and haloumi (from Cyprus) are particular favorites. Her favorite European dish is Tarte Tatin—a French upside-down apple pie. "I like to make soups, stews, comfort food, nothing too exotic. For about the last ten years I've had the same thing every morning—a fruit smoothie, usually with orange juice, banana, apples, grapes, and ginger. It's the best kick. I'm no different from any other woman. I watch what I eat, but if I gain weight on my thighs, I don't obsess."

On a quiet day, they eat breakfast out on the terrace looking at the Alps—"They are gorgeous in the morning; even in winter I can just wrap a duvet round myself and sit there for hours." She rides one of her horses—Tango, Queensy, Olé (who she rescued), and Big Chief—for hours at a time. (The much-loved Dancer died in 2002.) She also found time to visit Portugal for two weeks to learn to play "horseball." It is a rougher version of polo—a cross between rugby and basketball—and is very popular in Continental Europe; France has more than seven hundred teams. "From what the Portuguese explained to me," she cheerfully told *Rolling Stone* magazine, "it's an old Asian game that they used to play with heads. One of those bar-

baric games with body parts. It's very hard—you have to stand up in the stirrups at all times. To pick up the ball, you have to be upside down and hold on with one leg while the horse is running."

On less active days, she stays in with Carrie Ann watching a movie, munching popcorn, and chatting all afternoon. Though she does have a part-time cleaning lady at the château, Shania likes to do her own housework. "I try to do everything I can myself. I wash the dishes after I cook. If the floor needs a vacuum, I pull out the vacuum. I clean my own oven, I do my own grocery shopping." She mucks out the stables.

Despite her determination to be the perfect housewife, she is getting better at chilling. One New Year's Eve, they just sat out on the veranda and watched the fireworks going off up and down the Rhone Valley. Mutt has learned to speak good French quickly, which drives her crazy—so she has regular lessons and insists Helene speak to her in French for at least two hours whenever they meet up.

As for those no-sex rumors, Shania has learned to laugh them off in interviews. Occasionally she lets something a little more personal slip out. "I like to feel like a woman," she says. "I feel sexy in a plain white T-shirt with nothing underneath. My husband disagrees. He thinks nude is sexy. He likes me naked. Still, I like the white T-shirt."

In the early days, when Shania came back from a promotional trip, Mutt needed to know everything that had happened. She just wanted to go for a walk, smell the roses, anything but go over the details once more. "He gets frustrated because he is interested," she said. "Sometimes it can be difficult, he's so involved—he wants things to be so great for me. Sometimes I can't escape the intensity of it, he wants me to be great all the time, I can feel that pressure. I am very hard on myself and I don't get to escape that when I'm with him. Sometimes I just don't want him to care about my career, but it's impossible because he is such a part of it." She made a rule never to talk business over dinner or in bed and teased him, "I have great management. Call them." He did call Landau and Lewis, asking questions while she was lying next to him.

Otherwise, they talk about everything under the sun. Mutt loves good conversation, he reads voraciously, knows his history and his sport and loves the movies. "He loves fashion and likes to keep up with the latest of everything; he's very into the aesthetic of things, which is real fun for a girl when we're shopping." The image that has been built up of Mutt as some shadowy recluse is a media invention. He has never done interviews because he does not see the need (nor does Clive Calder). The Langes regularly make weekend trips to London for a mix of sanity and culture. Friday night watching Swan Lake at the Royal Opera House, take in a Spurs match with David Rose on Saturday afternoon, dinner at the Bombay Brasserie, back home on Sunday. Nobody, not the management, not the record company, knows. No fuss, no bother.

That is the way Shania likes it. On Saturday August 5, 2000, she stunned Timmins by turning up unannounced at her high school reunion. Helene spoke to her on the phone on that Friday night and should have realized something was up because the conversation was over in two minutes . . . and Shania never gives up the phone that quickly. The next morning Helene was sitting on the deck out at her cottage on Star Lake when Shania came out of the trees, laughing fit to burst. For a long time she had dithered about going, then she thought, "I can't miss out on everything normal in life," and flew to Toronto. Carrie Ann picked her up in a rental van, and the pair drove the six hours to Timmins "telling jokes and man-bashing, eating dill pickle chips and listening to Journey and AC/DC."

Shania and Helene spent the day out at the cottage, yakking away before she went back into town and got ready for the homecoming. Shania knew that if people were expecting her it would change the whole tenor of the event. So she turned up without security, simply dressed in a sleeveless top, black pants, her hair tied back, and only light makeup. Carrie Ann was worried. "We walked in, and it took only seconds before everyone realized it was her, and it turned into a photo-autograph lineup. "I kept saying, 'Enough!' But she kept saying, 'No, no, this is fine.' "

Shania happily chatted away, signed autographs, and posed for photographs with any of the two thousand–odd guests who wanted them. Eventually one of the organizers announced, "She's done her thing. Now she's Eilleen, she's one of you guys, she's here for the same reason as everybody else, please let her have a good time." The other alumni did exactly that, and she mingled with her friends, chatted to former teachers, and had a wonderful evening.

The next morning she had breakfast with Karen Twain and Don and Jan Fraser, went to see Grandma Selina, and left for Huntsville with her sisters. It was a most gracious performance. Small wonder Timmins loves her and was prepared to build a museum in her name.

At heart, Shania will always be a tomboy, a jeans-and-sweats girl happy riding her horses, but she has learned to accept the compliments of beauty. On July 27, 1999, Revlon announced that she had been appointed a company spokesperson—joining the ranks of such notable faces as Cindy Crawford, Melanie Griffith, Salma Hayek, and Halle Berry. She starred in a series of TV and print ads to help launch the cosmetic manufacturer's new product range, ColorStay Liquid Lip and Crystal Glam. "It's incredibly flattering to be recognized with some of the most beautiful women in the world," she said disingenuously. "My image and music fits their campaign perfectly and I don't have to compromise at all. They just let me be myself and that's what makes it the perfect relationship. Also it's an extension of what I already do in my own job—dressing up and playacting. Except this time they are paying me to do it." Shania earned some $3 million for the campaign, which was cunningly designed to tie in with the release of her single "Man! I Feel Like a Woman!" Part of the appeal was that both the photo session for the ads and the television commercial were shot by photographer-to-the-stars Herb Ritts. The sight of twenty flunkies running around after the flamboyant Herb amused her greatly.

Such over-the-top pampering has always made Shania uncomfortable. She knows how easy it is to get lost in stardom. Several times she has told Helene Bolduc, "If ever you see that I'm going the other way, please make sure that I come back this way, bring me back to earth."

She is worth at least $100 million. Mutt Lange is worth maybe twice that—excluding the value of his stake in Zomba. (Industry observers estimate his shareholding at 5–7.5 percent, which will have netted him a further $150–225 million.) Most of their wealth has come from writing songs rather than the record sales. The initial songwriting royalties on the sixteen songs on *Come On Over* have earned Mutt and Shania $18,374,803. That does not include performance royalties, which are payable on a sliding scale related to radio airplay, film, and TV license fees. In the case of a massive pop hit, this can add millions to a song's income. In America, every week a record is at number one it generates about $500,000 in performance royalties. Then there is the ancillary income. When Britney and her pals were singing along to "Man! I Feel Like a Woman!" in the movie *Crossroads*, or "Still the One" is playing in the background of the Queen Vic in the English soap opera *Eastenders*, money is coming in. Picking "You've Got a Way" for the soundtrack of Notting Hill would have cost the filmmakers anywhere between $100,000 and $250,000.

Despite all that money, for a long time Shania was uneasy, not with having money, but with spending it. When they first married, she refused to let Mutt buy her anything expensive, decreeing, "No jewelry, no vehicles, no expensive gifts, nothing." Secretly she wondered whether she should quit music altogether, but the hard-ass Eilleen reasserted herself soon enough. "All of a sudden, I'm completely provided for, for the rest of my life," she says. "It was too much change. I couldn't cope. And I had a strong need and desire to do it myself."

After her first tour, Shania had a tailor remake her stage costumes into more practical day clothing. "I hate waste," she says. "I wear track pants and a sweatshirt I've had since we first came to Huntsville fifteen years ago. Why get a new one if the old one still works?" Every Christmas, Carrie Ann gives her the same present—a sweat suit for her power walking and exercise. She'd wear until it wore out unless she was given a new one.

"Finally she can go out and shop for expensive clothes and

won't feel guilty about it," laughs Helene Bolduc. "She used to. Eilleen was so dirt poor, and without so much, she doesn't want to forget that, she would die before she goes back there. She makes me laugh every time, but she still likes to find a bargain, it's a kick with her. She's all excited about that, she loves saying, 'Hey, boy, did I ever get a good deal.' "

Old habits die hard. The first place she heads in a clothes store is the sale rack. "I am cautious with money," she told GQ magazine. "I never take it for granted. I now have enough I don't need to be cautious, but it doesn't matter, it's just in me. I still think it's indulgent to buy things you don't need. I still think it's careless to max out your credit cards. That'll never leave me now, I'm sure. I'd been poor and I became rich, so I know that if either was going to make me insane then that would have happened by now. I'm just not the sort of person who's going to go nuts.

"I would stress too much about blowing a million pounds down Bond Street. I'm just not that kind of shopper. I have to rationalize everything I spend. Call it a hang-up, I don't know. I bought myself a car four years ago, but it was a BMW roadster so that was a real splurge. But you don't have to be rich to have one and I haven't bought one since."

Her worst weakness is for shoes and she will spend $1,500 on a nice pair, but if she doesn't get enough wear out of them she happily gives them away. Nor does she spend a fortune on beauty products. Her favorite skin care product is called Bag Balm and is normally used to keep cows' udders soft and supple for milking.

"Remember I'm a country girl," she laughs, "and this is a pure country product. It's so country that only farmers use it—and me, of course. I use it all over my body from my face to my fingernails. I buy it in Canada from farm supply shops; it doesn't cost much but it is brilliant. And I promise it doesn't make you smell like a cow . . ."

One place Shania is certainly not stinting on is her new "cottage" on the Lake of Bays. She bought four lots of prime waterfront near Port Cunnington, forty-five minutes from Huntsville, tore down some of the buildings, and had one refurbished in time for her to spend Thanksgiving there with her family in 2000. Her long-term plan was that Carrie Ann and Jill have adjoining cottages. The best-appointed cottages in Muskoka are closer to mansions made from wood, beautifully fitted-out by craftsmen used to dealing with serious money. She has never asked for an estimate, just told them to get on with it.

Parsimonious with herself, she is exceptionally generous to her close family and to those who work for her. If she gives a present, it is one she has personally picked out and paid for. She has a remarkable memory for details and if anyone mentions they like a particular wine, there it will be in their Christmas hamper. The cards she sends have handwritten notes inside.

Switzerland may not hold her forever. Its manufactured perfection of nature set against a stunning background may wear thin. It's easier there for her to start up her chain saw and light a fire, but it is not the same. She has a place in Florida and now the cottage in Muskoka, where she can snowshoe through the woods and portage her canoe from lake to lake to her heart's content. In 2004 the Langes bought a huge estate in New Zealand that will fulfill any lingering need for privacy.

She is as close to happiness as she has ever been in her life, which scares her. "Ever since I met Mutt, ever since I got married, I don't feel the need to struggle anymore," she says. "A lot of the fight is gone, and I find it hard to keep myself going. Sometimes I get so fluffy and emotional, I don't like this person, it isn't me. I guess it is better to be sensitive than not to be. I am so much more aware of people around me, of things going on."

Because they want nothing more of her than her attention, Shania can be more herself with children. She does not care if they are sick, dying even, but engages with them on their level, asks all kinds of questions. "She is wonderful with kids," says Helene. "I see her with her nephews and nieces and she'll be with them hours, playing any game they want her to play, she's really good with that. Kids were attracted to her even before she became a star; she used to babysit here, and the kids just loved her. I don't know if it's that beautiful face she's got or her smile; kids would just automatically go to her . . . they need to touch her, they need to talk to her, it's always been that way."

Her own childhood, she acknowledges, was largely lost, and the memories of cold hungry days haunt her still. But she has no regrets, for the past cannot be reclaimed, only remembered. "When I look back at my childhood, I don't carry that grief with me," she says. "I feel like it was another person. I've gone through some very dramatic stages in my life, and I feel three different people lived through those stages. It's funny, I often feel like I'm on my third lifetime. My greatest fear is losing someone in my life, because I know what it's like and it is a very scary thing and I know how vulnerable life is, that it could happen at any time.

"If anything happens to my husband or my child I won't get through it," she says. "I just love my husband so much. He's like the most special person. He is part of me: Without him I'll be half a person. I really would be lost; you might as well just cut off my arms and my legs."

For Shania, kids were never an option until she was through the first part of her career, the tour was done, and she was established. For years, she agonized about having children, wanting them one moment, not the next. It was not an easy choice, for Mutt was in his fifties and as wedded to his muse as he ever was. He had never planned on having a family. One of the reasons his marriage to Olga had foundered was that she wanted children and he didn't. The thought also frightened her, for she grew up in a dysfunctional family—loving but dysfunctional—and she knows how easy it is to repeat the patterns of our past. She has taken comfort from the way her sisters, albeit with a few hiccups along the way, have "broken that cycle, raising their families in a higher standard of living than we were."

Her first experiences raising Mark and Darryl had not been a huge success. Mark, however, has managed to put his past misdemeanors behind him. He lives in British Columbia, works in the computer field, and has his life mainly on track. Darryl spent a few years drifting but then appeared to have settled down in Edmonton; he married his girlfriend and started raising a foster baby. "Nothing has changed, they are still finding themselves," said Shania in 2002 before howling with laughter. At that time Darryl was no longer in disgrace. "Not in my book," she said. "I am a very forgiving person now. It's all gone. Past."

Sadly, Darryl's life continues to hover over the abyss between disaster and disgrace. At 10:30 P.M. on Thursday, August 21, 2003, Darryl was out with his brothers-in-law Franklin and Jason Logan when their car was pulled over by the police at Jasper Avenue and 90th Street. Their Pontiac Grand Am was stopped because it fit the description of a car suspected of being involved in a shooting from the previous month. Inside the car Constable Dean Boyer and another officer allegedly found 170 spitballs of crack cocaine valued at C$7,000 ($5,600). Darryl and the Logan brothers were arrested and charged with drug trafficking.

"There were over 170 of these spitballs throughout the car," said police spokesman Andy Weiler when announcing the arrest. "It's significant. Officers are happy whenever they can get illicit drugs off the street." Darryl's bust was an international news story and the Edmonton police glowed in the praise and publicity.

However, on April 29, 2005, Darryl walked free. The judge tossed out the police evidence after ruling the officers had unlawfully detained him, failed to read him his rights, and only later found drugs. "The breaches of the accused's Charter rights were serious, if not egregious, and I am persuaded that the admission of the evidence in this case would bring the administration of justice into greater disrepute than would its exclusion," said Court of Queen's Bench justice Eric Macklin, explaining his decision.

Shania has never said a word about her half brother's arrest, and in fact interviewers have been warned not to bring it up. Those close to her are convinced that she paid for his lawyers and that she will continue to support him come what may. Inside she despairs because she knows that he is now a thirty-one-year-old set in his ways, heading down a dark tunnel with scant light at the other end. The family ties remain, but now Shania has a child of her own to be concerned with.

The decision to start a family came suddenly. "Up until the time we decided to have a baby, we weren't thinking seriously about it," she says. "When I got off the road and I'd been home for a few months, I said to Mutt: 'If we don't have a baby now we may never have one, because by the time this record is finished and I finish working it—the last one went on for ever and ever—it could be so far down the line I might not be up to it anymore. If we are going to consider it, let's consider it now.' I was getting tired of being a star and didn't want to be famous for a while.

"We both thought long and hard, talked about it for a month. Then we decided let's try it. If it's never meant to happen, it won't, and that's the way it'll have to be. And six or eight months after we got home . . . voilà Eja."

In late 2000, when Shania suspected she might be pregnant, she and Carrie Ann rushed to a pharmacy in Tour-de-Peilz to buy a testing kit. All the instructions were in French and although Shania's command of the language had become pretty good, she didn't want to make any mistakes. "So we did all of them," says Carrie Ann. "The one with the cross, the one that turns pink. Five positive signs later we all hugged and broke out the champagne."

The champagne was nonalcoholic, of course, and Shania had to wait a further two weeks before the doctor would confirm her condition. "It drove me crazy. But I knew in my heart I was pregnant." She told her close family the good news over Christmas, and it was officially announced in March 2001. Shania was, she admits, lucky. She had an easy pregnancy, though she gained twenty-five pounds; her face, neck, and arms got very round. "I ate really well," she said, "but when I wanted to have a banana split I had it. I ate very sensibly and nutritiously. I didn't use my pregnancy as an excuse to eat. I did a little bit of a trade-off, I'd take a half-hour walk, have my banana split, and walk home."

"I was at the point where I was like, 'I've already been there, done that—so what if my stomach never comes back? Vanity wasn't an issue. I didn't care if I ended up with a million stretch marks, my stomach never went flat, and I never showed it again." Fortunately for her millions of male fans, that didn't arise. The weight came off right away because she was a nursing mother. She was riding her horses six weeks later and the most famous stomach in show business soon regained its old shape. Shania confessed that like many women she felt under pressure to get back into shape—but at least she could write songs about her feelings, which was the genesis of the song "What a Way to Wanna Be!"

Eja D'Angelo Lange was born on August 12, 2001. It was an easy delivery, though the downside came a few days later. "I didn't cry when he was born," she has said, "but afterward I must have had the 'baby blues.' For a few days I would just cry for no reason. The nurses were like, 'Don't worry, this happens to everyone,' but it didn't make me feel better." Her biggest problems were actually physical, after her breasts became engorged with milk. "I think that, at times, was more painful than the actual birth. It was the day after labor, and now you are engorged because the milk doesn't have anywhere to go. That was so painful, I was in tears."

The baby's name caused a certain amount of surprise. Eja is a variation on the Indian (Hindi) word for angel and was invented by Mutt. "I thought I'd be more controlling about it," admitted Shania, "wanting to be the one who came up with a name, but I actually think it's really sweet that he did it. I love the name. It's just a creative name, short, sweet, different, and something we were going to use whether the baby was a boy or a girl."

Just two weeks after he was born, Shania, dressed in a white blouse and blue culottes, took him for a two-hour stroll into Vevey, pushing him in an old-fashioned pram. She stopped in a little café overlooking Lake Geneva and sipped a banana-flavored iced drink while Eja slept. When he woke up and began to cry, she calmly covered herself with a towel and breast-fed him.

While the locals studiously ignored her, the outing was photographed and reported in an American tabloid magazine. While the pictures were not very flattering, it was not that but the invasion of the baby's privacy that worried her. Shania herself hates having personal security; Eja is a different matter. When he travels with her he is heavily protected. "I am not big on having half the football team walking me around," she admits, "but for Eja I'll use the whole team if I have to. I want to make sure he's safe. Mutt is going to be around home so he'll be with his dad a lot."

According to Shania, Eja has inherited his looks from all sides of the family. He has Mutt's head shape and some of the Edwards mannerisms; his eyes and mouth are similar to Shania and Carrie Ann's. "He's got our smile," she says, "but he has so many of Mutt's ways about him already. He's got a very easygoing nature, but he's very certain of himself, very focused but calm about everything. He wants something, he doesn't throw a fit about it, he just keeps going until he gets it. He's a very level kid. I see so much of Mutt in him, it's really cute.

"They have a really close bond, the two of them. The baby really cries and is so unhappy when Mutt leaves, but when I leave he is okay," she laughs. "He has more of an attachment to Mutt than he does to me. He loves his mom and we have a really nice relationship, he is really affectionate with me, but he has something about his dad. When his dad comes in the room I don't exist. I'm doting, but that's probably normal with your first child. I'm always worried he's gonna fall or go too fast on his bike. I'm more stressed about that than I should be. He's a very sweet guy, he only fusses when he wants something specific."

From the start, Mutt was very involved in baby care, bathing the baby and changing his diaper. Like his parents, Eja is being brought up a vegetarian, with no meat or dairy in his diet. "I'm a nursing mother, so he doesn't need dairy," said Shania soon after his first birthday. "I'm very conscientious about his eating habits. I'm going to educate him about the reasons why not to eat meat, so he will grow up with that mentality. It will be more unnatural for him to eat meat. Of course, he can make his own choices when he is out independent and doing his own thing. I'm not going to control his life, he is his own person."

As soon as Eja was weaned, Shania took over preparing fresh food—beans, carrots, root vegetables, soy, tofu, soups, stews. He hasn't been allowed to guzzle any sweets and candies, except for crushed almonds and almond milk. For his first birthday, Shania baked him "my famous double-layer chocolate cake. And, being one year old, he's not exactly going to be knowing what's going on. So I figured I'll take the photos with the cake and candles and Mommy and Daddy. But there's no gifts or anything." Having come from nothing to acquire fabulous wealth, she is deeply concerned that he not grow up spoiled. However, like any loving mother she cannot resist buying him things. "I buy things mainly for Eja— books and soft toys. I try not to buy him too much because I don't want him getting spoiled. He doesn't own any designer clothes be- cause I don't agree with that sort of pressure." Eja's mother tongue will be French and when Shania wants to know if he's hungry, she'll ask, "Est-ce que tu as faim?" His reply, which cuts across all linguistic boundaries, is generally "Yum-yum."

Shania is hoping that Eja won't go into the family business. That may be hard to stop. Even aged two, his favorite Shania song was "Nah!," which he would sing along with. He also knew the chorus to ABBA's "Mamma Mia." Like his parents, "He's not a hyper kid. I was always happy playing by myself, and he's very much like that."

Eja's arrival has certainly changed the tempo of Mutt and Sha- nia's life. It has made them even closer. Perhaps more important are the changes he has encouraged in Shania's personality. Now that she no longer has anything to prove, neither as an artist nor as a woman, she is freer than she has ever been before. This is reflected in every- thing, from her body language to the clothes she wears and the way she feels. The wolf in her has finally answered the cries of nature.

"With this new little thing there is so much more love in our fam- ily now. He has so much love. He is just like Mutt. Mutt is so loving. I'm not like that," she says. "I'm a giving person, but I'm just such an independent entity that I'm not as easy to reach all the time. I don't reach out often, but Mutt and Eja are both very open, loving, and warm. They're good for me, both of them. Good for my soul.

"I have been unwinding myself ever since I met Mutt. I am trying to be a better person. I really am, because there is no point in being anything else. The only thing that gets you through is to approach everything with a light and loving heart. Nothing else works. No matter what shit life throws you, if you cannot take it graciously, it will only hurt you more."

The bad dreams have stopped too. She used to dream about Sharon and Jerry regularly, but those dreams, and their accompanying nightmares, have ceased. It has been three years since she had her last dream about them. "They said to me, 'You're okay now. You don't need us anymore. We're fine, and we're happy with the way everything's turned out.' "

Chapter Twenty-Three

MAKING *UP!*

WHILE THE HAPPY DOMESTICITY of Shania's life did not prevent her from working on her fourth studio album, it certainly delayed the process. *Up!* was finally released in November 2002, five years after *Come On Over.*

Ever the pragmatist, Shania consistently refused to let that record's success overshadow writing new songs. "*Come On Over* was more of a pressure because the last time out I was happy to have the first album be so big," she says. "At that time I thought it would be a miracle to do it twice in a row, but I still felt the pressure to follow up well, because if I hadn't I would have felt like a failure. I don't know if I can do that again . . . so the pressure's off."

"*Come On Over* was so big I don't know if anyone can do that for two records in a row," she admitted before *Up!* was released. "I'm a bit too realistic to set that goal for myself. I did want to put a better record together and I think I have. If the fans come back and agree with me, then I'll know I've done it."

There were differences in the working arrangements right from the beginning, as she told British DJ Bob Harris at the 2000 CMA Awards. "This one we are doing more together than we did the last two. Because I was gone so much he would do bits on his own, I would do bits on my own, and we'd get together and sort of blend everything together and make it work that way. Now we are to-

gether all the time, so our ideas are melding right from the beginning, which is a new way for us to do things. I'm liking it a lot.

"It's been nice to have the control from the beginning. I need to
grow, I need to have somewhere to go, I want to have some variety.
It is more interesting for me, so I'm pretty excited."

Although Mutt had built a state-of-the-art studio in the
château, Shania had problems writing songs at home. She found it
difficult to concentrate, a sign that perhaps finally she has found
somewhere where she can truly relax and be herself. "I get into domestic mode," she says, "and I'm more worried about what I'm
going to make for dinner. Being home is a real break for me, somewhere to rest my brain, but I found I was never in the frame of
mind to be creative because of all the cozy distractions I have
there. Travel inspires me. I need to travel to be creative, to focus. I
go to museums, the ballet."

During Shania's pregnancy, travel was limited to places they
could reach by car and train. She has been used to driving long dis-
tances all her life and her home is only a short drive from four
other countries. Milan is under four hours away, while Paris is just
over three hundred miles. "When we felt like we needed a surge of
creativity, we'd just get in the car, or hop on the train. We just find
it easier to go visit a museum and then go have a nice dinner and
think about what to write as opposed to who's calling and what we
need at the store."

Wherever they go, Shania is never without a notebook and a
small tape recorder, because she never knows when an intriguing
lyrical twist or a flash of melody might pop up. "We did a lot of the
writing at meals in restaurants or walking the streets," she laughs.
"Inspiration often strikes at awkward moments; sometimes we get
carried away and forget that there are people around us! I often
wonder what people must make of us, but as Mutt's got really long
rock and roll hair, I figured they probably assume we're in a band
and are more or less forgiving about the whole thing."

The writing habits they had developed on the previous albums
were refined further. "I don't find it difficult to write a song," she

says. "I find it difficult to write a good song. We rewrite our songs until we get to the point where we are both satisfied and that can take a while when you have two people to satisfy—and we're both perfectionists."

In the early stages, they went right back to Shania's old writing tapes, even toyed with ideas from the songs on the Harry Hinde sessions. "I'm Jealous" was from one such old tape. "If we look at a song from a long time ago we never take the whole thing we might take a melody, maybe a snippet of the chord structure. Generally, old material inspires us more than anything." Mutt often listens to Shania singing and writing on her own. He has a phenomenal memory for little flashes of lyrical inspiration or melody that Shania can forget. He'll tell her "that's not the line I was talking about." So he will fish and dig about in her tapes, forcing her to play it over until they finally come up with the one little thing he wanted to put in.

Watching the two working together often makes Helene Bolduc laugh, for in Mutt, Shania has finally met the only taskmaster who is harder on her than she is herself. "Mutt is more of a perfectionist than her," she says. "Sometimes he'll make her start, and start, and start, and she'll say, 'It's good enough, it's okay.' He just goes, 'No it's not.' "

"We are a good team," says Shania, understating the obvious. "We make interesting records together because he really understands how to make things sound. When you listen to a Mutt record, it can turn your head, it sounds different. He just has a talent for that. I don't know how he does it and I don't think anybody else does either; all the people who have ever worked with him go away without being able to do it.

"I wouldn't say he's a hard taskmaster, but he has a lot of energy and if you can't match it, you'll find it hard to keep up because he is such a machine. He knows when I'm my best, and he'll keep me going until he feels I've reached that. That's his job and because he knows me so well I can't get away with anything. But the guy is brilliant, so I pretty much have to just sit there and say, 'Okay, tell me what to do, give me some direction.' He's my mirror, I rely on him a lot . . . and he's always right in the end.

"My approach to writing songs hasn't changed at all. The musical flavor is where people are going to hear the differences, the vocal style, too. I am singing differently from the way people are used to hearing me, more intimately," she says. "Mutt told me, 'I want you to sing the way you do when you are just with your guitar.' I have always found it hard to go from my acoustic voice and then sing the same way to a track on a microphone. Mutt stayed with me until he got the natural, more intimate vocal sound he loves in my voice."

Eja's birth did change Shania's recording routine—though not Mutt's, as he has always worked through the night. Although they had a nanny to help out, Mutt and Shania liked to spend as much time as possible with their newborn while he was awake, pushing him down to a local bistro overlooking the lake, where they drank hot chocolate and snacked on French fries. At night, Shania says, "I'd just put Eja to sleep in his stroller and wheel him over to the studio. Mutt would be in the booth, I'd be in the singing room, and the baby would be in his own little spot with a monitor. And every few hours I'd stop and nurse him."

The terrorist attack on New York on September 11, 2001, shook Shania to the core; for the first time in a long while she doubted what she was doing. Coming so soon after Eja's birth, it reminded her once more of the fragility of life and the tragedies of her past. "It jolted me into the realization that life is more fragile now than ever before. Life is fragile anyway: I understood that a long time ago, when my parents died, I understood that any minute, anyone can be gone. I started questioning my purpose in life," she says. "For a while there I was wondering. Why bother even making a record? It seemed so frivolous."

Equally shocked by the events, Mutt, the master of happiness shrapnel, pulled her back on track by telling her, "No, no, you're looking at it all wrong. What we do is we create music which affects people's lives. Right now people need music."

Shania had already written and recorded "Up!"—a trademark country number driven by its fiddle and some typical Twain lyrics ("it's about as bad as it could be/everybody's bugging me/my skin's acting weird/I wish I could grow a beard")—and that decided her to make it the title track. "I realized, wow, that's the perfect title, we really do need to stay up. More than anything, people need—I don't want to say a diversion, but some release and relief. A positive distraction from all the anxieties everyone is experiencing. I have always tried to affect people in a positive way. I want my music to be uplifting, for the listeners and for myself, because I have to go out there and perform it and live with it, day after day, for months on end."

With each collaboration, Mutt and Shania have become more withdrawn from and oblivious to outside influences. After the multiplatinum success of *The Woman in Me*, any financial restraints were removed, and by the time *Up!* was being written, Mutt could indulge himself however he wanted. And he did. During the early stages, rumors flew about that the whole record was being recorded using machines and Pro Tools. While Mutt was assisted throughout on Pro Tools by Kevin "vOlt" Churko, an expert programmer and editor from Moose Jaw, Saskatchewan, and his brother Cory, who is one of the three fiddle players in Shania's live band, it was always his intention to use living, breathing players.

"Mutt doesn't like machines when he can use musicians," says Shania. "We used a lot of different musicians on this record, many more than usual." After Eja was a month old, they ventured further afield to record in Vienna, and twice traveled to Nassau in the Bahamas to record at Compass Point. Although there are dozens of players involved on the record, only a handful are from Nashville. Guitarists Brent Mason, Heitor Perreira, and John Willis, Paul Franklin on pedal steel, and fiddler Jon Yudkin went down to Nassau. For the first time ever, Paul Leim does not play on a Shania Twain album, though he is credited on "Forever and for Always" for a drum break originally recorded during the *Come On Over* sessions. Group fiddles were supplied by Leahy—a Canadian group who had supported Shania on her first tour—and Indian percussion sounds by Simon and Diamond Duggal. Two string sessions, both with very different feels, were recorded in Ireland with the forty-piece Irish Film Orchestra and in Mumbai (Bombay) with a very different orchestra using traditional Indian instruments. Mutt went to India alone because of the baby.

"I wasn't in a rush anyway and we did it in little pieces here and there," says Shania. "We had extra time because of the baby, which added something really great. We didn't focus too strongly on the lyrics until closer to the end, because I wanted the songs to be fresh, to reflect what I was currently thinking and feeling. By that point we had lots of music, lots of song structure, an entire chorus here, little bits and pieces, ideas and snippets there, but we were mostly missing the words. We had a lot of lyrics to write in a short period of time, but we did it and it all flowed."

Throughout her career, her most vociferous critics have suggested that Shania is little more than Mutt Lange's puppet; he's the Svengali, she's a disposable country songbird. That is too simplistic a rendition of a deeply complex relationship and occasionally Shania has snapped back at the rumors about her role. "It is frustrating," she told one interviewer, "especially because he [Mutt] doesn't do interviews. I mean, if he could have just said, 'Look, this is the reality.' But for me to say that wasn't acceptable. As people get to know me, though, they realize that the writing of the music is directed by me. The production of the music is directed by him. So even though we're involved in both aspects, the songwriting is my direction, and he wants it to be my direction."

"It might be fair to say it is more of a Mutt record than the last one," says Luke Lewis, "though Shania would sit here and say that is bullshit. I know she worked on it darn hard. She told me some of the ideas two years ago. I know he is dependent on her when they write songs to come up with ideas and hooks."

However the songwriting duties get split, Shania made a telling point, as well as showing that this cat still has claws, when she told another interviewer, "Mutt alone has never had this much success in his career. Never as consistently and never as big. It's what we do together that makes it so great."

On the surface, *Up!* has all the ingredients of a classic Mutt Lange soundscape, but plucked from the spice rack, not the kitchen sink. The first single, "I'm Gonna Getcha Good!," had big hit stamped over it from its opening shout of "Let's go." Each song is full of his little touches, a hard rock guitar on top of a compelling pop hook, country fiddles contrasting with Indian strings, a mariachi feel in one song, a touch of calypso in another, jangling guitar on one chorus, buzz saw on the next. When even the hooks have hooks it can get a little overpowering, but then there are also some radical departures, like "Juanita," a Latin ballad with sparse, simple production.

As Shania points out, "If it was all production and there was nothing else there, then this success wouldn't have lasted so long. The songs themselves, the attitude, the personality, are all from my personal character. I am a commercial singer. When I write a song, I'm thinking about the people who are going to be listening to it. The whole process is done with that in mind. I hear other singers say, 'What I do is artistic, and I do it for myself.' I don't get that. If you're making it just for yourself, why sell it?

"My own personality is evident in all my songs. I am really into the lyrics and the concept of the song, the meaning of it. I think hard about that. I think that has been a big part of my music. I still like to take the cheeky humor approach to things, to be very conversational and quite straightforward. I like the songs to be easy to read. I like to take an inspirational approach. I don't see myself as a hard-core feminist. I am more old-fashioned than that."

On "She's Not Just a Pretty Face," Shania took a lyrical stance—"She's an astronaut, a valet at the parking lot, a farmer working the land . . . She's not just a pretty face," that is bound to upset somebody, whether it be feminists or conservatives. "It relates to me, but that's not why I wrote it. There was a time when I felt more like a cover than content, but I don't really feel that way anymore. The song is just about women in general who often don't get taken seriously if they happen to be pretty. There is just so much more to us than that.

"I think women can be taken much less seriously if we pay attention to our femininity. That's the thing I can't grasp, why the song was written," she says. "I definitely believe that women's talent and ability gets overlooked by their beauty—or even the fact that they are a woman. When I am at home doing my everyday things, I wear frumpy clothes and I'm very light on the makeup. I'm sure I wouldn't turn your head. But I bet I would be taken more seriously than if I was dressed the way I am on my videos. I don't like that, because I am the same person. I have the same brain, I have the same idea. It is a complete prejudice."

Chapter Twenty-Four

SELLING *UP!*

ONE THING *Up!* is not is a pure country album. It's an international pop record crammed with nineteen tracks mixing up pop hits, Latin ballads, country swing, and hard rockers . . . and a rather strange collection of bhangra and Hindi pop mixes.

"We have made it much more international sounding," says Shania. "There are a few different sounds and styles that haven't been on other records of mine. On the last album, we played catch-up a lot, trying to keep up with all these new audiences that kept surfacing. It was great but not really that fulfilling creatively. I would have liked to have spent more time making it and then it just kinda ran off on its own. This time we were aware of the different types of people that were listening to the music and their different tastes."

Early in the recording process, Mutt and Shania played Luke Lewis some of the many songs they had. Lewis suggested to Mutt, "Why don't you fill up all seventy-four minutes of the CD for added value?" While he was expecting something different, what Shania and Mutt suggested took him by surprise. They wanted to release the album as a double CD package in three different formats. The "Red" CD can best be described as the international pop album; "Green" had a more country, acoustic feel; while "Blue" was more rhythmic, designed to be a dance record with a strong Indian influence.

North America got the Red and Green double package while

international fans got the Red and Blue CDs. "The whole different, two-mixes package was a sincere effort on Shania's part to ensure that the fans got what they deserved," says Luke Lewis. "So if their tastes were toward twang or pop they got the choice. Last time we had this overseas version, which we didn't sell in the US for a couple of years. But if we were to do that again, how would people know the difference when they go in a store?

"I know it sounds like bullshit, but it was never about marketing, it was fan driven—that was the spirit in which it was conceived. I discovered a way to package two CDs so it didn't cost that much more. Basically, we shared the extra expense so we could sell it at a reasonable price. I was concerned that it seemed overlong and that the project could seem a bit contrived. However, Shania has always had a very keen sense of how to market herself and she hadn't got it wrong yet."

While Mutt knows how to make records that spring out of the radio and mug the unsuspecting listener, he doesn't know what makes the clubs jump. So he turned to Simon and Diamond Duggal, well-respected Indian brothers brought up in Birmingham, England. They played in reggae, funk, and heavy metal bands before moving on to garage, house, and hip-hop as songwriters, producers, remixers, and DJs. They have worked with cult reggae artists Maxi Priest and Sly & Robbie, as well as Apache Indian, Stereo Nation, and Gurdas Maan, the new breed of British and Indian artists who fuse hip hop with bhangra and Hindi pop.

Simon Duggal was very surprised to be approached by Shania and Mutt in April 2002. "They told us that they wanted to have some of the tracks remixed. When they realized that nobody has come up with an entire album of such remixes, they decided to give us all the nineteen songs." Shania gave them the vocal tracks of each song, without playing the original versions. "Since we didn't have any idea of what the originals were like, we approached the project with an open mind. We decided to use Indian instruments like the bansuri, sitar, santoor, and tabla, and besides Indian elements, use some Middle Eastern and Oriental influences, too."

Unfortunately, even in a remix-crazy Europe, the Blue CD was not well received. It was a good idea, poorly executed. Some of her overseas country fans felt cheated—a concern that Shania dismissed in interviews. Getting to know nineteen new songs is hard work, even for the most devoted fan, without throwing in a radical reinterpretation that, at times, sounds like two cats fighting or mating. Reviews for *Up!* in Europe were muted at best, while in America it pulled in raves from *Rolling Stone* and even the iconoclastic *Blender.*

Whatever she might say in her songs, Shania knows she has to look good in her videos. The shoot for the first single, "I'm Gonna Getcha Good!," was straight-back to sex kitten land. It was a slick, expensive production—an unlikely cross between *Tron* and *Blade Runner*—that featured Shania in a skintight black leather catsuit, racing through a futuristic city on a motorcycle, and dodging a giant robot along the way. "I look the way I want to look," she says. "I am not going to sit here and say, 'Boo hoo, everybody is looking at me instead of listening to me.' I don't go for that. I want to look good on my videos. I want to have an image, but now people know who I am there is no mystery there. They are anticipating the music much more than they are anticipating seeing me."

If anybody doubted Shania's commitment to *Up!*'s success, the wolf showed she still had her teeth. Early in August 2002, the business was stunned by the news that she had split from Jon Landau Management. JLM issued a statement that typified their gracious, noncommittal, and noncontroversial management style: "After six great years together, Jon Landau Management and Shania Twain have decided to go their separate ways. The split is amicable and they wish each other much success." Neither party has said anything more.

Shania's choice of replacement—on August 14, 2002, she signed with Peter Mensch of Q-Prime—showed that she was expecting the next few years in the business to be tough. Where Landau's management style is passive aggressive, she has picked a man who is pure aggression, who will shout and fight, do whatever it takes to get the job done. JLM has concentrated on a few very select artists who strive for musical and lyrical sensitivity. Q-Prime's roster is altogether harder.

Hardworking, hard sell, hard rock bands like Def Leppard, Metallica, the Red Hot Chili Peppers, Garbage, Muse, and Fountains of Wayne.

Mensch and his partner Cliff Burnstein have known Mutt and Clive Calder for over twenty years, since Mutt produced AC/DC's *Highway to Hell* in 1979. During the eighties, Mutt produced all Leppard's biggest sellers. In 1998, Q-Prime bought half of the Volcano/Zoo record company (home to Tool and Matthew Sweet) from Zomba. They are friends as well as business acquaintances. Burnstein complements Mensch perfectly. He is a much mellower, cerebral character who looks like a roadie for the Grateful Dead, and fronted Metallica's attack on the Internet music sharing company Napster. Q-Prime has been among the most powerful management companies in the business for a long time.

In 1999, the company was rocked by the departures in quick succession of Madonna and Smashing Pumpkins. After Courtney Love's Hole fled their joint tour with Marilyn Manson and announced they were going to dump Q-Prime, the company responded by sending in the lawyers, demanding remuneration of $180,000 in outstanding management fees as well as compensation for the remainder of the agreement plus ten years. In *The Village Voice*, a record executive who had worked with Courtney Love was quoted as saying: " 'Cliff and Peter are peerless when it comes to handling business matters. But they're not as good at the kind of hand-holding and ego-stroking that this new breed of performer seems to need more than anything else."

While Shania Twain does not need that level of hand-holding and ego-stroking, she did not like being second to Bruce Springsteen. The bond between Jon and Bruce goes back almost three decades. JLM and Bruce are friends, Shania and JLM had a business relationship. Once Springsteen was spurred into action by September 11 to record *The Rising* and go back out on the road, he took most of the management's time. Jon is a laid-back man, but in early 2002 he was rocked by a serious illness and had not fully recovered. There were also rumors that he did not display sufficient enthusiasm when Shania and Mutt played him the new material.

Luke Lewis will have none of that. "Jon and I had just come

back from Europe, we both came back from listening to the material happy. It's not true he wasn't enthused, and I felt really bullish. The deal was up and they were trying to renegotiate. It was shocking to both of them that they couldn't come to terms. Their wires crossed, but there weren't any hard feelings. I bet she was surprised and disappointed they couldn't come to terms. I don't think either of them saw it coming."

JLM did their job when they helped Shania break internationally and set her first tour up to succeed. However, changing circumstances contributed to her need for somebody new. The real reason behind Shania's sacking of JLM may have nothing to do with music but everything to do with big business. In late 2000, Vivendi, a French multinational headed by the acquisitive Jean-Marie Messier, bought Universal Music from Seagram's. During Shania's ten years on Mercury Nashville, the label has been bought three times. She has certainly contributed to the company's value.

The massive international success of *Come On Over* turned Shania Twain from an important commodity into a vital one. Entertainment conglomerates deal in numbers and sales projections, so Vivendi's number crunchers would have been licking their lips waiting for *Up!* If the Shania graph followed its established path, the album would sell close to sixty million. Except record sales don't work like that. They never have. *Come On Over* is a freak—one of those records that becomes the soundtrack of its time and everybody has to have. Shania knows that. And so, for all their bravado, does her record company. *Bad* and *Dangerous*, Michael Jackson's two follow-ups to *Thriller,* each sold twenty-three million copies—extremely high sales figures, but to get that Sony had to market the hell out of both records. Jackson went on a two-year world tour. Both Shania and Mutt knew that for *Up!* to do that well the company would have to get right behind it with all the marketing muscle they possessed.

Unfortunately, 2002 turned out to be an *annus horribilis* for Vivendi Universal. In late 2000, the share price stood at just under $80 on the New York Stock Exchange. In January 2002, it was a respectable $57.90. But in the aftermath of September 11, Enron, and other corporate misdemeanors, the stock market became extremely volatile. Vivendi was perceived as vulnerable and Messier was forced out. The share price went into free fall. By August, it was hovering at $12.50—a phenomenal 75.74 percent decline since the beginning of the year. In the eighteen months since that low, Vivendi have been putting their house in order in a music business rocked by falling sales and the threat of downloading. By late spring 2005, share prices had stabilized at around $30, but the company lacked the clout of old.

Because of the tightly controlled way Mutt and Shania work, they do not have an especially close relationship with their record company. Nashville is nearly five thousand miles from Geneva. While Luke Lewis, her major business confidant, has become a much bigger fish with each takeover, his pond is now an ocean. When a company is in such trouble, budget cuts are inevitable and the marketing pie will get smaller. Peter Mensch's job was to make sure that the Twain slice was as big as it needed to be and that the record company remained on its toes.

The country music business was also in decline. In 2003, there were half as many people listening to country music radio as six years earlier. "There is not as much juice in the base," says Luke Lewis, "there are not as many people listening or watching. That makes you lean a little harder on the other pop side, dress a little different, do a lot of things to keep pace." The math is simple but scary for a record company: *The Woman in Me* sold ten million records, almost exclusively to a country music fan base. In today's country market, the same album with the same number of hits would only sell five million.

Up! was never going to sell itself. Shania knew that. In early September 2002, at the Montreux Palace, Twain electrified every national managing director of Universal. In a short speech, she committed herself to working *Up!* for the next three years. She announced she would start an eighteen-month tour that would crisscross the world the following autumn. Until then, she declared, she'd do any promotion, any high-profile TV show, any major radio or print interviews they wanted her to do, anywhere in the world. Artists of her stature simply don't say that . . . and if they do they don't really mean it, or their ever-expanding list of diva demands makes it exceedingly expensive. Shania meant every word and then proceeded to back up her promises with action.

The biggest problem Shania faced in promoting *Up!* was time. With *Come On Over* she had been able to crack the States first, then move overseas. Now everybody wanted a piece of her at the same time. The media blitz started in August with a series of magazine and TV interviews in the Royal Parc Hotel in Evian, a fast boat ride over Lake Geneva from her home. Once she was back in the cut and thrust of a relentless promo schedule that would make a workaholic whimper for mercy, the time for social niceties soon vanished. When she is working, Shania fills every spare moment, whether it be buttering up record retailers, shaking hands and smiling at a hundred new faces at a pre-gig meet and greet, or doing a phone interview in the car on the way to a radio station.

In a world of multiple consumer choices and declining CD sales, the industry requires more of her time than ever before. But because Shania had done so much in the past, she is her past. While Clear Channel with its multiple tentacles can always call on her services, smaller radio stations cannot. Six years ago they met her and they've been playing her records ever since, but this time around she was too busy, and so the disgruntled DJs started to grumble: "We used to talk to her, but now we can't because she's become a diva." They are missing the point. In radio, numbers count, and if yours aren't big enough you don't get the biggest stars.

There's never enough time and Shania knows it, which makes her chronically impatient. Personal security guards used to standing around and snarling, "No, you can't come in" are run off their feet. Once her car stops, Shania's out the door and halfway to her destination before anybody else has left her black people carrier. "I calculate things quickly, and I tend to be ahead of everybody. I just wish people could read my mind a lot of the time," she sighed to *Rolling Stone.* "It's not a great quality."

She spoke to Lewis once about a member of his staff who had been upset by her brusque, matter-of-fact attitude. "Why," she said, "does he think I have to pat him on the back? We're all members of the same team. There isn't time for that; I'm not patting anybody else on the back."

Luke Lewis says that the third time around, Shania is "still the hardest worker I have ever seen at it in my life. One of the worst raps she gets is that she gives off an ice princess vibe. Yes, she is so focused she will walk right past people. Yes, she's guarded in public, but she's not icy. It's all business. She's like a diamond cutter. You don't look up from your work in case you fuck up the diamond." Or in Shania's case, her third diamond album.

The first stage of promotion in the autumn of 2002 was to hit major TV shows. On November 6, she opened the CMA Awards in eye-catching fashion, appearing to enter the auditorium on a motorcycle (a clever nod toward her new video), roaring up an aisle onto the stage with fireworks exploding around her. In the excitement, nobody noticed it was a double. Dressed in a Marc Bouwer pantsuit that appeared to be constructed entirely from fishnet, with her band in biker leathers, Shania gave a hard rocking performance of "I'm Gonna Getcha Good!" Later on, she changed into a gold gown and presented Alan Jackson with his Male Vocalist of the Year Award. Backstage, Shania told the media: "I'm basically a bar singer. I am a bar singer who ended up on a concert stage." Given the nature of her performance and her attire, it sounded as if she was deliberately trying to appeal to her roots audience.

In the final weeks before the album's release, she appeared on the *David Letterman Show*, the BBC's *Fame Academy*, and *Star Academy* in France, duetting with the show's wannabes on each occasion. The initial push worked well. When *Up!* was released internationally, it went straight to number one on the US, Canadian, and Australian album charts, to number two in New Zealand, and number four in the United Kingdom. According to the official Nielsen SoundScan figures, during the first week it sold 874,000 copies in the United States and over 150,000 in Canada. The following week, it sold another 625,000 copies in the States and ended as the ninth biggest-selling LP of the year, with over 2.9 million sold.

Football fans got an eyeful and an earful of Shania during the winter with some high-profile halftime shows. During halftime at the ninetieth Grey Cup—the Canadian Superbowl—at the Commonwealth Stadium in Edmonton on November 24, 2002, she sang "I'm Gonna Getcha Good!" and "Up!," dressing down in a Canadian toque, yellow ski jacket, dark ski pants, and furry boots.

The big one, however, came two months later when she opened the Super Bowl XXXVIII halftime show, ahead of Sting and No Doubt. "I like football," she told a surprised reporter from *Sports Illustrated*. "I played a lot of football when I was younger. I'm a good receiver, actually." She opened, appropriately enough, by singing "Man! I Feel Like a Woman!," dressed in another Marc Bouwer outfit that somehow combined a bare midriff, a silver bra, a full-length black leather coat, assorted chains, and knee-high black boots. She strutted down the stage to high-five the fans, sang "Up!," and then she walked onto a camera crane that lifted her into the air above the crowd.

Because she moved around so much, there was some criticism that she was lip-synching the whole performance. Paul Liszewski, who produced the sound for the show, says Shania's mike was hot and her vocals were live. The musical accompaniment was what is called a "band in a box"—prerecorded. So while Shania was singing, her onstage drummer was thrashing away merely for effect. Not surprising, as sound engineers at the Super Bowl have five minutes—rather than eight hours—to set up. When U2 played the previous year, Bono's voice and the Edge's guitar were played live, while the rhythm section was prerecorded. There is always a backup tape just in case of problems. When Shania ran back to the stage after mingling with the crowd and didn't appear to be singing, her vocals came through loud and clear.

Two weeks earlier, at the American Music Awards on January 13, she sang the same songs while climbing up a flight of stairs to the fans in the balcony. The following night she performed "Up!" on the *Tonight Show with Jay Leno*, wearing a self-mocking black top with the word DIVA embroidered on the front and a wide black hat.

Yet despite this media blitz, fanned by a steady stream of cover stories and major features in *People, Rolling Stone, Redbook, Time,* and *Entertainment Weekly,* album sales failed to ignite in the way Universal hoped. For the first time, Shania and Mutt's preternatural ability to tap into the soul and sound of middle America was off beam. You can only seize the zeitgeist if you are part of it. After three years away in Switzerland, Shania had inevitably drifted away from American popular culture. Suddenly she wasn't listening to the radio, watching TV, or shopping in the malls. The cultural nuances that had surrounded her for thirty-five years were gone, with their subtle but inescapable pervasion. The Swiss towns—Vevey, Montreux, Lausanne—along the northern shore of Lake Geneva are inhabited by old, cultured, multilingual money, stuffed with expensive but traditional boutiques. To fit in there requires personal changes, and by 2002, whether she realized it or not, Shania had changed her style and image.

It was such a subtle thing. She still used Marc Bouwer to design her clothes. (He does design wonderful things for her; his outfits based on Canadian hockey team colors, which she wore for the Junos, combined humor, patriotism, and sex appeal in one package.) But the costumes she wore for the CMA Awards and the Superbowl disconnected her from her audience. Where once she was a jeans and T-shirt girl who loved to dress up for the big occasion in something glitzy and gorgeous, now she was seen as the international superstar gracing the little people with her presence. That was, and is, not true of Shania, but stardom is all about public perception.

Luke Lewis was concerned. "I don't know whether it's a country point of view or a middle America point of view, but I felt it was making her a bit more inaccessible. My take on her success was that her appeal was she was the all-American girl, but I think she had lost that, taken her finger off the pulse; maybe she was trying too hard. I had never had reason to speak to her like that before, but after the Superbowl I told her that jeans make her look more American and she got crazy at me." Shania reminded him forcefully that she was Canadian, but she took the point.

The video for "Ka-Ching!," Shania's song about conspicuous consumption, was not originally shown in America because Universal was concerned that while the expensive jewelry and fancy clothes worn by Shania accentuated the irony, viewers wouldn't get the satire involved. "We backed off that," admits Lewis. For her next three major TV appearances, Shania deliberately dressed down. On April 7, she won the "Concept Video of the Year Award" on the CMT Flameworthy Awards show, but celebrated by singing an acoustic version of her new single, "Forever and for Always," with Alison Krauss and Union Station, the exquisite champions of roots country. Two days later she was onstage at the Beacon to celebrate Willie Nelson's seventieth birthday. Shania joined the all-star cast and sang two songs with Willie, his "Blue Eyes Crying in the Rain" and her "Forever and for Always," dressed in a simple white T-shirt and black cap. On May 22, she flew to Las Vegas for the VH1 show "Divas Duets 2003," where she finally fulfilled one of her childhood dreams by singing with Stevie Wonder.

Lewis loved her duet with Union Station. "It was really magical," he said two months later, "slimmed down and acoustic. It was all anybody in Nashville has talked about since, it reminded everybody of how engaging she is and what a great singer she is." The pairing was so successful that on November 3, she recorded *Up! Close and Personal*, a one-hour TV special for NBC, with Alison and Union Station as her backing band.

Shania had long been a fan of the bluegrass star's music, while in a neat twist Alison had always admired Mutt Lange's productions. "I wanted to go back to something stripped-down and rootsy," Shania explained. "I've been doing big concerts for quite a long time, and I love it, but I just want that contrast. Wanting to break the music down, there just didn't seem to be any other way. They were the ones. There is no second choice."

The show was recorded at an intimate club in Nashville in front of a crowd of three hundred people. Shania wore a black leather, long-sleeved jumpsuit with a wide rhinestone belt and matching rhinestone choker. Between songs, when the cameras weren't rolling,

Shania chatted about how women get as hairy as gorillas during the winter when they don't shave, cellulite, burning a hole in a leather purse with vodka, sucking, and spitting snot, among other down-home topics. Seven of the twelve songs she recorded came from *Up!* while the closer was something of a surprise: a new version of the AC/DC classic "You Shook Me All Night Long," with lyrics rewritten by Shania.

At the 2003 CMA Awards, Shania gave an altogether more low-key performance, singing "She's Not Just a Pretty Face." She also found time for an extended conversation with her onetime label-mate and Triple Play touring partner Toby Keith, who had been nominated for seven awards but went home with nothing. "Here she is, completely ignored by the CMA this year," Toby told Country-stars.com, "and yet there she was singing on the show. Then she seeks me out to talk. We talked about a lot of things, she asked about my family, and things that are really important. She's just a class act."

In the States, Shania was constantly reinforcing her country roots. "I mean I'll never not be country, how can you not?" she said. "How can you be something and then not be it anymore? Country is so deep in my roots and such a huge part of my youth, my most impressionable years, that it's just not going anywhere and I think even for people who listen to me in pop, the style of the way I write, which is very conversational lyrics, very real lifestyle lyrics, comes from my country roots."

Long before her Nashville rehabilitation was complete, Shania had started to gear up for her biggest ever tour. In July, she warmed up with two shows in Europe—Kilkenny in Ireland and London's Hyde Park—before recording a TV special for NBC in Chicago's Grant Park in front of fifty thousand fans. She reassembled the same band from the Come On Over Tour, which gave continuity and en-ergy to the live performance from the very first show.

Following the Chicago concert, Shania decided to radically re-think her stage set. The original plan was to tour with a smaller ver-sion of the rig used in Grant Park, but she felt that lacked intimacy beyond the first twenty rows. There was less than five weeks to re-design and build the stage before starting three weeks of stage re-hearsals at the Copps Coliseum in Hamilton, Ontario. Mark Fisher, whose track record with the Rolling Stones, Pink Floyd, and U2 has made him the most in-demand set designer in the music world, con-ceived of an in-the-round stage that literally allowed front row fans to get so close to Shania that if it wasn't for the many security guards surrounding the stage they could jump up and dance with her.

The stage was a large oval, eighty feet long and forty feet wide, with a runway around the perimeter that was only four feet high and designed in such a way that Shania could interact with fans without missing a beat. At many of her shows, she signed over a hundred autographs. A pair of ramps at either end led up to the eight-foot-high central platform. Shania wanted the center plat-form of the stage to have a floating feel, so Fisher designed it with a frosted plexiglass floor.

There were a couple of extra intimate flourishes on the ballads. Shania and one of her guitar players (the job has rotated through the tour, with Brent Barcus, Marc Muller, and Randall Waller each taking their turn in the spotlight) appeared seated in the audience to sing "The Woman in Me." During "Forever and for Always," she sat down on a stool on a small, circular rotating stage.

The lighting designer, Peter Morse, has worked with Madonna, Michael Jackson, and Tina Turner, while the pyrotechnics designer, Doug Adams, was a veteran of Kiss, Metallica, and Britney Spears tours. "With many acts," says Morse, "your job is to make the artists look better. With Shania, she already is a truly natural beauty, so my job is to make sure I don't detract from that in any way. It is very easy with the wrong angle and color choices to make an artist look bad."

Shania had promised her fans more bang for their buck and the show used fireworks, firebursts, streamers, and confetti to dramatic effect. There were a few problems caused by the low outer perime-ter, which meant the pyros could not be placed around the edge of the stage. With nine musicians and Shania hurtling about, there was also little room onstage. During the last few days of the rehearsals, Shania kept standing so close to one pyro that the opera-tor refused to fire it in case he blew her up. Once she learned that, Shania stopped the rehearsal mid-song and started over standing in the right spot.

"The effects we designed were tasteful rather than explosive," says Adams. "For 'From This Moment On,' we had special slow-burning glitter mines designed, which did a chase up each of the ramps, cer-tainly one of the most tasteful effects I've designed and one that was completely unexpected from an audience point of view."

The tour proper began on September 25 in Hamilton, Ontario, a few miles from her birthplace. The concert sold out in forty-five minutes. By July 2004, she had played some 130 shows in eleven countries to over two and a half million people, breaking box office records all around the world. The first leg of the tour in the fall of 2003 generated over $35.5 million. In North America, her average box office gross per city was $1,121,822, with an average ticket price of $67.53. When her European tour reached the M.E.N. Arena in Manchester, she sold over 18,300 tickets and grossed £750,000 ($1.35 million) to break the house record.

The arrival of Eja meant more additions to the touring party. On the road he was looked after by Simon, his English nanny. Shania and Mutt tried hard not to let their blond toddler get too accus-tomed to the backstage lifestyle. When he did appear at sound-checks, he wore outsized headphones to protect his hearing. "He's usually off doing other things, like swimming, ice-skating, or going to museums," says his mother, who might have been trying too hard to educate her toddler. She, after all, never saw the inside of a mu-seum until she was in her twenties. "He's on my sleeping schedule. I put him to bed every night."

Eja enjoyed life on the road. "He did great," says his mother. "He was a real trooper about it all. He had his bed on the bus. He loved the bus. Whenever we'd leave it to go somewhere, and the bus couldn't come with us or whatever, he'd go, 'Where's my bus? I want my bus!'"

Backstage, sometimes it must have seemed that the whole Twain clan was on tour—dogs, horses, nephews, and nieces. Mutt, too, spent much more time on the road than he had done previously. Once the front-of-house sound was up to his exacting standards, he stayed on to be with his wife and child. Tim, Shania's German shepherd, guarded her tour bus with his customary ferocity. Except for the one time when Shania walked in and startled him so much he jumped on the kitchen counter and turned on the faucet in the sink. By the time she realized what had happened, the whole bus had been flooded.

Shania was much more comfortable with touring the second time around. "To be honest, your concert becomes your home base," she said. "You get comfortable after a while. Once your show is up and rolling, it's your comfort zone. You eventually become more relaxed because the environment is pretty much the same every night. Your show is your show every night. And there's definitely a sense of stability there. That's the one thing that never changes."

Helene Bolduc chose to stay home in Timmins and her role as Shania's personal assistant, general chivvy, and on-the-road confidant was taken by Carrie Ann. Ariane Martin, a twenty-year-old Toronto fashion designer, was hired as wardrobe mistress. During each concert, Shania had eleven and a half minutes flat to get through three complete outfit changes. "Everything is laid out face-down on a table in the order she puts it on," Ariane told the *Toronto Sun*. "So when she runs into the change booth I help her rip off her clothes, pull on the new ones, and make sure her jewelry is on, boots are laced, and zippers zipped. If she's putting on a fishnet stocking and it rips, we have to hide the rip or mask it."

Shania's wardrobe changed every night. At every show she wore a home team jersey—but never the same one twice just in case fans attended more than one show. If there was no local sports team, Ariane bought a local tourist T-shirt and customized it by cutting it low, tying it high and adding rhinestones and Swarovski crystals.

While the actual outfits evolved over the tour, perennial favorites included silk cargo pants, jeans dotted with studs and crystals, sparkly tops, and Cosabella mesh tank tops layered in bright colors. She also liked wearing large glittering pieces of jewelry, especially chokers covered with crystals, which show up well in the stage lights. Her wardrobe, said Ariane, also carried "gowns for award shows, and over thirty pairs of boots and shoes (size 6)." Her favorite stage footwear is brightly colored boxing boots, custom designed by Steve Madden, worn with contrasting laces to match her outfits. Although Shania is tiny, she never wears stilettos onstage, only boots and platforms, because the slim heels can get caught in the step grates, with potentially dangerous consequences.

Traditionally, support bands on major tours are treated marginally better than the venue janitor, limited to two-minute sound checks and a part of the stage smaller than a gym mat, and not allowed to enjoy any of the backstage catering. That isn't the way Shania treated her support band, Emerson Drive. After their first show in Toronto, the band were in their dressing room when there was a knock at the door. It was Mutt and Shania. Mutt said, "I want to welcome you guys on the tour. Sorry we took so long at sound check."

Lead singer Brad Mates virtually went into in a state of shock after Shania added that they "could use the whole stage if we wanted. Her generosity is amazing. She's so down-to-earth and sweet. Not only is the gig a dream come true, but the catering backstage is amazing. It's like going to a five-star restaurant every night . . . Subway kind of goes out the window."

After Shania discovered Emerson Drive were fellow Canadians, she chatted with them daily, even sat down with them at mealtimes. "We talked about where we're from, how the group got started, and our plans—and about where Mutt's from, what he's done. And Shania—you can talk to her about anything. She's almost like your next-door neighbor. She's that nice and down-to-earth."

On the Up! Tour, for the first time, Shania felt fully at ease with her onstage persona. Performing was now fun, a joy, an inspiration, and a buzz—not a chore. And it helped record sales.

Part of the massive financial success of *Come On Over* was that its sales life stretched over three holiday seasons. For *Up!* to emulate that feat in a declining market was always unlikely. In December 2003, Mercury announced that the record had been certified diamond—ten times platinum—by the Recording Industry Association of America. It is considered a double LP, which puts actual sales at half that—five million. However, this does make Shania Twain the only artist in history to have three consecutive diamond-certified albums.

Disappointing perhaps for the record company—she still represents 71 percent of Mercury Nashville's sales—but substantially more than any other country act. (The next-best seller in 2003 was the Dixie Chicks, whose *Home* sold six million. Their sales stalled somewhat after their anti-Bush pronouncements.) Shania topped the *Billboard* Year-End Charts as the Top Country Artist (singles and albums), Top Country Artist—Female (singles and albums), Top Country Album Artist, Top Country Album Artist—Female, Top Hot Country Singles and Tracks Artist—Female, and with the Top Country Album *(Up!)*.

The worldwide sales of *Up!* have been considerable—a very respectable eight hundred thousand in the United Kingdom, a million plus in Germany—which will push the eventual total above ten million units. By any standard, that is an impressive achievement and Shania worked her butt off for every single sale. But was it enough?

Probably not. Hindsight is a terrible thing. It always has 20/20 vision. By Shania and Mutt's own high standards, *Up!* could be considered a failure. Her second tour, though hugely successful, failed to ignite album sales enough. Three years down the line one has to wonder whether *Up!* was as much of a Mutt production masterpiece as Luke Lewis claimed. There is a hurried quality to the album. After repeated plays, small things start to niggle, the odd tuning in the voice, lyrics that don't flow quite so smoothly as they did in the past. That is so unlike Mutt, who has always been the perfectionist's perfectionist.

It begs two questions: Was *Up!* more Shania's album? Can Mutt and Shania ever re-create the magic of their first two collaborations?

Chapter Twenty-Five

MARKING TIME AND HEADING SOUTH

IT HAS LONG BEEN record company practice to add several new tracks to a greatest hits package. They claim it gives added value—though die-hard fans might disagree. In November 2004 Shania released her *Greatest Hits* album. It debuted on the *Billboard* charts at number two behind Eminem's *Encore*. It sold 535,000 copies in the first week, a record for a compilation album, second only to the Beatles' *1*. It has since sold 3.5 million copies in the United States and a further 3 million around the world.

It offered three new songs, two different versions of "Party for Two," "Don't," and "I Ain't No Quitter." While it's hard to judge by just three songs, Shania's direction seemed to be heading back to Nashville rather than targeting the pop charts.

The original plan for "Party for Two" was for Shania to duet with Toby Keith. Instead she sings a country version with fellow Mercury Nashville artist Billy Currington and a pop version with Mark McGrath, lead singer of funk-pop outfit Sugar Ray, who never quite capitalized on their hits "Fly," "Every Morning," and "Falls Apart." Mark also coanchors the entertainment tabloid show *Extra* with Dayna Devon.

"'Party for Two' is kind of picking up where I left off on *Up!*" explained Shania. "It's a pretty typical Shania-type lyric and feel. And there's not really a gap between the last CD and this CD per se. I had just got off the road so the flow just continued. It's really just a fun, flirty song. You know it's not sexual. It's a party. It's very flirty but obviously when we get there we just have fun 'cause I'm not into that kind of sexual thing."

"I don't even know if we had decided at the beginning that we were going to have two versions," she said. "We knew we were going to do country for sure. We fished around for a lot of different options. Time was a big issue for so many people. I asked Toby if he would do it. He said yes, but then it interfered with his record. He's probably the only other person I approached.

"It was getting complicated to find somebody who was going to have the right timing. So Luke [Lewis] said, 'Maybe we should look at somebody new. It's not like you need the name. Just find the right voice.' He said, 'Listen to this guy Billy Currington.' I wanted to have somebody who was a strong contrast to me. He's got the real deep, southern voice, couldn't be more opposite from me."

The country theme was confirmed by the down-home honky-tonk of "I Ain't No Quitter." Shania says, "It's going to be one of my favorites, out of all the stuff I've done. I really love that very traditional, straight-ahead country stuff, and Mutt does, too. This is real barroom, classic stuff."

"Don't," in contrast, was written for the movie *An Unfinished Life,* which stars Robert Redford, Jennifer Lopez, and Morgan Freeman, and is directed by Lasse Hallström. "Mutt had the title 'Don't' for a long, long time," she says. "Since the last album. And I had this melody that I was singing. He had this chord progression. But the sentiment of the song had not reared its head. What do you do with 'don't'? The movie dictated where we went with it. The movie is really all about the struggle of relationships—forgiveness, anger, some really deep things. So we had to dig deeper."

Shania also found the time to make her first appearance in a movie, playing herself in one scene in David O. Russell's film *I ❤ Huckabees.* "It was such a great experience 'cause I've never been on a set before. All I had to do was slap Jude Law around a little bit and get mad at him. It was fun."

She beats up Jude Law (he had personally written to her, asking her to appear) in an elevator—a well-deserved punishment since he has spent the entire movie telling other characters how he made the pop world's most famous vegetarian eat a chicken sandwich. "I loved the experience, but I also realized that these are real actors; they know what they're doing. I don't know if I could do that. It was a bit intimidating in that sense, but great fun."

Her acceptance by the American heartland was further confirmed on Valentine's Day 2005 when Stetson, the original icon of the American West, announced that a Canadian from the backwoods was going to create her own fragrance line for the company. "Shania Twain is a modern-day symbol of what the Stetson Fragrances embody—independence, originality, and accessibility," gushed the press release, which also claimed she accepted the deal because "like a favorite song, a scent evokes a memory, creates a mood, and inspires a feeling." The new fragrance will be out in fall 2005.

Her limited promotional schedule for the compilation culminated on November 2, 2004, when Shania finally made it back to Timmins to cut the ribbon at the Shania Twain Centre. It looks far better now than it did on the day of the opening: well organized, with a variety of memorabilia, outfits, handwritten lyrics of the songs, and even her tour bus.

Whenever she returns to Timmins, Shania has to spring a little surprise. She popped in unannounced to Timmins High and Vocational School. "This is awesome," said Principal Wendy Adams. "I'm sure our kids are never going to forget this." Her former math teacher Gord Spylo came to the school and "he actually gave her a little five-question quiz about some math things related to her," said Adams. "And then they walked down to a music room . . . and they went to see some of the practice rooms. When she was a student here, she would go in there and write music, so she had some pretty fond memories of the music room and just wanted to see what that looked like."

At an assembly of about five hundred students, Shania presented the school a C$10,000 grant from the Canadian Academy of Recording Arts and Sciences for the purchase of musical instruments. In return the principal gave Shania school hockey jerseys— one for her and a pint-sized version for Eja.

Just as they had done for the official opening of the Centre, the chilly weather and light snowfall reminded her of hometown conditions. "I apologize for this taking so long," she told one thousand fans gathered outside of the Shania Twain Centre. "I was very far along in my pregnancy and I've been touring for the past few years. I finally made it. Thank you for your patience.

"I hope that now it's paying off and attracting people to this beautiful place," she said, adding that visitors would enjoy things like fishing, snowmobiling, visiting the mine, and "learning about us northern Ontario people."

Whether the Centre is actually working for Timmins is open to debate. The original estimates of fifty thousand visitors a year were always hopelessly optimistic—Jean-Paul Aubé reckons twelve thousand to fourteen thousand are expected this year. It was never going to match Graceland, which attracts eight hundred thousand visitors a year to Memphis, and with all due respect to Shania, she is not Elvis. Geography is against Timmins, which will always be a dot in Northern Ontario, a long drive and an expensive flight from Toronto.

"Financially it has been a bit of a struggle, but it is now at a break-even point," says Aubé. "I would say that overall the local businesses and most people believe that the Centre has played a role in attracting more people to visit Timmins. There is no doubt that Shania's visit in November 2004 and her enthusiastic personal seal of approval will help in the future."

Provided local politics don't get in the way. The Centre has become a political hot potato—some local residents and city council members say it's a waste of taxpayers money. Nobody is saying officially how many people come through, or how much it costs. The Shania Fan Convention is held in Timmins every August, and while it now attracts over a hundred people, that is not enough. In April 2005 Will Saari, who has run the Centre from the beginning, was fired after his position was cut from the city budget.

It's a tough call for Timmins. At least now, after years in the doldrums, the mining industry has finally picked up steam with a diamond mine up the James Bay Coast scheduled to open soon, as well as some new gold and nickel mines. Mines create jobs. When Shania is there she gives Timmins an international presence and PR most small towns only dream about. Timmins now exists in the world outside of Canada. Shania has done that for them. Nobody else. The fans inject money into the city that was never there before, but it may not be enough. Having built a monument to their favorite daughter, could the the town dare close it down? If that happened would Shania ever visit again?

Shania turned forty in August 2005, an age that marks a time of transition and change for a woman. She has said many times that she does not intend to have anymore children; she may instead be planning a fundamental move to the other side of the world.

In 2004 Mutt and Shania bought a perpetual lease to the Motatapu ("sacred river") and Mt. Soho stations, 61,000 acres of high country behind Glendhu Bay on Lake Wanaka in New Zealand's South Island. Lake Wanaka, in Central Otago, is 250 miles from Christchurch. It is close to Queenstown, the Southern Hemisphere's capital of adventure sports—it's where the bungee jump was invented—and home to several ski areas.

The station was previously owned by Sally Mackay, who in her twenty-eight years at the remote ranch had created a world-renowned three-acre perennial flower garden, which became a popular tourist destination. Popular, that is, for such a remote region. The station also includes the Motatapu Chasms, a craggy area that is a favorite of climbers and campers.

Just as they had done in St. Regis Falls, the Langes excited controversy when they decided to buy such a huge, beautiful property. They paid NZ$21.4 million (US$15.66 million), which was apparently four times the going rate. The news upset New Zealand's powerful outdoor lobby, who feared the sale would deny climbers, hikers, cyclists, and campers access to the land.

Documents issued by the Overseas Investment Commission (under the Official Information Act) outlined the Langes' commitment to spend an additional NZ$3.2 million (US$2.34 million) to develop the two ranches by farming merino sheep (bred for the fine quality of their wool, not for their meat) and creating a thirty-thousand-acre conservation estate. Their business would require six full-time employees and another fifteen staff over the course of three years to work on development projects, including a NZ$1.5 million (US $1 million) home for the Langes. They would also need US$183,000 to build woolsheds and sheep yards, US$73,000 for shearers' quarters; US$263,000 for fencing; and US$58,000 for roads and an airstrip—which would certainly cut down travel time from Auckland International Airport. Interestingly enough, there is no mention of plans to build a recording studio, which in the past has always been Mutt's first priority. They also promised to spend at least four months of the year at Motatapu "to escape the pressures of their public careers."

Their original business proposal claimed that by 2007 the combined sheep station would be making a profit of US$200,000, thus turning "a non-performing farm into a viable economic unit." This cut little ice with the commission, which doubted whether "it really is a viable farming investment" and originally planned to reject the request.

However, the deal was made after Shania and Mutt promised to provide a public walking track linking Wanaka with Arrowtown, to build two tramping huts (for walkers to sleep in overnight), and to let the Department of Conservation manage the conservation estate and tramping facilities.

"It's just a property to visit, Switzerland is our home," Shania insists. "We're not moving. We're staying here. Eja will go to school here. I look forward to it. He speaks French fluently. It's his first language. It's really just for the future. We live in Switzerland. That's where we'll spend most of our time. But we'll definitely go there for a couple of months every year, in their summer, because of opposite seasons. And ride on the range!"

Others wonder how long the manicured charms of Switzerland will keep Mutt and Shania content. For a driven superstar, it's a perfect base that provides easy access to the rest of the world, but that access can easily backfire on a couple who relish their privacy as much as the Langes do. Mutt and Shania can write songs and record anywhere, so why not New Zealand?

Living at the end of the world has other advantages. The Langes are extremely health-conscious (though Mutt is prepared to give Eja too much chocolate) vegans. Shania has spoken about her concerns for Eja; living at Motatapu would be secure and private, and would give him the outdoor life she craves. Although the ozone layer in South Island is thin, the air is clear and clean and the views spectacular. Mutt already appreciates that New Zealanders are fanatical sportsmen: rugby and sailing are the twin national religions. It is a great and safe place to bring up a child, to be a family.

Shania's career is on hiatus. The members of her live band have been told that she won't be performing for the foreseeable future and have been given small retainers. Her tour bus is currently parked up at the Shania Twain Centre in Timmins, where visitors can pop in and have a look.

"I need to write again," she said during interviews to promote the Greatest Hits album in the fall of 2004. "So I don't know when the next album's going to be. I don't know when the next tour is going to be. And I think that what this album represents, for me, this greatest hits, is a period of pause.

"I've entertained the idea of doing a really rootsy, country sound; it would be more on the bluegrass side. Would I want to do a straight-ahead pop record? I've entertained the thoughts of doing just duets with all my favorite artists. I've thought of maybe doing an album of covers of my favorite classics. And so what kind of album is the next album going to be? I don't know. I have to think about it a little more.

"I've already got ideas. Because we're married, we don't have to arrange getting together. When we feel ready to get back in the studio, we'll go."

As Shania Twain likes to take five years between albums, she is unlikely to release a new record until 2008. It may well take longer.

Meanwhile, she has a lot of living to catch up on.

CODA: THE REAL EILLEEN?

THREE MONTHS PRIOR to the release of *Up!*, I was invited to interview Shania on the first round of media interviews she gave at the Royal Parc Hotel in Evian, France. The very different Shania who confronted me was a revelation. Three years out of the spotlight had visibly softened her buttoned-up, formal edge.

The small-town girl had become a European sophisticate, but more than that she was calm, relaxed, natural, glowing with health and confidence. Her hair tumbled onto bare shoulders, she was dressed in casual chic, a pair of red and black combat trousers slung low off her hips and a skimpy waistcoat over a leopard-skin print bra. I spent much of the hour-long interview forcing myself to look into her eyes rather than her breasts—something she was fully aware of and deeply amused by. There were moments when I felt I was sitting down with Eilleen, not Shania.

Some things had not changed. Physically, she still preferred to keep her distance and will only kiss or hug those people who really matter to her. "People do find me a little formal," she says. "Canadians are more reserved, but with people we know we're comfortable. I have never been a huggy feely person. I'm better now than I was. I didn't even want my mother to hug me and when it comes to someone who I've never met expecting me to throw my arms around them, that is too much.

"People ask me if I feel sexy. No, I don't." She says, "I think it's quite funny. Maybe if I was Pamela Anderson, if it was my career to be a sex symbol, then it would be one of my goals. I am an artist, but I have to be a model half the time. I have to go through these paces which I find very unusual and uncomfortable. It's just not my scene. I still won't go on a beach in a bikini."

That relaxed attitude quickly vanished once Shania's relentless, largely self-imposed promotional schedule kicked in. Press interviews were fixed at thirty minutes, regardless of circulation and cover promises, enough time to cover the bases and rehash the legend, but not enough to delve too deeply. In the subsequent features, interviewers complained of the time allotted (as if it were their sacred right to have more) and how Shania's answers were often curt, short, and simple. Well-rehearsed, sometimes she gives away more than at others, whether it be snippets about Mutt or Eja or being described as a robot by Darryl. The chill professionalism that seemed to have gone in Evian had returned, diamond hard and twice as shiny. "I don't think she wants to connect with the press," says Luke Lewis. "There are a couple of places where you just can't go."

She admits to feeling "smothered" by fame. It is not yet a comfortable place for her and indeed may never be. "I struggle with fame, because the reality is that I'm naturally a withdrawn person," she says. "I can sit here and talk about my music, but I don't feel like I'm a star. I don't feel I'm sitting here as some famous person. I just like to be normal. I accept fame as part of what I do and I love the fans, but I'm the type of person that needs to be cut off. That's why I don't let cameras into my private life. I don't want to be a hypocrite that way.

"I love singing, but it's just not the thing I wanted to be famous for. I never wanted to be a star. When you sing, you are asking people to look at you and that's just not part of my personality. I consider myself a songwriter first and foremost. My goal has always been to get to the point where I can write hits that I don't have to record in order for them to become hits. I've written for other artists such as Celine Dion and Britney Spears and I loved that."

One day, perhaps she will be content with just writing, recording, and being a mother. For the moment, she is a superstar, albeit a reluctant one, driven by her need to compete and win. (Magnified also by her husband, who, beneath his laid-back charm, is even more fiercely competitive.) Her expectations are grounded, but then she has always been a girl whose feet remain rooted in reality. She knows she earns a great deal of money and publicly wonders if it isn't too great a reward for what she actually does.

"I've often thought about that," she told GQ. "Entertainers, sports people, movie stars: We work hard at what we do, there is no doubt about that. If you are going to succeed at the top of your field then you have to work unbelievably hard. No one in my life works as hard as me or makes a sacrifice I have to make. But the payoff is huge and I don't know how to gauge that. Then you think about the coal miners and they work much harder than I do but they don't make what I make. And then they die of lung cancer. That's where it's not right."

Shania Twain tells the world that she wants to be a songwriter, that is what she was born to be. Frequently she is asked about the other songs, the personal songs, the ones that articulate the rage and pain of her upbringing and her parent's deaths. The ones she locks in a box and won't let Mutt hear however much he begs. Luke Lewis, too, wonders about those songs. "There are certain artists you have to wait for a relationship to go sour before they write a great song. I know Shania has songs stashed away from the past and maybe they're too hard for her to hear. God knows there is enough pain in her past."

"They're musical thoughts or musical emotions. Sometimes it's even gibberish," she says. "I go back to my tapes from when I was twelve or thirteen and I think, 'No one's ever going to understand this stuff.' I wrote a song one time called 'Feeling Invisible.' It's all about being a teenager and there's a guy in the school you absolutely adore and he is so gorgeous but he'd never notice you, so it's just painful. You're so hurt and it's not even the guy's fault."

Shania has thought about her personal songs and comes up with a series of glib responses, some contradictory. "The purpose of them is simply for my own self-indulgence. They maybe wouldn't be valuable to anybody else. The reality," she says, "is that it takes you into a whole other place. And I just don't wanna go there. And the stuff that I do write that's like that—sad, that is—I enjoy by myself. Once I share it, it's not there anymore. I just don't have the urge to commercialize and to record it. Who's gonna relate to that, anyway? People are going to go out and pay for the record, and I want my music to relate to their lives, not vice versa."

Then she cuts to the chase. "I would lose them."

But would she? Sometimes a sad song affects its listeners far more than a perky, bouncy, upbeat number. Shania doesn't understand why those are the songs that people want to hear and that journalists want to ask her about. Isn't it enough, she asks, that she gives the world uplifting positive messages? That these might be the songs people want to hear in the future frightens her and so she dismisses them as of no consequence.

But they are not of no consequence. What they are not is Shania Twain™ songs. They are not Shania Twain™ songs because they have not been buffed and polished until they shine brighter than the stars in the sky. They are not Shania Twain™ songs because they may be so very personal that they might help explain away some of her enigma, and lay bare the unhappiness and tragedy that drove Eilleen Twain to become one of the few true superstars in the music firmament.

NOTES AND SOURCES

To avoid confusion, I generally refer to Shania Twain as Eilleen (her given name) until 1992, when she signed her record deal with Mercury Records in Nashville. Thereafter she is Shania, unless I have quoted directly or used nonoriginal material in which she is commenting on past events.

Occasionally, quotes may refer to her as both Eilleen and Shania in the same paragraph. These quotes are taken from other published sources.

BOOKS

Barnes, Michael. *Timmins: The Porcupine Country*. Erin, Ontario: Boston Mills Press, 1991.

Clarke, Donald. *The Rise and Fall of Popular Music*. New York: St. Martin's Press, 1995.

Gray, Scott. *Shania Twain: On Her Way*. New York: Ballantine Books, 1998.

Guralnick, Peter. *Lost Highway: Journeys & Arrivals of American Musicians*. Boston: D. R. Godine, 1979.

Hager, Barbara. *On Her Way: The Life and Music of Shania Twain*. New York: Berkley Boulevard, 1998.

Kane, Peter. *Shania Twain*. London: Aurum, 2000.

Kennedy, Laura, with Celia Finley. *Deerhurst Resort*. Erin, Ontario: Boston Mills Press, 1996.

Larkin, Colin. *The Virgin Encyclopedia of Country Music*. London: Virgin in association with Muze, Inc., 1998.

McCall, Michael. *Shania Twain: An Intimate Portrait of a Country Music Diva.* New York: St. Martin's Griffin, 1999.

Porterfield, Nolan. *Jimmie Rodgers: The Life and Times of America's Blue Yodeler.* Chicago: University of Illinois Press, 1992.

Vaughan, Andrew. *Shania: Feel Like a Woman.* London: Andre Deutsch, 2000.

WEBSITES

Shania Twain is a true child of the World Wide Web. Most of the minutiae of her career can be found on the Internet on a series of linked sites collectively christened the Shania Forums. Particularly informative are the North American Online Fan Club (www.shania fans.com) and Shania Net (www.shania.net).

The official david malachowski zone! (www.davidmalachow ski.com) provided useful background information and quotes on Shania's first backing band. Other Shania band member websites include:

Randall Waller—www.randallwaller.com

Marc Muller—www.marcmuller.com

Cory Churko—www.corychurko.com

J. D. Blair—www.jdblair.net

Roddy Chiong—www.roddyonline.com

Allison Cornell—www.allisoncornell.com

Brent Barcus—www.mileyandbb.com

Dan Schaefer—www.danschaefer.com

Official websites and links to Shania's favorite charities include:

Shania's own website—www.shaniatwain.com

Shania's official fan club—www.fanclub.shaniatwain.com

Shania's Mercury site—www.shania-twain.com

The Shania Twain Centre—www.shaniatwaincentre.com

Mercury Nashville Records—www.mercurynashville.com

America's Second Harvest—www.secondharvest.org

Breakfast for Learning—www.bfl.org

The Mutt Lange Zone—www.bigbro.ca/zone.html

For my take on Ojibwe history, I am indebted to Lee Sultzman's First Nations Histories at www.tolatsga.org/ojib.html.

Castles of Switzerland (www.swisscastles.ch) provided much of the background information on the Château de Sully.

NEWSPAPERS AND MAGAZINES

Other than the quotes from my own interviews, I have taken from other interviews first published in: *Rolling Stone, Q, The Daily Mirror, The Times, Redbook, Macleans, Cosmopolitan, FHM, The Toronto Star, Country America, Music City News, Total Style, Country Music News, People, The Calgary Sun, Country Wave, The National Enquirer, Entertainment Weekly, Billboard, The Timmins Daily Press, The Sudbury Star, The Huntsville Forester, OK, TV Guide, USA Today, Flare, Eve, GQ, High Life, Toronto Sun, InStyle Magazine, TIME, Sports Illustrated, American Way Magazine, Professional Lighting and Production, The Telegraph Magazine, Lifetime Magazine, The Sunday Times* (South Africa), *The Sunday Express, The Sunday Mirror, The Irish Independent, Animal Fair, Glamour, In Touch Total Productions,* and *E! Online.* Apologies to any other sources I may have inadvertently left out; the fault is mine.

TV AND RADIO

TV and radio sources include: VH-1 *Behind the Music,* the CBS TV interview *From Rags to Riches,* and BBC Radio 2 interviews by Mindy McCready and Bob Harris.

INDEX

A&M Records, 133, 137, 159, 203

AC/DC, 86, 186, 188, 190, 330

Acuff-Rose, 141, 143

Adams, Bryan, 83, 177, 190–92, 197, 205–7, 238, 257

Adams, Doug, 331–32

Adams, Wendy, 338

Ade, King Sunny, 174

"Ain't Nothin' Like the Real Thing," 119

Allan, Bruce, 238

Allen, Rick, 187, 192, 196

American Music Awards, 236

ANC (African National Congress), 181

Anderson, John, 157

Anderson, Pamela, 343

Andrews, Eamonn, 183

Andrews, Patty Lou, 230, 235

An Unfinished Life, 337

Apotex, 125, 129, 138

Appalachian mountain music, 145

ARIA, 289

Armstrong, Louis, 147

Arnold, Eddy, 149

Atkins, Chet, 158

Atlantic Records, 181

Aubé, Ben, 80, 81

Aubé, Charmaine, 210

Aubé, Jean-Paul, 80–81, 82, 89–90, 210, 339

Autry, Gene, 148

Ayres, Brian, 110, 117–18, 129–30

Back in Black (AC/DC), 186

Backstreet Boys, 180

Bad, 323

Bailey, Mary, 140

    agrees to manage S, 91–92

    argues with S, 92, 95

    attends the Twains' funeral, 107

    Egypt, 235

    fired by S, 233–34

    first speaks to Mutt, 204

    follows Mutt's spiritual path, 201, 208, 230

    impressed by S's talent, 90–91

    invites Dick Frank to see S, 141

    loves S as a daughter, 229–30, 234

    overworked with cash flow problems, 230–32

    S calls for help, 107, 109

    S opens for (in Sudbury), 43

    S turns to again, 139

    S's first video, 162–63

    S's personality, 161

    S's relationship with Bell, 100–02

Bailey, Mary *(cont.)*
  S's second album, 225
  S's stage name, 144–45
  tries to get S's songs recorded, 157
Baird, Ron, 163–64, 227–28, 234, 266, 270
Baker, Carroll, 42
Barcus, Brent (B.B.), 267, 268, 331, 348
Bartz, Paul, 247
Bates, Dave, 201
Baxter, Craig, 139
BBC, 326
Beach Boys, 171
Bear Island, Lake Temagami reservation, 28, 53, 54
Beatles, the, 75, 83, 174, 175
Beaver Wars (1630–1700), 26
Beck, Richard, 280–85
Beer, Michelle Marie, 126–27, 134
Beginnings 1989–90, 285–86
Belinkis, Joe, 75
Bell, John Kim, 119, 124, 128, 244
  Deerhurst, 129, 131, 134, 137–38
  drives S back to Timmins, 106
  ends relationship with S, 107
  foundation, 95–96
  gives S opportunities, 101
  half Mohawk, 95, 99
  relationship with S, 95–107
  S's voice, 95–96
  told of the Twains' accident, 103–4
Bell, Kevin, 99, 104
Benatar, Pat, 73, 84, 137
Benson family, 14
Bernstein, Leonard, 101, 129
Big Country Show (traveling concert party), 42
Billboard, 152, 179, 225, 236, 335, 336

Black, Clint, 153
blackflies, 64
Bladon, Glenn, 142
Blair, J. D., 142, 267, 271, 348
bluegrass, 146, 148
blues, 146, 147
Blunder, Markus, 235
BMG Records, 181
BMI country awards, 158, 242
Bogguss, Susie, 164
Bohler, Jenny, 248
Bolduc, Helene, 2, 185, 272–73, 290–91, 292, 299, 300–302, 313, 333
  close confidant of S, 124, 272–73
  meets S, 124
  Regina's reconciliation attempt, 250–51
  S's breakup with Paul, 209–10
  S's Come On Over Tour, 272–74
  S's songwriting, 254–55
  S's wedding, 212
  Twains' deaths, 107
Bolduc, Larry, 2, 212, 272
Bolduc, Paul, 123–25
Bolton, Michael, 191–92, 205, 226, 254
Bond, Lynn, 46–47, 50, 56, 59, 265
Boomtown Rats, 182–84, 186, 190, 193
Boston, Massachusetts, 153
Boucheporn, Baron Bertrand de, 293
Boucher, Dan, 17
Bouton Bruce, 258
Bouwer, Marc, 326, 327, 328
Boyzone, 289
Brannen, John, 163
Brit Awards, 285
Broadway, 95, 101, 129
Brooks, Garth, 151–153, 192, 237, 257, 271, 277, 278

Broughton, Steve, 185
Brown, Arthur, 181
Brown, Carrie Ann (née Twain, S's
    sister) born Edwards, 50, 70,
    299, 301, 333
  birth, 21
  Huntsville, 110–12
  Jerry adopts, 30, 245
  S shares a room with, 51
  S's marriage to Mutt, 211–12
  Twains' accident, 105–6
  works at McDonald's 71, 106
  works in Jerry's reforestation
    business, 64–65
Brown, Charity (Phyllis Boats), 126
Brown, Junior, 241
Brown, Steve, 184–85, 188
Browning, John, 45, 48–49
Brulé, Étienne, 24
Buck, Gary, 43
Buffett, Jimmy, 159
Burke, Gary, 226
Burnett, Gordon, 95
Burnett, Suzanne, 95
Burnstein, Cliff, 322
Byrds, 171, 178
Byrom, Larry, 216, 218

CAA (Creative Artists Agency),
    163, 227, 230
Caby, Shirley, 249, 251–52
Calder, Clive, 178–81, 184, 201–2,
    225, 239, 299, 322
Campbell, Glen, 43
Campbell, Stan, 89, 91
Campbell, Vivian, 196
Canada
  education system, 28–29, 338
  musical periphery, early 1980s,
    88
  Pearce family sails to in 1912, 9–10
  wane of French power, 26

Canada Day, 1, 3
Canadian Country Music Associa-
    tion, 95, 241
  Awards, 231, 233, 295
Canadian Living Foundation, 276
Canadian National Railways
    (CNR), 21–22
Canadian Pacific Hotels, 139
Canadian Pacific Railway (CPR), 44
Cannon, Buddy, 143, 144, 214
Capital Radio, 282, 289
Carey, Mariah, 122, 137, 266
Carpenter, Karen, 91, 137
Carpenters, the, 35, 51
Carr, Barbara, 239, 275, 283
Carrette, Karen, 119, 121
Cars, the, 188
Carson, Phil, 181
Carter Family, 37, 147
Carter, A. P., 147
Carter, Carlene, 147
Carter, Ezra, 147
Carter, Maybelle, 147
Carter, Sara, 147
Cash, Johnny, 147, 150, 159
Cash, June, 147
CBC, 77, 101
Chabot, Mike, 78, 81, 83, 87
  meets S, 77
  S's first lover, 74, 84
Chapleau, Ontario, 13–14, 16, 21,
    248
Chapman, Steven Curtis, 268
Charles, HRH The Prince of Wales,
    274–75
Chase, Diane, 88
Château de Sully, Vaud canton
    Switzerland, 293–94
Chemay, Joe, 215, 258, 259–60
Cherokee Rose, 110
Children's Aid, 54
Chiong, Roddy, 268–69, 348

Churko, Cory, 268, 315, 348
Churko, Kevin, 315
CIBC bank, 65–66
Ciccone, Tony, 72–73
Cichon, Andy, 267
City Boy, 184, 185
CKGB radio station, 37
Clark, Guy, 150, 220
Clear Channel, 325
Clearmountain, Bob, 190
Cline, Patsy, 150
Clover, 182, 192
CMT (Country Music Television), 154, 162, 163, 203, 223, 329
CMT Europe, 164
Cochrane, Tom, 210
Cockburn, Bruce, 210
Cole, Nat King, 142
Collen Phil, 196
Collins, Bootsy, 267
Collins, Phil, 293
Columbia, 149, 182
Columbine High School, 277
Come On Over, 5, 84, 215, 255–62, 278, 280, 289, 323, 325, 334
Complete Limelight Sessions, 287–88
Connors, Stompin' Tom, 37, 40, 80
Cook, Jack Kent, 8
Copper, Cliff, 44
Cornell, Alison, 226, 267, 272, 348
Country Edition, 42
country music, 145–54, 159
Country Music Association (CMA), 141, 326, 328, 330
Country Music News, 89
country radio, 153–54
Country Weekly, 236
Cousineau, Paul, 3, 83
Cree, 42, 63
Crosby, David, 164
Crowder, Gillie, 230–31
Culture Club, 88

Currington, Bill, 336, 337
Cyrus, Billy Ray, 155, 206, 213, 221, 279

Daily Press (Timmins), 107, 210, 243, 246, 251
Dalhart, Vernon, 147
Dancer (horse), 274
Dangerous, 323
David Letterman Show, 326
Davis, Dr., 72
Davis, Linda, 216
Deal, Roland, 170
Decca, 149
Deerhurst Hotel, Huntsville, 115–28, 131, 266
    A Touch of Broadway, 131, 135–36, 137, 139, 142, 144
    Bell's arrival, 129–30
    Canadian Pacific Hotel, 139
    Cypress Lounge (Green Room), 110, 117, 135, 140
    expansion, 129
    Four Winds Cottage, 117–18
    Frank sees S at, 141–42
    Kelso incident, 124–25
    Kotowski issue, 126–28
    Kotowski's vision, 125
    Pavilion, the, 129, 137, 139, 142
    recordings, 134, 142, 285
    S leaves, 139–40
    S marries Mutt, 212
    S signs at, 119–20
    S's fling with Pierre le Gendre, 121
    Viva Vegas show, 117–18, 124, 126, 131
    Waterhouse sells to Apotex, 125
Def Leppard, 88, 120, 177, 185–88, 190, 191, 196, 203, 220, 271, 322
Degazio, Mike, 117, 126, 128, 132, 135, 136, 138, 140

Del Frate, Colette (née St.
    Amande), 43, 56, 59–60
Denis, Tim, 89
Derasp, Kenny, 51, 65
    denies S was an alcoholic, 252
    recordings with S, 38
    S's demo, 42
    S's musicality, 36
    Twain household, 55
Derasp, Romeo, 36
Derek, Bo, 221–22
Derek, John, 221–22
Des O'Connor Show, The (TV), 280
Detroit, 16
Dileo, Frank, 224
Dion family, 46
Dion, Celine, 261, 344
Dion, Rick, 78, 84
Dionne quintuplets, 116
Dirk, Dieter, 183
Divas Live show (VH-1), 269
Dixie Chicks, 335
dobro, 147
Dolby, Thomas, 188
du Plooy, Johan, 168–70, 172, 197
Dubois, Lise, 70
Duncan, Stuart, 258
Durning, Charles, 165

Eagles, 150, 153, 178
Eagles: Their Greatest Hits
    (1971–75), 5
Earle, Steve, 243
EastEnders, 301
Easton, Sheena, 84
Eastwind, 42
Easy Country (TV show), 43
Eddy, Duane, 218
Edmonton, 327
Edwards family, 13, 18–19, 30,
    243–44, 245, 249
Edwards, Clarence (S's natural father)
    appearance, 16–17
    background, 13
    commits himself to a mental
        hospital, 21
    controversy over him, 243–46,
        248–51
    home in the bush, 253
    leaves Sharon, 21
    marries Sharon, 78
    meets Sharon, 13, 17
    military career, 17
    singing voice, 16
Edwards, Desi (S's uncle), 18, 249
Edwards, Eilleen Regina *see* Twain,
    Shania
Edwards, Gordon (S's uncle)
    attitude toward Jerry, 30
    Clarence's singing voice, 16
    Harold's bootlegging, 15
    Sharon's jealousy, 19–20
    Sharon's pill-taking, 19
    tries to dissuade Clarence from
        marrying, 18
Edwards, Harold (S's grandfather)
    alcoholism, 15, 250
    birth in 1906, 14
    bootlegger, 15
    falls in love with Regina, 14
    marries Regina, 1927, 14
    music, 16
Edwards, Lori, 250, 251, 252
Edwards, Walter (S's uncle), 14, 18
Egypt, 235
"Eight Days a Week, 75
Elliot, Joe, 186–87, 189, 191
Elvis, 339
EMI Music, 151
Eminem, 336
EMI Records, 179
Emms, John 68, 82, 86, 210
Entertainment Weekly, 320
Escher, Wilhelm, 294

Estefan, Gloria, 136
Eurythmics, 88
Evans, Sara, 143
Evans, Ted, 48–50, 57
Evian, 343–44
Everly Brothers, 158, 171
Everly, Don, 141
Ewing, Skipp, 157
Extra, 336
Ezrin, Bob, 132

Falconbridge, 44
Fame Academy, 326
Fan Appreciation Days, 237–38, 262, 265
Fan Fair (International Country Music Fan Fair convention), 205, 236–37
Farian, Frank, 242
Fender, Freddie, 42
Fender guitar, 72–73
FHM magazine, 74, 281
Fiddler's Green Amphitheatre, Englewood, Colorado, 277
Field, near Sudbury, 12
Fingers, Johnnie, 184
Finley, Celia, 113, 118, 120–21, 130, 247
Fireside Studios, 144
Fisher, Mark, 331
Fleetwood Mac, 51, 83
Flirt, 88–89, 93
Flying Burrito Brothers, 178
FM radio, 67, 154, 189
Fontayne, Shane, 226
Foreigner, 84, 88, 188, 194
Foster, David, 185
Foster, Lynn, 130
Frank, Dick, 141, 158, 233, 246
Franklin, Larry, 258
Franklin, Paul, 258, 315

Fraser, Don (S's uncle), 2, 35, 108, 244, 300
    birth in 1933, 11
    lives with his grandparents, 11
    marries at nineteen, 12
    mother's dying wish, 31
    Sharon's marriage to Clarence, 22
    Sharon's mental health, 12
    Sharon's wedding, 18
Fraser, Jan (S's aunt), 2, 300
Fraser, Walter, 11
Freedom's Children, 179
Freeman, Morgan, 337
Frick, Julie, 123

Gabriel, Peter, 226
Gaye, Marvin, 119
Geldof, Sir Bob, 186
    Is That It? 83, 193
Gibson, Debbie, 238
Gill, Vince, 26, 248
Gilles (Jill's father), 13, 18
Glasgow, Renfrew Ferry club, 279
Globe, 242, 248
Gogama, Ontario, 63
Goldman, Steven, 162
Goldswain, Alan, 177
Goodman, Bennie, 148
Gootch, Don, 133
gospel, 146
Graceland, 339
Grady, John, 160, 220, 225, 263
Grainge, Nick, 193
Grainge, Nigel, 182, 183, 184
Grand Ole Opry, 148, 149
Grant, Amy, 215
Grateful Dead, 322
Greatest Hits, 336, 342
Green, Alison, 194, 195, 201
Green, Nigel, 190, 269
Guerette, George, 143

Guess, John, 216
Guralnick, Peter: *Lost Highway*, 146

Hagen, Cynthia, 75
Haggard, Merle, 150
Haidasz, Walter, 286
Hajacos, Rob, 216, 217, 258
Halfway Lake, 48
Hamilton, Mike, 122
Hanmer township, Ontario, 52–53, 67, 71, 252
    described, 45
    Gravelle Drive, 46
    Proulx Court, 44, 60, 265
    S's education, 46–52
    Twains move back to Timmins, 61
    Twains move to, 39
    winters in, 53
Harris, Bob, 295, 311
Hartt, Dave, 78, 81, 87, 107
    appeal of Longshot, 82–83
    compositions, 83
    real name (Guy Martin), 78–79
    S's songs, 84
    suggests S joins Longshot, 77
Harvey, Retta, 165, 223, 235, 264
Haselden, Tony, 157
Haverland, Kelita, 92
Hawaiian guitar, 147
Hawkes, Greg, 189
Heart, 120, 137
heavy metal, 153
Hemphill, Hardy, 268
Hendrix, Jimi, 175
Hey Hey Saturday (TV show), 284
Hidden Valley, 116, 118
Higgins, Sherrie, 119, 121
Hill, Chris, 183
Hill, Lynn, 119, 121, 139–40
hillbilly music, 146

Hinde, Harry, 126, 132–34, 136, 137, 139, 143, 244, 285–87
Hinduism, 199
Hocus, 176–78, 193, 198
Hollies, 171
Hollywood, Barry, 281
Holz, George, 281
Horne, Lena, 142
Houston, Whitney, 137, 151
Howard, Steven, 214
Hubbard, Gary, 136
Huey Lewis and the News, 192
Huff, Dann, 216, 258, 259
Hughey, John, 216, 258
Hungate, Dave, 216
Hunley, Con, 144
Huntsville, 110–13
    Mark and Darryl's criminal behavior, 246–47
    S moves to, 110
    Shoppers Drug Market, 111
Hynde, Chrissie, 122
Hurst, Brian, 75–76, 78

Ilovar, Marjan, 71
I ♥ Huckabees, 337
Inco (International Nickel Company), 44, 45
Ireland, 330
Irkin, Jon, 315
Iroquois Point, 26
Islam, 199

Jackson, Alan, 326
Jackson, Joe, 226
Jackson, Michael, 5, 88, 151, 160, 219, 224, 271, 289, 331
Jennings, Waylon 35, 150, 156, 159
Jive Records, 180, 194, 208, 238
Johannesburg music scene, 177
John, Elton, 51, 136, 177, 261
Johnson, Brian, 186

Jomato Records, 286
Jon Landau Management, 239, 280, 321
Jones, George, 143, 150
Jones, Jessica, 179, 203
Jones, Quincy, 219
Jones, Tom, 150
Journey, 83, 88
Judd, Wynonna, 153
Judds, 157

Kapuskasing, 14, 16
Kardas, Pam 65–66
Kasner, Bob, 90, 231, 233
Kasner, Bobby Jr., 91, 94, 143, 230
Keating, Ronan, 289
Keith, Toby, 155, 163–64, 330, 336, 337
Kelso, Mia, 124
Kelso, Sammy, 124
Kentucky Headhunters, 143, 155
Kerns, John, 269
Kerr, Julie, 230
Kershaw, Sammy, 143, 155, 236
Kidd Creek mine, Northern Ontario, 8, 28
Kiraga, Carole, 66
Kirkland Lake, 43, 92–95, 232
Kiss, 152, 331
Koch Records, 287
Korsten, Ge, 175
Kotowski, John, 125–28, 129, 133, 137–39
Kotowski, Mona, 127
Kragen, Ken, 92
Krauss, Alison, 329
Kreiner, Kathy, 8
Kristofferson, Kris, 34

Lake of Bays, 116, 302
Lambier, Eric, 93, 227
Landau, Jon, 239, 266, 321, 322, 323

Lange family, 174
Lange, Bill ("Slug," Mutt's brother), 170, 291
Lange, Eja (S's son), 306–9, 332, 339, 341–42, 344
Lange, Elizabeth (née von Wartenburg, Mutt's mother), 167
Lange, Ivan Gary (Mutt's father), 167
Lange, Olga (Mutt's second wife), 194–95, 201
Lange, Peter (Mutt's brother), 168–70
Lange, Robert John "Mutt" (S's husband), 170, 242, 344, 345
    ambition, 174
    appearance, 164, 206, 211
    birth in 1948, 167
    Come On Over Tour, 267–70
    disciplined lifestyle, 184–85
    education, 168–70
    finances, 301
    first band, 3
    Hocus, 167–78
    marriage to Olga, 194–95, 201
    marries S, 192, 212
    marries Stevie, 178
    master of double entendre, 257
    move to Switzerland, 291, 293–94, 297–98
    perfectionist, 183, 185, 188, 190, 343
    record producing, 183–92
    relocates to London, 181
    remains wedded to his Muse, 304
    S's second album, 213–25
    schools
        Belfast High School, South Africa, 168–69, 197
        Guinea Fowl, Gwelo, Southern Rhodesia, 168, 169
    songwriting, 185, 187–90, 254–56

Sonovision, 175
spirituality, 195–201, 211–12
success, 181–82
views on having children, 304–6
voice, 177
workaholic, 194
Lange, Stevie (Mutt's first wife) see Van Kerken, Stevie
Lanoir, Cyril, 283
Lansbury, Angela, 103
Lanthier, Gilles, 119, 121, 125, 131, 139
Las Vegas, 115, 118
Latchford, 28
Lauzon, Tom, 78
Lavigne, Avril, 275–76
LD Publicity, 280
Le Blanc, Larry, 225
le Gendre, Pierre, 121, 142
Leadon, Bernie, 153–54
Leamer, Laurence: Three Chords and the Truth, 54, 248
Led Zeppelin, 67, 154
Leim, Paul, 214–19, 257, 259, 315
Lennon, John, 175
Leno, Jay, 227, 268, 327
Lepine, Gaet, 37
Letterman, David, 236
Levack mine, 18, 44
Levy, Alain, 159, 221
Lewis, Huey, 182
Lewis, Luke, 159–60, 163, 204, 213–14, 220–25, 227, 229, 232, 234–35, 238, 241, 263, 270, 279, 319–320, 322, 324, 326, 328, 329, 337, 344, 345
Lillywhite, Steve, 190
Liquor Licence Board of Ontario (LLBOA), 81
Liszewski, Paul, 327
Live! (TV show), 227

Londin, Larrie, 158
London
  Alberta's bar, Sloan Street, 282
  Bombay Brasserie, 284, 299
  Hyde Park, 330
  Milestone Hotel, Kensington, High Street, 278
  no bodyguards, 284
  Royal Opera House, Covent Garden, 299
  Venom club, 279
Longfellow, Henry; The Song of Hiawatha, 25
Longshot, 93, 119, 210
  appeal of, 82
  disbands, 86–87
  hardworking, 86
  last gig, 87
  limited ambition, 87
  name, 78
  residency at JP's lounge, 81
  S joins, 77
  S's songs, 84
  songs performed by, 83–84
  start, 78
Lopez, Jennifer, 337
Lord Design Studio, 4
Lorrie Myrna, 35, 39, 42
Louvin Brothers, 149
Love, Courtney, 322
Lovett, Lyle, 216, 267, 288
Lynn, Loretta, 150, 216
Lynne, Shelby, 267

Maby, Graham, 226
Macdonald, Laurie, 47–48, 52
MacInnis, Jeff, 64
Madonna, 151, 266, 322, 331
Mahovlich, Frank, 68
Mahovlich, Peter, 68
Make-A-Wish Foundation, 286
Malachowski, David, 226, 236

Malton, Dean, 114, 122–24, 126, 134, 142, 209–10
Malton, Wayne, 122
Mamas and the Papas, the, 35
Manchester, La Gitaine club, 279
Manitoba, 10
Manitoulin Island, 63
Mann, Manfred, 171
Manson, Marilyn, 322
Mapfumo, Thomas, 174
Marsh, Dave, 239
Martin Ariane, 333
Martin, Lawrence (aka Wapistan), 41–42
Martin, Guy *see* Hartt, David
Mason, Brent, 216, 258, 315
Mates, Brad, 334
Mattagami First Nation, 28, 31–33, 52–54, 245–46, 276
McCoy, Neal, 227
McCready, Sammy, 143
McEntire, Reba, 153, 248
McGrath, Mark, 336
McKay, Willis (Jerry's cousin), 29, 31–32, 52, 54, 246
McKinnon, Don, 28
McNamara, Steve, 173, 176, 198
Meatloaf, 59
Melissa, 114
Melody Maker, 177
Mensch, Peter, 321, 322, 324
Mercury Records Nashville, 143, 155, 159–60, 162, 163, 206, 213, 220, 222, 228, 232, 237, 241, 263, 280, 323, 336, 347, 348
Mercy Brothers Show, The (TV show), 43
Merman, Ethel, 134
Merseybeat, 170
Mersham, Leah, 48
Messier, Jean-Marie, 323
Metallica, 331

Metroland, 226
Midler, Bette, 136
Miller, Glenn, 148
Mills, Gordon, 150
Milsap, Ronnie, 43, 157
Minneapolis, Mall of America, 237, 262
Mitchell, Mike, 78–79
Moeketsi, Kippie, 175
Mohawk, 24, 26, 95, 99
Montgomery, Hilda, 110, 118
Montgomery, John Michael, 226
Moose Factory, 63
Moosonee, 63
Morris, Doug, 263
Morrisette, Alanis, 256
Morrison family, 12, 35
Morrison, Bert (S's great-grandfather), 12, 31
Morrison, Mary (née Brisbois, S's great-grandmother), 12
Morrison, Van, 177
Morrison, Eileen (née Pearce, then Fraser, S's grandmother), 22, 244
    birth in 1911, 9
    dying wish, 31
    falls in love with George Morrison, 11
    ill health, 12, 13
    looks after her granddaughters, 22
    love of music, 34–35
    marries Walter Fraser, 11
Morrison, George (S's grandfather), 11–12
Motatapu, 340
Morvan, Fabrice, 242
Morsen, Peter, 331
Motors, 182
MTV, 67, 154, 223, 282
MuchMusic channel, 67, 88, 222
Muller, Marc, 226, 267, 271, 331, 348

Munns, David, 279, 281

Munsey, Stan, 157

Murder, She Wrote (TV program), 103

Murray, Anne, 136

Music Row, 157, 224, 228, 229

Muskoka, 116, 303

Nanak, Guru, 198–99

Nashville, 42, 139, 140, 148–49, 204, 330, 336

    attitudes, 150

    boom, 152–53

    conservatism, 241

    country radio programs, 154

    Cowboy line-dancing club, 221

    demos by S in 1984, 89, 91

    described, 153–56

    Mary Bailey takes S to, 1985, 92

    Masterfonics Tracking Room, 258

    pop crossovers, 88

    S's record deal, 3, 142–45

    Sound Stage studios, 215

National Aboriginal Achievement Foundation (previously Canadian Native Arts Foundation), 95, 99, 101, 129

National Enquirer, The, 113, 121, 127, 248, 290–91, 342

National Lottery Show, The (TV program), 281

NBC, 329, 330

Neese, Sandy, 241, 242, 254, 266

Nelson, Willie, 150, 329

New Liskeard, 28, 113

New York, 266

New York Times, The, 151

New Zealand, 340

North Bay, 116

North Carolina Ramblers, 146

Notting Hill (film), 288, 301

*NSYNC, 180

Nutbrown, Regina (née Benson, then Edwards, S's grandmother)

    claims that S ignored her relatives, 243

    death, 251

    Harold's bootlegging, 15

    marries Harold in 1927, 14

    Native ancestry, 14

    reconciliation with S attempted, 249–50

    remarriage, 250

O'Kelly, Fachtna, 184

Ocasek, Ric, 189

Ocean, Billy, 180

Ojibwe

    conflict with other tribes, 26

    culture, 27, 100

    dual citizenship, 246

    geographical remoteness, 24

    hunter-gatherers, 25

    Jerry's employer, 62

    language, 28–29

    loss of lands and self-respect, 27

    meat preservation, 32

    names, 24

    peace treaty, 26

    population, 27

    storytellers, 25

    trade, 25–27

Ontario, 24, 141

Ontario Provincial Police (OPP), 15

Onwatin Lake, 265

Oprah Winfrey Show, The, 251

Opry North (country radio show), 42

Orbison, Roy, 141

Orleans, 84

Orono, near Toronto, 94, 96

Oslin, K.T., 155

Otis Waygood Blues Band, 179
Ottawa, 45
Outlaw movement, 150

Palmour Tavern, 87
Paquette, Gerry, 72
Parker, Graham, 182, 184
Parsons, Gram, 150, 159, 220
Parton, Dolly, 34, 35, 88, 137, 146, 150
Party in the Park (Hyde Park, London), 274, 289
Patsy Cline's Greatest Hits, 238
Pearce family, 9–11
Pearce, Francis George (S's great-grandfather), 9–11
Pearce, Frank Jr. (S's great-uncle), 10, 11
Pearce, Grace (S's great-aunt), 10, 22
Pearce, Jack, (S's great-uncle),10, 12
Pearce, Lottie Louise (née Reeves, S's great-grandmother), 9–10
Pearce, Roger (S's cousin), 10, 35
pedal steel guitar, 147
Penn, Sean, 164–65
People, 328
Pereira, Pete, 142
Perras, Anita, 43
Perrault, Mike, 59
Peters, Bernadette, 101
Peters, Gretchen, 157
Peterzell, Lynn, 220
Phonogram Records, 184
Pilatus, Rob, 242
Piney, Manitoba, 11, 35
Pink Floyd, 69, 266, 331
Poco, 178
Police, the, 88
Polydor Records, 181
Polygram Records, 143, 221, 263, 279, 281

Port Cunnington, 302
Porterfield, Nolan, 146–47
Post, Debbie, 43
"Pour Some Sugar on Me," 120, 187, 221
Power, Vic, 4, 76
Presley, Elvis, 158, 174
Pretenders, the, 122
Pride, Charley, 34, 35
Prince Buddy (pony), 46
Pro Tools, 260–61
Prophet, Ronnie, 42

Q magazine, 30
Q-Prime, 321, 322
Q107 rock station, 94
Quicksilver Messenger Service, 182
Quirion, Georges, 4

Radhasoami Satsang, 198–99, 200, 296
Rambeaux, Leonard, 136
Randy (brand member, Kirkland Lake), 93–95
rap, 153
Rawson, Cyril, 92
record sales manipulation, 224–25
Redbook, 328
Redford, Robert, 337
Red River Rebellions, 26–27
Reeves, Cyl (Cecilia, S's great-aunt), 10, 11
Reeves, Sidney (S's great-great-grandfather), 11
Reid, Marg, 127, 131, 135, 140, 145
Rendazzo, Charley, 222
Reverdon, Emile, 293
Revlon, 300
Rich, Charlie, 143
Richie, Lionel, 92, 119, 136, 215, 277
Riel, Louis, 26
Rising, The, 322

Ritter, Tex, 148
Ritts, Herb, 300
Robbins, Kent, 157
Roberts, Julia, 288
rock and roll, 146
rockabilly, 149–50
Rodgers, Jimmie, 16, 146–48, 151
Rodrigues, Dave, 64
Rodrigues, John, 64
Rogers, Kenny, 88, 92
Rogers, Roy, 148
Roland Michener High School, South Porcupine, 12
Rolling Stone, 68, 325, 328
Rolling Stones, the, 277, 321, 331
Rollings, Matt, 216
Roman (family pet), 114
Romeo's Daughter, 195
Ronstadt, Linda, 84, 150
Rose Tattoo, 267
Rose, David, 203, 299
Ross, Diana, 119
Ross, Don, 101
Rowan, Brent, 216
Rush, 68, 266
Russell, David O., 337

Saari, Will, 339
SABC, 175
Sabu, Paul, 132–34, 139, 143, 285–86
Sachsalber, Jenny, 48
Sadie (family pet), 114
St. Regis Falls, New York state, 226, 230, 268, 292, 293
Sant Mat (Path of the Masters), 199, 212, 291
Saturday Night Fever Original Soundtrack, 5
Sault Sainte Marie, 24, 26, 29, 43
Science of Spirituality/Sawan Kirpal Ruhani Mission, 200

Scott, Bon, 186
Second Harvest/Kid's Café, 276, 286
Sex Pistols, 154
Shaefer, Dan, 227, 348
Shania Twain, 5, 155–61, 166
Shaver, Billy Joe, 150
Shedd, Harold, 144, 155, 157–59, 214
Sherman, Dr. Barry, 125
Sherrill, Billy, 143
Shining Tree, 28
Sikhism, 198–99
Silver, Rhonda, 117, 126–27, 128, 132, 136, 140, 141, 142
Silvertone, 195
Simon, Ralph, 175, 178–79, 181, 186, 187, 196, 202, 257
Sinatra, Frank, 51, 142, 174
Singh, Darshan, 200
Singh, Gobind, 199
Singh, Kirpal, 200
Singh, Rajinder, 200
Singh, Shiv Dayal, 198, 200
Singh, Thakar, 200, 291
skiffle, 150
Skyler, Phil, 226
Smith, Ian, 168
Smith, Richard Jon, 179, 181
Snow, Hank, 16
Sondheim, Stephen, 136
SoundScan system, 152, 225, 326
South Africa
    hippy revolution, 175
    music scene, 174
South Porcupine, 12, 20, 86
Spears, Britney, 180, 238, 301, 331, 344
Spence, Kim, 64
Sphour, David ("Spooky"), 197
Spirit, 182
Spivey, Joe, 216, 258

Sports Illustrated, 222, 327
Springsteen, Bruce, 226, 239, 266, 322
Stabile, Jan, 275, 283
Stanley, Allen, 68
Star Academy, 326
Star, The, 242, 248
stardom downside, 240
Steely Dan, 182
Steinman, Jim, 190
Steps, 180
Stetson, 338
Stevenson, B.W. "Buckwheat," 190
Stewart, Rod, 192
Sting, 192, 327
Stock, Darrell, 247
Strait, George, 151
Struthers, Evelyn, 13
Sturgeon Falls, 13
Sudbury High School (Kid's Telethon), 38
Sudbury Star, The, 42, 51
Sudbury, Ontario, 17, 42
    Bureau of Indian Affairs, 44, 52–53, 61
    casual racism, 53
    described, 44
    King Street apartment, 36
    Native Friendship Centre, 41
    Sorento Hotel, 36
    Twains move to, 36
Sugano, Aileen, 132
Sullivan, Steve, 8, 68
Sultzman, Lee, 27
Supertramp, 68
Supremes, the, 35
Surch, Laura, 51, 58
    lifelong friend of S, 60
    lives in high-rise with S, 96
    loss of S's songs, 70
    sees S in Flirt, 89
    Twains' poverty, 56

Sweetfish recording studios, Argyle, New York, 226

tabloid newspapers, 242
Take 6, 267
Taylor, Christina, 140
Taylor, Mike, 111–15, 127
Taylor, R. Dean, 133
Terrell, Tammi, 119
Texas Gulf, 8
The Box (TV show), 281–82
Thomas, Randy, 227
Thomas, Rufus, 146
Thompson, Hank, 149
Thompson, May (née Pearce, S's great-aunt), 10, 11, 12, 22, 244
Thompson, Rick, 75, 93, 94
Thomson, Roy, 8
Thorn, Sheri, 234–35
Thriller, 5, 160, 224, 323
Tim (dog), 272, 333
Time, 328
Times, The, 281
Timmins and District Hospital, 272
Timmins Youth Singers, 75
Timmins, Ontario, 40, 42, 88, 274, 338, 339, 340
    42 Montgomery Avenue, 69, 110
    137 Balsam Street South apartment, 61, 78–79
    294 Birch Street North, 23
    attitude toward Native Canadians, 27–28, 29–30
    Bannerman Avenue house, 36
    Canada's largest city, 7
    Chez Nous, 7
    described, 67–68, 79–80
    Don Fraser born in 1933, 11
    Don's Pizzeria, 6, 79
    Escapade Hotel, 71, 80–81, 210
    first album sleeve for S, 3

GV Hotel, 80, 86
high school, 299–300, 338
Hollinger gold mine, 8
Hollinger Park, 3, 67, 86
Jerry and Sharon's burial, 107
JP's lounge, 80–81, 85
Maple Leaf Tavern, 6, 38, 80
Mattagami Hotel, 6–7, 34, 35
McDonald's, 67, 71, 77
Poplar Street, 12
Riverview Hotel (the "Riv"), 80
S leaves in 1988, 2
Senator Hotel, 3
Shania Twain Centre, 1, 3–6,
    338, 339, 342
Shania Twain Day, 3, 253
Shania Twain Heritage Festival, 1
staking mining claims, 67
Theriault École Secondaire gig,
    210
Twain family moves to, 27
Twains leave, 36
Zudel's Fresh Mart, 65, 78, 108
Titanic, 9
TNN, 223
TNT, 154
Tom (band member, Kirkland
    Lake), 93
Tommy Hunter Show, The (country
    music TV show), 43, 77, 128
Tonight Show, The (TV show), 227,
    327
Toronto, 141, 238
    27 Indian Grove (Bell's home),
        96, 100, 103
    Clarence in, 21
    High Park, 96
    Longshot records in, 78
    McClear Studio, 134
    Orchard Park, 42
    Roy Thomson Hall, 101
    S lives in high-rise with Laura, 96

    S plays at Rockhill Park, 42
    S's voice lessons, 39
    Sharon visits S, 100
Toronto (band), 83, 85
Toronto Star, 102
Toronto Sun, 333
Toronto Symphony Orchestra, 101,
    129
Toto, 216
Travis, George, 266, 268
Travis, Randy, 153
Triangle, 180
Tribe Called Quest, 180
Triple Play Tour, 163
Tucker, Tanya, 34, 35, 58, 90
Turner, Tina, 236, 293, 331
Twain family, 28–31
Twain, Audrey (Jerry's sister), 23,
    30
Twain, Carrie Ann see Brown, Car-
    rie Ann
Twain, Darryl (Audrey Twain's son
    adopted by Jerry and
    Sharon), 30, 70, 106, 140,
    244, 344
    birth in 1974, 30
    criminal activities, 246–47
    Enquirer story, 291
    fired from S's tour, 275
    ice-hockey, 70
    Jerry adopts, 30, 245
    John Kim Bell, 100
    lives in Edmonton, 304
    lives with Jill, 113
    military school, 112–13
    out of control, 112
Twains' deaths, 104
Twain, Gerry (Jerry's father), 28,
    30, 31, 33, 245, 246
Twain, Jerry (S's adopted father), 100
    adopts Sharon's daughters, 30, 245
    ambition for his family, 28–29

Twain, Jerry (S's adopted father)
(cont.)
appearance, 24
birth in 1947, 27
burial in Timmins cemetery, 107
death in car accident, 104–6
education, 28–29
encounters ignorance and prejudice, 27–28
Gordon's animosity, 30
hunting, 29, 32
job with Indian Affairs, 44, 52,
61
lack of steady work in winter, 53
marries Sharon, 30
meets Sharon, 23, 29
moves to Sudbury, 37
personality, 24, 52–53, 58
reforestation business, 61, 62–67,
105, 107–8
relationship with Sharon, 29, 60,
70
runs a mining service company,
67
sacrifices for S, 39, 56
teaches S basic guitar chords, 37
works for Don McKinnon, 28
Twain, Jill (S's half-sister), 53, 98,
106, 108, 244
birth in 1963, 13
Darryl lives with, 113
father, Gilles, 13, 18
guitar, 37
Jerry adopts, 30, 245
leaves home, 57
S's marriage, 211–12
Ted Evans on, 57–58
Twain, Karen (S's aunt), 2, 300
encounters ignorance and prejudice, 27–28
family name, 28
Jerry, 24

Jerry and Sharon's relationship
29, 60
Jerry's business, 107–8
living in the bush, 33
S reveals where she writes songs,
51–52
Twains' strictness, 50
works in Jerry's reforestation
business, 63–64
Twain, Mandy (S's niece), 57, 100,
106, 212
Twain, Mark (S's half-brother), 60,
70, 140
birth in 1972, 30
criminal activities, 246–47
Huntsville High, 112
ice-hockey, 70–71
Jerry adopts, 30, 245
John Kim Bell, 100
military school, 113
out of control, 111–12
settles in British Columbia, 304
Twains' accident, 105–6
Twain, Mark (the writer), 145
Twain, Selina (née Luke, Jerry's
mother), 5, 28, 31, 33, 34, 36,
63, 98, 103, 245, 300
Twain, Shania (Née Eilleen Regina
Edwards, married name
Eilleen Lange)
affair with Paul Bolduc, 123–25,
156, 207, 209–10, 290
answers her accusers, 244–45
appearance, 1, 49, 59, 66, 71–72,
82–83, 95–96, 97–98,
119–20, 161, 279, 281
appears with the Big Country
Show, 42
awards, 4–5
birth on August 28, 1965, 18
breaks the rules about keeping
country pure, 241

breaks up with Paul, 209
charities, 276–77
christened Eileen Regina Edwards, 18
country/rock issue, 88, 92
death of her parents, 103–6, 137
debut album, 132, 155–61, 166
early songwriting, 51–52, 62
education, 46–52, 60, 67, 72–77, 87, 89, 95–96
family's poverty, 52–56
finances, 277
financial independence, 231
first appearance in public in 1873, 6–7, 34
first conversation with Mutt, 204–5
first guitar, 38
first visit to Mattagami reserve in 1970, 31
Flirt, 88
follows Mutt's spiritual path, 200
high school reunion, 3
honored in her hometown, 1–3
influences, 91–92
Jerry adopts, 30, 245
learns the guitar, 37–39
learns to dance, 131–32, 136
learns to hunt, 33
leaves Timmins in 1988, 2
Longshot, 27, 78–87
marriage to Mutt, 272
moves to Huntsville, 110
moves to Sudbury, 36
moves to Switzerland, 291, 293, 297–98
Nashville demos, 89
personality
    ambition, 86–87, 101, 121, 122, 133
    enthusiasm, 76
    family-oriented, 122–23
    inner strength, 234
    love of animals, 122
    love of children, 303–4
    love of solitude, 33, 52, 120
    perfectionist, 48
    respected, 66
    sense of humor, 84, 144
    temper, 99, 102, 124
    will of steel, 92, 104
personal songs, 345
pregnancy, 4, 201, 304
record deal, 142–44
recordings with Kenny, 38
records second album, 213–25
records third album, 254–55
records fourth album, 311–17
records a demo with Eastwind, 42
refines songwriting techniques, 254–56
relationship with John Kim, 95–107, 124
schools attended
    Capreol High School, 46, 60, 72
    Pinecrest Junior High School, 45–46, 47–49
    Redwood Acres Public School, 46, 265
    Timmins High and Vocational School, 72–76, 78–79, 89
sings at the Maple Leaf Tavern, 6
sings country songs at Mattagami, 32
songs performed in youth
    "Before the Next Teardrop Falls," 42
    "Coat of Many Colors," 34
    "Crying Time Again," 43
    "Delta Dawn," 34, 43, 58
    "Harper Valley PTA," 43
    "Honky Tonk Angels," 43

Twain, Shania (Née Eilleen Regina
    Edwards, married name
    Eilleen Lange) *(cont.)*
    "I Wish I was a Teddy Bear," 43
    "I'm So Lonesome I Could
        Cry," 40
    "Jambalaya," 43
    "Just When I Needed You
        Most," 48
    "Kaw-liga," 34
    "La Vie en Rose," 131, 136
    "Me and Bobby McGee," 34,
        43
    "Over the Rainbow," 119, 136
    "Pure Love," 43
    "Queen of the Silver Dollar,"
        43
    "Say You'll Stay Until Tomor-
        row," 43
    "Take Me Home, Country
        Roads," 35
    "Tennessee Mountain Home,"
        43
    "What's Your Mama's Name
        Child," 43
    "Wind Beneath My Wings,"
        136
    songs written/recorded by
    "Any Man of Mine," 207, 216,
        221, 222, 224, 226, 236
    "Black Eyes, Blue Tears," 254,
        257, 271
    "Dance with the One That
        Brought You," 165
    "Diamond in the Dark," 142
    "Don't Be Stupid (You Know
        I Love You)," 257, 262, 268
    "Feeling Invisible," 72
    "Forever and for Always," 331
    "From This Moment On,"
        261, 264, 271
    "Go and Be Gone," 142

"God Ain't Gonna Getcha for
    That," 157, 161
"God Bless the Child," 256,
    271, 275, 276
"Heavy on the Sunshine," 89
"Home Ain't Where His
    Heart Is (Anymore)," 205
"I Thought I Left the Storm,"
    143
"I'm Gonna Getcha Good,"
    317–21, 326, 327
"I'm Holdin' on to Love (To
    Save My Life)," 257
"I've Seen Better Days," 143
"If I Were You," 143
"If You Wanna Touch Her,
    Ask!," 257
"(If You're Not in It for Love)
    I'm Outta Here!," 218,
    224, 235, 271
"Is Love a Rose?," 51
"Ka-ching!," 329
"Just Like the Storybooks," 51
"Lay Down Your Arms," 143
"Love Gets Me Every Time,"
    257, 262
"Love in My Pocket," 142
"Man! I Feel Like a Woman!,"
    257, 264, 270, 280, 300
"No One Needs to Know," 224
"Raining on Our Love," 205
"Rock This Country!," 254,
    271
"Send It with Love," 137, 256
"She's Not Just a Pretty Face,"
    317, 330
"Stepping Stones," 84
"That Don't Impress Me
    Much," 5, 257, 264, 289
"This Man of Mine," 205, 207
    (*see also* "Any Man of
    Mine")